THE
CITY PLANNING
PROCESS
A Political Analysis

THE
CITY PLANNING
PROCESS

A Political Analysis

ALAN A. ALTSHULER

Cornell Paperbacks
Cornell University Press
Ithaca and London

First published 1965 by Cornell University Press.
Published in the United Kingdom by Cornell University Press Ltd.,
2–4 Brook Street, London W1Y 1AA.

Second printing 1966
Third printing 1967
First printing, Cornell Paperbacks, 1969
Second printing 1970
Third printing 1973

International Standard Book Number 0-8014-9081-2
Library of Congress Catalog Card Number 65-25498

Printed in the United States of America by Vail-Ballou Press, Inc.

To my parents

Acknowledgments

I have incurred many debts in the course of preparing this study. There is no way that I can ever repay most of them, but I wish here at least to record them.

First, my informants in the Twin Cities, most of whom are named in their capacities as actors in the case studies of Part One, gave (if they are taken together) many hundreds of hours of their time. Their knowledge and opinions provided the bulk of the data on which this study is based. Without their generosity, which never ceased to amaze me, it could never have come into being.

On the academic side, my primary debts are to Professors Edward Banfield and Herbert Storing, who supervised my work on the dissertation from which this book has emerged. Both devoted enormous amounts of time to counseling, questioning, and encouraging me, and to criticizing early drafts of the work. Their contrasting viewpoints never ceased to provoke me to develop and clarify my own thoughts, and their influence is apparent on every page of this volume. Although of course they bear no responsibility for its flaws, they certainly deserve a good deal of the credit for whatever virtues it may have. I am also grateful to C. Herman Pritchett, Martin Meyerson, Lloyd Rodwin, John R. James, William L. C. Wheaton, and Grace Milgram for reading and commenting upon the whole or portions of the manuscript.

My research in the Twin Cities was supported by a Social Science Research Council Research Training Fellowship. A supplementary grant from the Inter-University Case Program enabled me to spend several months longer in the Twin Cities than might otherwise have been feasible. A grant from the Ford Foundation permitted me to spend the summer of 1962 studying British town planning. I owe a special debt to Sidney Baldwin, formerly of the Inter-University Case Program, who devoted a good deal of time to editing the case studies that appear in Part I and who bore some of the burden of "clearing" them with participants.

Versions of five chapters, in whole or in part, have appeared previously: Chapters I, II, and III as Inter-University Case Program studies; Chapter V as an article in the *Journal of the American Institute of Planners* (August 1965); and Chapter VI as an article in the *Public Administration Review* (September 1965). I am grateful to their publishers for permission to reprint them here.

The staff of the Cornell University Press provided highly valuable counsel and editorial suggestions that improved the book substantially. Marguerite Gigliello and Jo Grodsky typed the manuscript, and deserve special thanks for the speed and remarkable accuracy with which they worked.

Finally, but also foremost, I wish to record my gratitude to Julie Altshuler for her patience, good humor, and constructive criticism at every stage in the life of this project. Fortunately for my professional standing (such as it may be), only she and I can know the full depth and extent of my debt to her.

A. A.

Ithaca
October 1965

Contents

Maps

THE
CITY PLANNING
PROCESS
A Political Analysis

Introduction

The job of the city planner is to propose courses of action, not to execute them. The standards prescribed by elected officials for his guidance are, when they exist at all, usually contradictory or ambivalent. Even the boundaries of his concern resist definition. Although his plans deal directly with only the physical city, their professed object is always to improve the total quality of urban living.[1] Some planners articulate this object purely in terms of physical and aesthetic satisfaction, preferring to de-emphasize the effects of physical design on economic and social problems. But most planners conceive the potential contribution of planning to urban life in grand terms. Charles A. Blessing, for example, in his presidential address to the American Institute of Planners (1959),

[1] Not all city planners agree that they should confine their attention to issues of physical development. A few theorists have contended that planning agencies should extend their jurisdictions to include general economic and social planning, especially since physical development plans must be based ultimately on considerations of economic and social forces and objectives. This view is not very widely shared, for reasons that will be discussed presently. A more generally accepted view is that capital budgeting should be considered part of the arsenal of physical development planning weapons. T. J. Kent, who himself appears to believe that planners should avoid involvement in nearly all detailed consideration of priorities, budgets, and legal land-use regulations, has discussed the various viewpoints on these questions in his book, *The Urban General Plan* (San Francisco: Chandler Publishing Co., 1964), pp. 46–53. Parenthetically, let me say at the outset that, despite specific criticisms made of it in this volume, Kent's extremely thoughtful study is probably the best history and critique of general city planning theory yet written by an American planner.

1

spoke of the value of planning for physical and aesthetic satisfaction in this way:

Our client is man—whose body and senses, conditioned through countless centuries of living near nature, yearn to see the sky and the earth and the green and trees, man who has instinctive feeling for space, for the beauty of fountains and squares and broad vistas and flowers. . . . Let us try with humility and insight to understand man's deep and timeless yearning for beauty, in this let us try to see beyond the seen and know beyond the known and thus give man back in fuller measure his birthright on the earth's own loveliness.[2]

In practice, unfortunately, even the most staunchly "physical" planners have found no way to isolate the effects of their work from the murky crosscurrents of economic and social conflict. Their failure to do so has been especially evident when their proposed objectives have been ambitious and their proposed mechanisms of change have been political. This has been the usual, and most significant, case. Planners aspire, as their theory says they must, to determine the overall framework in which urban physical development takes place. To do less, they say, is not planning but tinkering. In order to determine the framework effectively, they generally feel that they must recommend public regulation of the uses to which every bit of urban-area land may be put. They wish to limit the height and bulk of all new structures; they wish to set criteria for the location, design, and adequacy of all public facilities; they want to take the profit out of "undesirable" private activities and make "desirable" activities profitable by vigorous applications of public power; and they urge the government in certain situations to take land from its private owners and subsidize its transition to new uses.

Planners typically defend the claim that their work can add to the sum of human welfare by referring to the "comprehensiveness" of their point of view. Since they also speak frequently of the "rationality" of their prescriptions, the implication often seems to be that their breadth of concern enables them to conceive clearly rational solutions to policy-choice problems. At other times they

[2] This address was delivered at the annual meeting of the American Institute of Planners in July, 1959. Excerpts were printed in the *American Institute of Planners Journal*, XXVI, No. 1 (February 1960), 2–4. The quotation appears on p. 3.

seem more modestly to mean only that planning can elevate the quality of democratic politics by broadening the perceived range of possible solutions, by pointing out ways in which specialist proposals affect each other, and by suggesting means of harnessing the techniques of modern specialists to serve broad visions of the public interest in concerted fashion.[3] In either case, the promise is

[3] The following articulations of the meaning of comprehensive planning may be useful. Four of them refer to metropolitan rather than city planning, but I assume that this is not crucial to their underlying conceptions of comprehensiveness. The first five tend to support the first conception of comprehensiveness outlined in the text. The sixth, which is too academic and sophisticated to make use of the word "comprehensive" at all, tends to support the second conception. This distribution, the result of a brief search for definitions, is accidental. I would not be surprised to discover, however, that it fairly accurately represents the distribution of views in the American planning profession—with most supporters of the first view being practitioners and a radically disproportionate number of supporters of the second being academics. Needless to say, this is purely a personal impression. The definitions follow:

(1) "Comprehensive has meant that the plan should encompass all the significant physical elements of the urban environment, that the plan should be related to regional development trends, and that the plan should recognize and take into account important social and economic factors" (T. J. Kent, *op. cit.*, pp. 95, 96).

(2) A metropolitan planning body with comprehensive planning responsibilities should review "all proposals affecting the metropolitan area" for "content" and "compatibility" (American Institute of Planners, *The Role of Metropolitan Planning*, Metropolitan Planning Conference, Findings and Recommendations [Chicago, 1962], mimeo., p. 5).

(3) For the purposes of the federal urban planning assistance program, "comprehensive planning is defined as including, to the extent directly related to urban needs, the preparation of general physical plans for land use and the provision of public facilities (including transportation facilities), with long-range fiscal plans to accompany the long-range development plans; the programing of capital improvements and their financing; coordination of all related plans of the departments and subdivisions of the government concerned; intergovernmental coordination of planning activities; and the preparation of supporting regulatory and administrative measures" (Legislative Reference Service of the Library of Congress, *Catalog of Federal Aids to State and Local Governments*, committee print, U.S. Senate, Committee on Government Operations, Subcommittee on Intergovernmental Relations, April 15, 1964, p. 124).

(4) "An effective and comprehensive planning process in each metropolitan area [will embrace] all activities, both private and public, which shape the

that cities whose development is publicly planned will become
(assuming that their planners are competent) "better" places in
which to live than unplanned cities. The purposes of the study
which follows are to consider the plausibility of this promise in
some detail and simultaneously (on the assumption that the two
issues are intimately related) to explore the political and administrative obstacles to more meaningful planning of land-use development in American cities.

Significant planning problems are never simply technical; they

community. Such a process must be democratic—for only when the citizens
of a community have participated in selecting the goals which will shape
their environment can they be expected to support the actions necessary to
accomplish these goals" (President John F. Kennedy, 1961 Housing Message
to Congress, as cited and adopted by the U.S. Advisory Commission on Intergovernmental Relations in its report, *Impact of Federal Urban Development
Programs on Local Government Organization and Planning* [Washington:
U.S. Government Printing Office, January 1964], p. 1).

(5) The federal highway program, as amended in 1962, "requires comprehensive *transportation* planning which must take into account studies of
community value factors, development controls, financial resources, and projections of economic, land use, and population factors" (*ibid.*, p. 17; italics
added).

(6) "The metropolitan planning that is envisioned is . . . that of a representative body working with a competent technical staff to provide a factual
context for the consideration of policy questions, to study the implications
of alternative development choices, and to promote consideration of two
currently neglected points of view: the areawide rather than the local, and
the long-range rather than the immediate. . . .

"A metropolitan planning agency will alert local governments to the
regional implications of their decisions, and will work to encourage informed
decisionmaking in place of fragmented policies that plan for the region more
by accident than by choice. An effective planning agency will also help to
resolve conflicts between localities and the larger region, when these conflicts
prejudice the development of the region. Metropolitan planning can make
an important contribution in these situations of conflict merely by posing
the issues and analyzing the effects of alternative courses of action. More
complete information, highlighting the regional implications of local actions,
will enable local decisionmakers to see beyond the immediate parochial
advantages and to consider alternatives more beneficial in the long run—and
to justify such alternatives to their constituents" (Joint Center for Urban
Studies of the Massachusetts Institute of Technology and Harvard University
[Charles M. Haar, Project Director], *The Effectiveness of Metropolitan Planning*, committee print, U.S. Senate, Committee on Government Operations,
Subcommittee on Intergovernmental Relations, June 30, 1964, pp. 1, 8).

always involve the determination of priorities among values. As noted previously, political officials seldom give planners any clear instructions to guide the value-choice aspects of their work. If planners are to conceive new policies, rather than simply to set forth means of executing old ones, perhaps a large part of this lack of explicit political guidance is inevitable. But there is also some evidence that local politicians in many American cities have elevated their inability to give detailed guidance into a principle of political prudence: that it is politically unwise for an elective official to say anything at all during the early life of any idea.[4] To the

[4] Theorists of planning have rarely come to grips with this problem, though until the past two or three decades many did wish to insulate planning from "politics." As will be seen presently, nothing could be further from my mind than endorsement of this prescription.

One recent writer who *has* grappled with the issue of what guidance planners can expect from politicians has come to radically different conclusions from my own. T. J. Kent believes that city councils will give planners all the guidance that they need if only the planners bring issues before them properly. In particular, he believes that city councils are eminently willing to articulate the economic, social, and political assumptions on which comprehensive plans must rest whenever the need is presented to them clearly. The two brief selections which best illustrate his viewpoint are perhaps the following:

(1) "The city council can be made to work effectively by clarifying its most important duties and procedures."

(2) "I believe that our municipal governments will continue to foster and to maintain several general planning activities, each one focusing on a subject-matter area of major importance. Each such activity should be characterized by continuing efforts on the part of those responsible to understand and state the basic social and economic objectives of the community that have special significance for their work. In recent years, an increasing number of city planning programs have produced plans . . . that illustrate, however crudely, the meaning of the quality of comprehensiveness called for here. They attempt to state openly the judgments made concerning the most significant nonphysical factors upon which the physical plan is based, they place directly in the hands of the council the task of setting the social and economic objectives which their physical plan seeks to accomplish, and, by an open statement of their limitations, they foster recognition by the city council of the need for a more effective system of social, economic, and physical planning than we now have."

(The quotations are from T. J. Kent, *op. cit.*, pp. 12 and 101–102. See also pp. 9–12, 16–18, 54–59, 84–85, and 101–102.)

Several criticisms of Kent's formulation may be made. First, he assumes

extent that this is so, it follows that city planning is one of the extreme examples of administrative discretion to be found in American government. It seems reasonable to believe that an understanding of the ways in which city planners approach their choice problems may shed some light on the profound questions posed whenever expertise and politics merge in public administration. I have entitled this volume *The City Planning Process* to indicate that it does focus on the ways in which city planners approach difficult professional and strategic choice situations, and not just—or even primarily—on the ways in which local political systems dispose of planning recommendations.

My primary scholarly interests are in the politics of American public administration and, more specifically, in the political obstacles to general planning at all levels of American government. From these points of view, there were of course some arguments against choosing city planners as the subject of this study. For one thing, American city planners have been notoriously unsuccessful in their political relationships, at least until recent years. Consequently, there are few or no cities where current planning can be studied in the context of a long tradition of effective planning. For another, city planning has its own unique concerns, instruments, and doctrinal controversies. These flow from a history which clearly distinguishes it from, say, national economic planning. In addition, one can never know just how comparable local politics is to politics on larger scenes.

On the other hand, the political failures of general planning have been notorious at all levels of American government. This relatively consistent pattern suggests that an analysis in depth of the causes of failure in particular situations may shed some light on fundamental characteristics of the American political system. Moreover, general land-use planning has enjoyed a dramatic up-

---

that municipal governments will support comprehensive social and economic planning efforts outside the physical planning agency. Second, he assumes that the only reason for the failure of city councils to articulate economic and social goals is intellectual confusion about "their most important duties." Third, he gives no guidance to planners whose city councils fall short of his ideal. More generally, it may be noted that throughout his volume Kent assumes that politicians are constantly striving to understand and serve the overall public interest. He says nothing at all about the impact of special interest politics on planning.

surge of respectability (and perhaps even of influence) in most large and medium-sized American cities since World War II; its recent history may, therefore, be suggestive of general strategies for making broadly oriented planning palatable to legislative bodies at all levels of American government. These strategies in turn, if numerous studies in a variety of situations confirm their applicability, ought to indicate a good deal about both the substance and changeability of typical perceptions of interest and distributions of influence in American political systems.

The argument that the history of city planning is unique in some respects would apply to any governmental function chosen for analysis. Similarly, whenever a study focuses on a small sample of decisions, a small number of political systems, and/or a single level of government, the objection may validly be made that the extent of their relevant uniqueness is unknowable with any certainty or precision.

A related charge that might be leveled is that the methods of information-gathering employed in this study were insufficiently rigorous. In fact, this study makes no pretensions of being "experimental" or in any other way rigorously "scientific." It does claim to be the product of informed and disciplined hard work. Its defense against the charge, which I consider the only legitimate defense against such charges generally, is that the greatest care for accuracy (of both fact and inference) consistent with the purposes of the study and the resources available for it has been taken. The actual quality of this care in any particular study is for the author to communicate in his writing and for readers to assess in accord with the rules of evidence appropriate to the classes of phenomena analyzed. The ultimate defense of this defense must in turn be that, if its validity were denied, scholarly consideration of nearly all important social and political issues would have to cease, pending the (unlikely) development of rigorous scientific procedures for dealing with them.[5] In the present case, it is only appropriate to add that the resources available were extremely modest—they

[5] These sentences are occasioned, of course, by recent trends in the social sciences. Within the field of public administration, the most forceful exponent of "scientific" study has for many years been Herbert Simon. See his *Administrative Behavior*, 2nd ed. (New York: Macmillan Co., 1957). The other side of the case is argued well by Philip Selznick in *Leadership in Administration* (Evanston: Row, Peterson, and Co., 1957). See also Edward

permitted, for example, little more than one man-year of field work—and that the objective from the start was to explore a rather wide range of phenomena in search of suggestive hypotheses rather than to come out with a few precise and rigorously tested propositions.

Two methods of information-gathering, both traditional, were employed. First, the existing published literature on the political and administrative aspects of city planning was reviewed; and second, four detailed case studies of planning in Minneapolis and St. Paul, Minnesota, were prepared. Two of the case studies deal with the development of general plans and two with decisions about where to locate specific public projects. (The most important specific decisions that planners are regularly asked to advise upon are those having to do with the location of new public facilities.) Minneapolis and St. Paul, adjoining "twin" cities, were chosen for study because of their reputations (among a group of academic planners consulted) for "good" planning. Similarly, the case subjects were chosen to represent the best planning work done in the Twin Cities just prior to and during the year in which the field work for this volume was conducted—July 1959 through August 1960. I did not begin research on any case until the planners involved in it assured me that they were well satisfied with the parts they had played.[6] The cases, which make up the four chapters

---

Banfield, "The Training of the Executive," *Public Policy*, X (1960). 16–43. The difficulties that Simon has encountered in attempting to establish a behavioral science of administration are chronicled in great detail by Herbert Storing in his essay, "The Science of Administration: Herbert Simon," which appears in Herbert Storing, ed., *Essays on the Scientific Study of Politics* (New York: Holt, Rinehart and Winston, 1962), pp. 63–150. My own methodological position, it should be noted, is essentially similar to that of Selznick and Banfield, not Storing. Storing's critical insights may be found extremely provocative, however, even by one who disagrees with his overall evaluation of Simon's work.

[6] At the other end of the research process, each case was circulated to all significant participants, and to a number of other knowledgeable observers, in numerous drafts prior to publication. Where suggestions for revision appeared to be based on compelling evidence, simple corrections were made. Where suggestions for revision appeared to be merely plausible, they were reported in the text—or, occasionally, in footnotes—as individual points of view. A few of the thorniest disagreements about the roles of particular in-

(Part One) that follow this introduction, have been written to emphasize the emergence and resolution of choice problems rather than for their story value. Their consistent object is to isolate and analyze fundamental obstacles to "rational" land-use planning in American cities, the kinds of obstacles that show up most clearly when base and trivial motives are eliminated, and when able men seek honest answers to urgent and puzzling questions.

The next four chapters (V–VIII), though grounded in the case study data of Part One, constitute a general criticism of some important city planning theory. Some readers may question whether a predominant theory of American city planning exists. In fact, so few planners have written systematic defenses of their discipline's claims that the query cannot be answered with a simple yes or no. This is one reason why I have found it necessary to supplement the literature by asking practicing planners to justify their actions in concrete case situations.[7] Justifications are always and necessarily couched in theoretical terms, though the theories on which they ultimately depend commonly remain implicit. Thus, I have had in large part to *infer* the theoretical foundations of American city planning. I am the first to admit that the reliability of inference gathers persuasiveness only as the number and proportion of justifications accounted for grows, and that consequently my inferences based on the inadequate pre-existing literature plus four new case studies can be no more than suggestive. My hope is no

---

dividuals were resolved in a manner tolerable to the participants only after I made two reinterviewing trips to the Twin Cities in 1964. Had it not been for the elaborate "clearance" procedure, this volume would probably have appeared at least two years earlier.

[7] One of my central objections to the work of recent "scientific" students of administration is relevant here: namely, that even when they have examined the administrator's own perspective, they have tended to ignore the distinctive kinds of work done by administrators at the highest levels. Most particularly, their anxiety to quantify and systematize knowledge of administration has led them to de-emphasize choice problems which involve judging the merits of complex value-loaded policy alternatives. Yet high-level administrators (*and* politicians) do their most important work in making such judgments. Perhaps the most fundamental assumption underlying this study has been that careful, even if unquantified, analyses of the ways in which such high-level judgments are made can yield some valuable insights into the nature of the governmental process.

more than that students of urban politics, public administration, and public planning may find them that.

The following, and final, chapter constitutes an attempt to indicate some of the most important ways in which my choice of perspective from which to observe American city planning may have influenced the tone or "mix" of my conclusions about it. Its method is to sketch—in very brief and highly impressionistic fashion—the kinds of conclusions that might have been emphasized by four studies with radically different, though still clearly political, perspectives. To notify unwary readers that the level of discourse here is far more speculative than even that of Part Two, I have placed this chapter in a separate Part Three.

Before concluding this introduction, a few more words about Minneapolis and St. Paul are in order. Because the analysis which follows tends to be critical, it is important to mention again that these cities were selected for study because their reputations were favorable, both in terms of the political environment that they provided for planning and the quality of practice which they received from their professional planning staffs. Let us take these two criteria up in order.

There do not seem to be any major American cities in which politicians have continuously displayed enthusiasm about systematic land-use planning for any sustained period of time, but there was a long tradition of concern for public amenity in the Twin Cities area. Reginald Isaacs, the distinguished Charles Dyer Norton Professor of Regional Planning at Harvard, has noted that at least in Minneapolis recognition of public responsibility for parks and civic beauty dated to the middle of the nineteenth century. By 1883, Minneapolis had eighty acres of parkland for its 100,000 residents, a newly created Board of Park Commissioners, and a long-range park plan prepared by a consultant. The same consultant in 1888 proposed a single park and major boulevard plan for Minneapolis and St. Paul combined. A decade later Minneapolis was seriously endeavoring to implement this plan. Isaacs writes that

the "city beautiful" concept and movement is attributed to the Chicago World's Fair of 1893. . . . Actually, Chicago was four times the size of the then-Minneapolis before it did anything about parks and beau-tification.[8]

He adds that these early plans for

park systems, lake drives and boulevards have been realized, at least in good part. Although compromise and encroachment have reduced their proposals, the Twin Cities present a beautiful aspect to the visitor. Homes and communities have been maintained in better con-dition than in any other city that I have visited. Residential property and areas of the same age, which in other cities would have become obsolete and undesirable places in which to live, are clean, well kept and stable in the Twin Cities.[9]

This was not to say, of course, that the Twin Cities had been comprehensively planned, or even that local government in *this* century had been unusually active. The uncommon stability of Twin Cities neighborhoods was attributable largely to the meager-ness, by comparison with other large northern cities, of the influx of Eastern and Southern European immigrants in the early part of this century and of immigrants from the American South more re-cently. By way of illustration, it may be noted that the Negro pop-ulation of the Twin Cities Standard Metropolitan Statistical Area in 1960 was 1.4 per cent.[10] In addition, the Scandinavians who first settled these cities and who still set their tone were people who cultivated their property more lovingly than most. This had not, of course, always made them particularly receptive to plan-ning. The plans prepared by consultants amid great fanfare in the first quarter of this century were ignored in practice. So were simi-lar plans in most other American cities, however. In the two decades after the start of the Great Depression the planning func-tion had been reduced almost entirely to routine zoning adminis-tration and the production of occasional studies. This, too, had been in accord with the national pattern. More recently, there had

[8] Reginald Isaacs, "Goals for 2012," lecture delivered at the University of Minnesota School of Architecture, April 6, 1962 (printed as a pamphlet by the School of Architecture), pp. 2, 3. The quotation is on p. 3.

[9] *Ibid.,* pp. 7, 8.

[10] Ninety-seven per cent of the Negroes lived in the two central cities, constituting 2.5 per cent of the cities' combined population. Negroes con-stituted .05 per cent of the suburban population.

been something of a revival of interest in planning in each of the Twin Cities. During the decade of the 1950's the St. Paul planning budget had increased by ninefold and the Minneapolis planning budget had quadrupled.[11] Civic leaders in both cities professed to be sympathetic to planning in principle, and most observers believed that the prospects for planning in practice were quite bright—at least by American standards. It may be noted, moreover, that these were cities in which political machines did not exist, elections were nonpartisan, and graft was almost unknown. If decisions were often made on grounds other than those stated publicly, they were seldom made for reasons of which ethical politicians thought that they ought to be ashamed. In short, if the Twin Cities had not recently been far ahead of their time with respect to planning, one searched in vain for periods in which they had lagged significantly behind; and currently they provided a political environment that most American city planners would have recognized—despite the frustrations of those actually working within it—as relatively hospitable.

So much at this point for the political environment of planning. The quality of professional practice in the Twin Cities was beyond my competence to judge. I have no reason to doubt the general view of those more knowledgeable on this score, however, that Minneapolis and St. Paul planning circa 1959–1960 met contemporary professional standards with a good deal to spare.

All this is mentioned only to add perspective to the study which follows. Written by a student of politics rather than of land-use planning techniques, it focuses necessarily on areas where professional doctrine is unsettled, where different professions come into conflict, and where professional men, though agreed among themselves, have difficulty persuading lay civic leaders and ordinary interested citizens. Unavoidably, it emphasizes conflict at the ex-

[11] The growth in St. Paul was from $12,780 in 1950 to $116,742 in 1959. The latter figure included part of a continuing grant for support of comprehensive planning work from the St. Paul Housing and Redevelopment Authority. The growth in Minneapolis was from $54,600 in 1950 to $208,592 in 1959. These figures should be related to population. St. Paul was only about three-fifths the size of Minneapolis. The exact populations of the two cities in 1950 were 311,349 and 521,718 respectively. The 1960 figures were 313,411 and 482,872. The population of Twin Cities Standard Metropolitan Statistical Area rose from 1,151,053 in 1950 to 1,482,030 in 1960.

pense of consensus. It deals critically with the actions of men who could not possibly have acted so as to forestall all possible criticism. The more important public actions are generally of this sort. My purpose has been to contribute to a more profound understanding of the moral and strategic dilemmas which planners and lay decision-makers inescapably face. My technique has been to probe, more thoroughly than men of action normally have time or inclination to do, the *social and political* consequences of alternative reasonable approaches to the exercise of discretion. I have not endeavored to pass overall judgment either on men or on plans, a task which would have required both wisdom and skill of a far higher order than I have been able to employ.

PART ONE

I

The Intercity Freeway[*]

Introduction

Most laymen tend to think of city planners as proposers, but in fact only a small portion of the time of any planning agency is devoted to developing independent planning proposals. Each specialized public agency generally develops its own project proposals. In virtually every city the total public expenditure on projects initiated by city planners is insignificant. No one would contend, however, that this fact establishes the insignificance of city planning. City planners themselves reject such a conclusion by stressing their role as evaluators of other people's projects. They claim to be the people best suited to formulate goals for project planning, to point out relationships between the ideas of different specialists, and therefore to criticize the projects proposed.

If ever there was a public works project worthy of careful evaluation, that project was the Interstate Freeway. Its sections in and around St. Paul constituted the largest public works project that the city was likely to witness for decades. Its influence on the city's future development would probably be monumental. Although the project was not initiated within St. Paul and the city would not bear any part of its cost or administrative responsibility for its execution, no action involving the freeway could be taken inside the city without the municipal government's approval. The city planners of St. Paul therefore had, and publicly acknowledged, a

* A shortened version of this chapter appeared as *Locating the Intercity Freeway*, ICP Case Series, No. 88 (Bobbs-Merrill, 1965), copyright © 1965 by the Inter-University Case Program, Inc.; reprinted with permission.

17

responsibility to evaluate the freeway project from a comprehensive point of view.

They knew that no highway could serve traffic needs without having innumerable other repercussions, often less obvious to the casual eye than its intended purposes. They also recognized that some of these repercussions would probably disturb the public if there were full and open public discussion. This was the source of much proposer-evaluator conflict: comprehensive and careful study tended to turn issues from black and white to gray, thereby sapping public conviction and enthusiasm, and undermining the chances for approval of projects. In other words, the public relations requisites of any project proposal, needed to give it political momentum, conflicted with the prime characteristics of comprehensive evaluation: detached, systematic curiosity about the pros and cons of every alternative. Therefore, the planner who conscientiously subjected a popular proposal to searching criticism risked his own, his agency's, and his profession's standing in the community.

Of the three sets of actors whose approaches to St. Paul's freeway program will be described—highway engineers, organized private interests, and professional city planners—only the first had technical procedures for predicting the precise benefits to be derived by building on the basis of any particular design. Only they and the private interest spokesmen had explicit notions of what they hoped to achieve. Only the planners lacked *both* a clear notion of what values their efforts *should* serve and procedures for discovering what values any specific proposal *would* serve.

Consequently, the planners' work with regard to the freeway should not be evaluated according to some abstract criterion of "rationality." The emphasis of this case study is rather on how well the planners of St. Paul articulated key questions about the relations of problems and proposals to community values, brought together available knowledge bearing on these questions, formulated arguments supporting the various sides of each question, and tried to bring these arguments before responsible officials for their consideration.

Genesis of the Interstate Freeway

As metropolitan area populations grew after World War II, the nation's rising level of personal income permitted massive switches by metropolitan area dwellers from bus (and in the largest cities, rail) transportation to the more comfortable—but also far more expensive and space-consuming—automobile. To move a given number of people, even on roads of the highest quality, automobiles had to use at least four times the space required by buses and up to twenty times that required by rail transit. Even aside from the public costs imposed by automobile habits and the fixed costs borne by automobile owners (whether they drove or not), the expense of driving (figuring one person to a car) often ran several times higher than travel by public conveyance. However, commuters throughout the country (who caused most peak-hour congestion) remembered the waiting out-of-doors, the crowding, the delays, the stale air, and the general discomfort of public transportation. In ever-increasing numbers they chose to pay the price of automobile travel.

Their choice both encouraged, and was encouraged by, changes in the physical layout and spatial relations of urban areas following World War II. The movement known familiarly as urban sprawl greatly reduced the number of people living near public transportation routes while greatly increasing the number of, and distances between, their desired destinations. With an ever-declining number of people to patronize public transit on any route, transit companies were forced to reduce frequency of service, to eliminate some routes altogether, to raise prices, and to neglect maintenance. The cycle of declining patronage and service turned steadily, while the future of self-sustaining—not to say profit-making—urban public transportation was seriously challenged.

In cities throughout the country, increased traffic volume was channeled into street systems that had been laid out before the invention of the automobile. Until the end of World War II, amelioration of congestion had seemed feasible in most cases through piecemeal efforts to raise the traffic capacity of existing streets. Bottlenecks had been eliminated, sidewalks had been narrowed to permit street widening, and various traffic-control techniques had been employed—staggered traffic lights, prohibitions against parking, restricted left turns, and experimentation in the use of one-way streets.

After the war there was a gradual exhaustion of the available techniques for solving the problems of traffic congestion. Where sidewalks had been narrowed, for example, the only way to widen existing streets was to tear down the structures that lined them. The buildings that lined the major streets of a city were generally the most expensive. Even if city governments wanted to purchase the properties and demolish these structures, the very act of doing so would reduce the need for street widening at the point concerned, while increasing the need elsewhere. Crowded traffic arteries were caused not by people driving randomly through the city, but by trips designed to accomplish particular purposes. The concentration of economic, social, or other facilities on a particular street or at a particular corner was the factor that generated the congestion.

Most trips were, from the driver's point of view, economic in purpose. The 1949 Twin Cities Traffic Survey revealed, for example, that three-fifths of all passenger-car trips were for work, business, or shopping. Assuming that all truck traffic was economic in intent, the proportion of all traffic undertaken for economic reasons was more than 75 per cent. Economically generated traffic tended to concentrate at places of employment and at retail centers, which together occupied only one-eighth of the area of the Twin Cities proper and a much smaller proportion of the metropolitan area. Highway engineers called such places, where people habitually congregated in large numbers, "major traffic generators." The efforts to widen streets by tearing down adjacent buildings had the effect of destroying these generators to provide room for street widening—which was like tossing out all the merchandise in a store to make room for a maximum number of customers.

The first clamor from automobile owners throughout the nation for massive highway improvements had been cut short by the depression of the 1930's. During that decade federal aid for highway construction had risen, but not sufficiently to offset the decline of state and local expenditures. Highway funds frequently had been used to provide jobs with little regard for the enduring value of the projects undertaken. Then came the war. During the period of hostilities, no new highways were built and the decline in highway maintenance that had begun in the 1930's continued. At the war's end street networks in many cities were in worse condition than they had been in 1929.

Cities in Minnesota, as elsewhere, lacked the resources to meet their transportation crises. All local needs had been neglected during the previous fifteen years. Voter resistance to tax increases had stiffened in response to the unprecedented level of federal taxation. Local tax revenues, based primarily on the property tax, tended to lag behind inflation, which had halved the value of each tax dollar. The raising of property assessments was no less sensitive politically than the raising of tax rates, and few assessors tried to keep pace with the cost of living. The cost of building new high-quality thoroughfares was enormous. Even in the Twin Cities, one of the least densely built-up of the nation's large urban complexes, the estimated cost of construction ran in some instances to $10 million a mile. There were not, of course, any $10-million miles built prior to 1956. Politicians who raised a city's taxes sufficiently to finance a new system of highways or a thorough revamping of public transportation facilities would have run the twin risks of overwhelming defeat in ensuing elections and of having numerous taxable activities flee the city.

Nevertheless, the mass conversion to auto travel seemed to be relentless. Auto registrations in the Twin Cities area increased by 58 per cent in the years 1947–1950 alone (twenty times the rate of increase during the previous two decades). The number of miles traveled by the average car also increased rapidly.

Highway engineers, who had refined their techniques dramatically since 1929, promised that they could give lasting relief if the money to build new highways were found. They had discovered that gently curving limited-access highways could carry twice as much traffic per lane—at higher speeds and with greater safety—as the best streets built previously. The immediate cost of building these highways was great, but they seemed certain to repay it by reducing taxpayers' expenditures on vehicle operation and insurance. For those who cared, there were bonuses—intangible benefits of time saved, injuries avoided, and greater driving pleasure.

The key concept in the new approach was "limited access." A limited-access highway was one that permitted vehicles to enter and exit only at designated points—interchanges—and then only at angles gentle enough to eliminate the need for other vehicles to slow down. Cross traffic was eliminated by providing bridges over and tunnels under the highway. Commercial development was forbidden along limited-access highways, so that there was no reason for vehicles ever to slow down suddenly or to turn off at sharp angles.

Highway engineers coined new names for the new highways: "turnpike," "tollway," "thruway," or "freeway." The engineers urged that tolls not be charged on the new highways, to avoid the danger of discouraging use, and that they be built in urban as well as rural areas, despite their great expense and the dislocation they would cause. This was conceived not as mere street widening, but rather as the creation of wholly new highways on new rights-of-way. The engineers confidently acknowledged that it was bold surgery. State and local officials liked the idea but were unable to finance it.

The Federal Aid Highway Act of 1956 offered a solution. It provided for construction of a 40,000-mile national system of freeways, 90 per cent of whose cost would be borne by the federal government and 10 per cent by the states. The excise taxes levied to pay for its construction would fall evenly on automobile and truck users throughout the country; no one could escape by changing his residence. The freeways would cut through, around, and between the nation's cities, serving local as well as intercity traffic. Many people compared the importance of this ambitious highway program with that of building the railroads in the nineteenth century. (For estimates of its total cost, see page 52, note 16.)

The highway program evolved from more than a decade of planning at all levels of government. Highway engineers expected the freeways to be paramount traffic carriers for at least fifty years. Their impact on national development and patterns of living would presumably reverberate long afterward. During the decades of construction a million people would be forced from their homes to provide land needed for rights-of-way, and countless businesses would be compelled to move or would find the values of their locations affected by the new pattern of vehicular transportation. Soon after passage of the Highway Act, the federal Bureau of Public Roads decided that the rights-of-way in cities should be 400 feet wide. Most street rights-of-way in St. Paul were 60 feet wide, although the widest street had a 200-foot right-of-way. The bureau wanted to ensure that it would never have to purchase additional right-of-way for freeway widening, or to eliminate the strips of greenery on either side and in the center of the freeway. The center strip was a safety factor; that on the sides was a health factor (designed to keep nearby residents from the worst concentrations of noise and exhaust fumes); and both were aesthetic factors.

The concept of a federally financed superhighway network first had arisen in response to the perceived needs of military security in World War I. The Roosevelt Administration had revived it as a potential public works project when, in 1939, the Bureau of Public Roads had recommended a 26,700-mile highway system. During World War II the idea had received further study; and in 1943 a presidential commission had recommended a 40,000 mile system, offering two major reasons: (1) to provide a system for the rapid movement of men and equipment in time of war, and (2) to provide jobs during the expected postwar depression. The relief of peacetime traffic congestion had been offered as a desirable, but distinctly secondary, purpose. The possible indirect repercussions of such a program had attracted little attention. Here, it had seemed, was a public works project meant to serve useful purposes, not *merely* to create jobs. In 1944 Congress had authorized the Bureau of Public Roads to supervise the planning of the proposed highway system. The bureau, in turn, had prescribed standards for state highway departments to use and had then delegated to them the task of actually selecting the routes.[1]

Two points characterized the original planning of the interstate system. First, engineers did the planning. In Minnesota, which was typical, their conception of the function of the highway system was highly specific: the solution of traffic problems. They frankly declared that they did not have time to concern themselves with other aspects of the program. Second, the engineers of the federal bureau and the state highway departments had hitherto worked primarily on rural roads. The cities had built their own streets, laying them out in most cases before buildings and other structures blocked the way. In Minnesota, the state Highway Department had had, beginning in 1933, some experience improving

[1] In practice, the Bureau of Public Roads almost never adopted standards except on the recommendation of the American Association of State Highway Officials. Approval and promulgation by the bureau, however, was necessary to give them binding status and thus to ensure uniformity throughout the nation.

urban routes, but it had had virtually none locating new roads in urban areas. Nonetheless, its engineers now had to work quickly. The war was rapidly nearing an end, and they wanted to be prepared to move quickly once the expected economic depression developed. There seemed to be no time to theorize about subtle differences between urban and rural planning problems.

Selection of the Freeway Routes

The men who had cut dirt trails and roads in the early days of St. Paul's history had not been able to alter the landscape significantly; they had simply had to go around major natural barriers while trying to create routes as straight as possible between major centers of activity. As of the late 1950's the main routes into and out of St. Paul were still located on the same land. Some of them, such as Route 61—the main artery stretching north from the St. Paul business district—twisted and turned. Others, on flat land, were straight throughout their length.[2]

Facilities for work, shopping, and entertainment concentrated along the few early roads. Although they were the best roads in the city, in time they became some of the most congested. They served well, however, and outside the central business district *peak-hour* traffic on the city's major routes still averaged twenty miles an hour in 1949, according to the state Highway Department. Within the central business district, however, traffic frequently moved more slowly than a man could walk.

At an early date St. Paul's street planners had decided that entirely new highways, close to the existing major routes and located on the more heavily traveled side of them, would provide more lasting relief than piecemeal improvement. On this basis the city engineer in 1920 had proposed routes for a new radial highway system, with four routes projecting from the center of the city. He had supplemented this radial principle with two subordinate principles: (1) right-of-way costs should be minimized and (2) severe natural barriers should be avoided.

He had reasoned, for example, that a route parallel to Univer-

---

[2] Some exceptions to this pattern were the sections of Routes 12 and 61 that had been planned during the 1930's and constructed at the close of World War II. The Mississippi Street development, later incorporated as part of the interstate system, had been planned initially in the 1930's.

sity Avenue—the main artery between the central business districts of Minneapolis and St. Paul—should be built. A concentration of industry and railroad tracks blocked any route directly to the north of University Avenue. (See map, page 47.) Bridging it would be difficult and expensive. Further north, residential development was sparse. A highway in this area would clearly be so far from any heavily traveled routes that it would attract virtually no traffic away from them. Eight blocks south of University Avenue, on the other hand, was Marshall Avenue, heavily traveled itself, carrying a trunk highway and connecting with one of the major east-west streets of Minneapolis.

St. Anthony Avenue was almost precisely centered between University and Marshall Avenues. When University Avenue curved northwest toward the Minneapolis central business district, which was one and one-half miles north and eight miles west of St. Paul's central business district, St. Anthony, but not Marshall, followed it. Of all the streets between University and Marshall, St. Anthony alone was platted through to Minneapolis. Moreover, it connected with a major thoroughfare in Minneapolis. St. Anthony Avenue, therefore, was proposed as the western radial of the system.

Highway engineers had begun to make traffic counts in the 1920's; methods for articulating the data developed later. A traffic count merely showed the number of vehicles passing a given point during a particular period of time. It did not, however, indicate the pattern of traffic on routes approaching the point; therefore, it was of very limited use in explaining *why* traffic volumes reached a certain rate at a particular point. During the 1930's the interpretation of traffic count data had been greatly facilitated by the development of traffic-flow mapping techniques. A traffic-flow map was a pictorial summary of many traffic counts; it showed the number of vehicles passing each point on the map during a given period of time. Assuming that the day or hour represented was an "average" one and that traffic patterns hewed closely to the same average, day after day, one map could show a city's whole existing traffic pattern accurately and clearly. Trouble spots, and the extent of the remedy required to relieve them, could be clearly revealed, if the design capacity of existing streets was known.

Traffic-flow information was, however, better suited to piecemeal remedies than to comprehensive ones. It did not fully explain why drivers used some streets rather than others, nor what location would enable a new highway to attract the most traffic from existing congested streets. It did not indicate how traffic patterns would change during the projected life of the new highway, let alone explain the manner in which it would be *desirable* for traffic patterns to change. In short, a traffic-flow map was simply a pictorial representation of a large number of traffic counts, making the information easy to read but not necessarily easy to interpret.

After World War II highway engineers developed a new tool—the desire-line map. This map was the product of interviews rather than traffic counts. It showed not the routes that people were currently using but rather the straight-line routes from their origins to their destinations, which they presumably would take if they could. A desire-line map purported to show whether people used existing heavily traveled streets because they were the shortest *possible* routes, or the shortest *available*, or the shortest *high-quality* routes available. Assuming that most people took the route that minimized their travel time, and that it was desirable for the new highway to attract the maximum possible amount of traffic to it, the desire-line map showed the technician who performed certain calculations where the "ideal" route should lie in order to serve *current* desire lines.

When the highway engineers first chose the freeway routes in 1945–1946, desire-line techniques were new. The routes were chosen partly on the basis of "control points," which were ascertained by means of a very partial origin-destination survey. For the rest, the "art" of highway location—the common sense approach—still prevailed. The method employed by the Minnesota Highway Department in selecting the route from downtown St. Paul to downtown Minneapolis was typical and can be compared with the city engineer's method of plotting the same route in 1920 (see pages 24–25, above).

The first question dealt with in 1945 was where the Mississippi River should be crossed. The new bridge bearing the freeway was going to be expensive, and it was intended to be very efficient as a traffic carrier. Since the purpose of the bridge was to relieve existing bridges as much as possible, the proper location for it was where it would attract the maximum traffic. Motorists crossing the river on the existing bridges were interviewed; their origins and destinations were plotted on maps. In the center of the greatest desire-line concentration was placed the freeway "control point."

Interviewers then moved to three of St. Paul's leading north-south streets: Prior Avenue, Snelling Avenue, and Lexington Parkway. Motorists crossing them in an east-west or west-east direction at any point were interviewed, and their origins and destinations plotted. At Snelling and Lexington the center of desire-line gravity was slightly to the south of University Avenue; traffic was somewhat heavier south of the center of gravity than north of it. At Prior Avenue the emphasis was further north, but to build the freeway through the desire-line center on Prior would require expensive overpassing of the wide railroad track and industrial complex described earlier (see page 25, above). Four control points were then known, and the long projected St. Anthony Avenue route suited three of them quite well.[3] Its single defect, from a traffic point of view, was that it was slightly south of the center of desire-line gravity.

As noted previously, St. Anthony Avenue was the only street between University and Marshall that extended from St. Paul's business district to the Minneapolis city line. It was the only east-west street in the city continuing to parallel University Avenue as it angled northwest toward the Minneapolis central business district. St. Anthony Avenue ran directly south of the University of Minnesota and the Midway Industrial District, the third and fourth greatest traffic generators in the Twin Cities area after the two central business districts. Although it ran for one and one-half miles through the center of St. Paul's Negro district, it cut through no other neighborhoods. For more than half its length, it passed to the north of residential sections and to the south of trucking terminals and railroad tracks. This latter portion would require demolition of some homes—St. Anthony Avenue was too narrow for a freeway—but thereafter it would serve as a convenient buffer between the residential and industrial land uses.

St. Anthony Avenue connected with Arthur Avenue S.E. in Minneapolis. The freeway could continue adjacent to a railroad spur line until it curved west for a river-crossing slightly to the

[3] Data gathered in the St. Paul Central Business District Traffic Survey, published in 1946, had also supported the St. Anthony route.

south of the University of Minnesota. However, the section from the Minneapolis city line to the river-crossing cut through a pleasant residential neighborhood (already cut by the railroad spur), inhabited largely by university employees. Nonetheless, analysis of the driver interviews had demonstrated that the river-crossing "had to be" slightly to the south of the university. A crossing further south, sparing the residential neighborhood, would not serve traffic to and from the university very efficiently.

The St. Anthony route proposed in 1920 would have connected in Minneapolis with Arthur Avenue S.E. and the Franklin Avenue Bridge. By 1945 the Franklin Avenue Bridge was itself overworked, so a new bridge was proposed for a location one-third of a mile north of Franklin Avenue and just south of the university. Otherwise, the Highway Department proposal was identical with that made by the city engineer twenty-five years earlier.

Development and Application of Traffic Forecasting Techniques [4]

When the Twin Cities freeway routes were selected in 1945–1946, little work on traffic prediction had been done anywhere. The Highway Department's engineers had relied on their knowledge of existing desire lines. To estimate future traffic, they had simply projected vehicle registration trends, assuming the following: (1) no changes in average annual mileage per vehicle and (2) no changes in current desire-line patterns. To the extent that these data were insufficient, they had relied on their engineering experience and common sense. They had had no reason to believe that future traffic patterns could be forecast with any precision or reliability.

When it became clear after World War II that there would be plenty of time to plan the freeways, the federal Bureau of Public Roads had begun to finance more elaborate traffic research. One result was that the Minnesota Highway Department conducted its first full-scale survey of driver origins and destinations throughout

[4] The following section, which runs to page oo, is included for those who wish to consider the ways in which technical developments in the dozen or so years after 1945 might, had they come earlier, have influenced the basic freeway route location decisions. Readers who skip the section will find that they are able to follow the rest of the narrative without difficulty.

the Twin Cities area in 1949. The Department's engineers were unworried about the possibility that they might have located the freeway routes erroneously in 1945–1946. They expected, indeed, that the 1949 survey would provide irrefutable proof that their route choices had been the best possible. The primary reason for their interest in a full-scale origin-destination survey was that they needed precise estimates of future traffic volume at each point on the freeway to help them determine the number of traffic lanes necessary, the capacity of entrance and exit ramps, and related features.

The raw material of the survey consisted of interviews with the occupant of every twentieth dwelling unit in the study area, the owner of every tenth truck registered in the area, and the dispatcher of every fourth taxicab. Each interviewee was asked to list the trips that had been taken in his vehicle(s) on the preceding day. At fifty-four entry points during a period of several months, trips originating outside the study area were counted and driver samples were interviewed. The accuracy of the survey data as an indicator of current traffic patterns was subsequently checked by traffic counts at selected points. Discrepancies between traffic volumes predicted on the basis of the survey and actual traffic volumes averaged about 10 per cent.

The prediction of future traffic patterns was a two-stage procedure: prediction of desire lines and prediction of route attractiveness. The latter was easier by far, and may be dealt with quickly. To determine the most attractive route between any two points, highway engineers sought the one on which the trip could be made in the shortest time. Standard tables were also being developed to indicate the proportions of drivers who were likely to use the slower routes in given prototypical situations. State highway engineers in general did not worry much about predicting the speeds that would be possible on alternate routes in the future. They planned most important changes in route quality and were informed about the others at early stages in their planning evolution. The basic problem, then, was to predict desire lines.

Most researchers approached the problem by assuming that certain constant relationships existed between land use and traffic. Minnesota state highway engineers assumed at the start of their work in 1949 that the important relationships between land use and traffic volume could be roughly stated without too much trouble. Since land use was the cause and traffic the consequence, they believed that their fundamental requirement was a set of reliable land-use forecasts for the Twin Cities area.

Unfortunately, no land-use, economic base, or population studies had recently been carried out in the metropolitan area or any part of it. The only zoning ordinances in effect had been enacted during the 1920's. They had been amended from time to time but were not adequately enforced. They did not appear to mold the pattern of land-use change in any fundamental way. Nevertheless, the engineers proceeded. They asked every local planning agency in the survey study area to make twenty-year predictions for those of the eighty-eight survey districts within its jurisdiction. The study area included more than the Twin Cities proper but considerably less than the census-defined metropolitan area. The survey districts were delineated solely for the study's purposes; twenty-four of them were in St. Paul and its suburbs. The planning agencies were asked the number of dwelling units and retail establishments, and the dollar volume of retail sales, that they expected within their jurisdictions in 1970.

Not even the two central cities, Minneapolis and St. Paul, were able to make these forecasts properly. As of 1950 the St. Paul Planning Bureau consisted of three persons—a secretary, a recently graduated planner, and a man of eighty-three. The Minneapolis Planning Department had a larger staff, but like its St. Paul counterpart it had conducted no land-use research in many years.[5]

[5] A note on the formal structure of planning in each of the Twin Cities will perhaps be helpful. The St. Paul Planning Bureau and the Minneapolis Planning Department were agencies staffed by civil servants and administered in each case by a planning engineer. (The title "planning engineer" was changed in both cities to "planning director" during the 1950's. This was in accord with a national trend, and reflected a broadening conception of the planning function.) Each legally served a committee, known as the City Planning Board in St. Paul and the City Planning Commission in Minneapolis. St. Paul's Planning Board consisted of fifteen citizen members appointed for overlapping fixed terms by the mayor and eleven ex officio members, including the city's eight elective office-holders. The ex officio members almost never attended Planning Board meetings. The Minneapolis Planning Commission consisted of four citizen members appointed for overlapping fixed terms by the mayor (with the consent of the City Council), the mayor himself, two representatives of the City Council, and one representative each from

None of the suburbs had a trained planning staff. Local officials were asked to make the best predictions they could under the circumstances. If a few of the resulting district predictions were based on careful analysis—none could have been based on extensive research—it was difficult to know which they were and impossible to compare their reliability with that of the others.

From the district land-use predictions, Highway Department engineers attempted to predict the number of trips that would end in each district twenty years later. Because most trips occurred in pairs—a round trip counting as two trips—the number of trips ending in a district was considered to be roughly the same as the number originating in it. First, the engineers distinguished between trips made for "residential" and those made for "commercial" purposes. The categories were inclusive ones. "Commercial" trips were those made for work, business, medical, dining, and shopping purposes; "residential" trips were those made for social, recreational, school, and "other" purposes. Next, the engineers increased the number of "residential" trips to each district in 1949 by the same proportion that they expected the number of dwelling units in that district to increase. They increased the number of 1949 "commercial" trips by the same proportion that they expected the number of retail establishments to increase. They predicted the number of external trips in two steps: (1) they projected 1947–1952 trends, as revealed by traffic counts, in a straight line to get the total number of external trips to be expected at given dates; and (2) they divided the total among the districts in accordance with their expected number of dwelling units and retail establishments.[6]

As a final refinement, the engineers predicted the districts in which large shopping centers were likely to be built in the twenty-year period and raised their trip-end forecasts for those districts

---

the school and park boards. In general, all except the mayor took full part in the Planning Commission's work.

[6] The engineers apologized—in their own memoranda, although not to local officials at the time—for basing their commercial trip predictions on just the *number* of retail stores that would be in operation. They decided not to use the dollar-sales estimates that they had collected; their studies revealed that the number of stores correlated more closely with traffic volume than did dollar value of sales. Neither correlated very closely, but no better indicator was available.

accordingly. They reduced the trip-end forecasts for several districts within the city, on the assumption that some shoppers would be diverted to the suburbs as the freeways made travel easier and as attractive suburban stores with ample parking facilities were built. They had no formulas for making these adjustments, which consequently were merely token acknowledgments of the direction of change. The possibility that freeways might hurt retail business within the cities proper was never mentioned publicly. Civic leaders and officials in each of the Twin Cities continued to champion the freeways as undoubtedly a requisite of their economic survival.

State highway officials, when interviewed in 1959 about the techniques they had used in 1950, claimed only that the concept of relating land-use projections to traffic projections had been an important advance over previous approaches. They admitted readily that the techniques used had been extremely crude, but they maintained that these techniques had been the most advanced available at the time. No one had yet recognized that land-use projection was as difficult as traffic-pattern projection. In fact, the land-use forecasts made by the city planners and suburban nonplanners in 1950 had proven virtually worthless.

There had been another kind of flaw in the 1949 projections. The hypotheses that the number of commercial enterprises provided an accurate gauge of business traffic and the number of dwelling units an accurate gauge of other traffic were extremely crude. There was no theory to explain why the equations involved, based on 1949 patterns, would hold true in the future. Thus, their use for purposes of prediction depended on the underlying assumption that change was too gradual to affect twenty-year estimates significantly. It was a valid assumption in many cases, but not in all. In recent years, for example, the trend from numerous small stores to few large ones had been quite rapid. Moreover, the equations might have depended upon coincidence. "Commercial" trips had included by definition trips to work and to visit doctors; yet no theory had explained why the number of retail establishments should measure factory employment or trips to receive medical care.

The forecasters had not made any effort to predict the emergence and growth of nonretail places of employment—industrial, office, wholesale, and others. They had made no provision for increases in traffic volume per family unit, although this had been the trend for some years. They had not estimated the extent to which the freeway itself might affect future urban development. They had considered none of the following questions: What proportion of workers would travel to their jobs on public transportation in twenty years? What provision would be made in each district for commuters and shoppers to park their automobiles? Would the tendency of those who drove be to come singly or in car pools? To what extent would downtown retail stores be able to compete with suburban stores if the latter were to offer comparable selections of merchandise? Would large employers of office personnel shift to automated processes to a significant degree and locate in the suburbs? Would other employers find employees easier to attract on the urban fringe by belt-line freeways or in central business districts? Would urban redevelopment create new traffic-generating centers or renovate old ones that seemed to be declining?

In 1958 the state Highway Department conducted another Twin Cities origin-destination survey. Its traffic forecasters claimed still to be in the vanguard of their profession. They now employed an urban geographer to make their land-use projections. He explained to an interviewer that the fundamental premises of traffic-forecasting theory had not changed significantly since 1949–1950. They were that the relationship between land use and traffic, and the principles of land-use change, were constant over time. If these assumptions were correct, then traffic prediction was a three-stage process. The first step was to discover present land-use/traffic relationships, expressed in terms of trips per unit of specific land use.[7] The second step was to forecast land use in great

---

[7] No one had ever categorized land uses on the basis of their traffic-generating power. Nevertheless, data on current land use had to be categorized in some tentative fashion before exploratory research could begin. The Minnesota forecasters decided to use a modified version of the U.S. Census Bureau's standard industrial classification, which listed more than 400 land-use types. They coded trip ends into 55 land-use classes, and based their floor-area survey on the same 55 classes. They based their generalized land-use survey on 9 general classes. They hoped to refine their category definitions as computer analyses of the traffic data indicated that particular standard classifications had similar traffic-generation rates.

They did not even hope to be able for this survey to deal with the problem

detail by projecting the constant "principles" of land-use change. The third step was to apply land-use/traffic relationships to the land-use forecast.

The 1958 study area was the entire census-defined metropolitan area. The Highway Department divided it into more than 400 districts and 2,200 subdistricts. Twenty-year land-use projections were made for 700 zones. The forecasters obtained their information on current land use in Minneapolis and St. Paul from the planning staffs of the two cities. In contrast to 1950, both staffs had recently conducted land-use inventories. Their data on central business district land use was particularly recent and detailed. However, suburban officials still were unable to provide up-to-date land-use information. The department, therefore, prepared aerial photograph maps of the entire suburban area and categorized each structure according to dominant *first-floor* use. It reasoned that multiple uses within a single structure were rare in the suburbs. In any case, floor-area totals and use data were not available.

The next problem was to predict future land use on the basis of current land use. The forecasters assumed, it has already been noted, that the principles of urban change were constant; but students of the subject had just begun to search systematically for these principles and to study their operation. The forecasters were therefore compelled to accept many approximations.

They began by imposing four overall controls on their results. They accepted the Metropolitan Planning Commission's forecasts

---

of subdivision (as opposed to combination) of the standard classes. Yet, in theory, they admitted, this problem was just as important as the other. Because the standard categories had not been chosen on the basis of their traffic-generation qualities, individual establishments within each were likely to differ widely in traffic-generating power. The search for an adequate land-use classification based on traffic generation was an integral part of the search for constant land-use/traffic relationships. Hypotheses would have to be developed with respect to which variables were most responsible for traffic generation. Each hypothesis would have to be tested not only in one city, but in many, and over time. The classification would not be complete until all the major variables were identified and until it could be ascertained that the traffic generation of each establishment within each category could be predicted. The process of identifying variables and testing their relation to traffic generation was an endeavor of sufficient magnitude to absorb the nation's traffic forecasters for decades.

for the whole metropolitan area of 1980 population (45 per cent larger than in 1960) and of 1980 dwelling units (175,000–200,000 more than anticipated for 1960). They also accepted the land-use and population forecasts that had been made for each of the two central cities by its own planning staff. They confined their own efforts, therefore, to projecting suburban growth and breaking down the urban forecasts into district and subdistrict forecasts.

The forecasters assumed that some of the near-in suburbs would be saturated by 1980. The area within each that was zoned for residential development, suitable for building, and presently vacant was calculated. Its density when built up was estimated by projecting the average density of areas within the same suburb that had been developed since 1950. The remaining dwelling units of the expected total were assigned to suburbs on the fringes of the existing major-expansion lines, on the basis of a projection formula that took into account the past magnitude and rate of expansion in every direction. This was not quite a straight-line projection of the past trend; some adjustments were made to eliminate from the forecast both land reserved for public uses and land unsuitable for construction.

Commercial development was forecast in a similar fashion. The 1980 map showed all existing commercial areas as unchanged. To estimate the development of new commercial areas, state Highway Department personnel projected current relationships—which they had translated into mathematical equations—between shopping center location, shopping center store area, size of trade area, and population of trade area. Nearly all their prediction work involved shopping centers. Research concerning trade area, shopping center floor area, and related factors was based on existing shopping centers, most of which had come into existence since 1955. Since trade area patterns had developed so recently, no significant previous research existed to indicate changing relationships. The forecasters' major problem was to discover the nature of such relationships in order to do any predictive work at all. Actually, they made a number of generalized assumptions concerning future trade area relationships. For example, nearly all the centers built to date had been located so as to encompass parts of the high-density population of Minneapolis and St. Paul within their trade areas. Therefore, centers had often been closely spaced. The fore-

casters recognized that a future second ring of centers would serve
trade areas of far lower density. This would necessitate more spacing between centers. The forecasters also assumed that very large
centers would become increasingly dominant over the present
pattern of many small centers. This would significantly affect trip
generation and center location. These assumptions, however,
could not be of much use in predicting where particular centers
would locate.

The forecasters made a serious effort to predict industrial, public, or semipublic land-use development, but their methods were
different from and less sophisticated than those used in other kinds
of predictions.

They knew that 95 per cent of industrial employment was currently within Minneapolis, St. Paul, and the first ring of suburbs,
and that 95 per cent of all trips to industrial land-use locations
ended within these limits. They also knew that although movement of industry to the suburbs was the trend, this movement was
not rapid, it was characterized by low intensity, and it was being
counterbalanced by an intensive effort at industrial redevelopment within Minneapolis and St. Paul. They had obtained 1980
Minneapolis and St. Paul predictions from the planning staffs of
the two cities. The forecasters also believed that they could make
reasonably sound forecasts for the first suburban ring. The communities within this ring were 50 to 75 per cent developed; they
had reasonably firm zoning ordinances; they had hired consultant
or resident planners; and they had well-established land-use patterns. With these two sets of predictions, the forecasters believed
that they had accounted for 85 to 90 per cent of all 1980 trips to
industrial land-use locations. Outside the first suburban ring, they
had access to some firm plans for industrial park development, and
a few of the outer suburbs had already developed more general
planning and zoning data. Since all industrial land generated only
10 per cent of total daily trips in the metropolitan area, and developed suburban industrial land typically generated well under ten
trips per acre a day, the forecasters believed at this point that they
had reached the stage of diminishing returns.

Public and semipublic land-use forecasting presented other, but
no less awe-inspiring, challenges. It was relatively easy to predict
that most men twenty years hence would drive to work each day,

that their wives would shop periodically at nearby supermarkets, and that similar patterns would prevail. But their "whims"—as opposed to their immediate needs—would have much more to do with whether they approved school bond issues, contributed to the building of new churches, or induced public officials to increase park land acreages.

Despite their complexity, land-use forecasting techniques still appeared to rest on highly simplified and frequently crude assumptions. The *residential* expansion forecast technique alone seemed to rest on moderately firm foundations. Urban geographers had observed, for many years and in many different urban areas, continuities in the directions of urban expansion and in the rates of "filling in" built-up sections. They had also observed, however, that the trends sometimes changed. For example, the prewar suburban expansion pattern in most large American cities took the form of narrow bands along public transit line routes. After World War II the predominant commuter route became the highway, and suburban expansion took the form of wide humps with highways up the middle. The Highway Department found that directions of expansion in the Twin Cities area had remained constant between 1945 and 1958. One reason may have been that no new major highway routes had opened up; the freeways were planned, however, and might have been expected to alter the patterns of expansion in ways difficult to estimate with precision. The Department's forecasters did not try to estimate them at all.[8]

Even if the residential predictions had been perfectly accurate, the Highway Department's most important prediction difficulties would have remained. Traffic in low-density residential areas did not clog all surrounding streets but only streets along the routes from these areas to the destinations of many people. The problem was not so much how to predict residential expansion as how to predict where residents would want to go. Presumably, for example, they would go to shopping centers with some regularity. But

[8] Nor had forecasters elsewhere. Three years later it was still possible for a nationally prominent planner to write: "Until the current Penn-Jersey study in the Philadelphia region, I know of no planning process which has taken account of the differing impacts of alternative transportation plans on land use change" (Robert B. Mitchell, "The New Frontier in Metropolitan Planning," *American Institute of Planners Journal*, XXVII, No. 3 [August 1961], 170).

it was not enough to declare that new shopping centers would probably be located according to certain principles. A traffic forecaster needed to know exactly where a center would locate if he was to plan adequate highway access to it. Under prevailing conditions, the only way to predict shopping center location with precision was to control it. Highway Department personnel were, it had to be admitted, in a position to feel confident on this point. Most developers tried to build their shopping centers near important street and highway intersections. Nevertheless, Highway Department personnel did not feel content with their work; they viewed their problem solely as one of prediction, not of deciding where shopping centers should go. They wanted to serve economic forces, not to guide them.

Despite their awareness of these obstacles to reliable prediction, the forecasters felt that their projections were adequate at the level of showing major corridor movements, and that at all levels they were far superior to any projections that it had been possible to make previously. They did not claim that it was yet possible to locate highways by the scientific application of origin-destination and land-use data. They did note that it was currently possible, using computers, to plot any given number of potential highway route lines in such a way that the *average* distance from each desire line to the nearest route line was minimized. Given adequate computers, this procedure was capable of extraordinary refinement. Trips considered unlikely to involve freeway use on any of the routes being evaluated at any given moment could be precluded from affecting the results. The computations by themselves, however, could not solve all highway location problems. Highway engineers spoke frequently of the "art" in highway location. They noted that highways could seldom be built on "ideal" route lines. After desire-line computations were completed, maps indicating the locations of structures and of topographic hazards had to be studied to discover lines of tolerable, if not of "least," resistance. Moreover, each stretch of highway was part of a larger system. Its relation to the whole limited the area in which it might be located. Since most trips were short, the "ideal" route line for one stretch of highway might fail to extend into the "ideal" for adjoining stretches. Adjustments had to be made to ensure that the end product provided a more or less direct route between major traffic-generating points as well as an attractive alternative to existing overburdened routes serving short-trip traffic along the way. No one had yet devised a formula for "scientifically" balancing these considerations with each other or with considerations of cost.

By the late 1950's, however, certain plausible ways of reasoning had become widely accepted. For example, in the interstate system's urban sections, local rather than intercity trip desire lines predominated. Through travel was diverted from the cities by belt lines around them. In the rural sections intercity travel was given primary consideration; and connecting lines, rather than diversions of the main route, brought freeway service near the lesser cities. At a much lower level of generality, standard tables had become available indicating that few drivers would habitually add more than 20 or 25 per cent to their mileage in order to use a freeway unless they could save significant amounts of time by doing so. These tables showed no more than averages derived from data collected at particular places, with particular driver samples, when all other relevant factors, such as aesthetic attractiveness of the alternative routes, appeared to be roughly equal. They nevertheless served as a basis for concluding that, since most local trips took no more than 10 or 15 minutes on the current routes, no urban freeway would attract much local traffic unless it hewed closely to the main desire-line concentrations. Highway engineers, therefore, disliked adding more than 5 or 10 per cent to the average distance between desire line and route line in the service of "art."

"Art" also played a significant part in the process of determining new highway needs. There was no way of deciding "scientifically" how much money should be spent on highways and, therefore, what initial assumptions about desirable levels of highway service should be made when designing test highway systems. At the same time, the Minnesota Highway Department's engineers almost unanimously contended that new highway construction generally paid for itself many times over by spurring economic growth, by reducing automobile maintenance costs and accident rates, and by saving the time of drivers.[9]

As a matter of fact, however, the Minnesota Highway Depart-

---

[9] See pp. 50–51, below, for an elaboration of these points in a discussion of the Report of the President's Advisory Committee on a National Highway Program.

ment was not planning many new routes as the 1958 survey conclusions became available (beginning in 1960). The primary use
it now had for traffic prediction was to help gauge the additional
capacity likely to be necessary on existing or previously planned
routes. This was an important use, but a very limited one, especially where the freeway was concerned. The freeway right-of-way
was intended to be so wide that additional lanes could be added at
minimal expense whenever needed, and entrance and exit ramps
could be built with wide margins of safety. The greatest future
problems involving congestion would be on city streets in the
vicinity of freeway ramps. These streets were, for the most part, in
high-density areas where simple street-widening could provide little relief. It would always be possible to overcome congestion in
specified areas by building freeways, provided enough federal
money were available. Eventually, however, automobiles would
always have to exit from freeways to drive toward and park near
the major traffic generators. Some architects and city planners had
suggested expensive solutions, but the question of whether many
cities were likely to spend enough money to make progress against
the treadmill remained unanswered.

An Old City Planner's Approach

George Herrold had been chief planning engineer of St. Paul
for a quarter of a century by 1945. He had drafted highway improvement proposals many times during his tenure and was one of
the officials who in 1920 had helped to develop the plan for a
major thoroughfare on St. Anthony Avenue. A still-existent drawing depicted what he had envisioned: a four-lane divided parkway,
landscaped and tree-lined. Limited access highways, of course, had
not been conceived in 1920.

A graduate in civil engineering, class of 1896, Herrold was a
product of the "reform" and "nonpartisan" periods of Minnesota
history. He thought rather little of politicians; and in turn he had
never been popular with local political leaders, many of whom
considered him impractical and unbending in his idealism. Consequently, Herrold had never had much influence in City Hall. On
the other hand, he had good relations with many of St. Paul's
older business leaders, and for many years he had enjoyed a measure of public renown as St. Paul's "founder of city planning."

The Planning Board had published dozens of reports during Herrold's tenure. All of them had reflected some research and had been highly competent pieces of work by the standards of Herrold's generation. The City Council had never granted him funds for professional staff, but at times during the 1930's he had had several hundred WPA employees gathering data under his direction. The research conducted had almost always been of an inventory nature, but it had provided Herrold with a considerable store of information on which to base his general views concerning community land-use problems and needs.

The fact was, nonetheless, that in the late 1940's St. Paul had a chief planning engineer in his eighties, working with virtually no professional assistance. Largely for this reason, the city planning tradition in St. Paul did not stress intensive research or general planning. Issues were dealt with in an informed intuitive fashion as they arose. Herrold cited planning literature and data published by other agencies with larger staffs. He believed that he could make a substantial contribution even working under these handicaps. His work, he felt, was primarily thought and recommendation based on long experience with the city's problems. He said that he did not see how planners newly brought to a city could plan well; even the best of men required many years to understand and feel the needs of a city.

Herrold had little faith in his political superiors and conceived his role as independent advisor to the community as well as to them. He saw that engineers and other specialists who planned public works generally prevailed within City Hall, and he doubted that they would ever take account of planning needs except under public pressure. He felt certain, therefore, that city planners were most effective when they kept the general public informed of their views. Planners usually would be defeated in public controversies, of course, but no more ignominiously than they lost any other kind of political controversy. At least public disputes might have educative value.

Herrold did not believe that the automobile should dominate cities, and he preferred to keep new highway construction out of built-up areas. He knew that the freeway routes had been chosen before any elaborate traffic studies had been done, and this led him to doubt the impartiality of all Highway Department traffic analyses that came out in the late 1940's and 1950's—especially since none challenged the original route choices.

Herrold's interest in St. Anthony Avenue dated back to his work on the 1920 city engineer's report which had recommended improvement of the avenue as a surface highway. In 1938 he and others had proposed a trunk highway on St. Anthony Avenue. In 1942, at the request of the chairman of the City Planning Board's Street and Highway Committee, he had prepared a report on highway approaches to the city and on needed street improvements. In the report he again had recommended the improvement on St. Anthony Avenue. Nonetheless, when Herrold discovered that St. Anthony Avenue was being proposed as part of the interstate system, with a block-wide right-of-way, he was very surprised. Parkways with intersections at every corner, he declared, lined and divided by well-kept grass and majestic trees, with truck traffic excluded from them, would grace a neighborhood. To provide room on St. Anthony Avenue for a parkway, a 200-foot right-of-way would suffice—half of that prescribed for the interstate system. A freeway might carry more vehicles more quickly, but in Herrold's opinion it would also be a gigantic, unshaded, unsightly, noisy ditch and an unwelcome concentrator of exhaust fumes. He believed it was foolish to concentrate traffic so heavily on one artery; the city streets near the freeway's exit points were sure to be swamped, and the cycle of piecemeal improvements would begin again.

Herrold was basically opposed to any freeways in the city: urban freeway mileage was very expensive; it divided neighborhoods; and it encouraged vehicles to enter the city. He believed that a belt-line freeway encouraging through traffic to bypass the city would alleviate traffic congestion adequately. A parkway on St. Anthony, from which trucks should be excluded, would eliminate completely the problem of serious congestion between the two central business districts. The parkway needed to be only four lanes wide; at peak hours three lanes could be used in one direction; left turns and parking could be forbidden.

In arguing against the freeways, Herrold occasionally referred to considerations of mass transit, the economic position of downtown, and urban sprawl; but his primary objections to the freeway were social, and he expressed them frankly. He wrote, for example, that "the freeway idea . . . requires the moving of thousands of people, who must give up their homes, churches, schools, neighbors and valued social contacts, who lose the institutions they have built for their pleasure and profit." When considering the intercity freeway, he typically emphasized that five-sixths of the Negro population of St. Paul lived in an area two miles long and one-half mile wide. St. Anthony Avenue ran the length of this area, precisely through its center. The prescribed right-of-way would take about one-seventh of the area. A comparable proportion of its structures would be destroyed and its population forced from their homes. Either of two results was likely: (1) displaced Negroes might try to move into other neighborhoods, public reaction would be extremely unpleasant, and Negroes would find it virtually impossible to buy or rent homes in the neighborhoods to which they aspired; or (2) the Negroes might remain within their ghetto—reduced in size, more crowded, more completely Negro in composition. Herrold did not presume to be a social reformer. He had no wish for dispersion of the Negro population throughout the city, but he believed that Negroes should be protected from encroachments upon their traditional community in St. Paul.

In reaching his conclusions about the proposed freeway route, Herrold did no original research and held no hearings. He analyzed the data that were available, however, and he wrote numerous memoranda setting forth his views. He contended that long experience and a disciplined mind could give a man familiarity with the "heart" of a city and enable him to make some wise judgments even if he did lack staff for conducting intensive research. Thus, whenever the opportunity arose he reiterated his arguments that no freeway should run on St. Anthony Avenue.

The engineers of the state Highway Department disagreed vigorously with Herrold's views. They believed that their task was to build highways, not ruminate about the general needs of cities. Their method was research that yielded quantitative conclusions; art, they reasoned, was needed only to fill in the gaps. Their commodity was expertness, not wisdom. They and Herrold shared the belief that the public could not contribute much to their thinking; the groups that approached them, they believed, were self-seeking. The vast driving and taxpaying public had no interest group spokesmen; the department should stand firm and "build the best damn highways possible." The public should be won over, however, not alienated.

The engineers admitted the importance of circumferential routes but said such routes would not significantly alter traffic volumes within the cities. After 1949 they pointed to their desire-line maps for "proof." Driver interviews had revealed that through traffic was only a minute proportion of traffic on city streets. Most trips within the city were no more than several miles in length. It would not pay drivers to go out of their way to use the belt-line freeway for such short trips. The largest proportion of traffic, particularly at peak hours, was generated by the central business districts, the Midway Industrial District, and the University of Minnesota. All were along a line bisecting a circle that would be formed by the circumferential route; few drivers to and from these areas would find the circumferential route of any use. Only routes through the cities would substantially relieve urban congestion. The engineers estimated that by 1975 the intercity freeway would be compelled to carry 5,000 vehicles an hour at peak hours, and that six lanes of parkway in the peak-hour direction alone would be required to carry an equivalent load. The cost of an adequate parkway would equal that of the four-lane freeway. A parkway would move traffic more slowly; furthermore, it would divide neighborhoods more seriously than the freeway, because freeway overpass and underpass crossings were safer to traverse than busy surface streets.

Herrold's attitude toward the freeway remained unchanged. State and U.S. trunk highways that were well-located in St. Paul, he believed, were being abandoned unnecessarily in favor of the freeway idea. After 1949 he pointed to a section of the origin-destination survey report showing that a vehicle starting from the center of St. Paul's central business district, except during the peak hour, could travel far past the city limits in any direction within fifteen minutes. The peak hour was defined as the four consecutive fifteen-minute periods during the day when traffic was heaviest. Generally, a morning and an afternoon peak hour were measured. During the peak hour, traffic moving north, south, southeast, and southwest could travel as far as the city limits in fifteen minutes. Traffic moving east, west, northwest, and north-east could travel two-thirds of the same distance in fifteen minutes. Congestion was no problem beyond the fifteen-minute zone, and Herrold did not object to building freeways beyond it. He believed it was a question of values whether so much money should be spent and so many people dislocated to save drivers a few minutes within the fifteen-minute zone.[10]

Herrold lamented the freeway's foreseeable impact on land use in St. Paul. Twenty-two railroad lines passed through the city. Most of the city's growth in the late nineteenth century had been due to its position as the railroad center of the Upper Midwest. The railroads, however, together with the city's main thoroughfares, divided the city into "islands," often too small and irregular to permit the establishment of attractive neighborhoods. The freeway would be likely to increase the number and decrease the size of these islands, unless it were built adjacent to railroad lines or existing main streets. The cost of land next to main streets prohibited construction next to them, but development was light in the immediate vicinity of most of the rail lines. If freeways had to enter the city, Herrold reasoned, they should be put next to railroad lines. Dislocation of people and commerce would be minimized. The city's minority-group housing problem would not be intensified.

Moreover, if the freeway route did not follow present desire-line patterns precisely, its construction would encourage deconcentration and the development of new lands within the city; both were desirable and over the years would tend to decrease congestion. Although this approach to highway location would fail to maximize the use of the freeway in its first years, drivers would travel further out of their way to use it when congestion increased on city streets in the future—if it increased. It was better, Herrold said, to cause drivers to go out of their way and to get less than maximal traffic relief than to destroy neighborhoods and exacerbate racial tensions.

Applying this approach, Herrold developed an alternative to

[10] A decade after completion of the 1949 survey, the city engineer of St. Paul told this writer that he thought traffic could still move about the same distances in the same time. He added that the freeway would reduce the commuting time to the city limits by only a few minutes because drivers would still have to make their way to its entrances on city streets.

the St. Anthony route proposal. He concentrated his fire on the St. Anthony route because he thought it would do the greatest amount of social harm. He hoped that if his views prevailed in this instance, city officials might listen when he spoke about other freeway sections. He viewed his alternative as a compromise between the Highway Department's proposal and his own belief that the freeway should be kept outside of the city. It became known as the "Northern Route" because it ranged from three-quarters of a mile to one and one-quarter miles north of the St. Anthony Avenue route. At one point it was almost a mile to the north of University Avenue. It ran adjacent to railroad tracks most of the way between downtown St. Paul and the city line. Herrold proposed to cross the Mississippi River at the same place proposed by the Highway Department, but he wanted to approach the river from a different direction, thereby eliminating most of the freeway section through the Prospect Park neighborhood in Minneapolis. The most important virtues of his alternative route were its avoidance of the Negro neighborhood of St. Paul and its minimal passage through the Prospect Park area. He also claimed, however, that the northerly growth of suburban communities eventually would justify the Northern Route in traffic terms.

Highway Department officials, on the other hand, argued against the Northern Route. It bordered the Midway Industrial District only at the district's northwest corner, whereas the St. Anthony route ran along the entire southern boundary. The St. Anthony location was a direct route between downtown St. Paul and the Midway District. The Northern Route was indirect; following it from the Midway District to the downtown area, one would have to travel north and then southwest. The time saved by using the freeway would not justify its use for other short trips either, although it was satisfactory for trips from the central business district of St. Paul to the University or to the Minneapolis central business district. Yet most trips were shorter than five miles. The freeway would not be certain to relieve existing streets substantially unless it hewed within one-quarter to one-half mile of the major desire-line concentrations. Moreover, the Northern Route would pass through extensive railroad and industrial property at the western edge of St. Paul. Any saving in right-of-way cost

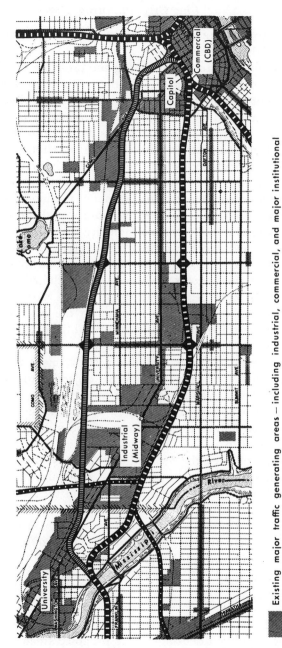

Existing major traffic generating areas — including industrial, commercial, and major institutional

The State Highway Department proposal for Interstate Highway route (St. Anthony Route)

Herrold's alternate proposal for Intercity portion of Interstate Highway route (Northern Route)

Connecting expressways

Map 1. Alternative proposals for the intercity route, St. Paul.

vis-à-vis the St. Anthony route would be offset by the cost of ele-
vating this section of the freeway.

Herrold wrote a ten-page report analyzing the probable social
and economic costs of building on the Northern Route as compared with the St. Anthony route, but he had no funds for collecting traffic data and thus could not estimate the amount of traffic
that would be diverted from existing streets to his proposed
freeway. Nor could he demonstrate with figures that a four-lane
parkway would suffice for thirty to forty years. The Highway Department had estimated that twelve lanes—the equivalent of a
freeway—would be needed. Department personnel reminded the
city that if fewer vehicles used the freeway, more would use the
city streets, thus increasing the city's maintenance bill. (The federal and state governments were to maintain the interstate system
as well as build it.) They reminded the driving public that it
would forego some of the benefits of freeway use if the freeway
were inconvenient for more people than it had to be. Moreover,
they declared flatly that the cost of a freeway on the Northern
Route could not be justified to the Bureau of Public Roads, in
view of the route's limited traffic-service potential.

City leaders, who had to approve Highway Department plans
for work within the city, considered still another objection to Herrold's plan. The parkway would have to be built with local tax
revenues; the freeway would cost the city nothing. Trucking interests in the Midway area were very conscious of the mileage and
travel time—equivalent to money—that they would save each year
if the freeway route followed the St. Anthony route. Midway retailers had noted that the St. Anthony route passed one-third as far
from them as the Northern Route. Commuters from the western
part of St. Paul, most of whom lived south of University Avenue,
knew that a Northern Route freeway would not save them time.
Minneapolis officials were pleased that the St. Anthony route connected conveniently to a projected river-crossing and to a locally
financed expressway in south Minneapolis.

The Highway Engineers Proceed

For a number of years prior to passage of the Highway Act in
1956 there had been public discussion of the proposed freeway in
St. Paul. Beginning in 1942, a number of civic organizations had

engaged in a study of postwar public works needs. Mayor Mc-
Donough, with the approval of the City Council and the Ramsey
County Board, had appointed an Improvement Coordinating
Committee, a civic group authorized to coordinate and activate
long-range plans for the improvement of the metropolitan area.
The St. Paul City Planning Board, the St. Paul Chamber of Commerce, the Midway Civic Club, and other organizations had contributed to the work of the committee. There had been public
meetings and press publicity, but little or no controversy appears
to have been generated. In 1947, despite Herrold's counterargu-
ments, the city had approved the Highway Department's proposed
route locations with little public dispute. After losing his fight in
the early postwar years, Herrold returned to do battle again after
1956. At the age of ninety, he took to writing long letters-to-the-
editor defending his position. He stirred some controversy, but
public officials ignored him.

As early as 1946 and 1947 the city engineer had begun informally to discourage new construction along the proposed freeway routes. His purpose had been to hold down the eventual right-
of-way cost. He had not had any legal authority to prevent new
construction, but he had found that few people were anxious to
build after he informed them of their property's uncertain future.
Of course, they might have gambled on being reimbursed adequately when the Highway Department took their land, but no
one had been certain what government appraisers and the courts
would think fair. Moreover, government agencies had seldom
compensated people for the mental strains and personal inconveniences of moving.

In 1949 Congress had authorized federal financing of urban
redevelopment projects. Mayor Delaney had been enthusiastic,
and had seen to it that St. Paul was the first city in the country to
win a project approval. To secure federal approval for its projects,
the city had been required to demonstrate that a market demand
for the land was likely to exist after it was cleared. The procedure
was for the Housing Authority to purchase the property, exercising eminent domain to force the hands of reluctant owners. The
land was then cleared and made available to private purchasers.
The Housing Authority might, and often did, sell land for less
than it had paid if it believed that the public interest would bene-

fit from such a transaction. The developer who purchased land from the Housing Authority was spared the pain of bargaining with large numbers of property owners, and he was assured of newly developed surroundings within the project area.

The Housing Authority located St. Paul's renewal projects adjacent to the proposed freeway routes. Its officials said that investors would clamor for land so close to the freeway, especially as the freeway would provide a buffer between the blighted areas proposed for renewal and those not so designated. The Highway Department assured local officials that Congress would eventually finance the freeway's construction. After work began on the renewal projects, the city's commitment to the 1947 route locations was deepened. Had local officials subsequently chosen to request that sections of the freeway be relocated, they would have embarrassed their colleagues who had to deal with the federal Urban Renewal Administration.

As the urban renewal program got under way, city engineer Shepard used his powers of persuasion more vigorously to discourage construction along the proposed freeway route. At his urging, the voters ratified a $200,000 bond issue in 1953 authorizing him to purchase property on the freeway right-of-way when the moratorium on construction imposed extreme hardship on specific owners. Still, most landowners who found themselves unable to sell or improve their property continued to suffer—not "extremely" in the city engineer's opinion—without compensation.

Meanwhile, the freeway program was making headway in Washington. It was also being altered somewhat in concept, if not in procedure. Although fear of depression had waned in the country and the national administration was trying to reduce defense expenditures,[11] urban traffic had burgeoned, and with it had increased political pressures on Congress to finance the interstate system.[12] The President's Advisory Committee on a National Highway Program, chaired by General Lucius Clay (ret.), re-

[11] The national administration was also pressing a policy of "no new starts" in the domestic public works field, but economic stabilization and defense had been the ostensible main purposes of the superhighway program according to official statements over the years.

[12] For a lively and useful, if highly critical, account of the political pressures in favor of the highway program, see Daniel P. Moynihan, "New Roads and Urban Chaos," *The Reporter*, XXII, No. 8 (April 14, 1960), 13–20.

ported in January 1955 that the total construction needs of the nation's highways required a $101-billion, ten-year crash program.[13] The interstate system accounted for $27 billion of this total.

The federal share of the proposed program was thirty times greater than the 1943–1953 rate of federal highway aid. The proposed rate of expenditure on streets and highways for all levels of government combined was four times greater than the 1947 combined rate, and twice the 1953 rate. The committee indicated, however, that the project would repay its cost with ease. It reported that "agriculture, industry, and our defense planning [are] closely geared to motor transportation" and noted a presidential statement that " 'an adequate highway system is vital to continued expansion of the economy. . . . The relationship is of course reciprocal; an adequate highway network will facilitate the expansion of the economy which, in turn, will facilitate the raising of revenues to finance the construction of highways.' " [14] As if this were not conclusive, the committee added that "the improvement of our highway systems as recommended herein would reduce transportation costs to the public through reductions in vehicle operating costs currently estimated to average as much as a penny a mile. Based on present rates of travel, this saving alone would support the total cost of the accelerated program." [15]

Although some city planners felt misgivings about the dislocation of people and economic activity that would accompany building freeways in cities, the hard political reality was that urban area residents constituted a national majority. They were the most conscious of traffic congestion. If the crash program were to be

[13] U.S. Congress, House, *Message From the President of the United States Relative to a National Highway Program*, 84th Cong., 1st sess., 1955, House Doc. 93.

[14] *Ibid.*, pp. 4, 7.

[15] *Ibid.*, p. 7. The committee carried the profit calculation a step further, citing the President's statement as follows: " 'A simple dollar standard will not measure the "savings" that might be secured if our highways were designed to promote maximum safety. . . . But whatever the potential saving in life and limb may be, it lends special urgency to the designing and construction of an improved highway network.' " The fact that automobile travel on the most modern superhighways involved accident rates many times higher than the national average for bus, train, and air travel was not mentioned.

supported by a general gasoline tax, as the President's committee proposed, they would bear the brunt of it. The committee had recommended financing by tax rather than user tolls because it believed that only 8,500 miles of the system could possibly pay for themselves in tolls; 5,000 of these miles had already been built or were under construction by the states. Therefore, the crash program had very little to do with this mileage.

After two sessions of debate, Congress voted in 1956 to authorize a crash program limited to the 40,000-mile interstate system, now officially christened the "National System of Interstate *and Defense* Highways" (emphasis added). The system was to be built over a period of thirteen years. No effort was to be made to relate the program to the business cycle. The long lead time between commitment to contractors and construction, it was now recognized, severely limited the usefulness of the program for economic stabilization purposes. Commitments made in time of economic recession might take effect in time of boom, and vice versa.[16]

As soon as the Federal Aid Highway Act became law, the Bureau of Public Roads asked the state highway departments to submit cost estimates for their freeway mileage within one year. The Minnesota Highway Department organized for the monumental task in four months; eight months remained until the deadline.

To make cost estimates, the state highway engineers had to know in detail the land over which the state's freeways would run. Of course, they used the routes approved a decade earlier. There was no time to argue with local officials; only the governments of the largest cities were kept informed of the decisions being made. Even they were told that if they wished to protest, they might do so after the deadline passed. Local protest was not, however, to be easy at any time. The state Highway Department had authority to determine the order in which sections of the freeway system were to be constructed. Right-of-way acquisition for each section had to begin eighteen months or two years before construction. If agreement with the officials of one city was not reached in time, the department could (and made clear that it would) simply shift its

16 Parenthetically, it may be noted that the Clay Committee's rough estimate of $27 billion as the total cost of the interstate program was revised to $41 billion by the Bureau of Public Roads in 1959. Early in 1965 the estimate was revised officially again, this time to $46.8 billion.

order of priorities. A section scheduled originally for 1960 might be delayed five or ten years.

The cost estimates submitted to the Bureau of Public Roads in 1957 had official status. The bureau's position was that future upward revisions should be made only in response to inflation, engineering improvements, or new traffic data. The Highway Department might propose changes for other compelling reasons, but the bureau did not intend to be very flexible. Inflation was already adding to highway costs.

The Highway Department had its own reasons for appearing inflexible. Traffic and cost data were recognized as authoritative and impartial by all parties. Such data could be collected without time-consuming political consultation. Secrecy could be maintained until the proper time for public announcement, thereby minimizing real estate speculation. At the stage of public discussion, inflexibility tended to hold down the level of controversy. Highway personnel noted that when the department acceded to the demands of one group of interested citizens, other groups were encouraged to make demands. If one group succeeded in having a freeway section removed from its neighborhood, residents near the proposed *new* location were extremely likely to protest. Every neighborhood and every property owner threatened in fact or fancy by the freeway had to be assumed to be watching closely to determine the potential rewards of complaint. Highway officials concluded that if they *were* flexible, it was unlikely that total public satisfaction from the freeways would be greater in the end. Every change would probably make the freeways more expensive and less efficient as carriers of traffic. There was no consensus about the extent to which other values ought to be served. If freeway plans were not completed on schedule, years of benefits to road users might be lost. Congress might unexpectedly cancel the program, in which case the state would never retrieve its loss.

City officials could not single-mindedly support displeased citizens because important pressure groups within the city wanted the freeways to be constructed *quickly.* Downtown businessmen and property owners wanted the task of driving downtown to be more inviting, and they wanted to arrest the flight of investment and consumer dollars to the suburbs. Truckers believed they lost money every moment that freeway construction was delayed. St.

Paul's Midway District was the third largest trucking center in the United States, and the truck owners were a force to be reckoned with when their interests were threatened. They knew much more precisely than private motorists how many dollars the freeways would save them. Labor was interested in the great number of jobs for construction workers that the freeway program would provide. Taxpayer groups noted that although the freeway would remove much land from the tax rolls, it was expected to encourage commercial development downtown and along its own right-of-way. By diverting traffic from city streets, it would reduce the cost of street maintenance. It promised an end to the cycle of widening old thoroughfares and constructing new ones. By carrying several times as many cars per lane as surface streets, the freeway might save land for the tax rolls in the long run. Booster groups emphasized that delay would sacrifice St. Paul's lead of several years over Minneapolis. Habits of shopping and working in St. Paul, if once developed, might persist after the Minneapolis freeways came into operation. The reverse might occur if Minneapolis took the lead.

The city's own engineers said freeways were needed desperately. The Highway Department had fine engineers on its staff. Only a fool would delay construction, it seemed, to satisfy specially interested voters who knew nothing about highway construction. St. Paul's elected officeholders, therefore, answered evasively the questions of citizens who complained, often implying that the Highway Department made all decisions without consulting the city. Every so often they quietly approved Highway Department plans at some new level of specificity.

A Young City Planner's Approach

Let us return for a moment to the period of the late 1940's, when members of the St. Paul Planning Board began to believe that the city needed more vigorous and politically acceptable planning. As a result of the Planning Board's dissatisfaction with the existing state of affairs, two young city planners were hired successively in 1947 and 1948 to assist Herrold. Both resigned after short periods.

In April 1950 C. David Loeks, recently graduated from Massachusetts Institute of Technology, became the third to try his hand.

Herrold's first assignment for Loeks was to study alternative routes for the intercity freeway. Loeks, unwilling to be impaled between Herrold and the rest of St. Paul officialdom, wrote a report urging further study. He soon found that city officials expected to talk to him rather than to Herrold when they entered the planning office. He said he felt sad to see them hurting Herrold in this way, but Herrold came to see him as a very ambitious young man. After a year of discomfort, Loeks prepared to follow his predecessors. The federal Housing and Redevelopment Act had been passed in 1949, however, and Mayor Delaney cared deeply about urban renewal. He believed that one prerequisite of a good renewal program was comprehensive planning, and he refused to accept Loeks' resignation. Instead, he created the post of Planning and Zoning Consultant and induced Herrold to accept the position.

In 1952, while still in his twenties, Loeks became St. Paul's planning director. He was almost sixty years younger than Herrold, and an entirely different kind of city planner. He was uncertain who, in theory, the planner was supposed to serve; but he was sure that in practice ineffective planning was worthless. The planner, he knew, operated in a political environment. He must gain the confidence of important community leaders, primarily within but also outside of government. He should never speak hastily. He should not only consider the validity of his statements but also the effect of making them in the form he did. If he alienated too many people, he would see his recommendations ignored, and make the task of his successors more difficult. The example of Herrold was before him.

Loeks chose to study as much as resources permitted and to confine his recommendations to matters on which he had highly persuasive evidence. He hoped to build a reputation for speaking only when he knew what he was talking about, even if this stand prevented him—with a total annual (1952) budget of $25,000—from making recommendations on all important subjects in the first years of his tenure. As far as his role within City Hall was concerned, he intended to be as deferential as possible without compromising his professional integrity. Although he realized that after study he might come to disagree with veteran city officials and political leaders on specific matters, his basic feeling was respect for their judgment. The avoidance of forceful opposition to their views seemed appropriate to Loeks, except in situations where he was certain the facts supported him.

Loeks did not question the concept of the freeway. He agreed with the engineers that because the automobile had inevitably come to stay, freeway construction was desirable. The route locations were, of course, another matter; but several factors dissuaded him from examining them seriously. First, he was confronted by the fact that the Highway Department and the City Council had approved the routes years earlier. Second, they neither asked nor expected him to evaluate these decisions anew. Finally, he believed that worthwhile route evaluations could only be made on the basis of intensive research. Given the governmental environment and his budget, this appeared to be an impossible condition to satisfy.

Loeks, an introspective man, later admitted that he might have considered the problem more thoroughly had he been City Planning Director when the Highway Department first presented its plan in 1946, and had the planning function in St. Paul been more secure at that time. Coming on the scene when and as he did, he deemed such a course unwise, especially since the decisions appeared to have been made intelligently on the basis of all available facts. He recalled that no drastic change in circumstance had ever made him feel that a comprehensive reevaluation of this position was necessary; therefore, in dealing with the Highway Department, he had focused his energies on particular matters of design rather than on general questions of freeway desirability or location.

Herrold remained as Director *de jure,* if not *de facto,* through 1952; and during the next two years, Loeks as Planning Director still had no planning staff. Moreover, during these years the attention of city officials was on urban renewal and public housing. Loeks worked closely with the Housing and Redevelopment Authority to provide an adequate community planning framework for the two major redevelopment project applications that were being prepared in this period. He also had to spend a substantial amount of time on zoning matters. At the request of the City Council he studied such problems as the possibility of a one-way street system for downtown, channeling traffic at downtown intersections, billboard control, junkyard regulation, and civil defense.

Some of his recommendations in these areas proved quite controversial, but he stood by them because he felt that he had done enough research to support firm professional judgments. On one occasion, as members of the City Council pressed him to withdraw on a controversial point, he explained that he would not appeal to the public over their heads but that he thought his usefulness would end if he became known as one whose professional recommendations were manipulable.

None of the studies he did in this period involved comprehensive planning, of course, but Loeks believed that it was necessary to demonstrate the utility of the planning approach by working on those matters that the community's leadership felt needed attention. If he won the leaders' confidence by serving them well, he hoped that in time he would be able to educate them to desire comprehensive planning. Throughout the period to 1957, when he left the St. Paul Planning Board to become director of the new Twin Cities Metropolitan Planning Commission, Loeks brought out about half a dozen publications intended for the general public rather than local leaders. None of these formal publications contained controversial recommendations. All were presentations of census data on the city or of already approved recommendations that had been conceived primarily by other agencies, namely the Highway Department and the Housing Authority. Shortly before he left St. Paul, however, Loeks acquired financial support for master planning, and he directed the first stages of work on St. Paul's comprehensive plan.

We have moved ahead of the story to set out Loeks' general strategy. There is a bit more to be said about his official environment on highway matters, however. The predominant figure in that environment was George Shepard, city engineer of St. Paul since 1922. Because the Planning Bureau had been part of the Public Works Department until 1947, Shepard had been Herrold's nominal superior until then. (Actually, the Planning Board, whose staff the Planning Bureau was supposed to be, was an independent body whose members enjoyed fixed terms of office.) While Herrold tended to be rather uncompromising and acid in his personal relations, Shepard got along well with nearly everyone. Since, in addition, his high professional competence was very widely acknowledged, Shepard's advice carried immense weight in

City Hall. Herrold had tended to look on Shepard as something of
an antagonist and to blame him in part for the Planning Bureau's
shortages of funds and staff, and for lack of political support on
policy issues.

Shepard's concept of planning led him to agree with the Highway Department that freeways were worthwhile and that engineers alone should determine freeway routes. In an address to a
businessmen's conference on urban renewal in 1947, for example,
he had described what he believed the planning function, operating independently of other functions, should embrace.

Planning Commissions or Boards should devote the greater part of
their time and energy [to broader matters of policy for guiding the
future growth and arrangement or rearrangement of our cities]. . . .
It is assumed of course that operating agencies, such as the Department
of Public Works, City Engineer's Office, park and other similar departments are adequately staffed with trained professional personnel
for the preparation of detailed plans and specification of approved
projects, and for supervision of such work when it gets underway.

He acknowledged the need for long-range planning, but emphasized that planners should not become involved in the "details of
administration."

Shepard resigned as city engineer to become city highway coordinator in 1957. His job was to help handle the increasing
burden of work in the city and to act as liaison officer between the
Highway Department and all city agencies. All official contacts
with the Highway Department were to go through him. He had of
course been the city's chief evaluator of highway plans for many
years before this, but his new position seemed to insure that no
challenge to the highway program by the planners could succeed
without his approval.

From the start of his tenure as planning director, Loeks sought
to maintain good relations with Shepard. He respected Shepard's
official responsibilities and professional judgments. In addition, he
felt strongly that planning was futile if ignored. His own future
and that of city planning in St. Paul, he later pointed out, depended on overcoming the legacy of hostility toward Herrold. One
of the most important ways to do this was to minimize conflict and
seek to enlarge areas of agreement. The fact that Shepard was an
engineer and tended to feel rapport with the approach of Highway

Department engineers suggested to Loeks that he should also strive to avoid conflict with the department engineers.

Loeks tried to keep informed about the Highway Department's intentions, and he frequently was asked to comment on new design proposals.[17] He maintained good relations with the personnel of the department and won some concessions by following three rules-of-thumb (outlined later to the writer): (1) never criticize the department publicly; (2) never claim authorship of a change accepted by the department; (3) rely on negotiations as much as possible, and force showdowns as rarely as possible.

In practice, Loeks later noted, no dramatic showdowns ever seemed necessary. The Highway Department seemed to make reasonable decisions, and it never presented firm plans at meetings with city officials. All plans were presented as tentative, and all meetings with city personnel were primarily to elicit ideas for further study. (Loeks later jokingly described the decision process as it appeared from his vantage point as "creeping *fait accomplism*.") If Loeks didn't approve of some detail, he usually would draft a map suggesting an alternative. Six months later, at the next meeting with Highway Department personnel, his alternative might or might not appear on the new set of tentative plans. Neither side ever intimated to the other that Loeks' suggestion had affected the new design. During the years that followed, this pattern of relationships between Loeks and the Highway Department endured.

Loeks published nothing on the freeways until June 1957, when he brought out a booklet entitled *The Proposed Freeways for St. Paul*. Despite its late date, this was the first effort made by any agency of the city government to explain the implications of the freeways for St. Paul in general terms. It was a rather sophisticated though simply presented functional analysis, and even years later Loeks was proud of it. In accord with his policy of not taking official disagreements to the public, Loeks did not include anything in the booklet that might give offense to other agencies. It was cleared with the Department of Public Works in its successive drafts and was approved by the City Council without controversy in July 1957. In one sense the booklet was a public relations effort

[17] The distinction between design and location should be kept clearly in mind. The latter had been settled for all practical purposes in 1945 and 1946.

because its whole thrust was to justify official policies rather than to call any into doubt. Loeks later commented that from his standpoint it had appeared to be a statement of planning conclusions that happened (largely as the outcome of a continuous process of discussion) to coincide with and reinforce the conclusions of the Highway and Public Works Departments. He further believed that justifying the freeways publicly in *planning* terms was likely to have a beneficial effect on future public discussions of highway proposals.

The Negro Community Reacts

Negro leaders first became aware that the city and state had approved the St. Anthony route as part of the proposed freeway system in 1953. In that year the school board recommended rehabilitation of an old elementary school in the Negro district. Residents of the district, led by Reverend Floyd Massey, Jr., of the Pilgrim Baptist Church, mounted a campaign aimed at persuading the board to build a new school instead. Massey learned from city engineer Shepard that the old school lay on the path of the proposed freeway route, and that therefore investment in it was likely to be wasted. His group used this argument to bolster its position, and it did achieve its objective. Negro leaders apparently thought little more about the freeway until 1955, when it became apparent that massive federal aid for freeway construction would soon become available.

Toward the end of 1955 Reverend Massey became aware that the City Planning Board, of which he was a member, would soon be asked to express itself again on the freeway proposals. He thought that the most effective way for the Negro community to impress its views on the Planning Board would be through a single organization. He therefore urged the members of his congregation to take the lead in organizing, and a number of them followed his advice. In January 1956 they established the Rondo–St. Anthony Improvement Association, the first property owners' group to appear in connection with the proposed Twin Cities' freeway routes.

The association, which soon included nearly 100 per cent of the threatened property owners and quite a few others as well, selected Timothy Howard as its president. Howard was a member of

Massey's congregation and a middle-aged bachelor with many contacts in the white community. He had long been active in Negro community affairs and was a vehement though seldom bitter critic of racial discrimination. He earned his living as a barber, but he seemed to have virtually unlimited amounts of time and energy to devote to causes that interested him.

Most of the members of the association viewed it as a mechanism for fighting the freeway right down the line. Howard and Massey, however, along with other Negro leaders whom they consulted, perceived the choice of objectives as a very difficult one.

On the one hand, it was possible to oppose construction on the St. Anthony route, pointing out that a St. Anthony freeway would split the Negro district and force one-seventh of its residents to leave their homes. Federally aided urban redevelopment projects had already displaced many of the district's residents since 1953. Although the district had been one of St. Paul's most densely populated areas even before 1953, few of the dislocated families had been able to find homes in other neighborhoods. It seemed likely that those displaced by the freeway would similarly contribute to overcrowding within the district.[18]

On the other hand, it was possible to emphasize the opportunities created by the freeway program. It would replace some of the most dilapidated structures in the district with a modern landscaped highway. By increasing pressure on the housing supply available to St. Paul's Negroes, it might help to justify an urban renewal project for the whole district. By giving displaced Negro homeowners ready cash, it might provide the impetus for some of them to buy homes in other neighborhoods. If they were prevented from doing so, even after being forced from their homes to make way for a public project, they could righteously demand passage of an open occupancy ordinance (i.e., a law making discrimination in the sale and rental of private housing illegal). Political leaders might recognize the moral justification of the Negro cause and appreciate the fact that Negro leaders had not tried to obstruct progress.

[18] The Housing Authority published data on a much larger area which included the Negro district in mid-1959. The area contained 2.8 per cent of the city's land, 10 per cent of its population, and 19 per cent of its substandard dwelling units.

Either of these two strategies might fail. The latter seemed more enlightened, however, and if it succeeded it might produce a significant victory for the cause of racial integration in St. Paul. This strategy also seemed more likely to succeed than its alternative. The few Negro leaders who had visited the Highway Department had come away convinced that the traffic data were conclusive; they had informed their colleagues that any effort to have the location changed would almost surely prove fruitless.

The leaders inclined to think, therefore, that they should accept the route line and focus on means of influencing its repercussions. They believed that their most feasible objectives were the following: to help the displaced Negroes find decent housing, to publicize their hardship as part of a continuing campaign for an open-occupancy ordinance, and to minimize the harmful effects that the freeway might have on the rest of the neighborhood. Massey and Howard accepted this evaluation, but most of Howard's "constituents" were primarily interested in saving their homes. He felt duty-bound to represent them. In addition, he believed that it would not hurt any other causes to make a fuss about the route line itself initially. If the Negro community began by opposing the route line, it would have a chance to air all its grievances and to dramatize the making of later concessions.

Howard did therefore protest the location of the freeway itself on every possible occasion, but he focused most of his attention on more limited objectives. Massey focused on the lesser objectives almost exclusively.

The first two of these objectives, helping the displaced Negroes and using their plight to advance the cause of open occupancy, were closely related. During the early months of 1956 all the city's major Negro organizations stepped up their continuing campaign for an open-occupancy ordinance. At the same time, Massey and Howard urged Mayor Dillon to request a city council appropriation for the purpose of supporting relocation services for those displaced by the freeway. When the Planning Board took up the St. Anthony route proposal in May and June, Massey argued that the displacement of Negroes by urban redevelopment and the freeway made the passage of an open occupancy ordinance and the establishment of a relocation agency imperative.

None of these efforts bore immediate fruit at the local level. The City Council showed no disposition to pass an open occupancy ordinance. Moreover, some officials professed to believe that Negro leaders were exploiting the relocation issue as just one more way of obtaining publicity for the cause of open occupancy. Mayor Dillon refused to ask the City Council for relocation funds, but after Massey and Howard reiterated their concern on several occasions he did agree to appoint a committee to consider what might be done to help those displaced. The committee never became active, however. The Mayor later explained that he had been unable to find a chairman. The Planning Board heard Massey sympathetically, but suggested only that the Negro leaders prepare a formal letter explaining in more detail what they thought the serious problems were. The board then adjourned for the summer.

Considering themselves rebuffed at the local level, Massey, Howard, and several other Negro leaders secured a meeting with Governor Orville Freeman and top Highway Department officials in the summer of 1956. The Negro leaders urged the Governor to assign responsibility for relocation to a state agency with legal authority and funds to act. The Governor said that he would refer the problem to the state Commission on Human Rights. The commission had no legal power of any kind and no budget.

The Negro leaders expressed their discontent vigorously in the last months of 1956 at hearings held by the Highway Department, the St. Paul City Council, and the State Senate's Public Highways Committee. Early in 1957 Governor Freeman created a subcommittee within the Human Rights Commission—the Committee on Housing and Relocation. It consisted of twenty-two members, most of whom were from St. Paul. Reverend Massey (a regular member of the Human Rights Commission), Howard, and a number of other Negro leaders were included. The committee held several meetings in its first months of existence, and decided that its first requirement was a census of the St. Paul families to be displaced by the freeway program in the next couple of years. The St. Paul Housing Authority, which already provided relocation assistance to families displaced by urban renewal projects, was anxious to make the survey but it had no funds available. The federal Bureau of Public Roads, which had estimated that a million people would be displaced nationally by the freeway program,[19] had a policy of contributing 90 per cent of the cost of relocation programs if the state contributed 10 per cent. The Highway Department reported, however, that no state agency had legal authority to contribute funds for this purpose. The next biennial legislative session was not scheduled until 1959, after most of the Negro families were scheduled to be displaced.

Finally, as the Highway Department began to file awards, the Housing Authority agreed to finance the census itself. It reported early in 1958 that right-of-way acquisition during 1958 and 1959 would displace 2,319 St. Paul families, and other public actions would displace another 592 families, for a total of 2,911. There were 399 Negro families in the total, with all but a handful scheduled to be displaced by the freeway during a period of several months early in 1959. Another 168 Negro families had been displaced by urban renewal during the preceeding five years. The total was well over one-fifth of the small Negro population of St. Paul.[20] The majority of the families—Negro and white—that would have to relocate were poor. Half had annual incomes of less then $3,500; more than five-sixths had incomes of less than $5,000. The Housing Authority offered to provide relocation assistance through 1959 for families displaced by the freeway program if the city or the Highway Department would pay it $30,000 to cover expenses. No money was found.[21]

During 1958 and 1959 the Housing Authority's Relocation Office did unofficially advise those threatened with displacement by the freeway who came in, but it could not actively seek homes for them. In addition, Timothy Howard informally sought them out. Aware that the lump sum payments were the largest amounts of money that many of the home owners had ever seen at once, he warned them of the ways in which they might be cheated if they

[19] These people were expected to be disproportionately poor, because highway engineers sought low cost rights-of-way and public officials generally liked to see dilapidated buildings go.

[20] About 2 per cent of St. Paul's residents were Negro.

[21] In its next regularly scheduled session, the legislature did authorize Minnesota cities to levy a one-tenth mill tax—worth about $25,000 annually in St. Paul—to support relocation services for people dislocated by public action. The St. Paul City Council enacted the tax rate in 1959 and designated the Housing Authority to provide the service.

bought homes in panic. When he heard of vacant dwelling units he passed the word along. He tried to ascertain which real estate men in the city could be expected to deal fairly with Negroes. Howard also maintained continuous contact with Highway Department officials. One of his objects was to persuade them that because of overcrowding within the Negro community and discrimination outside it, any given house represented a greater investment when owned by a Negro than it would when owned by a white man. It was imperative, Howard contended, for the department to use appraisers in the Negro community who were sympathetic to the Negro plight and who would let it affect their awards.

Looking back in 1960, Howard and most other Negro leaders agreed that the relocation had proceeded smoothly and with less inconvenience than anyone had expected. They believed that the department had used sympathetic appraisers and that its awards, for whatever reasons, had been generous. It had also declared a policy of permitting residents a full year in their homes, rent free, after awards were filed in court. The Negro leaders' original hopes, however, on which they had based their strategy, had not borne fruit. The great majority of those displaced had found it impossible to buy or rent outside the boundaries of the Negro district.[22] The city government had failed to provide official assistance for those displaced. It had also ignored the Negro community's pleas for an open-occupancy ordinance until 1959. Then, with the Negro leaders conducting an extremely vehement campaign, the St. Paul city attorney had written an opinion contending that the state constitution precluded local action an open occupancy. He had insisted that his opinion was devoid of political motivation and was offered as advisory only. Negro leaders had urged the City Council to pass an ordinance and let the courts decide, but they had been firmly (though politely) rebuffed. The Council had refused even to discuss the issue.

Massey's and Howard's third objective, after relocation and open occupancy, was to control the impact of the design of the freeway on the Negro district. Their primary concern in this regard was that the freeway might be elevated as it passed through part of the district. The Highway Department's preliminary pro-

[22] The district had experienced some contiguous expansion, however.

file as of early 1956 showed the freeway elevated over Lexington Parkway and Victoria Street, the two major north-south streets in the western half of the Negro neighborhood. Department personnel claimed that economic considerations might make at least this amount of elevation unavoidable. The land was low-lying, and drainage would be expensive if the freeway were built below existing sewers. Moreover, it was normal procedure in building roads to balance cut and fill between depressed and elevated sections. It cost money otherwise to haul away the unneeded earth. The cost of depressing the section shown as elevated in the profile might be as much as $1 million.

Massey, Howard, and their associates envisioned a raised freeway as a massive ugly barrier running through their neighborhood. They thought that rubbish would collect under it and that hoodlums would terrorize citizens who had to traverse the underpasses at night. They noted that the grass slopes next to a depressed freeway might muffle the noise and channel the fumes skyward to some extent, but that an elevated freeway would not. They pictured vehicles in accidents on an elevated freeway as occasionally escaping onto adjoining streets. The blighting effect of an elevated freeway on residential property, they said, would surely extend several blocks on either side, and the Negro district itself extended no further than that.

As noted earlier, the City Planning Board took up the St. Anthony route proposal in May and June of 1956. Massey acted as the Negro spokesman. After demanding passage of an open-occupancy ordinance and establishment of a relocation agency, he expressed the view that an elevated highway in particular would ruin what remained of the Negro neighborhood. Loeks reminded the board that he had previously mentioned the possibility that depression might be desirable. He believed, however, that city engineer Shepard might be inclined to favor elevation if the Highway Department found that engineering considerations made it necessary.[23] The board confined itself to asking Massey for a

[23] On reading this, Loeks commented that he had believed that "necessary" was a relative term, the applications of which depended on judgments of priorities. He had thought that engineering and planning priorities might legitimately differ—even when the relevant "facts" were established—leading to differences of opinion between engineers and planners about what was

formal letter stating all the positions of the Negro community in detail. The Negro leaders did prepare a letter, which the board considered at its October meeting. The board did not take a position on the relocation and open-occupancy issues, but it authorized Loeks to send a letter in its name recommending depression of the freeway in the Negro district to the extent feasible in engineering terms.

The Negro leaders, fearing that the Highway Department might not give the Planning Board recommendation sufficient weight, continued to press for some stronger official commitment by the city. They demanded and secured a hearing before the full City Council in the fall of 1956. At this meeting, Commissioner Marzitelli of the Department of Public Works—St. Paul had a commission form of government; each commissioner both sat on the City Council and headed an executive department—proposed that the matter be referred to a special committee representing the Department of Public Works, the Planning Board, and the Traffic Engineering Office, with their report to constitute the city's official position upon approval by the City Council. This proposal was adopted.

Before the committee had a chance to formulate its views, the Highway Department's first public hearing on the St. Anthony freeway occurred in December 1956. The department's spokesman noted that they still had only a preliminary profile to discuss, because engineering consultants to prepare a detailed design of the St. Anthony freeway had not yet been appointed. Massey argued, as he had previously, that if the freeway had to run on St. Anthony Avenue it should certainly be depressed through the whole Negro district so as to protect adjacent properties. The Rondo–St. Anthony Association as a whole went on record as opposed to the St. Anthony route but as very anxious to have the freeway depressed if the route were adopted over its objections.

Two weeks after the Highway Department hearing, City Engineer Shepard advised former Chief Engineer Kipp of the department, who was now a consultant to the department, that he thought depression would be desirable if it could be afforded.

"necessary." The author would add that, in the rhetoric of public life, the term "necessary" tends to be used to indicate that grounds for legitimate controversy are lacking.

(Shepard later recalled that this did not represent a change of position for him, only a slight shift of emphasis.) When the department selected its engineering consultants for the St. Anthony freeway in March, Shepard wrote in a similar vein to Chief Engineer Zimmerman of the department.

Meanwhile, Timothy Howard had independently continued his campaign for depression at the Highway Department. He had been told, he said, that the Bureau of Public Roads would be very unlikely to sanction a million-dollar expenditure for depressing the freeway. Hearing one day that a high bureau official was in St. Paul, Howard cornered him and was told that the bureau probably would not object to the expenditure if the Highway Department recommended it. Howard told Shepard of this, and Shepard agreed to investigate the matter more intensively by writing his friend, the city engineer of Detroit, to ask about that city's experience with elevated highways. His letter, dated March 13, 1957, said in part:

In connection with the planning and construction of the Interstate Highway system in St. Paul, we are confronted with a problem of whether or not the highway shall be depressed or raised. In some locations physical conditions definitely determine the issue; in others, the matter of complete depression has been weighed by the Highway Department as against a balancing of cut and fill. In the particular instance which I have in mind: namely, the intersection of the Interstate system on St. Anthony Avenue with Lexington Parkway, depression, which I believe to be preferable, will require the wasting of nearly a million cubic yards of dirt.

I am advised that over the years in which your Detroit expressways have been planned, a general policy of depression has been adopted. Will you kindly advise as to the principal reasons for the adoption of such a policy and also as to whether or not any particular problems were involved in the wasting of dirt.

The response, received early in April, noted that elevated highways in Detroit had created serious noise, fume, and crime problems. This answer apparently helped to convince Shepard that the matter was important. He decided to make this one of the few issues on which to recommend that the city stand firm. The Highway Department thereafter raised no serious questions about the desirability of depression, though it delayed making a firm decision (on the ground that economic questions still remained) for some time.

Finally, with Shepard clearly in favor of depression and the Highway Department agreeing that depression was desirable in principle, the doctrine that freeways in residential areas should be depressed received formal public expression in June 1957 with the appearance of the Planning Board booklet, *The Proposed Freeways for St. Paul.* In it Loeks wrote that although it was regrettable when freeways passed through residential neighborhoods, such routing was sometimes unavoidable. There was, however, no need for alarm in these cases; if the freeway were depressed and frequent bridges built over it, "the divisive effect on the neighborhood can be less than that of a moderately heavily traveled city street." The effect on property values of a depressed freeway with gradually landscaped slopes alongside it was "not too different from a narrow park strip; in view of the well-known beneficial effect of park areas on residential values it appears the net result of such a highway design would be reasonably favorable."

Thus, some social consequences of running freeways through residential neighborhoods did receive consideration, although not until late in the planning process. The task of dealing with these consequences fell primarily to engineers rather than to politicians or planners. Perhaps for this reason, they were articulated essentially as aesthetic rather than social problems. The Negro leaders found it discouraging that their only important victory had been on the issue of depression, and they attributed the decision to depress almost solely to the continuous pressure they had brought to bear. Loeks agreed that they had done well on the depression issue. He noted, however, that he had joined them before any other public official, that he had spoken favorably of depression to other officials at every opportunity, and that the Planning Board had been the first city agency to go on record in favor of depression. He felt that it was impossible to know whether the final decisions would have been any different if pressures had never been exerted, if he had never used his persuasive powers, and if the Planning Board had not blazed the trail for other city agencies at the level of public expression. He did feel certain that his "non-antagonistic" mode of operation had constituted an intelligent and sensible approach to a highly complex and potentially explosive situation. City Highway Coordinator Shepard contended that the pressures exerted had had virtually no effect and that he had expressed himself officially in favor of depression almost as early as Loeks. He had always hoped that depression would be feasible, he said, and his decisions throughout had been based on engineering and aesthetic, not political, considerations.

Other Reactions

The St. Paul Negro community was not the only group to react unfavorably to aspects of the intercity (St. Anthony) freeway in 1956 and the years immediately thereafter, and several other controversies arose.

One had to do with the impact of the freeway on related streets in western St. Paul. Snelling Avenue was three-fifths of the way from downtown St. Paul to the western city limit. From Snelling to the city line, the freeway would run along the northern edge of St. Paul's greatest concentration of middle and upper class neighborhoods. Home-owners' associations in several of these neighborhoods became vocal in 1957 and 1958 when they realized that two freeway interchanges were planned between Snelling Avenue and the city line. Two streets, previously moderate traffic carriers, were suddenly to become major arteries. The increased traffic and any street widenings that became necessary threatened considerable annoyance and perhaps eventual dislocation to property owners along these streets. Parents of children who had to cross either of these streets on their way to school were concerned about safety aspects. Highway Department officials contended that the neighborhood as a whole would benefit, because total north-south traffic in western St. Paul would remain constant and it would now be concentrated on two streets whereas it had previously been dispersed over many. Local residents were not mollified, however, because they believed that the freeway would generate enough new traffic to cancel this benefit quickly. In support of their position, they cited the Planning Board's 1957 booklet, which had observed that

freeways will generate traffic which previously did not exist. When a new high-speed, congestion-free route is opened, many people will find they can drive to their destinations in a shorter time and with greater ease and comfort than before, with the result that more people will be induced to drive.[24]

Highway personnel assigned to deal with the residents vigorously rejected this view. Along with supporters of highway construction throughout the nation, they insisted that highways themselves were not traffic generators. They inclined to feel that the whole controversy was essentially a public relations problem. The city officials immediately concerned with highway matters agreed. In truth, however, the department was not in a position to do much for the distressed residents even if it had accepted their forecast. The traffic engineering need for the two interchanges was undeniable. Snelling Avenue was already congested. If all the freeway traffic destined for parts of St. Paul west of Snelling were dumped on it, the resulting congestion would be intolerable. Moreover, vehicles coming from west of the city line would be forced out of their way.

A second controversy had to do with the impact of a section of the intercity freeway on the Prospect Park neighborhood in Minneapolis. Residents of the neighborhood asked simply that the freeway be placed *on* a right-of-way currently used as a railroad spur line, rather than adjacent to it. They contended that their proposal would save several hundred fine homes and would thereby serve some important social objectives.

Prospect Park was the only family neighborhood within walking distance of the University of Minnesota. Many of its residents were faculty members. Another portion of them were occupants of a public housing project, the only one ever built in Minneapolis outside the Negro section. The residents had deliberately permitted the project to be placed in their neighborhood—their alderman could have prevented it—hoping to set an example for

[24] Walter Blucher, then Executive Director of the American Society of Planning Officials, had made the point even more strongly as early as 1953: "Is there any instance in this country where a new expressway or highway or elevated street hasn't invited so much additional traffic as to almost immediately create congestion?" (*Problems of Decentralization in Metropolitan Areas*, Proceedings of the First Annual University of California Conference on City and Regional Planning, 1953 [Berkeley: Department of City and Regional Planning, University of California, 1954], p. 12.)

others in the city. They now maintained, contemplating the projected freeway, that the Highway Department's plan would leave the neighborhood 50 per cent middle class and 50 per cent project residents. It could not long survive as an "integrated" community with that ratio, they said. Middle-class residents would move out, leaving a predominantly lower-class and Negro neighborhood behind them. Not only would a noble experiment have failed, but another of the nation's big city universities would be plunged into a "neighborhood problem." The consequences in terms of the university's attractiveness to students and faculty and of its evening activities would be difficult to calculate. The consequences for the city's tax base would also be noticeable, as its supply of attractive middle-class homes would be diminished by several hundred units.

The Governor of Minnesota, Orville Freeman, was a former resident of Prospect Park. He took a personal interest in the threat to the neighborhood posed by the freeway, but he knew that railroads had the right of condemnation in Minnesota and would merely condemn a new right-of-way if the spur were taken. If an efforts were made to prevent them from doing so, the result would be prolonged legal suits and intense lobbying by the railroads at the State Capital. Freeman therefore did not believe that it would be feasible to build at ground level or below on the railroad property. He wrote the state highway commissioner a confidential note, however, asking whether the freeway could be elevated above the spur line. The commissioner replied that building over the tracks would bring about "benefits desirable and real for the community," but that such an approach would be "economically unsound from the standpoint of funds available for trunk highway improvements." In other words, the highway budget was tight, and its purpose was to improve traffic service, not to conserve middle-class neighborhoods. The exchange between the governor and the commissioner was never made public. The department maintained in its dealings with the residents of Prospect Park simply that sound engineering principles had dictated its original recommendation. It apparently persuaded a good many of the residents. The controversy gradually died without any concessions having been made by the department.

A third controversy had to do with the impact of the intercity freeway on business in downtown St. Paul. Until 1957, St. Paul's downtown retailers and property owners were ardent proponents of the freeway program. They reasoned that traffic congestion was a major cause of downtown decline and that improved access was the key to revival, or even survival. They overlooked, or preferred to ignore, the possibility that the most important consequences of the freeway might be to accentuate the trends toward urban sprawl and downtown decline.[25] Between the 1948 and 1954 censuses of business, as "sprawl" had become the dominant pattern of Twin Cities development even without the aid of new freeways, retail sales in the St. Paul central business district had—whether coincidentally or not—declined by 15 per cent (in constant dollars).

Most students of urbanism believed that highway improvements encouraged urban sprawl by making possible commuting from greater distances in any given travel time. Suburban residents tended to drive to work and to shop, in part because frequent and inexpensive transit services were impossible to sustain in low-density residential areas. Transit services had traditionally converged on downtown, making radial travel far easier than circumferential travel for most urban residents. For the driver, however, free parking at his destination tended to be more significant than central location, or even distance. Consequently, shopping services and employment tended to follow residents to the suburbs, seeking cheap land near major highways. Moreover, as residential sprawl continued, a larger and larger proportion of central area employees and shoppers would rely on their automobiles to bring them downtown. A survey published by the City Planning Board in 1958 would show that the number of *persons* entering the central business district each morning had increased by only about 25 per cent since 1944, but the number of *vehicles* had increased by 150 per cent. The city's traffic planning in the late 1950's was based on an estimate that traffic converging on downtown would increase by only 50 per cent more to 1980. If the rise were much greater, highly expensive street improvement and

25 Blucher had written: "I am convinced that the expressways leading to the centers of our cities will be one of the most important instruments we have created toward the cities' decentralization. I marvel that downtown merchants are usually in the van in urging their construction" (*ibid.*, p. 13).

peripheral parking ramp projects were expected to become necessary. No money for them was in sight.

Consequently, there was reason to believe that unless great investment could be generated to make the central business district more attractive and less congested, the impact of the freeway on balance would be to harm downtown. No state or local agency encouraged businessmen to think seriously about this prospect, however, until 1958. The Highway Department emphasized the importance of access to downtown and denied that highway construction bore any relationship to such phenomena as urban sprawl and the decline of public transportation, except that all reflected popular preferences. The city's engineers agreed with this position. The city's planners did not, but they kept their views on this subject within the official family. In their 1957 booklet on the freeways, they devoted almost a page to the question: "How can public transit make best use of the freeways?" They did not mention the possibility that the two might be in conflict. In view of the fact that the freeways were definitely on the way, they explained privately, it seemed reasonable to focus on the opportunities they created rather than on their unfortunate and unavoidable side-effects. The planners did not turn their attention to the general outlook for downtown until 1958. Then they maintained in a published survey and economic analysis[26] that great investment was needed to improve the attractiveness of the downtown area. They noted, however, that such action would, if successful, bring about an "unprecedented traffic demand in the core area." Downtown businessmen received the report antagonistically because it publicized a number of unfavorable economic trends. Ironically, therefore, even it failed to spur much serious thought about the future requirements of downtown economic health.

An event had already occurred in 1957, however, which, although it had not involved sprawl beyond the city limits, had significantly reduced the enthusiasm of downtown businessmen for the freeways. For some years St. Paul's largest department store had been Montgomery Ward's, situated on University Avenue midway between the central business districts of St. Paul and

[26] *St. Paul's Central Business District,* Community Plan Report 7, December 1958. This report was completed and published under the direction of Loeks' successor as planning director, Herbert Wieland.

Minneapolis. It had a vast parking lot surrounding it. The freeway was destined to pass a quarter of a mile from the store, making it more than ever accessible from all parts of the metropolitan area. In 1957 the St. Paul Housing and Redevelopment Authority sold a 24-acre tract in its Western Redevelopment Area to Sears Roebuck for construction of a retail complex comparable to Ward's. The freeway was scheduled to pass adjacent to the tract, which was itself adjacent to the major state government office buildings but not within easy walking distance of competing downtown stores. Government employees had long provided a large part of downtown retail trade.

When downtown businessmen learned of Sears' plans, they were outraged. One group of them brought an unsuccessful legal suit challenging the basic principle of urban redevelopment—acquisition of land by government for resale to private developers, often at noncompetitive prices. They simultaneously hired planning consultant Victor Gruen to propose an alternative freeway route line. Gruen came up with a proposed route line that cut across the planned Sears parking lot. It was received unfavorably, however, by both the Highway Department and the city's own engineers. They noted that it would serve traffic bound for downtown less adequately than the original route line, and that it would require substantially larger collateral expenditures by the city.

The reaction of downtown businessmen came too late, and although their legal suit brought urban renewal work in St. Paul to a halt for two years, they obtained no concessions. When it became apparent that further protest could only postpone freeway construction, not alter the route, many downtown businessmen gloomily urged an end to obstructionism. If there must be a freeway in the present location, they said, let us at least have it before Minneapolis has its freeway.[27]

The groups that had occasion, for one reason or another, to oppose some aspect of the intercity freeway never joined forces.

[27] It was expected that the freeway would be completed several years earlier in St. Paul than in Minneapolis, partly because no central Minneapolis plan existed. St. Paul did not have a downtown plan either, of course, but the downtown was smaller and its problems were less complex. Also, Minneapolis planners were considering construction of ramp garages adjacent to the downtown freeway interchanges.

The Negro community, the Prospect Park community in Minneapolis, the neighborhoods concerned about the interchanges in western St. Paul, George Herrold, and the downtown businessmen opposed to the Sears Roebuck store all sought objectives that not only did not conflict, but that might have been coordinated to form the basis of a single intercity route proposal. Herrold supported the businessmen, recognizing that the Gruen proposal fit in better than the Highway Department's plan with his own northern route proposal; but his interest in potential allies appears to have been unique. The Highway Department managed to deal with each irate group individually, and to focus attention primarily on traffic data and approved techniques of route location. It apparently convinced many of those who attended its meetings that, even though they might be inconvenienced by the freeway plan, the traffic data left no doubt as to the interest of the entire public. The department's success in this endeavor could not help but sap the will to battle of the groups concerned. Moreover, each irate group was interested in a different section of the freeway. People who rejected the Highway Department's arguments concerning their own source of dissatisfaction were likely to accept easily its arguments concerning someone else's.

Finally, the Highway Department's carefully cultivated image of rocklike strength plus amiability seemed to have persuaded many otherwise intractable opponents that pleading would prove more effective than fighting. The strategy of pleading assumed that the department could not be *forced* to do anything; therefore it was incompatible with the formation of alliances. In reality, neither the strategy of pleading nor the strategy of fighting (when indulged in by particular groups, such as the downtown businessmen in St. Paul or Prospect Park residents in Minneapolis) ever induced the department to move a route line or relocate an interchange.[28] The Negro leadership's persistent pleading may have been responsible for the official decision to depress the freeway as it passed through their neighborhood. The plans still provided, however, for elevation of the freeway as it passed through other

[28] For a case study of an instance in which another state highway department *was* induced to move a route line, by a strategy of fighting, see Polly Praeger, "Extinction by Thruway: The Fight to Save a Town," *Harpers*, No. 1303 (December 1958), pp. 61–71.

neighborhoods whose residents had abjured organized action altogether. The Negro leadership could also claim that it had induced the department to give displaced Negro residents generous prices for their homes, plus a year of rent-free occupancy. The department found these financial inducements to peaceful acceptance of its plans so useful, however, that they were soon extended to all Minnesota residents threatened with displacement.[29]

Conclusion: Standards and Political Influence

The relative influence of engineering and city planning considerations on decisions concerning the intercity freeway illustrated a fairly simple point: clarity of standards and strength of conviction were extremely important political variables. When standards were clear, and a profession felt confident that they were right or "the best available," conscientious men could look to them for guidance and take on from them the energy that flowed from unclouded conviction. If those who proposed a project were perceived as moral and realistic men, their passionate conviction as technicians was likely to persuade doubting laymen to support their project. The formula was not perfect, of course. The project might seem too expensive, or it might threaten important vested interests or sacred beliefs. Some other group of technicians might testify passionately against it. But observers of politics had long recognized that, other things being equal, the political value of having a clear sense of direction and honest conviction was substantial.

It was a crucial advantage of the highway engineers in freeway disputes that they possessed and believed implicitly in a set of clear normative propositions, applicable to the most important of their problems and convincing to the vast majority of the people with whom they had to deal. The most important of these propositions, in their general order of priority, were the following.

(1) Highway improvements were desirable. Although a satura-

---

[29] While it was difficult to prove that the state was following a policy of paying generous prices, there was widespread agreement among local officials and the homeowners involved that the department's awards were higher than the properties taken would have brought on the open market. The law authorized payment only of "fair" prices, but appraising was not a precise skill.

tion point was conceivable, St. Paul was so far from it that one could say with confidence that the cost of foregoing new highways was almost always higher than the cost of building them.

(2) The location of highway routes should be determined according to engineering criteria, of which by far the most important were traffic service and cost.

(3) The articulate public should never be confused with the entire public. The former should be won over to the department's point of view, if possible, but not at the cost of traffic inefficiency, excessive expense, or undue delay.

(4) It was preferable, engineering considerations being equal, not to build a highway through a residential neighborhood or very far from existing areas of heavy investment, since the highway would tend to stabilize existing investment if built near it, while it might bring about costly shifts of economic patterns if built elsewhere. Engineering considerations were, however, seldom equal. Since centers of heavy investment were generally major traffic generators, there was seldom any question of building far from them. As there were usually no vacant corridors of land near such centers, it was sometimes necessary—more candidly, less expensive —to go through the residential neighborhoods that surrounded them. In such cases, it was reasonable to show the utmost consideration for those inconvenienced: e.g., by landscaping the road as attractively as possible, by giving displaced home-owners fair and prompt compensation for their property, by allowing them more than ample time to find new homes, and by building pedestrian overpasses and underpasses at locations chosen by the neighborhood's own leaders.

Highway Department engineers later explained that they had seen no reason to lament the side-effects of progress. They admitted that change inevitably hurt some people but maintained that great nations had never been built by foregoing progress to pamper people. Those hurt by any project should be treated fairly and kindly, they explained, but should never be allowed to obstruct projects designed to benefit everyone.

The engineers did not have to worry about the allocation of all public resources or the abstract meaning of progress. They had only to ask themselves whether highway building was a significant contribution to progress, and they responded affirmatively and unhesitatingly. Of all the groups involved in this narrative, the engineers were the least susceptible to political pressure. Their pride in their techniques permitted them to scoff publicly at irate interest groups, and they pointed out that any change in plans to satisfy self-interested groups would cost taxpayers and drivers unnecessary millions of dollars. So long as the owners of property along the freeway right-of-way received fair compensation, they could only be protesting to safeguard their own convenience or, as in the case of the slum speculators, their immoral profits. In the first case, the property owners' convenience should not be allowed to outweigh the convenience of millions of drivers for years to come; in the second, society had no moral obligation to satisfy their demands.

Highway engineers emphasized that traffic and cost data were quantitative and impartial. They believed they were able, therefore, to prove that they had selected the highway routes without favoritism toward any group or interest. The department enjoyed an additional advantage, although one it did not boast about— traffic and cost data could be compiled without time-consuming consulation with the public. Such data were conclusive, while public consultation was seldom so. One could never be sure which interests had failed to appear at the hearings, nor which might appear if a new proposal were made. The only thing one could be sure of was that the general public had been inadequately represented.

The Highway Department was not completely unbending, but it had to guard itself against the appearance of weakness. So many people were going to be inconvenienced by the freeway that the first sign of "softness" by department officials would open the floodgates. The department had to deal more candidly, however, with the governing bodies of the state's large cities, which had their own disinterested engineers. Consequently, the department made its concessions only to those interest groups that were championed by their own local governments.

Department officials knew, of course, that the local mayors and councilmen were themselves in an embarrassing position. Virtually any change in plans intended to appease one set of constituents would antagonize some other set. Local officials had no desire to alienate any group, and therefore they tended to deny that they had any voice in freeway planning. When any group approached the Highway Department, it received courteous but firm treatment. Occasionally, when some group became particularly adamant, the department induced local officials to defend the engineers' position.

To department officials, this method of handling complaints was not only the most practical but also the most ethical possible. If every pressure group were granted the concessions most desired by it, they said, public satisfaction would probably be no greater, while public officials would constantly be accused of favoritism. In short, Highway Department engineers who reflected on their position generally concluded that ethics and engineering, in most cases, simply happened to coincide.

Next in certainty that his position was righteous was George Herrold. In some ways he was even more certain than the engineers, but his assurance was less convincing to others. In part, his inability to persuade others was due to the situation and his own personality. It was also due to the nature of his standards.

Herrold was fighting what he perceived as a federal-state offer to spend $400 million in the Twin Cities area and well over $100 million in St. Paul alone, in return for nothing but freedom to do so in accord with "sound engineering principles." Had the federal and state governments offered the city the same sum of money and told the city to spend it "rationally," the question of whether to spend any portion thereof on highways would have been approached in quite different fashion. As it was, local officials had the choice of taking the whole sum for freeways or taking nothing. Furthermore, highway congestion was a problem about which many voters had strong feelings.

Herrold had no standards that he could say he *always* applied to highway proposals. Because he also had virtually no resources for acquiring statistics to bolster his recommendations, he was generally limited to examining data made available by others and pointing out implications that they had ignored or de-emphasized. When he discussed possible repercussions not clearly pointed to by Highway Department traffic and cost analyses, he generally had no means of proving that they would occur; in many cases highway officials denied that they would. When highway officials admitted that certain repercussions *would* occur, Herrold had no general

standards to cite in support of his judgment about their importance. He could only assert his opinion and let the engineers assert
theirs. Without some invocation of general standards, the public
could not understand the dispute.

The Highway Department could set plausible specific standards
for the amount of traffic service needed to justify each unit of
expenditure. Herrold, on the other hand, wanted to bring in any
other values whenever he believed they were important. Although
he recognized that his beliefs did not add up to a tight theoretical
system and that some critics thought his policy views stemmed
from nostalgia for the horse-and-buggy age, his conviction did not
waver. The components of decency, he felt, did not change overnight; they did not have to be systematized to acquire validity; and
technical computations should not be allowed to obscure them.
An engineer himself by training, Herrold was not awed by engineers or engineering competence. The automobile was merely a
gadget of convenience, he believed, and tens of thousands of
people should not be put out of their homes simply to save drivers
minutes and pennies. His experience told him that many sets of
road improvements in the past had been treated as "final
solutions"—and that each had brought more unpleasant and costly
congestion to the city. The whole approach, he thought, was a
cruel distortion of the meaning of progress.

Herrold's standards could not be analyzed as a "system," but he
believed in them and insisted that he was more capable of expressing the public interest than were local politicians. In pursuit
of his mission, he rather disdained political caution. To his successors, however, Herrold's career proved that "those who speak
too frequently and dogmatically, and who ignore the requirements
of political prudence, cannot accomplish anything as planners."

C. David Loeks lacked Herrold's generalized sense of righteous-
ness. There appeared to be three major reasons why this was so.
First, Loeks felt a need to justify his recommendations in terms of
systematic and well-articulated normative theories, but his profession had not made much progress in developing such theories
since Herrold's day. Second, Loeks' standards of empirical theory
and research required to support strong policy views were as high
as those of the engineers, but his financial and manpower resources
were hardly less limited than Herrold's had been. And third,

Loeks felt a more compelling obligation than Herrold had to nurture the planning function's store of good will in the community. Each of these factors tended to sap Loeks' sense of conviction on most issues.

Loeks fully appreciated the paradox that although his profession enjoined him to plan comprehensively, it did not provide him with a comprehensive set of criteria for making value choices. He attributed the lack of systematic planning theory to the diffuseness of planning objectives. This was not very helpful, however. He understood that he needed such criteria before he could successfully argue against specialists' recommendations in their own fields. It was necessary to present alternatives and demonstrate their superiority, not merely to argue abstractly that many values should be considered. Yet Loeks had scarcely more resources than Herrold had had for conceiving independent alternatives. His standards of theory and research prevented him from taking his own capacities seriously in this area. One might add that the whole planning profession seemed to have been similarly inhibited in developing a distinct viewpoint on highway matters. It rather tended to accept the basic highway engineering viewpoint and to argue, if at all, about occasional and highly marginal (though important to the individuals affected by them) design details.

The depression controversy may be taken as illustrative. Loeks felt that the Highway Department's original proposal to elevate part of the freeway in the Negro neighborhood was a rather clear-cut instance of insensitivity to social values. It aroused him to opposition more than any other issue involving the freeways that arose during his tenure as St. Paul planning director. To the Highway Department the issue of elevation or depression was extremely marginal, however. More to the point, it was marginal from the standpoint of land-use planning: that is, in the context of the overall impact on land use of the whole St. Paul freeway program.

Loeks did not consider himself obligated to assert jurisdiction over subjects simply because their significance for planning objectives was great. He did feel obligated, however, to tell the unvarnished truth when his opinion was asked and to mention courteously to the officials directly responsible when it occurred to him that obvious injustice was likely to flow from one of their projects. Loeks tried to keep his unsolicited references to injustice at the level of quiet suggestion. He said that he believed his capacity to do good would increase proportionately with his willingness to let others get the credit. This was reasonable, but it was also true that Loeks had no theoretical basis for *arguing* with officials who might maintain that the obvious injustices to which he called attention were unavoidable. If he were to decide impressionistically that some injustice was avoidable—that the expense of avoiding it was justifiable—he had no professional standard to help him in determining what his political obligations were. Thus, even on the fairly simple issue of depression, the Planning Board qualified its recommendation by noting that it might not be feasible in engineering (a euphemism for "economic") terms.

This is not to say that Loeks or the staff he was gradually building up lacked ideas about how cities should be laid out. Their profession did provide them with such ideas, but not with standards for determining when and how to strive for their effectuation. Planners recognized that many important aspects of life had no price because they could not be bought or sold. They seemed to have made little progress, however, in defining these aspects, discovering how they were affected in specific situations, or evaluating their importance. Consequently, planners in St. Paul were more or less forced to accept on faith the Highway Department's assumption that other effects of the freeway besides those involving traffic would somehow "balance off" or prove beneficial on balance. Lacking conviction that another plausible viewpoint was available, they accepted the engineering point of view—except on a few matters of detail—as their own.

It was possible, of course, to contend that planners and highway engineers independently agreed on all except matters of detail. Loeks himself believed that he had brought a distinct point of view to the discussions of detail in which he had engaged. He also thought that he had probably had some influence on the highway engineers' thinking. He pointed out that one does not leave a public record—may not even leave a record in men's minds—when he exercises influence by subtle and continuous suggestion. Perhaps Loeks had served the cause of comprehensiveness better than a case writer could know.

II

A Land-Use Plan
for St. Paul[*]

Introduction

A fundamental instrument in comprehensive city planning has long been the land-use plan. It does not present a detailed program for curing civic ills, but it suggests the goals toward which public planning policy should be directed. It does not deal with all civic problems, but emphasizes those that can be resolved most directly by regulation of the uses of land and the dimensions of structures built upon it. A land-use plan, therefore, does not indicate where each school, park, street, factory, and shopping center should be located, but rather states principles of desirable spatial relationships between them. A land-use plan's most general conclusions are supposedly expressed on the land-use plan map, which shows the use or uses that should be permitted on each parcel of land in the city. Planners believe that the more detailed conclusions should be applied by those who plan specific public projects and who approve plans for private construction within the city. Furthermore, for the plan to be fully effective, private developers must use it as a guide in those phases of their own project planning that are beyond the reach of public regulation.

It has long been orthodox planning doctrine that no other phase of city planning can be successful unless the basic land-use pattern is satisfactory. Consequently, city planners have tradition-

* A shortened version of this chapter appeared as *A Land-Use Plan for St. Paul*, ICP Case Series, No. 90 (Bobbs-Merrill, 1965), copyright © 1965 by the Inter-University Case Program, Inc.; reprinted with permission.

ally made the preparation of a land-use plan an early step in the development of any comprehensive plan for a city. Ultimately, of course, land-use regulation affects every aspect of life in a community, and the effect of any land use on its surroundings differs from that of every other. The completely comprehensive land-use plan would therefore have to deal exhaustively with the use of each parcel of land in the planning area. As the formulation of such a plan would be an impossibly difficult task, planners have always had to simplify. Their first and most important method of simplification has been to divide all land uses into a very few categories. The establishment of categories, in turn, has involved assumptions about the most important objects of land-use regulation.

The general categories of land use now commonly employed by city planners, and which were employed by St. Paul's planners, were chosen in response to conceptions of importance—from a legal rather than a planning point of view—which prevailed in the courts four and five decades ago. During this period the first important technique of modern land-use regulation, zoning, was striving for legal respectability in the United States. In order to win court approval of zoning ordinances, planners tailored their principles to fit the prevalent legal doctrines of their day. English and American courts had long permitted public action under the common law of Nuisance to prevent one property owner from harming the market value of another's property. Accordingly, zoning was defended as a way of preventing mixtures of land use that would harm market values.[1]

The planning doctrines of several decades ago, which are still reflected in St. Paul's zoning code—originally enacted in 1922—had it that land uses could be ranked according to their effect on each

[1] The two best brief and general sources on the history of zoning and the development of judicial attitudes toward it are the following: John Delafons, *Land-Use Controls in the United States* (Cambridge: Joint Center for Urban Studies of the Massachusetts Institute of Technology and Harvard University, 1962), pp. 17–60; and Robert Walker, *The Planning Function in Urban Government*, 2nd ed. (Chicago: University of Chicago Press, 1950), pp. 50–89.

In addition, excerpts from leading court decisions on zoning, along with some history and analysis, are offered by Charles M. Haar, *Land-Use Planning: A Casebook on the Use, Misuse, and Re-use of Urban Land* (Boston: Little, Brown and Company, 1959), pp. 147–346.

other's values. It was thought that those uses high in rank could not harm the market values of those low in rank. Thus, the early zoning ordinances prohibited "lower" uses from locating in districts reserved for "higher" uses, but not vice-versa. Consequently, cities like St. Paul have had many residential structures in districts zoned commercial, and residential and commercial structures in districts zoned industrial.

The system's descending order of rank generally ran as follows: single-family residential, two-family residential, walk-up apartment residential, high rise apartment residential, commercial (retail and office), light industrial, and heavy industrial. Needless to say, infinite subdivision of these categories was possible. Perhaps the most common form of additional subdivision involved single-family homes. It was demonstrable, for instance, that the construction of inexpensive homes on small lots could harm the marketability of expensive homes on larger lots nearby. It was also clear that racial and ethnic mixing could harm market values.[2]

Certain land uses did not easily fit within the ranking system on the basis of their nuisance qualities. The most important of these were categorized public and semipublic land uses. These were distinguished by being (1) intended to serve those on the ranking scale, and (2) both nonresidential and nonprofit in character. They were distinguished from each other by their ownership. Planners were never able to declare that all uses within either category had a similar effect on surrounding land values. They therefore treated subcategories within each—streets and alleys, schools, parks and playgrounds, churches—separately. Probably in order to avoid unmanageable complexity, they tended to ignore the effects of other land uses on the values of public and semipublic property.

More recently, planners have come to reject notions of rank among uses. The newer fashion has been to emphasize that every

[2] The Supreme Court declared zoning to achieve racial segregation unconstitutional in 1917 (*Buchanan v. Warley*, 245 U.S. 60). As late as the 1940's, however, federal home loan authorities expressly encouraged racial and ethnic neighborhood segregation as a way of securing their loans. For a brief account of federal practices in this period, and the no more than gradual change since, see Charles Abrams, "The Housing Order and Its Limits," *Commentary*, XXXV, No. 1 (January 1963), 10–14.

land-use type can in some circumstances harm the value of property in every other use-type. Planners have recognized that even the traditional pariah, heavy industry, serves indispensable functions and has special needs that are difficult to satisfy in neighborhoods interspersed with homes, schools, and stores. They have therefore come to the view that the objective of land-use planning should not be to protect "higher" uses from "lower," but rather to protect all uses from each other by suitable segregation.

Two important issues have emerged: (1) do the traditional categories provide proper criteria for the segregation of land uses? and (2) how well are city planners equipped to indicate which kinds of land-use patterns are desirable? In recent decades the courts have liberalized their interpretations of "value" and "harm" beyond the monetary. Consequently, it has become permissible, even *de rigueur,* for planners to say that the ultimate objectives of their work involve social welfare. Thus, St. Paul's planners wrote in various sections of the land-use plan to be considered below that good plans "must promote the common good," that planning "can assure that the entire city will become a better place in which to live," and that "land use policy should not only concern itself with the efficient functioning of a city, but also [with] its appearance and liveability." [3]

This narrative focuses upon the extent to which the planners of St. Paul gave practical evidence of having cast off the market bias of early land-use planners. This is far easier said than done. Criteria of social desirability cannot be defined objectively or noncontroversially. There are mighty pressures on planners to avoid the question of "proper" objectives for social policy and to emphasize instead the social benefits that flow from protecting market values. Full discussion of any plan, therefore, requires some consideration of the subjects on which it is silent as well as those on which it lavishes attention.

[3] These and all other quotations from the St. Paul Land Use Plan in this book are from the published plan report, entitled *St. Paul's Preliminary Land Use Plan* (City Planning Board of St. Paul: Community Plan Report Number 8, July 1959). Unless otherwise indicated, all passages quoted appeared in substantially identical form in the first draft of the plan submitted by Carl Dale to his superiors in December 1958.

The Decision to Plan

No politician, city official, or influential group of private citizens in St. Paul ever asked the City Planning Board for a land-use plan. The plan whose evolution we shall examine came to be written because the Housing Acts of 1949 and 1954 required each city desiring aid for urban renewal and public housing to produce a comprehensive city plan. Specific urban renewal proposals invariably stirred controversy in St. Paul, but the abstract ideas of urban renewal and federal aid were popular. At least no organized groups in the city opposed them. It was taken for granted, therefore, that eventually the city would comply with the requirement.

Few communities anywhere in the nation produced comprehensive plans between 1949 and 1954. Consequently, the 1954 Act provided that, in future, federal assistance for urban renewal projects would be granted only to communities that had adopted, and had had certified by the Housing and Home Finance Administrator, "workable programs for community improvement." Each community's "workable program" was to demonstrate that steady progress was being made toward completion of a comprehensive city plan; adequate codes and ordinances; neighborhood analyses; plans for urban renewal project financing, for administrative organization, and for relocating displaced families; and citizen participation. With respect to the comprehensive plan, each locality's "workable program" was to describe the progress being made toward completing it, the extent to which it was being used as a guide to the locality's development programs (most particularly, its urban renewal and public housing programs), and the staff, funds, and current work program of the planning agency. The comprehensive plan itself was to include *at least* four general elements and two detailed regulatory ordinances. The general elements were to be:

(1) a land-use plan, showing the location and extent of land to be used for residential, commercial, industrial, and public purposes;

(2) a thoroughfare plan, indicating the system of existing and proposed limited-access, primary, and secondary thoroughfares;

(3) a community facilities plan, showing the proposed distribu-

tion of schools, parks, playgrounds and other public facilities; and

(4) a public improvements program, identifying the specific public works required to implement the first three plan elements, and recommending priorities for their execution.

The regulatory ordinances were to be:

(1) a zoning ordinance, designed to set precise legal constraints on the uses of land and the locations, heights, and land coverages of buildings in the community; and

(2) a subdivision ordinance, providing for planning agency review of proposed subdivisions of undeveloped plots of land to insure conformance to the general plan, adequate lot sizes, appropriate street grades and widths, provision of adequate street and utility improvements, and the establishment of proper official records.[4]

It was to be expected that the six elements of the comprehensive plan would be prepared in roughly the order of the above listing, and that the general land-use plan would provide the overall assumptions on which the other plan elements would rest. The Housing and Home Finance Administrator had no thought (nor did he have any mandate from Congress) of reviewing "workable programs" or comprehensive plans for substantive policy content, or of retarding urban renewal activity while full-scale comprehensive plans were being developed. The only immediate objects of the "workable program" requirement were to force local communities to organize their ideas with respect to physical development, to take stock of their planning operations, and to put firm promises concerning the levels of their future efforts on the record.

A gradual expansion of city planning activity had begun in St. Paul shortly after passage of the Housing Act of 1949. By 1954 the City Planning Board's budget had tripled—from $12,780 in 1950

[4] Advisory Commission on Intergovernmental Relations, *Governmental Structure, Organization, and Planning in Metropolitan Areas,* committee print, U.S. House of Representatives, Committee on Government Operations (Washington: U.S. Government Printing Office, July 1961), pp. 79, 80. See also Advisory Commission on Intergovernmental Relations, *Impact of Federal Urban Development Programs on Local Government Organization and Planning* (Washington: U.S. Government Printing Office, January 1964), pp. 17, 68–70, and bibliography on p. 70.

to $37,872 in 1954—and its staff included four professional planners, as compared with two in 1950. However, zoning administration, one-shot reports on issues of interest to the City Council, and public relations dominated the staff's energies. Not until the beginning of 1955 was a man assigned to work full time on research preparatory to long-range planning. That man was Rodney Engelen, who joined the planning staff in January 1955, only eighteen months after leaving planning school. Although Engelen's work was considered a prelude to work on a comprehensive plan, C. David Loeks, the Planning Director, maintained that his staff was still too small to undertake comprehensive planning. The "workable program" submitted to the Housing and Home Finance Administrator in March 1956 stated only that the development of a community plan was a goal. "It is well recognized," the report said, "that not enough resources are yet being applied to the planning of the city." It went on, however, to contend that: "As a continuing policy the budget for planning is being gradually increased to bring it up to generally accepted national standards. The city will continue to push its planning program forward until it has developed all the major elements of a community plan and, in order to meet changing conditions, will provide the means for their continuous review and revision." [5]

Even as this was being written, however, Loeks fully realized that it would not satisfy the Housing and Home Finance Administrator for long. His strategy was to exploit the fact that the St. Paul Housing and Redevelopment Authority would bear the brunt of any federal pressure to demonstrate continuous progress on the comprehensive plan. The Authority was responsible for the detailed planning and execution of urban renewal projects in St. Paul, and it was the local body that dealt with the Housing and Home Finance Agency. In addition, it had independent taxing powers that were more than ample. The one-mill property tax that its enabling legislation permitted it to levy for planning and internal administration was worth almost $250,000 annually, but the Authority had seldom found it necessary to levy more than half that amount. The main body of the city government, on the

[5] City Planning Board of St. Paul, *New Life in St. Paul* (St. Paul: City Planning Board, March 1956), p. 13.

other hand, was forced to pinch pennies mercilessly to stay under its chartered spending ceiling.

The Housing Authority might have produced its own plan, because its enabling legislation provided that "when a comprehensive or general community plan is not available by the planning agency, [the Housing and Redevelopment Authority can] make or cause to be made such plans as a guide in the more detailed planning of housing and redevelopment areas." The Authority preferred, however, not to do so. The federal regulations assumed that where possible comprehensive plan preparation would lie within the jurisdiction of the local planning agency and, in any event, the Authority had no desire to compete with an agency that was potentially its closest ally. It was receptive, therefore, when Mayor Dillon, at Loeks' urging, asked it to help finance development of the comprehensive plan by the Planning Board. The two agencies approved a contract in January 1957 providing that for $80,000 the Planning Board would develop the four general elements of the comprehensive plan called for by Housing Act. Loeks promised to complete the work within two years from July 1, 1957, and, simultaneously, to prepare drafts of a new zoning ordinance and a new subdivision control ordinance using funds included in the Planning Board's regular budget. The contract with the Housing Authority, however, did not *require* that the Planning Board produce these ordinance drafts.

Before proceeding with work on the comprehensive plan, Loeks was compelled to settle some questions of strategy. The first was whether to prepare an economic base study and a study of the central business district in conjunction with the plan reports. Preparation of an economic base study was clearly justified in terms of planning doctrine. Although the Housing Act did not specify that comprehensive plans should include base studies, many planners believed that wise planning was impossible without reliable information about market forces. Loeks therefore decided to prepare such a study as part of the total work program.

The second, whether to do a study of the central business district, had political implications. A committee representing certain factions in the downtown business community had employed the nationally prominent consulting firm of Victor Gruen Associates to prepare a central area plan. The businessmen asked Loeks to furnish the consultant data. Loeks decided, however, that if he were going to gather the data in the first place, he might as well get a published report out of it and, consequently, public credit for the work. He also felt certain that no plan sponsored by the faction that employed the consultant could ever win the support of the entire downtown business community.

Loeks was also faced with questions of priorities and timing in work on the various studies and reports proposed. He believed that it would be particularly desirable for a central point of view to permeate the whole plan. If the parts were written separately, only the last could embrace an overall perspective.[6] Some planners admitted the logic in Loeks' approach, but disagreed with its feasibility. They believed that each study and plan tended to develop at a different rate of speed and that an overall point of view would be more likely to evolve if a sequence of steps could be designed, with all participants working together on one or two steps at a time. One planner employed by Loeks explained later, perhaps with the wisdom of hindsight, that the sequence of work should have been: (1) economic base and existing land-use studies, (2) preparation of a land-use plan and zoning ordinance, (3) development of goal-setting plans in addition to land use, and (4) development of a detailed public improvements plan. In the spring of 1957 Loeks decided, however, that work should proceed simultaneously on the first three parts of the comprehensive plan (land use, community facilities, and thoroughfares), the economic base study, and the study of the central business district.

With the Housing Authority contract in hand, Loeks had to build a comprehensive planning staff almost from scratch during 1957. Rodney Engelen had moved to the Housing Authority in June 1956 to become that agency's assistant director for planning and development. In this position he continued to work with the planning staff on all of its reports that appeared up to the end of Loek's tenure as planning director in January 1958. None of these

---

[6] Some of the problems that have been caused by piecemeal plan preparation and adoption over the years are discussed by T. J. Kent in his book, *The Urban General Plan* (San Francisco: Chandler Publishing Co., 1964), pp. 40–43. He also discusses important related problems of general plan preparation on pp. 33–40, 43–53.

reports represented original research or planning by the planning staff. Engelen was not available to direct the work on the comprehensive plan itself.

In June 1957 Loeks hired the first of the new staff members. He was Carl Dale, who had worked in Duluth, Minnesota, since his graduation from planning school two years earlier. During Dale's tenure in Duluth, a land-use plan had been prepared by the well-known consultant, Harland Bartholomew. Loeks knew that a land-use plan was customarily the first phase in comprehensive planning and believed that Dale's participation in Bartholomew's work qualified him well for the task of preparing one for St. Paul. He recruited three additional planners for the permanent staff of the Planning Bureau during the summer of 1957. He also hired a student for the summer to collect data for the report on the central business district and a recent planning school graduate for five months' work on the economic base study.

Loeks expected to have an ample budget. The Planning Bureau's budget increased from $56,024 in 1956 to $82,171 in 1957. In 1958 he would be able to spend $115,554, including more than $45,000 from the Housing Authority.

Formulating a Strategy

Dale's superiors gave him considerable freedom in planning and carrying out work on the land-use plan. It was understood, however, that he would keep C. Allan Blomquist, a senior planner on the staff, constantly informed of his progress, and that Blomquist in turn would converse frequently with Haluk Tarhan, head of the comprehensive planning section. In practice, the staff was small enough so that Dale and Tarhan also had frequent informal contact. Dale resolved to try to complete the first draft within a year, if possible; then, if all went well, the plan might be published before the end of 1958. Such a schedule seemed necessary if the other three parts of the comprehensive plan were to be published by June 1959 in accordance with Loeks' promise.

So far as Dale knew, there were no how-to-do-it books on land-use planning. The literature of planning included many volumes dealing with specific aspects of land-use plan preparation. These books were valuable and included discussion and criticism of planning methods, but none contained a step-by-step formula for the preparation of a complete plan nor any criteria of a "good" plan. He found that the few authors who had a clear conception of a "good" plan were interested almost exclusively in real estate or market values.

Dale found that most land-use plans that had been prepared in other cities seemed to have some common characteristics. Virtually all consultants and most planning commission staff members geared their work to the funds available. Dale believed that he could have written some of the plans he examined in no more than two or three weeks. Even the better plans generally offered only an inventory of facts about existing land use, and then a map showing land use for some future time. Those who prepared the plans had seldom bothered to discuss their methods or to tell how they had proceeded from inventory to proposal; none had done so in detail or self-critically. The plans that Dale considered most comprehensive, however, did tend to contain the same kinds of inventory and projection materials. The authors of these plans, perhaps because they read the same books and copied from each other, had probed for similar categories of information. Dale decided to follow the pattern of those plans that were in agreement. Where they disagreed, he would be compelled to select among the differing approaches. In cases of doubt, he would draw on his own experience, which was greatly influenced by Harland Bartholomew's work in Duluth. It seemed reasonable to depend upon that experience because Bartholomew had long been recognized as one of the leading land-use planning consultants in the United States.

Dale believed that the broad objectives of land-use planning in St. Paul would not differ significantly from those of Duluth. Therefore, he did not dwell on the theoretical problem of how to work out a research program that would produce the facts about land use most relevant to the accomplishment of the city's goals. Instead, he assumed that it was possible to select the relevant facts without clearly articulating the problems and goals involved. At no time did he ever set forth a list of the problems on which he hoped to shed light. He felt that there would be time to articulate the plan's objectives *after* a survey of the facts had uncovered St. Paul's important land-use problems. He believed his reasoning was plausible, but it depended on three assumptions: (1) that land-use planning faced similar problems in most cities; (2) that other planners had discovered the types of facts most relevant to these problems; and (3) that they or Dale had some adequate means of determining the existence and importance of a "problem." Dale instinctively believed that these were reasonable assumptions, but he had neither the time nor the inclination to analyze them seriously.

One of the books that Dale found most useful, especially with respect to methods of fact gathering and prediction, was a volume written by F. Stuart Chapin.[7] Although he believed that Chapin's book was too academic for easy application, it was profound and had been written with planners in mind. One of Dale's colleagues had taken courses with Chapin in planning school and had been greatly impressed by him. The book had been very favorably reviewed. Chapin frankly and fully discussed the poverty of most existing forecasting techniques, but he was of little help on the problems of compensating for faulty projections and in the difficulties of moving from diagnosis to prescription. None of the methods discussed by Chapin dealt with forecasting the consequences of specific proposals. Dale believed that Chapin's methods would work well on the metropolitan level, but that his techniques were of less value in land-use planning for a city that was only a part of an urban complex. In its field, however, Chapin's book had no competitors, and Dale concluded that he had no alternative but to rely heavily on the volume. As a matter of strategy, it was important to use forecasting techniques developed by recognized experts. If parts of the plan should become law and were challenged in court, the legal argument would likely revolve around whether the planners had been arbitrary. The use of methods approved by reputable planning authorities seemed to provide the best defense against such a charge.

Preparing a Land-Use Inventory

To implement his work program, Dale prepared a two-part land-use inventory; one part dealing with land use and the other with market trends. He himself would do the work of the first part; for the second, he expected to use data that his colleagues on the economic base study would collect.

[7] F. Stuart Chapin, *Urban Land Use Planning* (New York: Harper and Bros., 1957).

He found most of the data for his land-use inventory in the files of various city offices, the office of the Ramsey County Assessor, and in fire insurance atlases. The Planning Board staff in previous years had mapped the city on 200-foot scale base maps (i.e., one inch on the map equalled 200 feet), showing the use and size of every lot in the city. Maps were now drawn on a 1,000-foot scale to permit greater perspective. Census data for each block in St. Paul were superimposed on the maps, showing types of structure, population density, number of dwelling units by type, number of dilapidated dwelling units, and similar information. The total amount of land in each category of land use, the net land per dwelling unit for each type of residential structure (single-family, two-family, three- or four-family, and multi family), the average number of dwelling units per net residential acre (for the city as a whole), and the average number of dwelling units per gross acre, were all computed by measuring the length of lines on existing maps. The tens of thousands of measurements on which the maps were based were available, but the staff time required to add them up was judged to outweigh the added precision that would be achieved.

Dale drove up and down every street in St. Paul, to get the "feel" of each street and neighborhood, to note extraordinary features not shown on base maps, and to discover changes that had occurred since the maps had been drawn. He computed past trends in population, land development, building construction, and rezoning from federal census materials and from data in the city government files. His draftsmen superimposed maps of the local water, sewer, and street systems on the base maps. He ascertained the reasons for inadequate service in some parts of St. Paul from city officials directly concerned. He studied the current zoning map carefully and tried to evaluate it according to the recent professional literature on zoning. He also asked experienced city officials why private developers had ignored certain lands in St Paul. According to them, the reasons were varied: some lands were subject to flooding; others were not served by water, sewers, or streets; some had poor drainage or severe topography; others were platted irregularly; others adjoined railroad lines. Dale made no attempt to suggest solutions to these problems, but he listed them in the plan as worthy of more detailed study.

In compiling his data, Dale was aware of the need for a study of social conditions and public attitudes in St. Paul, but he made no formal attempt to carry out such a study. For one thing, there was no evidence that other land-use planners had ever done it. Aside from the racial and ethnic composition of the population, which the federal census recorded, very little dependable data on social groups or intergroup relations existed. Dale realized that a great deal might be gained from knowledge about the aspirations and concerns of St. Paul citizens, but he had no idea about how to seek this information, even if adequate time were available. Furthermore, he reasoned, no one knew what to ask in opinion surveys. They were too expensive, and planners disagreed over how much importance should be attributed to glib opinions. It was well known that public opinion at any moment was a poor predictor of its own future character. Not even the most optimistic planner thought that the general public could be induced to inform itself about comprehensive planning alternatives or to evaluate them carefully. Dale agreed with what he considered a prevalent attitude among planners, that they and politicians should lead the people, not merely follow uninformed majority whims. If public opinion were permitted to dictate policy decisions, there could be neither rational planning nor informed government. The proper places for the people to exercise their judgment were the marketplace and the voting booth.

On the basis of similar reasoning, Dale never seriously considered the need to consult with organized groups in St. Paul. Herbert Wieland, who replaced Loeks as Planning Bureau Director in January 1958, believed that city planners should only consult with organized groups for the purpose of obtaining information and sampling neighborhood sentiments. Planners generally maintained that organized groups represented only a part of the community, while the purpose of general planning was to determine goals for the entire community. They acknowledged that specialists in the municipal administration might be compelled to work with such organized groups, but this was unfortunate. In any event, planners should avoid interest group politics.

The land-use inventory, therefore, was no more than a compilation of available data about the physical aspects of St. Paul. It dealt neither with social problems nor community opinion. It was not intended to illuminate specific problems. Finally, while Dale believed that the purpose of the general planning was goal determination, no procedures were designed for ascertaining community values.[8]

Interpreting the Facts

Dale believed that simple presentation of the facts was not enough if his inventory was to have any influence. Interpretation was a necessary part of land-use planning. What, for example, were St. Paul's foreseeable future problems and needs? What contingencies might arise? What might happen if the city should do nothing? What could the city do to alter its prospects? In his analysis Dale eschewed social problems per se, as he had in his inventory. He realized that most physical land-use problems involved nonmonetary as well as monetary values, but he chose to concentrate on only those nonmonetary or "social" problems that he believed were associated in the public mind with good business and progress. Therefore, although he considered the metropolitan area's expected population growth at length, he did not consider racial segregation or the migration of nonwhites into St. Paul. He estimated the rising demand for new housing, but not the expected shortages of housing for low-income groups.

Dale did not believe that he was defaulting. None of the land-use plans he had examined had dealt extensively with difficult social issues, and he had heard other planners discuss approvingly the principle that "planning is more important than any plan." On the surface this principle suggested that a planner pursuing specific planning goals should never neglect the need for a long-range strategy to improve the good name of planning in his city. In application, it inevitably meant more, for there were no reli-

[8] Dale commented: "The types of social problems and community opinion which [the author] has in mind have been a matter of concern for many people since the beginning of time—we would have been mighty indeed to have attempted to solve them with our minute effort in St. Paul. Procedures for goal determination? Ascertaining community values? This is school talk which I have found makes no impression upon laymen, politicians, decision makers, or anyone else outside of the university and planning circles. I don't believe that planners who talk about community goals know what they are all about! Specific, urgent issues—yes; long range policy and goals—no! Our society has not evolved to that point yet."

able means of predicting what strategies would be most successful in the long run. Caution, therefore, might lead the planner to shape specific goals according to the immediate tactical needs of the planning agency. These practical needs, in turn, depending on how they were perceived, were likely to dictate a deliberate avoidance of "problems" for which technical or noncontroversial solutions were not available.[9]

The "problem" that seemed to concern most St. Paul civic leaders was the attraction of business investment to downtown. They believed that of the groups that the city might deliberately attract, only employers would pay more in taxes than they would require in public services. "Boosterism" had never been a major force in St. Paul. For decades the city's business and political leaders had accepted economic stagnation as normal and rather pleasant, even aristocratic. Only in recent years had opportunities for federal aid and fears of rising taxes roused them from this complacency. Some of these leaders by 1957 feared that traffic congestion, housing obsolescence, and technological unemployment would ruin the city financially if new investment should fail to produce enough jobs and if federal aid opportunities were lost. One of St. Paul's most important assets, they believed, was its low property-tax rate. No community in the Twin Cities Metropolitan Area could boast of a lower one. But they also realized that St. Paul had many miles of poorly paved streets, inadequate water and sewer systems, outdated school facilities, understaffed and undersupplied fire and police departments, and similar municipal faults. Costs of services were constantly rising. The only way to hold the tax line while maintaining or improving the level of service was to attract industry. Moreover, this appeared to be the best means of avoiding technological unemployment in an era of automation and expanding population. With luck, new industry might even provide new markets for existing businesses.

From available literature Dale informed himself about the criteria that businessmen allegedly used when seeking sites for new

[9] Dale commented: "We *did* consider the social problems and we were quite aware of their importance. These problems have been with us for well over 2,000 years and *planners* are not going to solve them with a land-use plan. In fact, it would be foolish to 'shoot for the moon' only to fall and break your neck."

structures. He examined the vacant land in St. Paul with an eye to industrial potential, but he made no attempt to evaluate the desire to attract industry. He knew that all efforts to prove that industry would improve the city's tax position had so far failed. Industries employed and often released from employment low-income workers who apparently consumed more services than they paid for directly. The combined balance of taxes paid by employers and employees, and the services consumed by both, had to date defied computation anywhere. Furthermore, even if such a balance might have been calculated for specific industries already located in St. Paul, no dependable projections could be estimated for all industries that might conceivably locate in the city.

Dale realized that tens of millions of dollars would be required to prepare some of St. Paul's most suitable industrial sites for use, and he knew that these locations were not at present really needed by industry. If improved at public expense, they would compete with industrial locations already prepared in suburban areas and in Minneapolis. The money spent to develop the land might not be recovered for many decades and perhaps could be applied to better uses.

If the financial balance defied Dale's expertness, the social balance seemed too complicated even to think about. For example, if a labor shortage attracted low-income earners to the city, it presumably was good that they would buy goods, pay taxes, increase the city's attractiveness to certain industries, and enable the city to boast bustling growth statistics. On the other hand, it was unfortunate that they would consume city services, add to the burdens of social service agencies, lower the level of intellectual attainment in the public schools, increase juvenile delinquency, and perhaps increase racial tensions.

Dale did not dwell on dilemmas such as these. He felt confident that his superiors did not expect him to question the desirability of worldly success for a city. American planners, unlike many of their European counterparts, almost never did so. It was taken for granted by St. Paul's planners that their position was far too weak for them even to consider embarking on such a controversial course. The issue was so academic that, so far as Dale could later recall, it never even came up over coffee or cocktails.

The form of the analysis was affected also by the dictum that politicians expected planners to know answers and to issue calls to action. According to this dictum, plan reports must have simple, straightforward, consistent themes; apathy was generally rife enough without a planner paralyzing the public will to act by emphasizing uncertainty. If civic leaders pressed for action on certain problems, with no one in opposition, then the planner should not issue public warnings unless he was sure that some other method would meet the public's desires more fully. The planners' definition of rationality, therefore, included political calculations "behind" the analysis of facts presented in the plan.

Throughout his analysis, Dale focused on a variety of factors sustaining or limiting the marketability of land in St. Paul. He defended this focus by pointing out that for the city to approach the ideal of reserving each parcel of land for its most desirable user, it had to discover who would demand what land if it were available, and for what purposes. His major findings were of the following order. Only one-eighth of the land in St. Paul was both vacant and potentially usable. A good deal of this land would probably not be developed unless replatted with some consideration for market demand. Most commercial areas in the city were short of off-street parking space and might be helped through cooperative ventures to provide parking space. Demand for apartment construction in St. Paul appeared to be on the western side of the city, where people who worked and entertained in Minneapolis lived. Industrial users of land preferred to be located near alternative types of cargo carrier, so they could take advantage of changing rate relationships and have insurance against tie-ups in any one type. St. Paul's most important vacant areas that might be suitable for industry were astride or adjacent to four means of transportation: air, rail, highway, and water. Heavy industry had used only one-eighth of the land allotted to it in the existing zoning ordinance, enacted in 1922, while light industry had outgrown its allotment of land and had spilled into heavy industrial areas. There was substantial reason to believe, therefore, that unless it was offered new sites and protected from heavy industrial neighbors, additional light industry would be deterred from locating in the city.

Predicting the Future

The work of the St. Paul planners was influenced by prevailing thinking in their profession about the goals and methods of land-use planning. A plan was meant to bring about a future state of affairs. A data inventory and analysis should therefore be the prelude to projection and goal determination. The projection phase of land-use planning served two purposes: (1) to indicate the direction that change would likely take in the absence of new governmental efforts to control it; and (2) to show the possibilities of purposeful action. The latter purpose was especially complicated, because a city could not concentrate its total energies on the accomplishment of any single goal. Multiple objectives added up to a complex resultant—a way of life for an entire community—involving a wide range of citizen choices. Planners tended to believe that they were unable to reduce all the possibilities to a significant few for a city to select without some theoretical guidance. A truly comprehensive planner should try to envision, in some detail, many possible goals for the future. His professional criteria should indicate the variation possible for each. He should also know the means by which each of these specific goals might be achieved and the expected consequences of achieving them.

The St. Paul planners' strategy was based upon imperfect projection techniques. Dale believed, therefore, that caution was desirable. City planners, he reasoned, concentrated their efforts on the anticipation of a future that no planner tried to change, and then estimated the various ways in which they might alter individual variables through specific, purposeful actions. They frequently tried to conceive the unintended consequences of these alternative actions, but they had no dependable techniques for delineating them. Nor did they frequently have grounds for believing that their governments would intervene to alter ongoing trends. Consequently, they typically (and, in Dale's view, wisely) endeavored in their recommendations to help the inevitable to occur in more orderly fashion, not to redirect the stream of change.[10]

The object of the forecasting effort was to determine the

[10] The remainder of this section, which runs to page 114, deals in some detail with the St. Paul planners' land-use forecasting efforts. Readers who skip it will be able to follow the rest of the narrative without difficulty.

amount of acreage that would be demanded for each major category of land-use in 1968 and 1980. The first step was to forecast population changes. Dale described his method of forecasting population in the plan report as "average 1945–1956 natural increase and 1940–1950 migration, modified by land development trends." It was actually simpler than that. The record of population increase during the three decades from 1920 to 1950 had been approximately the following: 37,000; 16,000; and 24,000. Data were available on the number of occupied dwelling units in each census tract at the beginning of 1957. Unable to do a complete census, and believing that any sampling techniques that he could afford to employ would be unreliable, he assumed that the 1940–1950 migration rates were still operative and that the number of persons per dwelling unit had remained constant since 1950. He believed that these were reasonable assumptions, although migration rates tended to be extremely unstable and the United States Census Bureau had estimated that the average number of people per dwelling unit in the nation's cities was declining markedly as families with children fled to the suburbs. The dwelling unit calculation, combined with a projection of the 1940–1950 migration rate, yielded a population estimate for 1957 of 335,893. The rate of increase from 1950 to 1957 was then projected into the future, yielding a 1980 population estimate of 415,800.

The planners did caution in the land-use plan report that their population forecast rested on an important assumption, namely that the existing ratio of single-family homes to apartment construction would be drastically altered. During the 1950–1957 period, two and one-half times as much land had been used up by residential construction as remained vacant and planned for residential use in the entire city at the end of 1957. Therefore, the projected growth could take place only if, as the land available for single-family home construction filled up, apartment construction increased rapidly enough to accommodate a population continuing to expand at the 1950–1957 rate. Exclusive of public housing, only 341 apartment dwelling units had been built in the city during 1952–1957, as against 6,263 single-family homes. There was some reason for optimism as the plan went to press, however, and this was duly noted; the total number of apartments constructed in the city had risen from 61 in 1957 to 240 in 1958 to 489 in the first half of 1959. There had been short-lived apartment construction booms before in St. Paul, most recently one that had lasted from 1949 through 1951, but the planners believed that the current boom would continue. Their faith rested on one salient fact: given current death rates and the numbers of people already born in each age group, it could be expected that the number of childless adults in the metropolitan area would increase rapidly during the twenty-year forecast period. They judged that a large proportion of these people would prefer to live in apartments and that apartments would be built to accommodate them.

Members of the planning staff acknowledged privately that older people, as a group, would probably not be able to afford any new housing. Therefore, the expected market would likely come from childless young people who worked in St. Paul. If these people owned cars, they might choose to live in suburban apartments and commute via the freeway. On the other hand, if they disliked the suburbs, they still might prefer to live in Minneapolis, which had a far more varied and colorful night life than St. Paul. The areas in Minneapolis where apartments were likely to be built would be closer (by the measure of time-distance) to downtown St. Paul, once the freeway was completed, than parts of St. Paul itself.[11] Furthermore, the average age at which young people became parents might drop. The projection of consumer demand was always hazardous, and few industries had confidence in sales projections more than a few months ahead. The planners based their projections of apartment demand, perforce, on less well-established trends than those which underlay most industrial forecasts.[12]

In his first draft Dale cautiously pointed out that most of the areas allotted to apartments in the plan, and the entire area allotted to high-rise apartments, were currently blighted and unpleasant. He wrote that public action would be needed to make

[11] The published plan mentioned only the reverse: that the freeway would put even some of eastern St. Paul—the side of the city away from Minneapolis, but also the major reserve of undeveloped land in the city—closer in time-distance to downtown Minneapolis than portions of Minneapolis itself.

[12] On reading this in 1961, Dale commented: "Our data may have been less than substantial but our estimates are proving correct. Data cannot be compiled about men's minds and their desires which affect the real estate market. A planner must use good judgment and 'cross his fingers' for luck!"

them attractive to developers. This warning of the possible consequences of inaction was later edited out by his superiors.

Dale also warned in his first draft that the plan's population
forecast rested on an assumption that the 1,877 vacant acres
allotted to residential use were as desirable as the 4,903 acres filled
during the 1950–1957 period. He noted that stockyard odors made
some of the East Side—the major reservoir of vacant land in St.
Paul—rather undesirable for residential use at the present time.
This, too, was later edited out by his superiors.

Dale's next step after making his population estimates was to
determine future land-to-population ratios for each major category of land use.

He began by trying to establish existing trends in St. Paul.
Unfortunately, the only two years for which land-use data were
available were 1934 and 1957. Dale realized that two points in
time a quarter of a century apart were hardly sufficient to establish
convincing trends, especially when a depression, a world war, and
a postwar boom had intervened. To make matters worse, the 1934
data had been collected by amateurs in the Works Progress Administration (WPA), working under professional direction; and
the categories they had used were in many cases quite different
from those employed in 1957. Dale suspected that even the categories that did sound comparable had in some cases been defined
differently. Still, he judged that some trend was better than none.

Next, he considered the relationships between St. Paul's land-to-
population ratios and those of seven other cities. Harland Bartholomew had published a book in which he had presented citywide
land-use totals for 53 central cities, 33 satellite cities, and 11 urban
areas.[13] Dale compared the proportions of St. Paul's land used for
each major purpose with the average for seven selected cities dealt
with by Bartholomew. On the basis of this comparison, he concluded that St. Paul was an average city in its size range, with
slightly lower residential density, considerably more light industry, and somewhat less heavy industry then the "norm." How
significant was this finding?

Bartholomew had dealt with only five cities above 250,000 in
population. These five varied so widely in size and range of their

[13] Harland Bartholomew, *Land Uses in American Cities* (Cambridge: Harvard University Press, 1955).

land-use proportions that Dale did not consider their average significant. He therefore decided to compare St. Paul with Bartholomew's seven cities in the 100,000 to 250,000 range. The seven cities varied in population from 106,000 to 247,000 and their average size was 147,000, while St. Paul's estimated current population was 343,000. Unlike St. Paul, none of the cities among Bartholomew's seven was part of a metropolitan area dominated by a larger city. The surveys on which Bartholomew's data were based had been made at various times between 1938 and 1948, averaging in 1944, fifteen years before the publication of St. Paul's land-use plan. Elsewhere in his plan Dale emphasized changes in construction trends since the war.[14]

The seven cities differed widely in the proportions of their land devoted to each use and seldom clustered around a norm. Dale's characterizations of St. Paul were based on deviations from the seven-city average that were miniscule compared to their own range. Perhaps this was to be expected, as the cities ranged in size from 111,000 to 667,000 acres, and the largest city in acreage was the smallest in population. The percentage of developed land devoted to industry ranged between 1.61 and 7.16. Parks and playgrounds consumed between 2.14 and 10.09 per cent. The space per one hundred persons devoted to residential use ranged from two to five acres. The total developed area per one hundred residents varied from six to twelve acres. St. Paul's acreage per one hundred persons devoted to the ten categories of land use for which comparisons were made deviated from the seven-city average in no case by more than .25 of an acre. In the case of that divergence, the seven cities differed from each other by as much as three acres. Bartholomew's book had not explained why cities divided their land as they did, nor had it indicated which of the distributions revealed by his data were desirable.

Finally, Dale proceeded to formulate specific acreage forecasts for St. Paul. He did this, according to the published plan report, in the following manner:

First, the characteristics of the 1957 land-use pattern were studied and, where possible, were compared with some limited data on 1934 land

[14] Dale commented: "The fact that some of Bartholomew's work is dated has proven to be of no importance; a city's land use pattern and composition does not change very rapidly."

use to arrive at growth trends in terms of acreage increases. Second, the population growth was projected to 1980 and, by comparative analysis (7 other cities), a projected land-to-population ratio was developed and applied to give a rough estimate of 1968 and 1980 land needs.

In other words, the plan's rough estimate of future land needs was based on 1944 land use in seven cities averaging 43 per cent of the current population of St. Paul. The exact nature of the relationship was not specified, but the central assumption appeared to be that the amount of land per hundred residents used for each major purpose in the St. Paul of 1980 would approximate the 1944 seven-city average.[15] The more precise estimates, however, were arrived at as follows:

Third, the Land Use Plan was drawn compromising the acreage projections from step two with the types of land available and its suitability to specific uses . . . Throughout step three every reasonable consideration was given to possible highway, school, recreation, urban renewal and other factors which influence the 1980 land use picture.

The planners did in fact have a better knowledge of existing plans for development than any other group of men in the city, but this knowledge was of substantial use only in the making of short-term projections. Beyond that, their estimates of future deviations from the expected patterns of development had to be purely speculative.

Descending to still a lower level of generality, let us turn to the ways in which acreage projections were made for each category of land use.

Dale's inventory revealed that 0.20 acres per hundred residents

[15] On receiving an early draft of this case study, Dale contended that the comparative analysis had been meant to be illustrative and that inadvertently the plan report had been printed in such a manner as to suggest that the comparative analysis had been the core of the forecasting procedure. In fact, several pages in the plan report were devoted to this analysis, and the effect of the "inadvertency" was to give readers the impression that the methods of the planners were scientifically reliable and nationally recognized.

On receiving a later draft, which contained the first paragraph of this footnote, Dale commented as follows: "We did base our final land use projections upon considerable 'professional judgment.' However, our methods were as 'scientific' as any that I am aware of today. The best anyone can do is make an educated guess."

were currently devoted in St. Paul to commercial uses. He forecast that the figure would rise to 0.23 acres in 1968 and remain at that level through 1980, even though population would continue to rise. His method was described in the plan report as follows:

The average now found in [Bartholomew's] seven cities is 0.23. Assuming that St. Paul will become more important as a regional center, that a considerable amount of parking space will be added, and that steps will be taken to improve the competitive advantage of its retailers, it is expected that the land-to-population ratio will increase, and be more comparable to that found in other cities.

His actual procedure, Dale later said, had been to assume that existing shopping centers would remain without important change through 1980. He had then used current trends in shopping center construction and location, together with his 1980 population estimate for each section of the city, and estimated the distribution and size of new centers that would be built by 1980. To be safe, he had added a margin of space for additional parking. The agreement between his estimate and Bartholomew's seven-city average, Dale commented, had been purely a coincidence. Unfortunately, the plan as written had inadvertently suggested otherwise.

Dale's assumption that St. Paul would become more of a regional center presented a two-part problem: would the central business district require more space, and would the shopping centers developed to serve St. Paul's growing suburbs be located within the city? St. Paul planners believed that the central business district contained so many old, low-rise structures that its future expansion, if any, would not require additional acreage. In any event, current planning doctrine was to aim at closely built downtowns with high-rise buildings, ring roads, peripheral parking facilities, and as few pedestrian interruptions within the core itself as possible. The planners also believed that new shopping centers should and would be located on the in-town edges of their trade areas. Traffic tended to be heavier and residences tended to be more concentrated on the side of any area closest to the core of the central city; private developers had, therefore, traditionally believed that the greatest number of people would find it most convenient to visit the in-town side of any normal area. According to this reasoning, local regional centers, defined in the land-use plan as centers built around a major department store and meant to serve more than 100,000 people, should, given the distribution of residences in St. Paul and its suburbs, be located inside the city.

There was, however, another possibility. The location theory outlined in the plan report had developed prior to the freeway era. Now an Interstate Freeway belt line was being built for the Twin Cities area, and its route was through the suburbs. Regional center developers might well opt for locations by it. Land for parking would be cheaper than inside the city, and customers might come from greater distances. A great shopping center, Southdale, had already been developed south of Minneapolis, drawing customers from the entire Twin Cities area. St. Paul's northern boundary was directly east of the Minneapolis central business district. Many trucking, warehousing, and manufacturing establishments had already moved out of Midway, the large regional center in St. Paul located midway between the central business districts of St. Paul and Minneapolis, to Roseville, a suburb immediately north of St. Paul and east of the northern half of Minneapolis.

No one knew whether steps would be taken to increase St. Paul's attractiveness to commercial investors, or whether any steps could succeed so long as the central city's blight continued to spread. The value, if any, of making the projection was in dramatizing possibilities for the public, perhaps thereby increasing its receptivity to planning proposals. The projection might also awake some local leaders to think in terms of longer time-spans than usually concerned them. But these benefits had nothing to do with the projection's accuracy.

Another key projection concerned industrial land use. During the 1946–1956 period, industrial expansion in St. Paul had absorbed an average of thirty-six acres each year. In his first draft, Dale noted that local industrial growth had been most rapid in the first postwar years and had declined since that time. He estimated that the average amount of land that would be absorbed each year until 1965 would be somewhat less than the 1946–1956 average, and that as the postwar babies began to come of age another ten years of rapid growth might occur. A straight-line projection of the 1946–1956 average, slightly optimistic on these assumptions, indicated that 828 additional acres would be required by 1980.

Dale's superiors, when they reviewed the first draft in December 1958 and January 1959, believed that this projection was too pessimistic. They contended that the 1946–1956 growth rate would be maintained until about 1965 and would approximately double thereafter. On these assumptions, they found, "as much as 1,477 additional acres may be required by 1980."

The plan recommended that 2,500 vacant acres should be zoned for industry, above the 2,000 acres currently in use. The stated basis for this recommendation was that industrial investors demanded a wide variety of sites from which to choose. Moreover, no one was able to predict the precise needs of the industries that might decide to locate in St. Paul. Finally, few of the 2,500 vacant acres could conceivably be used for any purposes other than industrial. More than four-fifths of the available acreage was currently unattractive because of flood danger. Most of this land, embracing 1,800 acres, was in the Pig's Eye Lake area, a section covered by marshes, water, and peat. Its water line with the Mississippi River was not clearly demarcated even in normal times and could not be secured against periodic flooding except at exorbitant expense. Dale and his fellow planners hoped that Congress would someday appropriate the tens of millions of dollars needed for the United States Army Corps of Engineers to stabilize the water line. The area might then be suitable for certain industries, such as gravel pits and bulk storage uses, which could bear the risk of periodic floods in return for cheap land, riverfront location, and ready access to four means of transportation. Another 250 acres were located in the proposed Riverview Redevelopment Area, directly across the river from St. Paul's central business district. To be rendered suitable for industrial development, the Riverview Area required a major urban renewal effort in addition to a floodwall, which the Army engineers estimated they could build in three years for $4.58 million. In this case the planners had good reason to expect that federal funds would be made available.

Some projections depended on the accomplishment of specific goals proposed in the plan. For example, in the final report the planners recommended that one acre of land for "Recreation and Schools" be maintained per one hundred inhabitants of the city. As the 1980 population estimate was 415,800, they estimated that in 1980 a total of 4,158 acres would be devoted to recreation and schools—2,000 acres more than in 1957. Dale and others admitted privately that St. Paul would never support such an expansion of recreation space and pointed out that the plan map itself allotted only 3,208 acres for 1980. They told the writer privately that the latter figure was the true one. In the plan report itself they explained the discrepancy differently:

Chart 43 (the Plan Map) shows only the larger existing parks [and several major additions already planned]. These areas together with existing smaller public parks, playgrounds and schools amount to 3,208 acres. The difference between the 1980 required recreation and school acreage (4,158 acres), and the 3,208 total, amounts to 950 acres. These 950 acres are needed in expanding some of the smaller public parks and certain existing playground and school sites and will be shown in the Community Facilities Plan to be published later this year.

The Community Facilities Plan in fact became available early in 1961. It stated that the national park standard was an "ideal," beyond St. Paul's resources over the next twenty to thirty years, and that sites of "reasonable minimum" size within a reasonable distance of most homes were more valuable than sites of standard size far removed from most homes. The plan did not set a specific target for 1980 park acreage.

Dale faced similar problems with respect to 1980 residential land use. He estimated that the supply of vacant land for one-family home construction would be exhausted by 1968. Between 1968 and 1980 the amount of land in one-family residential use would decline by 1,800 acres—one-sixth of the total. An additional 49 acres would be devoted to two-family use through conversion of older one-family homes. The amount of land in multifamily use would almost double, rising from 877 to 1,643 acres. The total amount of land in residential use would decline by 985 acres.

These estimates were educated guesses. It was certainly true, for example, that after the city's land filled up, the amount in residential use could not increase. Meanwhile, certain uses—parks, schools, churches, shopping centers, roads—would probably require more land if the city's population should continue to grow. Unfortunately, no one knew exactly how much or which land would be taken. The multifamily residential projection was based on similar reasoning. Dale postulated that as the city's one-family neighborhoods filled out, presumably with the same population densities as those of recently developed one-family residential areas, its population would continue to rise at the 1950–1957 rate. If the assumption were true, the increased demand for dwelling units would have to be satisfied through conversions and new apartment construction. Dale assumed that the average population density in the new apartments would equal the average for apartment houses built between 1950 and 1957. He believed that this was an improvement on the plans of other cities that he had examined. The authors of most of them had projected the average population density for all of their cities' existing apartment dwellings. Dale considered this unreasonable, in view of the changes in construction practice that had taken place over the years. He therefore excluded all buildings constructed before 1950 from his computation of the average population density to be expected in multi-dwellings.

Dale was confident of his ten-year projections, except for those concerning industrial and recreational land use. Industrial demand was not predictable, he maintained, particularly for an area as small as St. Paul. The recreation prediction depended not on market demand but on public action to achieve a recreational standard seldom approached in any city. However, he believed that the population forecast on which his other projections were based would prove to be highly accurate, at least for the shorter (ten-year) projection period. It was revealed later, unfortunately, that even his estimate of *current* population was wrong. Dale concluded from his calculations that the 1957 population of St. Paul was 335,893 and that the 1960 population would be 347,000, an increase of almost 36,000 over 1950. When the census figures became available they showed that St. Paul's population had risen by less than 2,000, to a 1960 total of 313,411. (Minneapolis planners made a similar mistake. Applying the same set of assumptions to their own city, they had anticipated a population increase for Minneapolis of 8.2 per cent, with a population total for 1960 of 565,000. But the census figures showed that Minneapolis' population, like that of most other large central cities, had *declined*—by 7.8 per cent, for a total of 481,026.)

Although he acknowledged that none of his assumptions were theoretically compelling, Dale could not bring himself to doubt that, in the absence of war or depression, recent trends would continue over at least the ten-year period. The assumption that all change was gradual was the key justification for his confidence. With respect to the longer period, to 1980, Dale privately disclaimed any faith in his own projections. He reasoned that when the city's land was filled up, demand for its reuse would not tend to develop until the government announced its intention to acquire land, clear it, assume responsibility for relocating the occupants, and put it up for sale. In the absence of such action, private developers could likely obtain land outside the city with far less trouble. The planner could only suggest the kinds of developers who *might* want land in a particular location *if* it were cleared and offered on the market.

More generally, it may be noted that methods of trend projection depend always on the assumption that the trends projected will persist. Dale did not examine this assumption seriously in any case, except where the obstacle to persistence (most notably, of the rate of single-family home construction) was an obvious shortage of land. It would no doubt have been unreasonable to expect him to do so. The planning staff's economic base section was not ready with its data as he worked, and in any event the forces that produced urban land-use trends were extremely complex and not very well understood. Moreover, the city boundaries within which Dale was forced to work formed a highly arbitrary area from the point of view of adequate trend projection; the forces that produced market demand and population increases largely ignored municipal boundaries.

In view of these factors, Dale could not help but realize that his projections were crude. He knew, however, that laymen expected planners to predict, and he believed that planners might *make* their forecasts come true if they won community approval for the execution of their plans. If planners projected a clear image of future conditions and requirements, they were more likely than otherwise to make an impression on busy civic leaders. The more that their recommendations could be made to appear inescapable, the less controversial they were bound to be. Thus, the easier it was likely to be for politicians to support them. At the same time, it was both risky and professionally unethical to express with certainty estimates which were likely to prove demonstrably wrong.

Therefore, Dale took care to note that all projections were uncertain, but at the same time he emphasized the sophistication and complexity of the methods he had used and endeavored to convey an overall impression of confidence based upon expertness.[16]

Delineating the Goals

Having prepared and analyzed his data inventory, Dale was faced with the task of delineating in greater detail the goals embraced in his emerging land-use plan. He recognized a dilemma. Planners generally subscribed to a modest view of their role in the community; they believed that city planning should be carried out within the framework of articulated public preferences, arrived at through the political process. Planners could contribute greatly to the goal determination process by generating data, by suggesting technical standards and principles to be observed in the selection of goals and in planning implementation, and by citing the anticipated consequences of alternatives, but they should not try to impose their own values and preferences upon the community. Rather, they should serve the goals, principles, and standards chosen by the community on the basis of adequate information. The planner's task, according to this view, was to discover the goals and then present plans for their achievement. It was not enough for him simply to list alternatives; he had a responsibility to recommend among them. In St. Paul, however, as in most cities, no authoritative effort had ever been made to formulate and articulate meaningful, long-range community goals, let alone to develop a system of priorities.

Dale knew that the City Council did not want to be bothered until the plan was completed, and perhaps not even then. He decided not to consult special interest groups in the city, because he believed it possible and desirable to prepare a plan that would be best for the city as a whole without such consultation. He understood that some people might be harmed, or at least denied benefits, by any plan that aided others, but he felt that certain broad principles of city development might be observed that would

[16] In reflecting upon this interpretation of his strategy, Dale has commented that while his discourses on scientific-sounding techniques "were admittedly window-dressing, they (also) had a more important function—that of showing how many of the old, so-called tried and true methods were totally impractical."

surely benefit the vast majority without imposing injustices on any individuals or groups. He did not hope to solve all the city's problems, and he resolved not to make any recommendations that could not be demonstrated as beneficial to the entire city. He expected that his colleagues and superiors on the planning staff and in the Planning Board would have an opportunity to review his proposals before publication.

Dale professed no articulated vision of the "good life." He did not believe that it was his task to tell people how to live. He saw his objectives as being the much more limited ones of making life more "pleasant" and investments more "secure." The first might be achieved by enabling people to do more easily what they were already doing, the second by enabling them to predict the future environment of any piece of land more accurately. He believed that working toward such goals was a rational pursuit of the public interest. He felt, however, that an unspoken consensus did exist in St. Paul on many issues. As the planners saw the city drifting toward blight and commercial decline, they were certain that they could offer means of reversing trends that everyone agreed were undesirable and accelerating other trends that were recognized as desirable.

On the basis of these assumptions, Dale began his exercise in goal articulation by preparing a statement of general objectives for land-use planning. He came up with a list, which read as follows:

1. Encouragement of large and small-scale enterprises to locate or to remain and expand in St. Paul.

2. Consolidation of business and industrial development at the most favorable locations.

3. Gradual elimination of excessive and marginal business locations and developments (strip-zoning and development, spot development, etc.).

4. Improvement of the conditions attending business operations at the selected locations, including traffic, parking, removal of obstacles to site expansion, elimination of land-use nuisances and eyesores, and other bars to progressive development.

5. Elimination of conflicts between residential and non-residential uses.

6. Evolution of St. Paul as a better place in which to live and work.

7. Encouragement of enactment into law of those land-use standards

which are considered as minimum and necessary to insure sound development.

8. Encouragement of public demand for development according to those sound land-use principles and standards which cannot be enacted into law because they are higher than those required for minimum health and safety reasons.

Dale had not used any formal method to discover these community objectives, nor did he suggest their order of importance. The sixth objective (evolution of St. Paul as a better place in which to live and work) presumably embraced all the others. He made no claim that these objectives were addressed to the most important problems of land use in St. Paul, nor did he attempt to justify their different levels of generality. He believed that greater specificity would have led to conflict and controversy—an eventuality that he and his superiors wished to avoid. For example, elimination of "conflicts between residential and non-residential uses" was quite specific compared with enacting "minimum land-use standards . . . to insure sound development." The objective of eliminating "bars to progressive [business] development" was just one means of encouraging enterprises "to locate or to remain and expand in St. Paul." These objectives, which Dale intended as expressions of community consensus, did not attempt to clarify controversial issues of public policy.

The eight objectives evoked little interest in the community when the plan was published in 1959. Political and other community leaders saw no practical implications flowing from them. This may have been because the goals seemed too vague to merit attention. In fact, however, certain meaningful policies were implied by them. The clearest policy was that St. Paul should encourage commerce and industry to locate and prosper within its boundaries. The city government could ease certain conditions that would deter businessmen from locating in the central city and should do so when it could. Some of these conditions were: traffic congestion, insufficient parking space, shortages of attractive sites, obstacles to site expansion, eyesores, and "conflict" between business and residential land uses.

The eight objectives were based on a number of premises that were not articulated by the planners at the time of their work but were implicit in the land-use plan and were later acknowledged privately: (1) the city was a going enterprise; therefore, its decline should be prevented at all costs; (2) the situation was not so desperate, however, that unprecedented public powers were required; (3) the city should be made as attractive as possible—by tried and tested means—to investors and to middle- and upper-class residents; and (4) the city had some responsibility to serve the needs of its own low-income residents, but it should not make itself attractive to a flood of low-income migrants. When the land-use plan was issued, the planners were challenged on only one of these assumptions: that the city had an obligation to make life in St. Paul more attractive to its own low-income residents.

Ostensibly on the basis of the eight general objectives, Dale next developed three series of goal statements, which he labeled: (1) planning *principles* to be observed; (2) recommended *policies;* and (3) *standards* to be enforced.

Principles

Seven "basic land-use principles" were listed. These were much less vague than the eight objectives, but no indication was given that they were meant to be subordinate to the latter. In practice, their greater clarity appeared to make them far more relevant to the choices that had to be made in writing the plan.

The first principle was that existing land-use characteristics "must be recognized and given due consideration." The destruction of existing patterns entailed costs that any planner with aspirations to rationality had to consider, but Dale intended a more precise and forceful meaning than this. He wrote that rezoning an area could be justified only when normal market forces were working to change a "substantial" part of it in a "desirable" direction. In practice, the land-use plan map as published would recommend no specific changes at all in the predominant uses of built-up areas, with the exception that redevelopment projects previously proposed by the Housing Authority were explicitly approved. The only structures designated as nonconforming uses were little shops, not representing "substantial" investment and standing alone in residential neighborhoods. If two or three "insubstantial" stores were grouped together, their sites were designated as commercial on the grounds that the planners had no choice. Dale and the planners who reviewed his work believed that the owner of even a middle-sized business establishment would prevail with the City Council if the Planning Board should try to designate his business a nonconforming use. If politicians had not been involved, planners would have judged each case on its merits, asking whether the commercial use tended to cause blight in the neighborhood and how heavily its loss would hurt the owner and patrons. The planners realized that they lacked dependable means for judging and weighing these factors.

Despite their prudence, the planners discovered soon after the plan's publication that some political leaders termed it "visionary." These politicians had seen that a couple of small sections, residential in 1959, were colored for industrial use on the 1980 plan map. Some of the planners later explained privately to the writer that they had based their art work on the fact that the transition was already under way and was certain to be completed before 1980, whether or not the land-use plan was implemented. The political leaders had not sought the planners' reasons.

The second "basic principle" called for a new zoning code, but suggested nothing about the code's contents.

The third provided that each land use should be concentrated in neighborhoods large enough to avoid becoming engulfed by other uses and protected by strong physical boundaries. Its premise was that mixtures of incompatible land use led to blight, making the city less attractive to residents and investors. Dale was convinced that residential, commercial, and industrial uses should be segregated. There was room for disagreement about details but not about the basic idea. He qualified his position, however, by indicating that his target was mixtures of land use "which will lead to blight."

The fourth principle was that "residential areas should be free of incompatible uses, large volumes of traffic, economic hindrances to development, and conditions of blight. [They] should maintain desirable densities and, above all, be liveable." Dale defined a "liveable" city as "one which has those qualities in the physical environment which tend to induce in its citizens a feeling of mental, physical, and social well-being."

The fifth principle was that schools, playgrounds, shopping centers, work areas, and leisure time areas should, to the extent possible, be located "in convenient proximity" to residences. The sixth principle was that "transportation, size of site requirements, nature of activity, utilities, and other factors must be considered in order to determine the location of work areas. They should be economical to develop, and attractively situated for the particular uses intended." The seventh principle was that major parks, in addition to being convenient to their service areas, should "take advantage of natural or unusual features of the landscape and provide for a variety of activities."

The most important of these seven principles were the first, third, and fourth. Taken together, they suggested that the major purposes of land-use planning were (1) to encourage the development of neatly defined, unsplit, homogeneous neighborhoods, and (2) to protect these neighborhoods from invading uses, large volumes of traffic, hindrances to development, and blight. Dale did not indicate any criteria for dealing with conflicts among these principles, or between them and other criteria of good public policy. In the case of the freeway being planned for St. Paul, however, the planning staff had recently supported proposals to run major new barriers through several existing neighborhoods. Nor did he advance any evidence to support his thesis that clearly defined neighborhoods should be a high priority object of public policy.[17] Nor did he make any effort to define the precise levels of homogeneity that he thought desirable in neighborhoods, except to say that levels of heterogeneity which produced blight were clearly undesirable. He also failed to articulate his view of the ways in which the principles would help to implement the eight stated general objectives of the plan. Consequently, it seems fair to say that the principles no less than the objectives were offered in every case as inherently and self-evidently desirable in themselves.

[17] In private conversations Dale and his associates contended that the reason for their stress on land-use segregation was that sufficiently high standards to allow mixing of types without detrimental effects were extremely unlikely to be adopted. They would be happy, they said, to approve controlled mixing of land-use types in any community willing to enforce an effective and comprehensive zoning ordinance and system of related controls. They believed, however, that St. Paul, like nearly all other cities, was far from ready to adopt such a program.

Policies

After his brief listing of objectives and principles, Dale devoted a lengthy section (which eventually ran to ten closely printed pages in the plan report) to articulating policies for each particular category of land use. In addition to the usual categories of residential, industrial, and so on, he discussed policies for utilizing vacant lands, for identifying neighborhoods, for selecting urban renewal projects, and for selecting public housing sites. It would be fruitless to summarize all these policies, but their major types are identified and briefly discussed below.

One type of policy recommendation consisted simply of points that Dale considered worthy of the attention of policy makers. For example:

1. The location of industrial sites should be one of the key considerations in developing a major streets plan.

2. In planning the use of St. Paul's vacant land reserves, the goal should be the proper balance of industrial, commercial, residential, and other land uses.

3. The location of new business areas should be justified by an adequate market radius, estimated customer potential, suitable location in the market radius, and consideration for the neighborhood circulation pattern. Proper design standards should include parking, loading signs, relative building hulk, and landscaping.

He defended these statements on the theory that many businessmen plunged into ventures without examining the market situation carefully. Large developers, he reasoned, had learned from experience how to avoid mistakes. By asking prospective developers to explain how they planned to avoid these pitfalls, the city might help some to avoid ruin by locating where they might more effectively serve themselves and the city. The test of significance was negative: the city should regulate factors that had caused difficulty elsewhere, according to intelligent—although generally unsystematic—and intensely interested observers, such as members of the Urban Land Institute and planning consultants working in the St. Paul–Minneapolis area.

A second type of policy statement consisted of clear proposals that the city government should act to accomplish specific objectives. They were likely to be noncontroversial in the sense that

virtually all planners could agree with them and that no vocal
public opposition to the abstract statements (as opposed to specific
proposals for implementation) was anticipated. Examples of such
statements were the following:

1. Non-industrial uses should be eliminated from industrial areas
whenever possible.
2. Future commercial development should be based upon the concept of the integrated business center . . . [one] developed according
to a specific site plan and justified by an economic analysis of the area
to be served.
3. Vacant land should be subdivided only when a specific demand
is evident.

Policy statements of the third type were similar but likely to be
more controversial if considered seriously. The following are
illustrative:

1. The policy of clearing the redeveloping slums should continue.
2. All future land-use allocation should be "according to the Land
Use Plan."
3. The zoning, health, housing and building codes should be
strictly enforced.[18]

The most categorical policy statements were often intended to
reassure property owners. The following are illustrative:

1. Established business areas should be zoned as "business" provided
that they now serve areas of at least neighborhood size.
2. All policy regarding industrial land use should be guided toward
making St. Paul more attractive to industry.
3. Each [semipublic] institution should provide its own off-street
parking.

The principle that land uses should be separated was repeated
frequently in the policy statements. It was amplified only once, in

---

[18] Paradoxically, the St. Paul planners considered the zoning, health, and
building codes to be outmoded, and they knew that, after fifteen years of
wrangling and rewriting, the city's proposed housing code was still awaiting
City Council approval. Dale did not indicate in the plan whether the policy
of strict enforcement should begin before or after new codes were passed. He
later commented privately that he thought strict enforcement was always
desirable, because it prevented apathy. Where codes were inadequate, strict
enforcement would inspire public demands for change.

the following terms: "Where practicable, those semi-public institutions which [serve an area larger than a neighborhood] should locate as buffers between residential and land used for other purposes. Those institutions which do serve a given neighborhood should locate in [its] center." The principle that existing land uses should not be disregarded was modified only by a statement that slum clearance should continue.

The meanings of the other "basic principles" were also left unclarified in the policy statements, although two of the thirteen policy headings did attempt to clarify the plan's "objectives." In the identification of residential neighborhoods, it was proposed that they should be large enough to support an elementary school, playground, and small shopping center. They should be small enough to permit the city to satisfy its needs for through streets without having any that ran through neighborhoods. Second, it was proposed that public housing sites should be within existing residentially zoned areas. Each site should be within walking dis-park, and neighborhood shopping center. It should be "con-tance of an elementary school, neighborhood playground, small venient" to a bus line, to a secondary school, and to places of work. The city's housing projects should be small and scattered; none should be completely within "an area inhabited exclusively by a minority group." They should replace substandard housing or nonconforming uses in residential areas, or they should be on vacant lots "leapfrogged" by private housing.

Dale and the other planners who reviewed his work were relatively bold on the subject of public housing, because, of all the programs with which they dealt or might have dealt, it was the one about which planners generally felt the greatest moral certainty. They were practically certain that those who opposed public housing projects were either misguided or simply unwilling to face up to their social responsibilities. Planners took heart from a large body of planning literature which indicated that the primary obstacles to effective public housing were political opposition and faulty design. Some planners went so far as to hope that it might be possible to dispel political opposition with design improvements. The most important new design principle of recent years was that public housing sites should be scattered, with each site containing only a small number of units. Many observers had noted a "project atmosphere" in the large projects and called its effect on public housing occupants pernicious. At the same time, many planners hoped that small, scattered projects might stir less neighborhood opposition than the large ones usually had. The federal Public Housing Administration officially changed its earlier policy in February 1958 to specify that it would look favorably on scattered site proposals.

Standards

The final, most specific, and most lengthy cluster of goal statements was concerned with land-use standards. The standards were almost the only recommendations in the entire plan capable of direct implementation. In a sense, they constituted the "heart" of the plan. The planners indicated some awareness of this when they declared in the plan report that "future land-use development should be guided by a set of locally accepted standards that are specific, clearly stated, just, and workable." [19]

Dale introduced the section on standards with a list of site characteristics sought by private developers. In doing so he modified one of the few clear policy recommendations made previously, namely that (as it was expressed in the published plan report) "all policy regarding industrial land use should be guided toward making St. Paul more attractive to industry." He explained that it was "oversimplified" to believe that a city could direct its efforts toward the narrow goal of attracting industry. The modern industrialist looks for a city that, among other things, is a "good place in which to live," and he

is not against high local taxes if he gets his money's worth in quality of service. The people must be satisfied and happy if they are to be productive. Cultural facilities, schools, housing, parks, and existing industrial and retail districts must reflect a high sense of civic pride. New store fronts, freshly painted houses, and adequate recreational facilities are important.

Presumably, then, the goal of industrial land-use policy, like all other land-use policy, was not simply to attract industry but also to help make the city a better place in which to live. The precise

[19] Dale commented: "The land use standards were intended only as an 'education' feature. When we *spoke* of standards, no one knew what we were talking about. We had to give some examples in the report, fully realizing that they would be greatly expanded in the hoped for new zoning and subdivision regulations."

components of a desirable or "liveable" place in which to live were never delineated in the plan.

In the statement of standards, Dale listed the precise spatial relationships that should exist among land uses. He explained the general criteria employed in determining what standards should be recommended:

Minimum standards are those necessary for reasons of public health and safety, and are enacted into law. [They] are not adequate for the many people in search of a better-than-average environment. To plan the future city on the basis of minimum standards would be the equivalent of no planning at all. Consequently, in city planning, the minimum standards are recommended for enactment into law and the high standards are encouraged by committee work, publicity, and meetings.

No criteria were offered to help distinguish "high" from "minimum," or even to define "wrong" standards. One standard was suggested for each topic, without any effort made to distinguish "high" standards from "low":

The land-use standards in this report are a compromise, neither too high nor too low, and represent a set of practical and desirable goals for both private individuals and public officials to attempt to achieve step-by-step over the next decades.

Dale and the planner who reviewed his work most carefully, C. Allan Blomquist, later explained to the writer how they understood the word "compromise" as used in the plan. They admitted that no explicit criteria had been applied. Most of the standards had been orginally suggested by national professional organizations. They had modified some to make them "reasonable" in the light of existing conditions in St. Paul. "Reasonable" had meant many things to them, the most important of which was: not too far from the *status quo*. Their judgment of human psychology was that the plan would produce a greater effect if its goals seemed within reach to minds of average boldness and imagination. There was no "technique" for making this judgment; it was based on intuitive knowledge, like decisions made by the mayor and other elected officials.

When asked to justify specific standards, however, Dale and Blomquist admitted that they had not always been faithful to this conception of compromise. They considered some of the recommended standards high, others low, and still others a compromise. For example, the plan proposed that the city should have one acre of land for recreational use for every 100 residents. It should, in part, be distributed as follows: every neighborhood should contain a playground one acre in size for every 800 residents. Every community—i.e., grouping of four or five neighborhoods—should also have an acre of athletic field for every 800 residents and an acre of park for every 400 residents. No residence should be more than one-half mile from the neighborhood playground, or more than two and one-half miles from the community park. Similarly, the following school acreage standards were recommended:

> elementary school: five acres plus one acre per
> 100 children;
> junior high school: ten acres plus one acre per
> 100 children;
> senior high school: twenty acres plus one acre per
> 100 children.

Dale and Blomquist admitted that these goals were "very high." They would not have recommended higher standards even if their power to determine land use in the city had been absolute. Moreover, they were not at all sure that the city *should* spend as much on parks as the park standard seemed to require.

Some of the standards were based primarily on current local practices and conditions. For example, the plan report urged that new homes be built on lots no smaller than 6,000 square feet. Dale explained that people seemed to desire lots of at least this size; in addition, maintenance levels seemed to fall rapidly in more crowded areas, and fire spread more easily. Larger lots than those recommended were not desirable because the housing market set the minimum effectively. If people wanted larger lots and were able to pay for them, builders would respond quickly enough.

The proposed time-distance standards governing travel from a person's residence to a regional shopping center, to his place of employment, and to the central business district were all twenty minutes. It was already possible to travel from the city's center to the city limits in most directions in twenty minutes, even during rush hours. There was no reason for anyone to travel longer unless he chose to live on one side of the city while working on the other.

Similarly, neighborhood shopping centers should be within "easy walking distance" of every home in high-density neighborhoods, and no further than six minutes' driving distance in low-density neighborhoods. One of Dale's associates explained that the city's low-density areas already supported neighborhood shopping centers at about six minutes driving distance from the least conveniently situated homes.

Dale used many standards recommended in the publications of national professional organizations. Park and school space standards were in this category. Similarly, the American Library Association (ALA) had recommended simply that a branch library be maintained for every 20,000 residents of any city. Any decision on how many branch libraries should be maintained depended in large part on the level of service considered desirable. With fewer libraries, a higher level of service in each within any given overall budget was possible. Nevertheless, in the final plan the planners urged adoption of the ALA standards without qualification.

Similarly, the St. Paul Zoning Board for several years past had, on the planners' recommendation, applied density standards adapted from *Planning the Neighborhood,* a 1948 publication of the American Public Health Association (APHA).[20] Dale incorporated these standards into his plan, with only minor revisions. Most notably, he recommended the provision of more land per dwelling unit in multifamily dwellings than was proposed by the APHA. Automobile ownership had become far more prevalent in the years 1948–1959. The authors of *Planning the Neighborhood* calculated their parking space requirement at one-half to two-thirds of a space per dwelling unit. By 1959 St. Paul had a city ordinance requiring the provision of a full space per dwelling unit.

Dale later expressed his belief, in conversation with the writer, that planners should avoid the standards proposed by business associations interested primarily in serving their economic self-interest, but he acknowledged no misgivings about using the standards proposed by park, school, library, and other experts interested in maintaining or expanding the values and roles of their specialized, professional points of view. Moreover, he found it virtually impossible to take account of the incomparability of the

20 Chicago: Public Administration Service, 1948, pp. 38, 39.

recommended standards with which he had to work. The professional associations seldom justified the standards they proposed. None specified the precise ways in which local conditions might justify revisions in their standards. The city planner trying to use their standards generally knew little about the size, density, and wealth of the "normal" city used by the associations as their model. The planner had no way of measuring the degree to which each set of standards was a compromise.

In some instances Dale openly acknowledged the inadequacy of his information and, instead of proposing standards, suggested further study. For example, he accepted the planning doctrine that industrial uses should not be segregated according to the casual impression of public officials as to their nuisance effect, but proposed that segregation should be based on scientific measurement of nuisance characteristics. He listed sixteen characteristics of industrial land use for which standards should be developed, ranging from "outdoor storage and waste disposal," to "emission of heat, glare, radiation, smoke, dust, and fumes." He and his associates conceded privately that no professional consensus yet existed as to the precise levels on each scale at which industrial uses should be segregated. Moreover, employing all sixteen standards in order to provide two or three general classifications of industry was a delicate affair. Therefore, Dale refrained from recommending specific performance standards; these rightfully belonged in a zoning code. He suggested that for the present the distinction between light and heavy industry continue to be made on the basis of impressionistic enumeration. The lists of light and heavy industries incorporated into the plan were the ones developed by Harland Bartholomew.

Many of the standards in the plan were compromises between competing planning principles rather than between high and low standards of performance. Theorists disagreed, for example, as to whether one-family, two-family, low-rise apartment, and high-rise apartment houses should be confined to separate neighborhoods. Mixing them tended to increase the likelihood of blight—to what degree in specific circumstances was never explained—but it also distributed the population more evenly and made it possible for people of all stages of life to mix freely. Some planning writers considered it very important for people beyond the child-rearing stage to be able to find housing in family neighborhoods, preferably the same ones in which they had made friends while younger. Other writers considered it essential to preserve the charm of chaos in cities. One writer, for example, had written:

The planner's ideal of complete segregation of land uses is absolutely the wrong answer for the city. . . . So don't plan the neighborhoods —plan areas of action, of life, which means, I say it again, areas which are unplanned except in the broadest sense, so that the urban pattern of confusion can develop as it will.[21]

Dale's solution was simply to recognize that he could not dispel the chaos of St. Paul's older neighborhoods. Most of these neighborhoods already contained many two-family homes; in others there was a scattering of apartment and rooming houses. He indicated, however, that his sympathies lay in the direction of greater segregation by allocating almost the entire vacant acreage of the city that was suitable for residential development to one-family residential use. The only new locations he proposed to open to apartments were those that might serve as buffers between commercial uses or heavy thoroughfares and one-family residences.

[21] Henry S. Churchill, "Planning in a Free Society," *Journal of the American Institute of Planners*, XX, No. 4 (Fall 1954) 189–191. Churchill said that the idea of a city included "a high degree of social anonymity . . . a very considerable freedom of action both moral and occupational, the stimulus of a variety of people, and the possibility of cultural improvement. If you are going to have these things, I maintain you cannot plan them. They are the essence of a city. All you can plan for is (1) a traffic pattern, (2) a concentration of population, (3) a way by which a measure of quiet and safety can be obtained within a high concentration without interfering with the mobility and action of the population, and (4) within such a framework *complete liberty for the development of typical urban life and confusion.*" (Italics added.)

For the attribution of charm to chaos see Vernon de Mars, "Townscape and the Architect: Some Problems of the Urban Scene," *The Future of Cities and Urban Redevelopment*, Coleman Woodbury, ed. (Chicago: University of Chicago Press, 1953), I, 90–99.

Dale commented on the points raised by Churchill and de Mars: "Planning has so little effect upon most Minnesota communities that the opinions expressed by these gentlemen are an actuality. Even if planning becomes more important in this state, we will not progress far beyond these quoted desires. The political, economic, and other factors will assure continuation of the confused urban pattern and the 'charm of chaos' will be in no danger from the planning profession."

Some of the St. Paul planners did not believe that residential neighborhoods should contain commercial buildings. Dale, on the other hand, maintained that locating shopping centers in the center of the neighborhood rather than on major streets, which formed the neighborhood boundary, encouraged people to walk to their neighborhood center and to shun other competing shopping facilities. If people were encouraged to drive and were required to use major streets, they might shop around. Some centers might therefore become very popular, while others might fail, thereby upsetting the neighborhood pattern and causing traffic congestion near the successful centers. Dale later acknowledged privately that his approach would probably tend to discourage competition among shopping centers for the consumer dollar, but he felt that the planning principle involved was a worthy one. A critic might have raised a variety of issues such as the following: whether free competition in most types of business threatened the forecasts of planners; whether planners should discourage competition among shopping centers, while encouraging it among other business enterprises; and whether the pressures on planners led them to have a bias against competition generally.[22]

The Planners' Review

Dale had resolved at the beginning of his work, it will be recalled, to try to complete the first draft of his land-use plan in time for publication before the end of 1958. Loeks, then the director of the Planning Bureau, had also determined that the other aspects of the comprehensive plan should meet a July 1, 1959, deadline. Early in 1958, while Dale was in the middle of his work, Loeks had resigned to become director of the newly established Twin Cities

[22] Dale commented: "Our plan would, I hope, prevent the process of one out of several shopping centers becoming so large that it became a subregional or regional shopping center when the site was better suited to being a neighborhood center; this would then allow the other centers in the area to maintain a larger (fair) share of the buying power and not slip into the marginal business category. Physical considerations were also involved; a neighborhood shopping center which grows in an *ad hoc* fashion presents all sorts of problems from signs, thru parking, to traffic control and pedestrian circulation." He also maintained that his decision to recommend shopping centers within neighborhoods was no more a mark of bias against competition than was a belief in zoning.

Metropolitan Planning Commission. Herbert Wieland, his successor, felt less compelled to meet the deadlines that Loeks had set.
Therefore, when Dale argued early in 1958 that the student hired
to conduct the central business district study had not had time to
do an adequate job and that Dale should be permitted to spend
several months on an elaborate study of the central business district, Wieland acquiesced. Consequently, Dale did not complete
his first draft of the land-use plan report until December 1958—six
months behind schedule. For various other reasons, work on the
economic base study and community facilities plan was even
slower; work on the zoning ordinance had not even started.

Dale's draft was reviewed and edited, for greater clarity and consistency rather than for content, by C. Allan Blomquist, a senior
city planner on the staff. By the time Blomquist's review was completed in February, Dale had left the Planning Bureau for a
position with the Housing Authority. He requested and was
granted permission by his superiors in the Housing Authority to
assist the bureau in "wrapping up the plan," but he was not consulted during the review process.

Next came the director's review, lasting from February through
May, which consisted primarily of a series of seminars, attended by
Wieland, the director; Burdette Teig, the assistant director;
Haluk Tarhan, the head of the staff working on the comprehensive plan; and Blomquist. Occasionally, other members of the staff
were invited to attend. Wieland led the discussion and, as planning director, made all the decisions. Blomquist rewrote where
necessary in accordance with Wieland's revisions. As planning director, Wieland believed that his primary responsibility should be
to assure that the plan would project a proper image of the
Planning Bureau and that it would not damage the agency politically. He believed that young planners had a tendency to press for
"ideal" goals without regard for political consequences. He maintained that his responsibility should be to determine what
statements might provoke controversy and when the publication
of such controversial statements might serve long-range planning
goals. Wieland insisted that "planning" as a process was more
important than any particular plan. Except where political difficulties might be involved, he was generally prepared to accept the
technical data developed by his subordinates without question.

Teig, his assistant director, agreed wholeheartedly. Teig and Wieland referred to the weakness of the planning function during the regime of Loeks' predecessor, George Herrold, and noted that such a period would recur if city planners were to antagonize too many men of power and influence in St. Paul.

At this time Wieland had been in St. Paul slightly over a year— a period of residence even shorter than Dale's. In December, at the same time that Dale's draft of the land-use plan was completed, Wieland had issued the first publication of his tenure, the central business district study. It had stated that vigorous action to preserve the economic position of the downtown area was necessary. The report's factual sections had indicated that business activity in the central business district was declining, not only relative to the suburbs and to the central business district of Minneapolis, but also in absolute terms. No one had charged that the study's data were false, but downtown groups and the local newspaper, anxious to promote an optimistic picture of St. Paul's future for business and industrial development, had responded to the report's publication with anger. Not a single individual or organization of importance had come to the planners' defense. This experience had been painful for the planning staff and its political friends.

Dale had been mindful of the pressure on the Planning Bureau from the Chamber of Commerce, booster groups, and others to present a rosy view of St. Paul and to avoid proposals for radical change. His selectivity in the inventory and analysis of data and his acceptance of existing averages as his land-use standards in many cases were illustrative of his sensitivity to this pressure. Wieland and Teig now suggested the addition of several sections to reassure various groups. They edited the factual analysis slightly to de-emphasize problems and to highlight opportunities. They altered some predictions to make them more optimistic, edited the section on prediction to make it seem less tentative, and softened Dale's few controversial recommendations. They deleted statements that implied that civic inaction would bring stagnation and eventual decline to the city. The following are illustrative of the revisions made by the editors.

Dale had written that unless public action made central areas more attractive to apartment developers, St. Paul's population might decline after 1968, when, according to the plan prediction, the city's vacant land for single-family residential development would be exhausted. The warning was de-emphasized, and the final draft of the plan predicted a constant rate of growth to 1980. Dale's estimate of the acreage that industry would absorb by 1980 was more than doubled. His recommendation that a market analysis be undertaken to determine the potential of the vast Pig's Eye Lake area was reduced to an aside; the final plan report urged that the area be zoned "industrial" because of its apparent "great potential as a future industrial park." A statement that St. Paul had no street plan for parts of the undeveloped East Side was altered to read "no final plan." A statement was inserted praising downtown merchants for the "renaissance" that had occurred downtown since completion of the central business district report less than a year earlier. Dale's discussion of the dearth of private apartment construction since the war was deleted in favor of a statement noting an upsurge during the early months of 1959, and his mention that unpleasant odors from the stockyards were a hindrance to residential development on the East Side was deleted.

Denouement

Early in the summer of 1959 the plan was reviewed by the Planning Board. Three meetings were held, each lasting about two hours. Only seven of the board's thirteen members attended as many as two of the meetings. Planning staff members presented the reasoning behind the chapters on policy and standards, but the board confined itself largely to discussing the plan's summary version, which had been prepared by the planning staff after their review. It suggested minor language changes, but tended to accept the view that laymen could not intelligently criticize experts. One member perhaps spoke for the others when he said that the detailed standards should be reviewed by some group with greater expertise.

The board urged, however, that the findings of fact in the plan be phrased more optimistically, particularly the discussion of the central business district. It deleted several findings of unpleasant facts. The board members also expressed their fear that opposition to the plan's general principles would be aroused if the plan were to contain many specific recommendations. For example, the planning staff had proposed that merchants in old strip commercial areas should be requested to invest money to solve their parking and other problems collectively. The board altered the wording to express a simple hope that some solution to their problems could be found. A recommendation that a particular proposed highway be rerouted to avoid splitting a neighborhood was deleted, leaving only a general statement that every effort should be made to keep highways from passing through neighborhoods.

When one board member questioned many of the specific standards in the plan as being unrealistically costly, Wieland assured him that it did not matter. The capital improvement plan, Wieland reasoned, set budget priorities. It was a *future* project of the planning staff, and work on it had not yet started. The same board member also objected to a recommendation that every house in St. Paul be inspected for violation of codes every five years. Most homes in the city were owner-occupied and obviously maintained above-minimum standards, so regular inspection would be an unnecessary nuisance to homeowners and an unjustified expense to the city. Accordingly, the planning staff altered the recommendation to read: "effective inspection at reasonable time-intervals."

The only subject that the Planning Board discussed at length was public housing. The members of the board appeared somewhat torn between their roles as homeowners, parents, and neighbors, and their roles as participants in the planning process. The plan draft submitted to them contained a rather bold statement: "The plans for new freeways, schools, playgrounds, commercial and industrial expansion, and urban renewal projects will greatly reduce the amount of private low-income rental housing and create a need for additional public housing." After long discussion, the board deleted the final eight words of the sentence and directed the planning staff to insert a substitute statement that "the need for adequate housing at low rentals must be met." Two board members opposed even this and vainly sought to have all reference to low-income housing removed.

Similarly, one member submitted a memorandum opposing the draft plan recommendation that public housing should be constructed on scattered sites. He argued that such a policy would plunge homeowners throughout St. Paul into a state of intolerable uncertainty. The planning staff, alerted to the political explosiveness of scattered public housing, stood its ground but submitted a paragraph to be added to the summary version of the plan:

The sites should be those which for various reasons will not be developed by private owners. So that their construction does not lower existing property values in the surrounding neighborhood, these housing facilities should be constructed to conform to applicable zoning regulations and enhance the architectural character of the immediate neighborhood.

Actually, the whole issue of public housing was rather academic. Politicians and others likely to be antagonized by proposals for more and better public housing had long been confident that there would be little more public housing in St. Paul.

The overall effect of the Planning Board's review was merely to eliminate several unpleasant truths about St. Paul and a few specific recommendations for public action. It did not change the plan in any fundamental way. Planning staff members commented privately that the Planning Board rarely contributed much, even politically. Although its members were prominent businessmen and civic leaders, none were active or influential politically, and none were likely to work politically for the plans that they reviewed and approved. They did not even appear to have any special ability to foresee political trouble. For example, they had not anticipated the hostile public reaction to the central business district study published late in 1958. And so far as the planners could tell, the board's hesitancy about public housing was personal rather than political.

In October 1959 the Planning Board submitted the land-use plan report to Mayor Dillon and the City Council. In addition, the staff explained it orally at a City Council meeting. When the plan was officially published in November, however, it produced no public reaction. No civic organization expressed more than mildly polite interest. The newspaper publicized the plan's findings and projections, but otherwise ignored it. No member of the

City Council made any public comment, nor did the council schedule any consideration of it. No apparent effort was made by the Planning Board's members to promote interest in the plan. The situation was unchanged when the writer left St. Paul a year later.[23,24]

[23] It may be noted in passing that when the contract between the Planning Bureau and the Housing Authority expired on June 30, 1959, the only portion of the comprehensive plan which was even nearly ready for publication was the land-use plan. Wieland argued that the original contract had been completely unrealistic, because no agency could produce a worthwhile comprehensive plan for only $80,000. After prolonged and occasionally strained negotiations, the Authority agreed in the spring of 1960 to contribute an additional $33,000 toward work on the comprehensive plan.

[24] It should be noted that Planning Director Wieland remained highly critical of this narrative from first to last. The author made several complete revisions in an effort to satisfy Mr. Wieland while retaining what the author considered fundamental accuracy and balance. In the end, it was possible to write nearly nothing about the role Mr. Wieland played in the planning process on the basis of interview material. For the most part, only his clearly documented actions have been reported.

After reading the final version of the case manuscript on June 30, 1964, Mr. Wieland wrote:

"I do not believe [the manuscript] could ever be changed sufficiently to have me agree with it. You have made several fundamental errors in your approach which I believe invalidate the major part of the report.

"1. You completely missed the point that this was a *PRELIMINARY* plan. Planning is an on-going process and over the intervening years, the plan *was* changed substantially before being incorporated as an element of the Comprehensive Plan. . . .

"2. You placed too much reliance on Dale, a very young inexperienced junior planner on the staff. He had the usual attitude of the new graduate: 'I'm going to remake the world overnight, I have all the answers.' Certainly it was my responsibility as Director to make changes and I did and time proved I was right. . . .

"Frankly, I'm more than ever convinced that your study adds nothing to the area of planning. It is so typical of the countless number of reports that are written that are highly critical of something that was done, but the author usually lacks the expertise to make constructive criticisms. This study in my opinion falls into this category.

"Under these circumstances, I could never give my approval to the publication of this report. If it is published, it will have to be over my objections and I hope you have the courtesy to record these objections."

In Retrospect [25]

The St. Paul land-use plan dealt with little more than one-fifth of the Twin Cities metropolitan area. The estimates of future conditions on which the plan was based were, unavoidably, extremely shaky. There is little more to say about these obvious facts. Taking a local perspective and considering only foreseeable conditions and consequences, however, one can still inquire as to whether the land-use plan was in any significant sense "comprehensive" or "rational"?

The plan was not based on any comprehensive or carefully articulated vision of the good city. Nor was it based on systematic study of articulate citizen fears and desires. No public discussion accompanied the planning process, though one was expected (over-optimistically, as it turned out) after the plan's publication. Thus, even when dealing with goals and means on which local consensus could be assumed, the planners lacked any systematic way of determining priorities. In addition, they chose, considering the land-use plan essentially a general goal statement, to plan without systematic analysis of costs, either public or private, financial or social.

This is not to say, of course, that the plan was based on *no* estimates of urban needs, probable costs, and political possibilities. It is merely to say that these estimates were based on professional training and experience, not systematic study. Academic planners familiar with the published plan have advised the writer that it was rather typical in its value premises of American land-use plans of the late 1950's.[26] Its overall objectives appeared to be the following: (1) to make the city a safe place in which to own property, primarily by stabilizing existing land-use patterns; (2) to reduce the tax burden on current residents by attracting new land uses that would pay more in taxes than they would consume in serv-

[25] This section is avowedly interpretative rather than narrative. Several participants in the land-use planning process have expressed disagreement with portions of it. Where they have failed to persuade the author, they have been offered the opportunity to state their views in footnotes.

[26] They have also considered it technically above average (judging on the basis of the published plan alone). They have not ranked it with the few very best plans published in this period, most of which were produced in larger cities than St. Paul, with far more money, and in more sympathetic political environments.

ices; (3) to enable people to go about their daily business more conveniently; (4) to offer residents more fresh air, outdoor recreation space, and physical safety from accident and disease; and (5) to make the city more pleasant to look at (for lovers of neatness and domesticated greenery). The relationship of these objectives to "goodness" in urban life was not elaborated in the plan.[27] To the planners, however, they seemed beyond controversy, subject only to the criticism of being insufficiently far-reaching.[28]

Of the concepts discussed at length in the plan report, only one reflected direct concern with a major cause of human unhappiness. That one was "blight," which the planners made clear was the

[27] John Dyckman has recently characterized "orthodoxy" in American physical plan-making as follows: "The approved physical solutions are marked by an enthusiastic tidying up of land-use mixtures, a restoration of more or less formal order, a segregation of uses, and the imposition of a middle-class aesthetic. Sometimes the . . . solutions are defended by arguments of the economic merit of the orderliness and the efficiency. . . . At other times, the aesthetic is defended for its own sake. . . . A ruling protestant ethic . . . prescribes healthy, outdoor participation activities." This quotation is from a preliminary draft of Dyckman's Introduction to a forthcoming book entitled *Readings in the Theory of Planning: The State of Planning Theory in America.* Dyckman indicated in a personal communication dated December 10, 1964, that the published version of the Introduction would be substantially changed from the preliminary draft, but that he still stood by the quotation cited here.

[28] Dale commented: "Any person who believes that the means at hand will allow us to plan major changes in the City environment belongs to the 'ivory tower' school of planning. He has not been through the *school of hard knocks* and practical reality. . . . The planning profession is full of dreamers who, in my *opinion,* are a danger to the survival of our profession. Planning is in trouble in Minnesota. . . . Ten years ago there were less than 10 professional planners in the State. The postwar building boom was accompanied by a rise in development problems. The planning profession was the sole voice crying out: 'We can help you solve your problems.' As a result, planning flourished —the State now has over 50 professional planners (including those who *claim* to be 'planners'). *But,* we do *not* have the answers, and unless we provide some practical answers soon, I fear that planning will again begin to decline, at least in Minnesota. Those planners who have big ideas about changing a City can never get specific, they can never tell you *how* it can be done, and they cannot even give you a specific idea of what the major changes should be. They always say, 'We are studying the situation.' . . . How long can we wait?"

archenemy of cities and city planners. Though never defined precisely, "blight" was apparently a close relative of the U.S. census term "dilapidated." The census defined a dilapidated dwelling unit as one that the census enumerator considered, on the basis of casual inspection, rundown, neglected, of inadequate construction, providing inadequate shelter against the elements, or endangering the safety of its occupants. The plan dealt with blight—which referred to neighborhoods rather than individual dwelling units —as if it were characterized by shabbiness, disrepair, a chaotic mixture of uses, and a general lack of community spirit.

According to the plan diagnosis, blight resulted from poor maintenance of property, which was caused, in turn, by mixtures of land use and by building obsolescence. For example, a homeowner found a major street built in front of his house or a garish store-front across the way. He decided that the neighborhood was declining and that further expenditure on his property would be throwing good money after bad. Elsewhere, old buildings that failed to meet current standards of density and construction were exploited by speculators who crowded in low-income tenants and ignored maintenance needs. The plan implied that government should prevent the first situation from arising by forbidding mixtures of land use. Where mixtures already existed, a palliative would be to form block clubs, which might inspire cooperation and assure homeowners that their high maintenance expenditures would be matched by their neighbors. The remedies for profitable obsolescence were enforcement of codes and slum clearance.

The plan did not explore the social causes of blight, such as the demoralizing effects of poverty, racial discrimination, overcrowding, and lack of hope. Nor did it explore the economics of blight in any depth: for example, it neglected to inquire whether owners, tenants, or both, had the ability or desire to pay for improvements of their blighted homes. Nor did it deal seriously with the organizational requirements of change. It proposed grass roots action through block clubs, but ignored the fact that block clubs had repeatedly disintegrated throughout the country—even in middle-class neighborhoods—unless prodded and aided by official agencies. The plan did not propose any program of official support for the clubs. Finally, the plan did not deal with the issue of whether better housing by itself, if it brought about increased financial pressure on low-income families or intensified overcrowding, contributed to the well-being of the community.[29]

On the whole, then, the plan was quite a cautious document. It focused on what the planners believed to be consensus objectives. It eschewed discussions of the political, social, cultural, and for the most part even the economic factors which had produced St. Paul's current land-use "problems." It avoided specific proposals for change on the ground that a land-use plan was no place for them, that its purpose was to teach general lessons and preach general solutions without inviting controversy over details. Even on the general level it did not suggest the need for any expensive locally financed public programs.

Nonetheless, few political or civic leaders paid any attention to the plan. A number who were interviewed in the months after the plan's publication expressed the opinion, largely based on reading the plan's summary statement, that it was "visionary" and that they could perceive no practical proposals in it that were likely to require their attention in the foreseeable future. By the fall of 1960 St. Paul planners generally agreed that their work on the land-use plan had produced few noticeable accomplishments. They professed to doubt that any elected official in the city had even thought the plan sufficiently important to read.

Dale in particular was shaken by this experience. He told the writer that he now doubted the utility of producing land-use plans separate from specific legislative proposals. The information on which any land-use plan was based soon became obsolete, he argued, and it therefore seemed ridiculous to gather data and formulate general goal statements, only to wait many years for legislation, by then probably out of date, to result. Furthermore, Dale now thought that no abstract plan was likely to have much educational impact. The acquired reflex of important groups in

---

[29] If the plan's discussion of blight lacked bite, it was apparently not atypical. Robert Mitchell has written: "Many American cities are engaged in preparing plans and programs for 'urban renewal.' Often this is thought of as a group or series of acts intended to remove, halt, or prevent 'blight.' But the very concept of 'blight' is unstructured, whether it be a condition or a kind of urban change. Its prevention or removal is essentially a negative objective aimed at an undiagnosed mixture of symptoms" ("The New Frontier in Metropolitan Planning," *American Institute of Planners Journal*, XXVII, No. 3 [August 1961], 170).

any community was to ignore the many goal statements issued by planning agencies and to conserve their energy for concrete proposals with price tags attached. Plans that failed to lead to discussion and action could have little educational or other value.

Dale was not alone, of course, in his view that general planning should be quickly followed up by legislative initiatives. The ideal companion to a land-use plan, according to orthodox planning theory, was a zoning ordinance. Zoning ordinances included immense detail, however; and it was difficult to justify the expense of their preparation unless demand for their enactment existed. It was possible to contend that a land-use plan was somehow useful even though no specific action was taken to implement it, but a zoning draft was clearly a total loss unless it provided the basis for legislation. Only rarely did public demand for a new zoning ordinance exist. In St. Paul it did not exist. The zoning ordinance of St. Paul, four decades old and loaded with amendments designed to satisfy individual petitioners, was regarded by the planners as inadequate to deal with current problems. Political leaders, however, valued their prerogative to zone constantly and without preset criteria. Many professional dealers in land liked the existing situation, in which zoning variances were easy to obtain. The value of their land depended frequently on speculation about its possible future uses. Any zoning ordinance based on abstract general principles would alter these speculative values, in some cases drastically. No one could predict with assurance who would gain or lose. Likewise, builders did not care to be subject to close supervision of the quality of their work. The owners of structures designated as nonconforming uses were unlikely to be happy with any new ordinance. And the great mass of property owners whose investment the planners sought to protect were apathetic. Few were aroused by the prospect of a city designed for greater "liveability."

A zoning ordinance proposal would have faced the same obstacles to rationality as the land-use plan. These obstacles would then have been even more apparent, because a zoning ordinance must embody hard choices about priorities. Its creators would have been compelled to deal with pressing issues and specific properties. The St. Paul planners believed that they had no political support for such an enterprise. The city administration, faced with biennial elections, had no wish to incur battles, especially battles to reduce its own prerogatives, when it could avoid them. The administration's lack of interest in the land-use plan reflected its certainty that the safest political path lay in not stirring up issues that voters hadn't troubled to raise themselves. Few political leaders cared to risk their futures in the service of abstract principles. If they did, they wanted the principles to matter to many people outside the civil service.

There was also probably a matter of temperament involved. Planners complained privately that the bias of councilmen was away from all abstraction. The City Council would debate for hours about "human interest" cases, in which the immediate interest of some individual or small group was at stake, but it seemed to prefer noninvolvement in the more complex and long-range issues of public policy. By some process of self-selection, it appeared, men who enjoyed study were more likely to become planners than local politicians.

Blomquist was somewhat less pessimistic than Dale. He thought that, regardless of the fate of the plan's recommendations, its inventory and analysis would prove to be of lasting value.[30] Their availability as reference works, he believed, would encourage the habit of informed decision-making by public officials. No agency had hitherto collected such data for convenient reference. Even before publication of the plan, State Highway Department engineers had devoted almost a full man-year to work with the large base maps that had been prepared as part of the land-use planning process. Consultants hired by the School Board and others appointed by the Chamber of Commerce had used the base maps intensively. Public officials continually used them as a basis for discussion with citizens irate about one public action or another. Private agencies had begun to use block-census data, which they had previously ignored, in deciding how to distribute their resources and personnel. The collected and organized data in the plan maps of current and projected future land use clearly indicated facts and trends that had previously been ignored. Dangerous street intersections, unused space near existing inadequate playgrounds, physical land-use barriers, residential enclaves being

[30] Dale was scornful of this argument. The Planning Bureau was supposed to be a *planning*, not a municipal research, agency, he commented.

devoured by industrial expansion, and other features of the city's layout were now more easily discernible.

Other planners stressed that the planning process enabled a few men, presumably well-trained, intelligent, and dedicated to the public interest, to think seriously about the city's major land-use problems. As it proceeded, the more obvious assets and liabilities of each section of the city were studied in detail and assimilated *in toto* by a few minds. The more obvious opportunities for public policy to aid development were inventoried and discussed. The conclusions were not profound, but no agency had previously endeavored to provide even this elemental base for informed consideration of alternatives.

The planners interviewed were disinclined to brood about the value premises of their work. Their faith, they said, was in the democratic process. Their methods of serving it were, essentially, (1) intuition about community values based on their experiences as professional public servants and as local citizens, and (2) analysis of the determinants of local land values. Their job, they said, was to propose goals for the community, taking care to consider not only popular desires but also the requisites of any social system in which those desires were likely to be met. The politician's job was to decide which of the proposed goals most interested his constituents, and which of the others were most important to their welfare.

When pressed for the reasons why the land-use plan simply listed goals and points to consider without exploring their conflicts, costs, and priorities, the planners were likely to answer as follows: The capacity to make a complete statement of the complex considerations underlying every planning recommendation does not exist anywhere in the planning world. Any statement the planning staff could have produced would have been so complex itself that it would have gone completely unread. Anyone who had read it would have been completely overwhelmed by the obstacles to action. The reasonable thing, perhaps even the "rational" thing, in this situation was to overcome self-doubt in order to set goals, to start people moving, and to inspire respect for planning.

Thus, goal-setting was in an important sense a technique of mass psychology, a way of arousing the public's interest by setting it definite tasks. At the same time, the planners strongly believed that their recommendations deserved implementation, or at least serious consideration and revision. They recognized that their intuitive perceptions of community goals were imperfect, and that their applications of them were bound at best to be "reasonable" rather than "rational." But they still considered the public regulation of land use according to the kind of plan they had produced a "good thing." When asked their reasons, they generally argued more or less as follows:

Within a given culture men can agree that certain objectives are desirable and that certain interpretations of general goal statements are "about right." No doubt the range of cultural agreement varies widely from one goal statement to another, and with every one is constantly subject to change. It is better, nonetheless, to seek collective solutions to problems which require them on the basis of this intuitively sensed cultural agreement than to accept public paralysis in the absence (which, after all, must be eternal) of total knowledge.

This was certainly a reasonable argument. It left unanswered, however, the question of how planners distinguished the problems which required collective solutions from those which did not. The St. Paul planners had no consensus on how to answer this question explicitly, but they seemed to have answered it implicitly in the land-use plan by showing great respect for the *status quo*. They had confined their recommendations to areas in which private parties did not commonly act (such as construction of public streets) or would be unlikely to act unless public action eased the path (e.g., by the use of eminent domain to assemble large tracts of land for industrial development). Within the sphere of activity to which they limited themselves, they had sought recommendations which they thought would benefit many while seriously harming no one and inconveniencing few. This was all in accord with their view of themselves as moderate and practical men, extremely cautious in the face of uncertainty but unwilling to be paralyzed by considerations that were of interest only to "ivory tower" theorists.

III

The Ancker Hospital Site
Controversy [*]

Introduction

In the development of general plans, conflicts between planning
principles and other principles worth defending are seldom mentioned. They frequently spring forth full blown, nevertheless,
when the moment comes to make a project decision. At such times
the planners and their antagonists cannot ignore the existence of
conflict, but they may have a very partial view of its significance.
Each may assume that the other has selfish motives and argues dishonestly. Some evidence can usually be found to support one or
both assumptions. The combatant who prevails in the end, if one
does, finds it most gratifying to think that the decision-maker
accepted his arguments. The defeated combatant is likely to think
that the decision-maker failed to understand, or that he had some
nefarious motives.

In the Ancker Hospital site controversy, city planners disputed
with forces led—at least intellectually—by a hospital architect.
Each side may have had some reasons for its position which it
never found convenient to discuss publicly. Arguments in debates
are bound, after all, to be selected in part on strategic grounds.
Still, there is no reason to think that either side doubted the wis-

[*] A shortened version of this chapter appeared as *The Ancker Hospital
Site Controversy,* ICP Case Series, No. 82 (University of Alabama Press, 1964),
copyright © 1964 by the Inter-University Case Program, Inc.; reprinted
with permission.

dom of its recommendation or the essential benevolence of its motives.

At the battle's end, the city planners saw their recommendation accepted. They not unnaturally judged that their ability as professionals to locate public facilities had once more been confirmed. This writer found in the course of his research, however, that the planners' recommendation had won acceptance in large part for reasons unknown to the planners; and that if the arguments the planners advanced had had to stand alone against those of their antagonists, the laymen who had to choose would have had a difficult time indeed.

The layman's point of view is crucial, because the conflicting claims of generalist planners and specialists must in the final analysis be evaluated by laymen. It seems fitting, therefore, for one of our cases to deal in part with the problems of conscientious laymen asked to choose between contesting experts. The Ancker Hospital Site Controversy provides an opportunity not only to examine the problems of laymen in such a situation, but also to contrast their approach to a single-choice problem with the approach of a group of generalist city planners and with that of an acknowledged specialist.

Background

The three largest hospitals in the city of St. Paul in 1955 were Ancker Hospital, a public institution with a rated capacity of 850 beds and administered by the Ramsey County Welfare Board; Miller Hospital, a nondenominational Protestant institution with a rated capacity of 360 beds; and St. Joseph's Hospital, a Catholic institution with a rated capacity of 260 beds.[1] The two private hospitals were separated by only a single city block.

For many years the physical plant of Ancker Hospital had been outmoded and uneconomical. In the early 1940's the Welfare Board had retained the local architectural firm of Ellerbe and Company to evaluate the Ancker Hospital heating system. Frank Rarig, who had served as Executive Secretary of the Welfare Board from 1935 to 1940 and then as a member, later recalled that he had hoped Ellerbe's findings would lead him to recommend con-

[1] By 1959 St. Joseph's Hospital had completed a modernization program that gave it a rated capacity of 407 beds.

struction of an entirely new hospital. When Ellerbe had reported that the most economical course at the time would be renovation, Rarig had been disappointed.

Even the need for improvement, however, had been essentially ignored until September 1952, when the Minnesota state fire marshal had threatened to condemn the hospital as a fire hazard. For about a year the County Welfare Board had discussed possible courses of action; then in August 1953 it had hired Booz, Allen, Hamilton, a leading management consulting firm, to evaluate the hospital's facilities and operating costs and to recommend necessary action. The consultants had submitted a 400-page report in July 1954, concluding that Ancker Hospital was a fire hazard and that its structures were outmoded and uneconomical to maintain.

Basing their recommendations on assumptions about the anticipated quantity and quality of service, which some local planners later believed were premature, the Booz, Allen, Hamilton consultants had concluded that the present site of Ancker Hospital should be retained and that the facilities of the hospital should be improved to accommodate a bed capacity of 1,025. They had suggested two alternative proposals for renovation. One approach, which they had estimated would cost about $2.25 million, was to improve only the most deficient of existing facilities. They had considered this, however, to be tantamount to throwing good money after bad and had pointed out that similar expenditures would be required periodically to bring the hospital's other aged buildings and facilities up to approved standards. A second alternative, while estimated to cost four times as much in the beginning, was likely to prove more economical in the long run. The older buildings were to be razed, several of the newer ones renovated, and two large new buildings constructed.

On January 31, 1955, largely in response to the report of Booz, Allen, Hamilton, several doctors on the staff of Ancker Hospital induced the County Medical Society to go beyond the consultants' formal recommendations and to pass a resolution favoring the construction of a completely new hospital at a more convenient location, preferably near Miller and St. Joseph's hospitals. Underlying the doctors' proposal was an idea that was being promoted by a small group of people in the community, the idea that a single medical center, embracing the three largest hospitals, should be established in St. Paul.

Advancing the Medical Center Idea

Over the years a number of influential men in the city other than doctors had also come to believe that a new Ancker Hospital was needed and that building it might provide the occasion for establishing a medical center. Among them were the following:

(1) Frank Rarig, Executive Secretary of the Amherst H. Wilder Foundation, an endowed, Minnesota, nonprofit corporation that operated the second largest outpatient clinic after Ancker Hospital in Ramsey County. Among other things, the program of the foundation included three day nurseries, a nursery school for handicapped children, and a child guidance clinic.

(2) Frank Marzitelli, a labor leader who served as a member of the St. Paul City Council from 1950 through 1957, when he became Deputy Commissioner of the State Highway Department.

(3) A. A. Heckman, Executive Director of the Louis W. and Maud Hill Family Foundation, a regional, grant-making foundation, functioning in the Northwest and focusing its program on research, experimental, and demonstrational projects in several fields, especially in science, education, health, and welfare.

(4) E. E. Engelbert, a St. Paul businessman who had assisted many community improvement efforts in the city.

On the subject of a new Ancker Hospital, these men were concerned about the outmoded nature of the Ancker plant and the fact that its maintenance costs were rising rapidly every year. They realized that renovation appeared politically more feasible at the moment than construction of an entirely new hospital, but they doubted that it would be more economical in the long run and found the idea of combining construction of a new Ancker with establishment of a medical center an intriguing one. They noted that the trend in medical practice was toward an ever more narrow specialization and that the small hospitals of St. Paul were finding it increasingly difficult to offer the full range of services required. Furthermore, there were many hospital facilities that the three local institutions could not justify financially because of insufficient full-time demand. Even if Ancker, Miller, and St. Joseph's

Hospitals administered all major facilities jointly, it was likely that these problems could be only alleviated, not eliminated. They reasoned that over time the cooperation of these three hospitals might encourage the city's remaining hospitals to join in helping to finance very expensive facilities for common use. The concentration of half of the city's hospital beds in a medical center would also benefit the community in other ways. For example, when moving patients from one hospital to another to utilize different facilities, the hospitals would less frequently have to take ambulances from emergency service. Similarly, the doctors of Ancker Hospital who practiced at Miller or St. Joseph's hospitals would be able to save time in driving to and from Ancker Hospital. More than nine-tenths of the doctors who contributed time at Ancker Hospital also practiced at Miller Hospital, St. Joseph's Hospital, or both; these men could avoid the necessity of shuttling between their private and public hospital patients. The construction of a medical office building nearby would also contribute to a more efficient use of doctors' time.

The champions of the medical center pointed out, further, that all hospitals depended heavily on interns and residents; each year 12,000 positions for interns and residents were available nationally. Public and university hospitals traditionally faced the least difficulty in filling their rosters because they offered young doctors the opportunity to learn by practicing on varied caseloads and by assuming responsibility for nonpaying patients. If Miller and St. Joseph's hospitals were permitted to participate in a medical center, they could offer more attractive opportunities to their younger staff members. Certainly, it was reasoned, the whole city would gain if the two largest private hospitals could attract more and better interns and residents.

During the summer of 1955, Mayor Dillon of St. Paul, induced by the proponents of the medical center approach, appointed a Citizens Committee on Ancker Hospital. The committee met for the first time in October 1955. Engelbert was selected as its chairman.

Engelbert, Rarig, Heckman, and their associates realized that the construction of a new Ancker Hospital would probably require a large bond issue. Since the hospital was a joint city-county insitution, in which the city financed about 27 per cent of the costs and the county about 73 per cent, enabling legislation would be necessary to permit elected officials to issue bonds without a public referendum. The legislature never acted on local problems unless the local legislative delegation involved exercised the initiative. The operating rules of the Ramsey County delegation allowed any three of the twelve representatives or any single senator to veto a recommendation. Thus, legislative approval of anything opposed by an influential segment of the community was unlikely. It was thought that significant opposition to the construction of a new Ancker Hospital would most likely come, if at all, from groups that generally opposed government spending. Support was therefore sought from tax-conscious groups in the community. During the early months of 1956 Julian Baird, chairman of the board of the First National Bank (subsequently Under Secretary of the U.S. Treasury) and one of the two or three most influential business-men in the city, was persuaded after several discussions reviewing the Ancker situation to help secure business support. Baird in turn persuaded many of the other top corporation executives of St. Paul to contribute their support. The decisive arguments seem to have been that the medical center would attract business from surrounding states, improve the quality of medical care in the community, perhaps inspire creation of a medical school before long, and contribute intangibly to the image of St. Paul as a dynamic metropolis. It should be noted that the businessmen gave their support primarily to the medical center concept, which they approved in large part for its dramatic, or "booster," qualities. This is not to say that their motives were crudely economic. Their taxes would be raised to pay for the medical center. If a medical school followed, they would also be asked to finance that.

The Mayor's Citizens Committee Report

The promotional effects of the mayor's committee continued during 1956 and the early months of 1957. The committee did not commission any new studies and it sought no new facts, but time was not wasted. When it reported in May 1957, it had achieved a large measure of internal consensus among its members, and several men who were prominent in tax-conscious circles in the community had been won to the cause.

The committee followed the lead of Ancker Hospital staff

members in recommending that a new 600-bed Ancker Hospital be built adjacent to Miller and St. Joseph's hospitals, so that the three institutions might operate as a single medical center. The committee also reported that in 1954 the Booz, Allen, Hamilton consultants had privately favored the building of a new Ancker Hospital adjacent to Miller and St. Joseph's. Representatives of the consulting firm, according to the committee, had suppressed their first choice for fear that the community would be unwilling to finance a completely new hospital.

During the period of the committee's work, Thomas Ellerbe, head of a local architectural firm and another supporter of the medical center concept, had privately estimated to Englebert, Rarig, and Baird that construction of a new Ancker Hospital in the location indicated would cost about $16 million. He admittedly had based his estimate not on a detailed analysis of the planned hospital, but on his long experience in designing hospitals elsewhere in the United States. His firm specialized in hospital work and was widely recognized as one of the leading hospital architectural firms in the nation. Ellerbe had grown up in St. Paul, had attended school in the city, and had enjoyed long personal friendships with some of the medical center proponents. As one of them put it later: "When you have one of the two or three most prominent hospital architects in the nation in your home town, you naturally turn to him for as much advice as he will give." The committee therefore accepted his estimate and urged that legislation authorizing a $16-million bond issue be sought.

Securing Legislative Authority

As the mayor's Citizens Committee on Ancker Hospital prepared to issue its report, it became apparent that haste was necessary if enabling legislation for a bond issue was to be secured. The legislature was in session, but would adjourn within several months and not meet again for two years. After some dispute about financing provisions a bill incorporating the committee's major recommendations was approved by the Ramsey County Board of Commissioners and the St. Paul City Council for conveyance to the local legislative delegation.

During this legislative campaign another figure, Edward Delaney, played perhaps the central role. Delaney had been mayor of St. Paul from 1948 to 1952 and a member of the County Board since 1954. As mayor he had relied heavily on Frank Rarig as an adviser on health and welfare matters, and had devoted a substantial portion of his energies to them. He had long been concerned about the dilapidated state of Ancker Hospital and had promised in his 1954 campaign for the County Board to bring about construction of a new Ancker Hospital. It should be noted, however, that he had no preconceptions about where the hospital should be located. Delaney was particularly proud of his role on behalf of what he called the "downtrodden," and it was generally believed that his fight for public housing and similar measures had cost him the mayoralty, despite St. Paul's traditional support of labor-endorsed candidates. A colorful figure, he recalled with pleasure that, as mayor, his first conflict with the St. Paul Chamber of Commerce had been over Ancker Hospital:

We made up the 1949 budget providing a large sum for desperately needed equipment and remodeling at Ancker. The Chamber resolved that $800,000 should be cut out. The City Council voted unanimously for the cut. But I convinced the Board of County Commissioners to restore it. When the board and council disagree over money matters on Ancker, the lower figure rules, so I had to get the council to reverse itself. The councilmen agreed, merely as a courtesy to me, to reconsider. For the public hearing we then scheduled, I hired a court reporter and rented a recording machine. I announced at the start of the hearing that every word would be recorded doubly and beyond dispute for posterity. Then I read the budget, item by item. I stopped after each item and asked for objections: for instance, "Does anyone think that Ancker Hospital should not have a cardiograph machine?" No one did. At the end, Rosen and Mortinson moved that $600,000 be restored. "Human misery leaves no room for compromise," I said. Rosen laughed and answered, "O.K., Simon Legree, you win."

In 1957 Delaney was chairman of the County Board's Welfare Committee and also of its Legislative Committee (which handled relations with the state legislature). He took responsibility for working out successive compromises that might win the support of the board and the St. Paul City Council, lobbied for passage in both, and lobbied almost every day for three months to secure passage of the bonding bill by the legislature. Throughout this period he received effective help from Marzitelli, who was chairman of the City Council's Legislative Committee and thus was lobbying continuously for a variety of legislation desired by the city. In addition, prominent businessmen indicated their support on a number of occasions and Frank Rarig frequently gave technical testimony in support of the bill at the Capitol. The bill was eventually enacted with several amendments in the final hour of the legislative session.

During the legislative campaign opposition sufficient to prevent passage of a less well-endorsed and well-shepherded bill became apparent. Some legislators differed about how the costs of the new hospital should be split between the city and the county. Others wanted to require a referendum before bonds could be floated. The bill as passed included a compromise provision enabling 10 per cent of the county's voters who had voted in the last gubernatorial election to petition for a referendum on the act within thirty days of passage. This was regarded as an impossible requirement, but it was the way of saving face for those who had pressed for a "strong" referendum provision.

Another and eventually more important controversy involved the composition of the Ancker Hospital Facility Building Commission that would come into being as a result of the legislation. The commission's key decisions were to require approval by both the County Board and the City Council, but as the initiating body it would be the central locus of official power in disputes over where and how to build the new hospital. Elmer Andersen, then a Conservative [2] State Senator from St. Paul and later Republican Governor of Minnesota (1961–1963), opposed the idea of permitting the City Council and County Board to appoint the commission. He knew that St. Paul's business leaders wanted a blue-ribbon commission to be appointed, preferably under the chairmanship of Engelbert, and he hoped to be able to bring about this result if the legislative delegation made the appointments.

D. D. Wozniak, a State Representative from St. Paul, had another reason to press for legislative appointment of the commis-

[2] The Minnesota legislature was one of two in the nation currently elected on a nonpartisan basis. Two factions operated within it, however. They were known as Liberal and Conservative, and generally corresponded to the Democratic-Farmer-Labor and Republican parties.

sion members. He represented the district in which the existing Ancker Hospital was located. Neighborhood businessmen, most of whom were proprietors of small retail shops, had been encouraged by the 1954 Booz, Allen, Hamilton report to hope that the neighborhood and their business interests would be benefited by major renovation and reconstruction of the existing Ancker Hospital. On the other hand, the recommendation of the mayor's committee, favoring a new Ancker Hospital located adjacent to the Miller and St. Joseph's Hospitals, seemed to suggest abandonment of the neighborhood. Organizing to prevent this, they were led by an undertaker who (according to his opponents) may have feared that he would lose his advantageous relationship with the hospital if it were relocated in another area of the city. He perceived himself, it should be noted, as simply a neighborhood civic leader. Although these businessmen were not influential on a city-wide or county-wide basis, they did manage to win the support of Representative Wozniak. He cooperated with Andersen in making sure that the final bill contained a provision permitting the local legislative delegation to appoint five of the nine members of the new Hospital Commission. Ironically, whereas Andersen supported the provision in hope of bringing about speedy execution of the recommendations of the mayor's committee, Wozniak supported it hoping he would be able to block committed proponents of the medical center idea from serving on the commission. In this Wozniak was to come very close to complete success.

Establishment of the Ancker Hospital Facility Building Commission

The nine-man commission that came into being contained only two men who had had any previous interest or involvement in the problems of Ancker Hospital (and none who had served on the mayor's committee). Delaney was a "natural" for one of the two County Board appointments, and Frank Marzitelli was a "natural" for one of the legislative delegation's appointments. Marzitelli had just resigned from the St. Paul City Council and, almost uniquely, enjoyed the warm support and trust of politicians, labor leaders, and business leaders throughout the community. He was, at this point, deputy commissioner of the State Highway Department; and the interstate freeway was expected to run between

Miller and St. Joseph's hospitals. If a site in that area were eventually selected for a new Ancker Hospital the closest cooperation
between the Hospital Commission and the Highway Department
would be desirable. There had to be a Highway Department
representative, therefore, and in addition to having strong local
roots Marzitelli handled these matters for the department.

The remaining members of the commission were: former St.
Paul Mayor Daubney (1952–1954), a Conservative member of the
County Board; a Liberal and a Conservative from the St. Paul
City Council; a Catholic priest; a Lutheran minister from the
neighborhood of the existing Ancker Hospital; an official of a local
labor union; and a contractor. The last four, together with
Marzitelli, were the legislature's appointees. In addition, one
Liberal and one Conservative member of the county legislative
delegation sat on the commission without voting rights.

Englebert, Marzitelli, Rarig, and others who had led in the
campaign for a new Ancker Hospital believed that there had been
more than enough study of the problem and that the time was ripe
for decision and action. They assumed that the new hospital would
have to be situated adjacent to Miller and St. Joseph's hospitals
and believed that the commission should proceed to the settling of
details. Of the commission members, however, only Marzitelli
seemed ready to decide. Chairman Delaney, despite his long-held
belief that a new Ancker Hospital should be built, had never
committed himself to the idea of a contiguous or nearly contiguous medical center. He declared his intention to search open-
mindedly with his fellow commissioners for the best way to spend
the authorized $16 million.

The Hospital Commission held its organizational meeting in
October 1957. Delaney was elected chairman, and then the commission proceeded to choose a consulting architect to evaluate the
present Ancker plant and later, presumably, to evaluate alternative sites for a new hospital. Eight architects presented their bids.
Admitting that its members lacked knowledge of technical standards on which to base a selection, the commission limited its choice
finally to the two local architectural firms, one of which was
Thomas Ellerbe's firm, Ellerbe and Company. During the following months the commission sought to make up its mind which
firm to retain. Rarig on one occasion testified to the commission

that Ellerbe was far better qualified for hospital work than the other local firm. Ellerbe was eventually chosen by a vote of 5–4, and on July 1, 1958, the agreement was formally approved.

Marzitelli appears to have been the only member of the commission who knew that Ellerbe already had rather well-formed views about the desirability of a new Ancker Hospital adjacent to Miller and St. Joseph's hospitals.[3]

Ellerbe's first assignment was to evaluate the existing Ancker Hospital plant. While he worked on this, the pressures upon the Hospital Commission began to crystallize. The local St. Paul newspaper, in its morning and evening editions, published editorials throughout the summer of 1958 arguing that a new Ancker Hospital should be built adjacent to Miller and St. Joseph's hospitals. On the other hand, businessmen with interests in the neighborhood of the existing Ancker Hospital attended in force a public hearing held by the Site Committee of the Hospital Commission in July 1958. They cited the Booz, Allen, Hamilton team's conclusion that a 1,025-bed facility was needed and could be secured at the existing site for half of what it would cost to provide a downtown hospital with 400 fewer beds. The millions of dollars that might be saved by reconstruction on the present site, they reasoned, might better be spent on other community needs. Several doctors on the Ancker Hospital staff countered that Ancker would experience increasing difficulty in attracting volunteer physicians unless the inconvenience of its present location were eliminated. Representative Wozniak, criticizing what he regarded as a "veiled threat" by the doctors, retorted that the freeways would make the mile from the downtown location of Miller and St. Joseph's hospitals an insignificant trip.

As opposition to the medical center concept grew, proponents of the plan moved to mobilize community support. Even before his report evaluating Ancker Hospital's existing plant was issued,

[3] It should be noted that Ellerbe and Marzitelli did not feel that they had been secretive about their views, though they had not advertised them. Indeed, anyone familiar with the history of efforts to improve Ancker Hospital should have judged them to be at least likely supporters of the contiguous medical center idea. In fact, however, the other members, aside from Delaney, had no familiarity with this history; and even Delaney did not realize that Ellerbe was committed to a contiguous medical center as distinguished from the need for a new hospital.

Ellerbe joined with Engelbert, Rarig, and several others in seeking the support of Reuel Harmon, president of St. Paul's largest commercial publishing company and a long-time member of the Chamber of Commerce's inner circle. He knew Rarig and Ellerbe well—in fact, he and Ellerbe had been boyhood friends, and their parents had been friends before them—and he was naturally inclined to defer to their judgment in matters involving hospital needs. They told him that political pressures were emerging, making imperative the creation of a blue ribbon committee to focus public attention on the facts. The committee should be composed, they thought, of community leaders having no direct interest or previous involvement in the dispute. If it did its work well, such a committee might mobilize sufficient public support to permit the Hospital Commission to stand firm against any parochial interests, however vocal. Ellerbe could not head the committee because he was the commission's consultant, and he hoped eventually to design the new hospital. Rarig had been the leading public advocate of a site near Miller and St. Joseph's. The members of the Mayor's Committee, including Engelbert, had endorsed the medical center concept. Harmon, on the other hand, had never mentioned Ancker Hospital publicly. He was asked to form and head the committee, and he agreed to do so.

Ellerbe, Englebert, and Rarig suggested candidates to serve with Harmon. With very few exceptions, those nominated were people who knew and trusted Ellerbe and Harmon. When Harmon explained its purposes, they generally expressed pleasure in lending their prestige to a committee that would speak for the "responsible" elements of the community. Only the medical members of the committee had any direct interest in the issue and that was presumably philanthropic rather than selfish. All ten of the doctors on the committee enjoyed appointments at Ancker Hospital.

Harmon's Ancker Hospital Volunteer Committee was unveiled to the public on November 13, 1958. It evoked immediate enthusiasm from the local newspaper. No one, including the members of the Hospital Commission, doubted Harmon's avowal that the Volunteer Committee started with no preconceptions. The newspaper quoted Harmon as saying that civic leaders had a duty to expedite "one of the half-dozen greatest civic enterprises in the history of St. Paul."

Ellerbe Reports

Meanwhile, in September 1958, Ellerbe had submitted a brief report on his evaluation of present Ancker Hospital facilities. He had concluded that "it is a physical impossibility to rehabilitate or modernize the institution. Even though it were possible the cost would be so excessive that it would be impractical to do so." He had not offered estimates of either the cost of modernization or of a new facility, but he had asserted that construction of a modern hospital would result in operating economies that should "carry the debt service on the institution without increasing the budget itself."

A few months later, in December 1958, Ellerbe told the Ancker Hospital Commission that as his next step he would evaluate five potential sites for a new Ancker Hospital, one adjacent to the present institution and four in the vicinity of Miller and St. Joseph's hospitals. No one on the commission objected, although Representative Podgorski, one of the commission's two legislative "advisers" without vote, suggested that Ellerbe consider a section of the Eastern Redevelopment Area along with the other alternatives. This area was a sixty-acre tract directly east of the State Capitol buildings and about one mile from Miller and St. Joseph's hospitals. Ellerbe amiably agreed to do so.

He presented his "Site Evaluation Report" to the commission in March 1959. In his report he discussed the merits of all six alternative sites, but three of those in the Miller–St. Joseph's area were shortly thereafter removed from consideration because of factors beyond the control of the commission. The commission confined its attention to the remaining three alternatives: Site A was adjacent to the existing Ancker Hospital; Site B-1 was located between Miller and St. Joseph's hospitals; and Site D was situated in the Eastern Redevelopment Area.

Ellerbe explicitly predicated his recommendations on his belief that the potential sites could not be evaluated "scientifically," but he went on in his report to claim that his staff had almost achieved such a feat.

Because there is no established formula for siting any hospital, and because it is impossible to satisfy everyone or even reach agreement as to the factors that constitute the basis for evaluating a site, Ellerbe

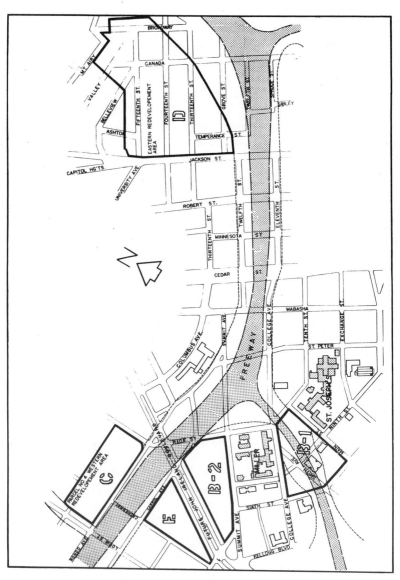

Map 2. Proposed site locations for new Ancker Hospital, St. Paul.

and Company has selected a series of factors for site evaluation which eliminates insofar as humanly possible: self-interest, sectional bias, unfounded personal opinion, and lack of understanding of problems peculiar to hospitals. To make this process as objective as possible, these selected factors have been incorporated into a chart, wherein each has been given a numerical value based on its relative rating to a theoretically perfect site, which would have a score of one hundred. . . . The result of this effort is graphically dramatic and conclusive. . . . The objective conclusion reached shows that Site B-1 is preferable to all others considered.

For his chart, Ellerbe had selected seven criteria: (1) relative convenience for drivers and pedestrians, (2) proximity to bus routes, (3) parking facilities, (4) distance from population center in the community, (5) absence of nuisances, (6) joint use of facilities, and (7) land cost. To Site B-1, located between Miller and St. Joseph's hospitals, he awarded 94 out of a possible 100 points. The three next highest sites were those never seriously considered and later dropped from the serious alternatives. Site D, located in the Eastern Redevelopment Area, received a score of 52; while Site A, adjacent to the present Ancker Hospital and at this time the only serious rival of Site B-1 for public support, received a dismal score of 28.

Ellerbe's report met with public acclaim from the newspaper and organized supporters; those who disagreed with it or who had serious doubts were not immediately vocal. The professional planners in St. Paul's Planning Bureau were severely critical of the report and of the "numbers game" employed in the chart, but in keeping with the bureau's policy of avoiding participation in public controversy, they kept their opinions inside their own circle. On the other hand, when Ellerbe's report was discussed at the March meeting of the Ancker Hospital Commission, several members of the Volunteer Committee were present to testify to their admiration for its content. The following day the St. Paul newspaper editorialized that there was no excuse for further delay. It cited its belief that Ellerbe's numerical scoring system was irrefutable evidence of the superiority of Site B-1 over all other choices. The newspaper continued to express this point of view vigorously throughout the subsequent controversy. Yet, during the commission's first discussion of the report in March, and at subsequent meetings on April 8 and April 10, it became apparent that there was sharp disagreement among the commission members over Ellerbe's methods and conclusions.

A leading source of their hesitation in supporting Ellerbe's conclusions was the fact that the favored site, B-1, lay athwart the right-of-way of a proposed freeway section that would become part of the interstate system. Ellerbe had explained that he would build the new hospital above the freeway. The newspaper gave this proposal a favorable presentation, and Ellerbe believed the idea sound, but the laymen who composed the Ancker Hospital Commission wondered if the technical complexities of construction in this situation might not prove prohibitively expensive.

Another leading source of doubt among members of the commission and others in the community was the proposed cooperation between Ancker Hospital and the two private institutions that was implicit in Site B-1. Commission Chairman Delaney, for example, believed that selection of Site B-1 would lead to particularly close operational relationships among the three hospitals, especially in view of the staff overlap involved, and he had conflicting thoughts about this close relationship. On the one hand, he reasoned, it would be wonderful to bring Miller and St. Joseph's hospitals into close cooperation, since they were the city's largest private hospitals—one Catholic and the other nonsectarian. Although they were separated by only a city block, each had been expanding away from the other. If Ancker Hospital were to serve as a catalyst in promoting cooperation between the two private institutions, the public would surely benefit.

On the other hand, physical contiguity, cooperative ownership of expensive equipment, and sharing of interns and residents would require that the three hospitals work out a system of cooperative decision making. Delaney considered it intolerable for two private hospitals to dictate to the city-county institution or for the public hospital to dictate to the private institutions. Participation by Ancker Hospital in a medical center would likely make one of these situations unavoidable.

The fact that St. Joseph's Hospital was a Catholic institution presented some additional problems. One of the most important features of political life in St. Paul was a rigid divorce of religion and politics. The crucial function of this divorce was to perpetuate majority acquiescence in leadership by the minority. The population of St. Paul was 40 per cent Catholic, but for as long as anyone could remember most of the city's political leaders had been Catholics. The city's labor leadership was also predominantly Catholic, while business and professional leaders were principally non-Catholic. In their political behavior, however, Catholic politicians and labor leaders had demonstrated an ability to ignore their religious affiliation. For example, Democratic-Farmer-Labor party (DFL) and labor organizations fought one of their most strenuous campaigns in history during 1958 in support of divorced Protestant Joseph Karth against St. Paul's devout Catholic mayor in the congressional primary. Karth surprised his staunchest supporters by winning more than two-thirds of the total vote cast. Similarly, Catholic politicians and labor leaders campaigned regularly for public school bond issues and tax increases, even though most of the city's Catholic children attended parochial schools. Furthermore, Catholic clergymen refrained conscientiously from speaking out on political issues.

Delaney thus seemed to be acting in harmony with local political tradition when he concluded privately that selection of Site B-1 might be interpreted by some Protestants as an improper boon to St. Joseph's Hospital and a repudiation of the larger community interest. He confided his thoughts on this issue to no one. His instinct as a seasoned politician was to wait and see. Furthermore, the technical difficulties involved in building a hospital over a freeway seemed to emphasize the need for a more cautious and studied approach. He thus induced the commission to instruct its Site Committee to resist the pressure for haste from the newspaper, the Volunteer Committee, and the Chamber of Commerce, and to study Ellerbe's report carefully and deliberately.

While the Site Committee proceeded with its study, battle lines took shape in the community. First, Ellerbe arranged to address the medical personnel of every hospital in the city. He had already spoken to a nonmedical gathering, even before presenting his report, and now enlarged his promotional activities, despite the belief among some community leaders that it was inappropriate for a hired consultant of the commission to generate public pressure upon it.

The developing controversy also revolved around the issue of the quality of medical service performed at Ancker Hospital. Ancker staff appointments had long been a matter of dispute within the Ramsey County Medical Society. Many doctors believed that their colleagues affiliated with Miller and St. Joseph's hospitals and a nearby institution, St. Luke's Hospital, had maintained Ancker Hospital as a special preserve for themselves. Ancker Hospital staff members, on the other hand, denied that they were cliquish and pointed out that any doctor willing to contribute sufficient time each week could practice at the public hospital. As a matter of fact, they added, the number of doctors from the other hospitals anxious to assume permanent staff obligations at Ancker Hospital had never been large. The other hospitals were situated less conveniently in relation to the existing Ancker Hospital than were St. Joseph's, Miller, and St. Luke's, and for their doctors to accept long-term obligations at Ancker would necessarily entail some financial sacrifice. Nevertheless, some doctors resented being denied staff opportunities at Ancker Hospital. Frequently, in prosperous times, all of the county's private hospitals were fully occupied, while Ancker had several hundred empty beds. Emergency cases thus were sent to Ancker Hospital, but a doctor not affiliated with Ancker could not treat his patient there. Consequently, the doctor might lose the patient. Doctors thus strove to keep their patients out of Ancker Hospital, it was said, even at the risk of patients' health. Few doctors at other institutions wanted to see the intimacy of Miller, St. Joseph's, and St. Luke's with Ancker formalized once and for all in concrete. Thus, there was little reason for surprise when, late in March, the medical staff of Bethesda Hospital, a Lutheran institution, listened to one of Ellerbe's presentations and then voted 43–3 *against* Site B-1. (Nonetheless, most of the commission's members were astonished.)

During the spring of 1959, after the publication of Ellerbe's report, letters began to appear in the newspaper opposing selection of Site B-1. Although all of the letter writers emphasized traffic congestion in the area of Miller and St. Joseph's hospitals and the apparent technical difficulties involved in building a hospital over a freeway, they fell into several categories. Some writers were prominent in Protestant churches, while others were doctors not affiliated with Ancker Hospital. And some of the letter writers were residents of the neighborhood of the existing Ancker Hospital.

On the other side of the dispute, Reuel Harmon's Volunteer Committee and the administrators of Miller Hospital became particularly active. They bombarded the commission with letters and telephone calls. The administrators of St. Joseph's Hospital, aware of the unspoken taboo against Catholic pressure, were more discreet, despite an interest in the issue that was almost as great as that of their counterparts at Miller Hospital. Miller administrators had a special reason for wanting Ancker Hospital built next door. Miller had left one floor unfinished in its latest addition in anticipation of an increase in demand. The planned interstate freeway, however, seemed likely to reduce the hospital's attractiveness. When it was complete, Miller would be surrounded by freeway or major city streets on all sides. The noise, according to all expectations, would be extremely disturbing. Ellerbe's proposal for construction of Ancker Hospital above the freeway promised to smother freeway noise at the point where it would pass most closely to Miller Hospital. St. Joseph's Hospital, on the other hand, was somewhat less vulnerable economically. It had just completed a modernization program, and since it was the only Catholic hospital in the city it could count on a steady clientele.

By early April 1959 the Site Selection Committee of the Ancker Hospital Commission seemed unsure as to how to proceed. It had heard no one effectively refute Ellerbe's technical analysis and therefore it had no basis for articulating its doubts about Site B-1. At this moment of indecision the planning staff of St. Paul's Housing and Redevelopment Authority advanced its case in favor of site D, located in the Eastern Redevelopment Area.

The Housing and Redevelopment Authority Promotes Site D

The next phase of the controversy can be understood only if the involvement of the St. Paul Housing and Redevelopment Authority is clarified.

During the first flush of excitement following passage of the Federal Housing and Redevelopment Act in 1949, a plan for the 60-acre Eastern Redevelopment Area in St. Paul had been rather quickly formulated. It had been intended to include multiple middle- or high-income dwellings, parks, schools, and a shopping center. The Housing Authority had acquired the area and had cleared it of slums between 1953 and 1957, but St. Paul still had a great deal of vacant land within its boundaries and no developers came forth. In 1957 the FHA had decided that it would be unable to insure loans for residential development of the area, even if private developers should appear. FHA officials had believed that there was no market for such housing.

A 75-acre tract to the west of the State Capitol, called the Western Redevelopment Area, had been cleared by the city at the same time as the Eastern Redevelopment Area, so that by mid-1958 the Housing Authority had possessed 135 vacant acres. The Western Redevelopment Area had attracted some prospective developers, but not enough. In mid-1958 the federal Urban Renewal Administration had declared that it would not approve new projects in St. Paul until the Housing and Redevelopment Authority found uses for its two existing redevelopment areas. To the Housing Authority's planning staff, far more had been at stake than bureaucratic survival. It had believed that the Eastern Area could be put to good use and that failure to identify such a use would be inexcusable.

Norton Kent, assistant director for planning of the Housing Authority, had been concerned about the lack of buyers for land in the Eastern Area since his arrival in St. Paul. In August 1958 he had conceived the idea of using Site D for Ancker Hospital, but had been warned that the location of Ancker Hospital was too "hot" a subject. He had dropped the proposal but had not forgotten it. Instead, he had sought all available information on Ancker Hospital, including the alternative proposals of the various consultants. Kent's study had reinforced his belief that the Eastern Redevelopment Project Area was a desirable site for the new hospital. On the other hand, he had strongly disapproved of using the land for public housing, the other leading possibility. A public housing project of 450 units was being erected at the time in a bordering area. The public housing proponents had envisioned the construction of 500–800 units within the renewal area. Both areas, according to plans at the time, would have been physically isolated from the rest of the city.

Within the Housing Authority there was some disagreement over the desirability of Site D for the new hospital. Housing Authority members believed that the issue was too controversial to risk a public commitment. Kent's immediate superior, Executive

Director Louis Thompson, had some sympathy for Kent's idea, but he preferred to remain publicly neutral. He had raised the question informally with the members of the Housing Authority; they had privately endorsed the proposal but had taken no public stand. Thompson also had informed Representative Podgorski of the suggestion for Site D, and in December 1958 the latter had proposed that Ellerbe consider the site in his evaluation study. In reporting to the Ancker Hospital Commission in March 1959, however, Ellerbe had ranked the site fifth on his list of locations.

Kent was undismayed. As he watched the Site Committee of the commission bog down following Ellerbe's report, he concluded that a highly plausible case could be presented for the selection of Site D. In late April he pressed his views during a chance luncheon encounter with Martin O'Donnell, the labor representative on the Ancker Hospital Commission. O'Donnell, like most of the commission's other members, already had doubts about Site B-1 and was not impressed by the argument that efficient medical practice required contiguous hospitals. He thus carried Kent's views to the commission, and it invited the Housing Authority to present its case.

Prior to the May 1959 meeting of the full Ancker Hospital Commission, the Housing Authority held two private meetings with the Site Committee, at which Kent made presentations in support of Site D. The chairman of the Housing Authority and Executive Director Thompson were present on both occasions, but the proposal was considered to be primarily Kent's. As a result of these meetings, a majority of the Site Committee privately agreed that Site D was superior.

On May 27, Kent appeared before the commission and argued as follows: The Housing Authority already owned Site D, so that legal suits with protesting owners would be unnecessary. The price per acre for land in Site D would run about one-sixth that of land in Site B-1; and the commission might, if it wished, purchase 19 acres at Site D, as compared with 7 acres at Site B-1. It would be possible on Site D, he reasoned, to provide almost limitless room for expansion, landscaping, cheap surface parking, living facilities for staff, and a medical school, should the opportunity to establish one develop. Kent also pointed out that adjacent land uses were amenable: to the north there was a public housing project and a park; to the west there would soon be located another renewal project; to the east and the south the interstate freeway would divide Site D from industrial and commercial uses. The site was also near the center of a "ring"—with a radius of one and one-tenth miles—in which all of the city's existing hospitals were located. Site D would be more conveniently reached than Site B-1 from all hospitals but Miller, St. Joseph's, and St. Luke's. Furthermore, Site D lay near the intersection of the proposed north-south and east-west freeway axes in the city and the St. Paul Department of Public Works was then considering two thoroughfare extensions which, if constructed, would serve Site D. Although bus service to the site was poor, there seemed to be no reason why buses might not be routed past it once the hospital was built.

Kent had anticipated that some critics would wonder aloud why the Housing Authority did not propose the construction of a public housing project at Site D. He therefore pointed out to the commission that a large public housing project had already been constructed adjacent to the site and that if another were built in the same area, isolated from other residential neighborhoods, the resulting ghetto might spawn the social problems associated with the slums of larger cities. He believed that every principle of effective city planning militated against another public housing project for this area. Those who wanted the Housing Authority to support another public housing project for the area, he declared confidentially, would have to replace him first.

After Kent's presentation, the commission made no commitment with respect to Site D, and at that moment Kent stood largely alone in his support of the proposal. Although he exercised strong influence and effective leadership over the two planners subordinate to him, the Housing Authority itself often avoided supporting him publicly. Actually, Kent had arrived in St. Paul at a somewhat peculiar moment. Both the previous executive director and the assistant director had resigned within a space of two months, between June 15 and August 15, 1958. Kent had joined the Housing Authority on June 16. The members of the Housing Authority as well as most municipal officials looked upon planners generally with some suspicion. Against such a background, the politically appointed executive director of the Housing Authority, Louis Thompson, assumed a cautious posture. His refusal to actively support Kent's proposal for Site D was part of his strategy.

Herbert Wieland, the city planning director, was sympathetic but warned Kent—according to the latter's recollection—that the Ancker Hospital controversy was too intense and too unrelated to the Planning Bureau's central concerns for him to court involvement in it. Wieland himself later recalled that his warning had been more conditional: "I said in effect that this was not the time to go after this site publicly and that we would become involved at the right time." In either event, Wieland's reticence was consistent with longstanding Planning Bureau policy. The previous executive director of the Housing Authority, for example, had addressed a written request to the Planning Bureau in 1957 for suggestions as to future uses for the Eastern Redevelopment Area; but C. David Loeks, then the director of planning, had failed to reply. In August 1958 Kent had suggested Ancker Hospital as a possibility for the area and had asked Wieland for suggestions. Wieland had replied early in September that he could not make a specific recommendation without more extensive study, and that the Planning Bureau's current work schedule would not permit him to make such a study.

The Planning Bureau's lack of interest in supporting Kent apparently stemmed from a strategic desire not to become involved in the affairs of the Housing and Redevelopment Authority. At least two plausible explanations of this desire were available. Kent, supported by several members of the Planning Bureau staff who were interviewed on this subject, believed the first. According to it, the key factor was the unpopularity of the Housing Authority in conservative circles. This unpopularity had stemmed initially from the Authority's identification with public housing and more recently from its sale of Western Redevelopment Area land to the Sears Roebuck Company for a huge retail store with free parking facilities. Central area businessmen feared that Sears would reap the benefits of centralized location—outside of and in competition with established businesses in the central district. Wieland, according to this first possible explanation, was anxious to demonstrate the usefulness of the Planning Bureau to businessmen and had no wish to earn their enmity by associating too closely with the Housing Authority. Whatever his motives, Wieland certainly had kept his distance from the Authority. Although the Planning Bureau's general planning activities depended on the Housing Authority for considerable budgetary support, Wieland had forbidden his staff to answer any requests for data from it without first securing his personal approval. He had also chosen not to seek the opinions of Housing Authority staff on his plans prior to their publication.

So ran one explanation. Wieland, supported by his assistant director, advanced another. According to it, the key factor was that Wieland lacked confidence in both Thompson, the Housing Authority's executive director, and Kent, its assistant director for planning. Thus, he did not care to release data to them indiscriminately, nor did he feel any need for their planning advice. In addition, he felt that the Housing Authority's financial contribution was not philanthropic; it was intended to help the city meet federal requirements for continued urban renewal assistance. That object could be accomplished without the Housing Authority being consulted on the substance of plans being produced. As executive head of the Planning Bureau, Wieland's own chain of command ran to the Planning Board and the City Council alone. Moreover, it was incorrect to say that he was unduly oriented toward business support. When a group of downtown businessmen had sued to prevent the Sears sale, he had firmly supported the official city position. When they had hired a planning consultant who had proposed running a freeway through the proposed Sears parking lot, he had opposed that as well.

The Religious Issue

While the Hospital Commission, after Kent's presentation late in May 1959, continued its leisurely pace and did not meet again for five weeks, the religious issue began to rumble discreetly in the community. Throughout the deliberations of the commission, the lone Protestant member, representing the neighborhood of the existing Ancker Hospital, had opposed Site B-1 vigorously. Meanwhile, many letters to the newspaper had come from people who were associated with the Protestant churches of the city. As time passed, Protestant discontent became more noticeable. The climax came on June 18, when St. Paul's official organization of Lutheran ministers formally resolved that the mixing of religious and public institutions would violate the First Amendment to the United

States Constitution. Its resolution charged that construction of Ancker Hospital on Site B-1 and, presumably, the establishment of close relationships with St. Joseph's Hospital, "would to a considerable degree establish a religious institution as a city and county facility."

The ministers sent their resolution to the office of the Ancker Hospital Commission but did not release it to the press. The commission likewise refrained from making the statement public. Kent and the city planners never knew of its existence. Nevertheless, for several weeks some of the insiders involved in the dispute believed a public explosion imminent. Although none occurred, the ministers emphasized privately that they would bring legal suit, based on the First Amendment, if the commission proceeded to select Site B-1.

Delaney, chairman of the commission, suspected a bluff, but he recognized that the very fact of its being made indicated how strongly the ministers felt. Religion had never been an open issue in St. Paul, although some Protestant religious leaders had protested privately on occasion to city leaders about the absence of Protestants from the City Council. There was no easy remedy for this condition in the City Council, however, for St. Paul was a nonpartisan city, whose councilmen were elected at large. Forty or fifty people filed for the City Council primary every two years; the top dozen won a place on the general election ballot, and at the general election the high six among these were elected. The absence of Protestants from the council was probably due in part to chance and in part to the unwillingness of outstanding Protestants to run. Catholic politicians, it will be recalled, leaned over backward to avoid the appearance of dispensing favors on religious grounds, and Catholic institutions were careful not to pursue their political interests conspicuously.

Delaney pointed out to intimates that if the ministers did sue, the dispute could be expected to drag out for many years. The advantages of Site B-1 to St. Joseph's Hospital would probably be emphasized out of proportion, even though Miller Hospital had more to gain and had been far more active in the current dispute. He feared that religious antagonisms, always present not far below the surface of politics, might emerge openly and paralyze effective government in St. Paul. The consequent conflict might lead to an intensification of charges and counter charges for an indefinite period. He could not anticipate with certainty what would happen and he deplored the threats already made. But he was certain that the unpredictable effects of a sharp religious issue should be weighed against the technical arguments stressed by Ellerbe and the planners.

The Planners Challenge Ellerbe

When the Ancker Hospital Commission finally convened on July 2, it found that a State Highway Department revision of the freeway plans had reduced the amount of land available for hospital use at Site B-1 from seven acres to three—one small city block. Ellerbe, seeking to console the commission, explained that he had included the block that was eliminated only because a member of the commission had indicated a preference for above-ground parking. The cost per automobile space of underground parking, he declared, would run about the same as for the multilevel above-ground ramp previously considered. The reduction in site size, moreover, would reduce the price of Site B-1 by 60 per cent, from $2.15 million to $0.85 million.

During the meeting a representative of the Northern Association of Medical Education, a group working to bring a medical school to St. Paul, informed the commission that his organization preferred Site B-1 even though the school would have to be located several blocks away. He believed that the city would be unable to secure a medical school unless it were able to establish a sufficiently large and elaborate medical center. He denied, however, that his group would abandon its efforts if Site D were selected.

Representatives of Reuel Harmon's Volunteer Committee also argued at this time that the medical center was what mattered; land cost and parking facilities were subordinate issues. The commission became more confused than ever. Chairman Delaney reflected that Ellerbe had gone "overboard" in his public defense of Site B-1 and that the commission might be placed in a difficult position if it were to choose another site. In an effort to secure a clearer understanding of the technical issues, the commission now decided to seek the views of the City Planning Board.

The planning *staff*, of course, could hardly claim to be impartial at this point. It had been critical of Ellerbe's report from the first and had agreed with Kent that any competent city planner would choose Site D over Site B-1. Although the planners had avoided public involvement in the issue, several members of the commission, including Delaney, knew of their low estimate of the B-1 proposal. These commission members may have asked for an opinion simply to assure that the majority of planning experts were formally and publicly on their side before defying openly the influential proponents of Site B-1. The majority of the commission members, however, apparently believed that the planning staff might contribute a fresh and objective professional viewpoint on the Ancker Hospital controversy and favored obtaining the staff's opinions. With this in mind, the commission's Site Committee formally questioned Wieland on July 8. He declared that hospital planning experts generally believed that there should be sufficient open space around a new hospital to permit 100 per cent expansion. Since he saw no opportunity to leave this much space available on Site B-1, he felt compelled to conclude that B-1 was a poor site. On the other hand, he cautioned, further study would be required before he or his parent body, the Planning Board, could recommend a more suitable location.

Following this meeting, Wieland assigned Haluk Tarhan, chief planner on his staff, to develop immediately a planning staff position with respect to Sites B-1 and D. He made no effort to suggest additional alternatives. Tarhan, feeling the pressure of time, seized upon a Planning Advisory Service Report on hospital location issued by the American Society of Planning Officials (ASPO). ASPO had prefaced its report as follows:

There is widespread agreement among hospital planners on the criteria for site selection. The following statements were excerpted from *Design and Construction of General Hospitals*, published by the Modern Hospital Publishing Company, Inc., Chicago. *Some of these may be modified where a medical center is the unit being planned instead of a unitary hospital.* [Italics added.]

Tarhan and his staff disregarded the qualification made by ASPO, even though proponents of B-1 considered the issue of whether to build a medical center absolutely crucial. Later, several of the planners maintained that a medical center might develop even if the hospitals were a mile or so apart, but they never tried to assess the likelihood that this would occur or the advantages that a contiguous medical center might have over one composed of hospitals dispersed throughout the city.

On the basis of the eight ASPO criteria, Tarhan judged that Site D was preferable to Site B-1. His analysis so confirmed his initial inclination to challenge Ellerbe's study and recommendations that he prepared for his own use an alternative scorecard evaluating Sites B-1 and D. He believed his approach would disqualify Ellerbe's scoring system. He acknowledged that any method of weighing criteria entailed a good deal of arbitrary judgment, but he thought that his own scorecard was superior to Ellerbe's. Somewhat paradoxically, Tarhan's system of weighting tended to emphasize factors having to do with the physical structure of a hospital itself, generally considered architectural matters, while Ellerbe's had allotted many more points to such factors as access, distance from the population served, and relations with facilities elsewhere in the city—generally considered planning matters.[4]

In his 100-point system Ellerbe, for example, had rated relative convenience for drivers and pedestrians at 35 points, and proximity to bus routes at 10 points. Against this 45-point total, Tarhan in his 100-point system presented a general category of "accessibility" which he rated at 15 points. Ellerbe had assigned Site B-1 44 points out of a possible 45 points on his two access categories and Site D only 16 points, while Tarhan granted Site B-1 14 points and Site D 13. Tarhan conceded that B-1 was presently much more convenient by bus, but contended that bus routes could be altered without great difficulty and that traffic congestion in the Miller–St. Joseph's area would make Site B-1 far less accessible by automobile.

Ellerbe had rated land cost at 5 points. Tarhan rated a general category covering cost of land and construction at 20 points. Ellerbe had granted both sites 4 out of 5 points, while Tarhan gave Site D 17 out of 20 and Site B-1 8 out of 20. Ellerbe's estimate

---

[4] On reading this, Tarhan commented that in view of his undergraduate training as an architect it was not surprising that he considered architectural factors very important. He also felt that the serious question was not who had more closely approximated the stereotype of one or another discipline, but rather who had balanced architectural and planning considerations more reasonably.

of land cost was especially difficult to understand. He had estimated that 19 acres at Site D would cost $600,000 and 7 acres at Site B-1 about $1.5 million. He later raised the latter figure to $2.15 million, then reduced it to $850,000 when the site was cut to three acres. Ellerbe had judged that foundation work would cost $100,000 to $300,000 more at Site D. However, Site D had already been acquired and cleared. He apparently had avoided embarrassment by writing that legal and site clearance costs could "not be determined at this time so were not included in the estimate."

Ellerbe later defended his scoring by asserting that he had counted on the State Highway Department sharing the purchase price of Site B-1. The department needed part of the site for right-of-way, he reasoned, and he intended to construct the underground parking facilities on either side of the tunnel. Frank Marzitelli, the State Highway Department's Deputy Comissioner and a B-1 supporter, had consistently said that too few engineering data were yet available for it to be possible to say what the Highway Department would be able to do financially. But he thought the commission should purchase the land and then find out. He believed that as owner of the land, the commission would be in a stronger bargaining position. High-ranking engineers on the permanent staff of the Highway Department who were consulted, however, tended to emphasize rather that it would cost a great deal more to construct the freeway under Site B-1 than it would to work on the surface. They strongly doubted that the department would be willing to end up paying more for that portion of the freeway than it would have paid without a hospital being built. They did not know how much the hospital would add to construction costs, but they did not imagine that it would leave much for right-of-way expenditures. Supporters of B-1 retorted to this estimate that even if it should prove correct—which they hoped it would not—it did not really matter whether the state or the city and county paid the purchase price. The central point was that Site B-1 would be purchased by the taxpayers and used for public purposes in any case, whereas Site D might be maintained on the tax rolls if a hospital were not located there. Tarhan and his fellow planners replied that St. Paul land was not in such demand that this issue should be an important consideration, and that the price and potential tax yield of the 1.8 acres not needed by the Highway Department almost equaled that of Site D's 19 acres. The newspaper repeatedly stated as fact that Site B-1 would cost the city nothing. Consequently, most observers and even some members of the Ancker Hospital Commission never ceased to doubt this.

Ellerbe and Tarhan each rated the relative absence of environmental nuisances at 15 points. Opponents of Site B-1, including Tarhan, believed that the tunnel underneath the freeway could be no more than 300 feet long, because the Highway Department had no intention of paying for the expensive ventilation facilities that a longer tunnel would require. Therefore, the distance from open freeway to the hospital would be short; noise and fumes from the freeway might disturb Ancker patients. Tarhan thus awarded Site D 13 points out of 15, Site B-1 only 7.

Ellerbe had contended that building over the freeway would muffle noise for the two private hospitals already located in the area and that this fact should influence the decision. The planners acknowledged that the two private hospitals were important community assets, but they saw no reason why public funds should be spent to muffle noise in the vicinity of private institutions. They denied Ellerbe's contention that the freeway passing adjacent to Site D on two sides would also create a problem of noise and they challenged his scoring on Sites B-1 and D with respect to nuisances. The Ellerbe and Tarhan scorecards, reproduced below, had no other criteria in common.

Tarhan's scorecard evoked a great deal of interest and support among the staff of the Planning Bureau. Wieland, the planning director, was especially impressed by Tarhan's reasoning with respect to the factors of parking, traffic congestion, expansion, and environment. In his final recommendations to the Ancker Hospital Commission he emphasized these four points.

Parking. Ellerbe, the consulting architect for the commission, had acknowledged that ramp parking would be necessary at Site B-1, whereas there was more than adequate room for parking at Site D. He had pointed out, however, that

parking ramps can have the advantage of being closer to the desired point of arrival than the five acres of surface parking for about 700 cars initially estimated as necessary. Because the cost factors for parking purposes are so nearly equal, the [scorecard] shows a level figure for this item.

Ellerbe Scorecard

Criteria	Maximum	Site B-1	Site D
1. Relative convenience for drivers and pedestrians	(35)	34	15
2. Proximity to bus routes	(10)	10	1
3. Parking facilities	(10)	10	10
4. Distance from population center in the community *	(15)	13	11
5. Absence of nuisances	(15)	13	7
6. Joint use of facilities	(10)	10	4
7. Land cost	(5)	4	4
Total score	(100)	94	52

* Although Ellerbe awarded Site B-1 a higher score than Site D on "Distance from the population center," the Ancker Hospital Commission's staff expert concluded from Ellerbe's own data that Site D was slightly closer. It was certainly in the direction of population movement from the center.

Tarhan Scorecard

Criteria	Maximum	Site B-1	Site D
1. Cost of land and construction	(20)	8	17
2. Accessibility	(15)	14	13
3. Nuisances	(15)	7	13
4. Dimensions *	(15)	7	15
5. Orientation and exposure	(10)	4	8
6. Public utilities	(10)	10	10
7. Topography	(10)	5	8
8. Landscaping	(5)	2	5
Total score	(100)	57	89

* The category "Dimensions" consisted of three sub-categories:
(1) Room for expansion (8 points)
(2) Possibility of orienting the building well (4 points)
(3) Possibility of separating different kinds of traffic (3 points)

He had awarded each potential site 10 points out of a possible 10. When challenged by the commission, however, he admitted that the initial cost of ramp parking would be about five times higher than surface parking—$1,200 as compared with $250 per space. He explained that he had based his estimate of equal cost on the fact that surface lots required nighttime policing and removed far more land from the tax rolls. When the Highway Department reduced the size of Site B-1 he contended that underground parking would cost no more than ramp parking. Tarhan challenged this statement on the ground that the underground rock formation in that location would add to the cost of the structure.

Tarhan also argued that the deduction of a hypothetical tax yield from the five acres at Site D was patently unrealistic because no demand for the land existed. If a demand that could not be satisfied elsewhere should develop in the future, there would be time then to build a ramp facility. If it were found desirable in the future to build additional parking facilities at Site B-1, on the other hand, there would be no way to expand the underground facilities. Ellerbe acknowledged that this was true.

In Tarhan's view, the most important factor was expense. The University of Minnesota had recently built an underground parking facility in Minneapolis at a cost of more than $3,000 per space. Tarhan saw no reason to believe that Ellerbe could improve on this price significantly. Ellerbe claimed that the university had done a fantastically uneconomical job. Accepting the university's figure as the best available, Tarhan compared the cost of structure plus rock excavation against development of surface land. He concluded that parking facilities would cost 12 times more at Site B-1 than at Site D—$2.1 million as compared with $175,000 for 700 spaces.

Traffic Congestion. Tarhan emphasized that the Miller–St. Joseph's area already had serious problems of traffic congestion and that the construction of a third hospital there might create a crisis situation. Wieland, in responding to questioning by the commission, dramatized this point by declaring that he feared that the area might become "a brick and mortar jungle." The commission seemed greatly impressed, while the proponents of Site B-1 were compelled to admit that Ellerbe had not considered the issue.

Ellerbe later privately gave these reasons for his silence when Wieland made that remark: (1) the commission had by this time made up its mind, (2) the commission had clearly demonstrated its lack of confidence in him as consultant, and (3) he did not wish to jeopardize his opportunity to become the architect for the new hospital by prolonging the site controversy. Ellerbe insisted, however, that Wieland was wrong. If parking were prohibited on the nearby streets, traffic would flow rapidly. Furthermore, the underground facility at the new Ancker Hospital at Site B-1, together with those that Miller and St. Joseph's hospitals would be compelled to build in any case (his imperative), would provide sufficient parking space. In any event, Ellerbe concluded, the overriding issue was not traffic congestion or parking, but whether to build a medical center.

Expansion. While Tarhan was working on his study, an issue of the magazine *Architectural Forum* appeared with an article about hospitals. Its author wrote that according to "official government surveys" the United States had a shortage of 900,000 hospital beds. According to these surveys, the United States currently had 7.5 hospital beds per 1,000 population. If the deficit estimate were accepted as literal fact, the proper ratio was between 12 and 13 beds per 1,000 population.[5] Tarhan pointed out that Ramsey County currently had only 6.4 beds per 1,000 population. If current population forecasts proved accurate, the county would experience a 40 per cent population increase by 1980. Merely to reach the existing national bed-to-population ratio—not even the desired level—Ramsey County would require a 61 per cent increase in hospital beds by 1980. Furthermore, as if to clinch the case, Tarhan recalled that the ASPO Planning Advisory Service Report, on which he had already depended so heavily, included the statement that "the plot chosen should allow for future expansion of at least 100 per cent in building area and still retain attractive grounds and obviate objectionable appearances of overcrowding." Tarhan emphasized that at Site D there would not only be room for 100 per cent horizontal expansion, but also for construction of any related facility that future administrations might desire to build.

Tarhan criticized Ellerbe's contention that although he could not provide horizontal expansion at Site B-1, he had intended all

---

[5] Edward T. Chase, "Revolution in Hospitals," *Architectural Forum,* CXI, No. 2 (August 1959), 127–129, 178ff. Chase is a free-lance writer who specializes in health, transportation, and city planning topics. In this article his approach to the estimates of hospital needs made by professional hospital administrators was totally uncritical.

along to provide foundation support for vertical expansion to a capacity of 1,000 beds. Ellerbe had maintained that he had built all of his hospitals for vertical expansion and that this was the best kind, since elevators are the most efficient form of transportation. He would design the same hospital at Site D as at B-1. He had to admit, however, that 1,000 beds was the maximum possible at Site B-1 and that no room existed for the expansion of parking facilities beyond 700 cars. Tarhan asserted that Ellerbe would find it difficult to design enough capacity on the lower floors—kitchens, laundries, laboratories, and similar facilities—to service such a vertical expansion and that in any event the 1,000-bed figure might in time prove well below community needs.

Environment. Ellerbe had maintained that the only relevant features of the environment were traffic noises and the possibilities for joint use of facilities. He had explained that since the average period of hospitalization had been reduced from twenty-eight to seven and one-half days during the past thirty years, the idea that hospitals should have parks surrounding them had become anachronistic. Today's patient, he reasoned, leaves the hospital as soon as he can walk. Landscaped gardens are little used and expensive to maintain. Architects continue to design them only because clients expect them.

Tarhan, on the other hand, insisted that an aesthetic environment still had important therapeutic value, and he pointed out that virtually all of Ellerbe's own designs included landscaping. He considered that Ellerbe's attack on greenery was motivated solely by the consulting architect's preference for Site B-1 where no room for landscaping was available. Tarhan also stressed that the architect who designed a hospital at B-1 would have little freedom to orient the building correctly with regard to prevailing winds, sunlight, and other relevant factors. He did not consider it his responsibility to determine whether the orientations possible at Site B-1 were desirable, but he was impressed by the fact that the ample size of Site D would permit orientation in any direction.

The professional planners of St. Paul believed that Tarhan's arguments, combined with those that Kent had made earlier, added up to a conclusive case against Site B-1. Throughout the period of Tarhan's work, the more active members of the Ancker Hospital Commission had maintained close private communication with Planning Director Wieland, and they knew the drift of planner opinion. (Delaney later recalled that he frequently had asked Kent and Wieland for data since the beginning of the commission's work and had always considered himself familiar with their general views.) The commissioners were also impressed by the fact that the ASPO criteria used by Tarhan had been developed outside the community by people having no special interest in the Ancker Hospital controversy. On the other hand, Ellerbe had cited only his own (admittedly long and distinguished) experience in support of his criteria.

By the end of July 1959, the commissioners were thoroughly familiar with the technical arguments concerning the two rival sites, but they remained confused as to what their decision should be. Two members of the commission favored Site B-1, one continued to favor the present location of Ancker Hospital, and two or three seemed inclined to favor Site D. The remainder had treated their membership on the commission casually and intended to defer to Chairman Delaney. The chairman by this time firmly favored Site D. Although he found it impossible to weight the factors that had influenced him, he endeavored some time later to list them for an interviewer in their general order of importance. First, he believed a prolonged and acrimonious struggle that might divide the community on religious lines was likely to develop if the commission chose Site B-1. This was of course highly undesirable in itself, but in addition he thought that such a struggle, accompanied by legal suits and taken together with probable delays before the Highway Department's freeway alignment plans became final, might prevent the start of hospital construction on Site B-1 for five or more years. Second, he had strong doubts that a 600-bed hospital with parking facilities and room for expansion could be built for $16 million on Site B-1. Third, he believed that when the freeways were completed Site D would be one of the most accessible spots in the county, within about twenty minutes of any point. And fourth, all the other arguments advanced by the planners seemed to lend additional support to his position.

One reason for the other commission members' indecision was their growing estrangement from Ellerbe. Even before Kent's defense of Site D in May 1959, many of the commissioners had begun to resent Ellerbe's ardent public defense of Site B-1. When he perceived this, Ellerbe deliberately retreated to the background, hoping to win the final architectural contract regardless of the site selected. Rarig also concluded that there was nothing further he could do. Reuel Harmon, chairman of the Volunteer Committee, and the newspaper continued to press for Site B-1, but because they lacked the status of professional planning experts they tended to rely on Ellerbe's reputation as the main intellectual support of their point of view. The commissioners became impatient with these constant references to Ellerbe's reputation and came to feel that the Volunteer Committee was no longer a disinterested study group.

On the other hand, there was a growing confidence among the commissioners in the ability of the city's professional planners. The commissioners were laymen and tended to feel more comfortable with the Housing Authority's recommendation favoring Site D. There had always been some doubt within the commission concerning the feasibility of constructing a hospital over a freeway, and its members easily understood that traffic congestion and parking difficulties might result if the new hospital were built at Site B-1. Some of the commissioners also believed that locating Ancker Hospital at Site B-1 would favor two of the city's hospitals over the others. The land that would be lost to the tax rolls at Site D hardly seemed worthy of concern; in a city of one-family homes with a stagnant core area, there could not be a need to spend great sums on underground parking facilities, buildings above tunnels, and other extraordinary structures. Furthermore, some of the commissioners tended to regard the professional city planners as relatively disinterested, whereas they were uncertain about Ellerbe's motives.

As a matter of fact, Ellerbe's motives became a favorite subject for speculation. Some people pointed out that he served as "house architect" for both Miller and St. Joseph's hospitals, but Ellerbe argued that he also worked regularly for every other hospital in the city. Some believed that he wished to design an architectural wonder over the freeway, while Ellerbe maintained that his firm had not become nationally renowned by indulging in monumental whims. Others believed that construction on Site B-1 would necessarily depend on Ellerbe's serving as architect, whereas an open competition could be held for the design of Site D. The supporters of Site B-1 insisted that there would be open competition for the contract to design a hospital if Site B-1 were selected and that Ellerbe, out of a sense of civic duty, had probably endangered his chances by publicly pressing his convictions.

The most important technical argument against Site B-1 seemed to be that it provided no room for expansion.[6] The proponents of Site B-1 denied that expansion was a serious problem. Ancker had not had more than 600 patients at any one time since the economic depression of the 1930's, and Ellerbe had given assurance that Site B-1 could sustain a hospital of 1,000 beds. If in some future depression the number of indigent patients should strain Ancker Hospital's capacity, some patients might be "farmed out" at public expense to private hospitals. Every private hospital in St. Paul had had a surfeit of empty beds during the last depression. This solution, they reasoned, would relieve the taxpayer of the need to maintain excess capacity in prosperous times and would provide the private hospitals with a form of "depression insurance."

Some of the defenders of Site B-1 also argued that the spread of private hospitalization insurance, together with medical progress, would in time reduce the need for public beds. Proponents of Site D, on the other hand, maintained that rapid population growth and the increasing proportion of older people in the population would make expansion of hospital capacity eminently desirable. No one really knew, however, how many beds would be needed ten or twenty years hence, nor did anyone conduct research to find out. Ellerbe and Rarig believed that it was absurd to sacrifice the medical center idea at this time simply because of the remote possibility that the public hospital needs of the community might eventually more than double. They were supported by those who expected to benefit from location of Ancker Hospital at Site B-1 and by those in the business community who believed that public hospitals should rapidly be supplanted by private insurance. According to Rarig, some of the business leaders in the community hoped to limit Ancker Hospital to a capacity of 350 beds.

---

[6] On reading this, Delaney said that he had not considered expansion *the* most important technical issue. It did dominate public discussion in the final phase of the commission's deliberations, however, and other members recalled it as the issue that had struck them as decisive.

Commission Chairman Delaney, on the other hand, believed that the community should maintain several hundred more hospital beds than were normally required in order to assure that unexpected emergencies might be met. He knew that the private hospitals could not afford to maintain any excess capacity, and spoke privately of building a 1,000-bed Ancker Hospital initially. He admitted that he had no idea whether expansion would be required in the future; the selection of Site D, however, would permit postponement of a decision on this question.

Delaney and some other members of the commission were favorably impressed by the planners' assertion that land on Site B-1 not needed by the Highway Department would be a logical place for expansion of the two private hospitals located there. For Miller Hospital, which would be bounded on all sides by the freeway and major thoroughfares, it would be almost the only available site for expansion. One member of the commission predicted publicly that the administrators of Miller and St. Joseph's Hospitals would curse the commission within ten years if Ancker Hospital were built on Site B-1. The incumbent administrators of these hospitals, of course, interpreted their interests differently.

Delaney also had serious doubts that a public hospital should own equipment or hire interns in partnership with any private hospital. He preferred to see the public hospital purchase expensive equipment and let the private hospitals use it on a fee basis. He also had wondered from the first whether administrators and practitioners at the other private hospitals in St. Paul would believe that a decision to build Ancker Hospital at Site B-1 had been arrived at honestly. No community, he reasoned, has any greater asset than the faith of its citizens that public officials are impartial and incorruptible. Regardless of the technical arguments favoring Site B-1, it seemed dangerous to appear to give two private hospitals such an advantage over the others in attracting interns, residents, and patients. Delaney knew that the leaders of the County Medical Society—all of whom were on the Ancker Hospital staff—continued to favor Site B-1, but he was also disturbed by the virtually unanimous vote against Site B-1 by the staff of Bethesda Hospital. These factors tended to reinforce Delaney's private inclination to favor Site D.

Some of the other commissioners, however, were still quite perturbed by the charge that in choosing Site D they would eliminate the city's opportunity to establish a medical center. Their sensitivity to this argument was only partially reduced when they learned that the professional planners knew of medical centers in other cities that were composed of noncontiguous hospitals. Rarig, Ellerbe, and the other leading proponents of Site B-1 contended that the city's hospitals had never cooperated in the past and never would in the future if Site D were chosen. If, however, Ancker, Miller, and St. Joseph's hospitals were once to begin to operate as a medical center—which they certainly (*sic*) would if Ancker Hospital were located at Site B-1—every other hospital in the city would be compelled to join them in order to remain on a competitive basis. Moreover, they reasoned, the efficiency of medical practice in a noncontiguous center could never match that of a contiguous center. A doctor, for example, can go to his car, drive from one hospital to another, find a parking space, see a patient, and return, but two such circuits a day waste an hour. Similarly, a patient can be moved from one hospital to another for treatment requiring expensive equipment, but the process upsets the patient and ties up an ambulance for considerable time. Ideally, they concluded, private and public hospitals, doctors' offices, and research facilities should all be within easy walking distance of each other. High rise brick "jungles" might be anathema to professional city planners (except in central business districts where business efficiency seemed to require them), but only in such structures could the limited supply of medical talent be efficiently utilized. Only by improving medical efficiency, they reasoned, could the cost of medical care be kept within the means of most people.

Denouement

When the Site Committee of the Ancker Hospital Commission met again on August 4, 1959, Delaney did not mention the religious issue that had influenced his personal choice but rather emphasized the technical arguments raised by the planners. He pointed out especially that at Site B-1 there would be no room for expansion, that underground parking would cost too much, that Site D was already under unified ownership and cleared, and that medical centers existed throughout the country without contiguous buildings. The committee, greatly impressed by Delaney's sense of conviction, immediately voted 3–0 in favor of Site D, with 2 abstentions.

Public reaction was immediate. For example, the Executive Committee of the Chamber of Commerce, which had earlier criticized the commission for its procrastination, now declared that the issues had not been adequately aired. The leaders of the County Medical Society announced that they were conducting an opinion poll of all Ramsey County physicians on the issue of a site for Ancker Hospital. The newspaper charged that Ellerbe's exhaustive, detailed, and scientific scorecard had never been refuted. (Tarhan's scorecard had never been made public.) It reminded its readers that the eminent, disinterested Volunteer Committee had, "after long and serious consideration," endorsed Site B-1 wholeheartedly. The newspaper considered the decision of the Site Committee to be "most surprising."

Despite the public protests, Delaney easily carried the full commission with him on August 12, when it voted 6–2 in favor of Site D. Former Conservative Mayor Daubney and Deputy State Highway Commissioner Marzitelli composed the minority. Monsignor Ryan, the Catholic clergyman on the commission, was out of town.

Two days later, on August 14, the City Council of St. Paul took up the commission's recommendation. The president of the County Medical Society, representatives of the Chamber of Commerce, and lead editorials in the newspaper implored the council to await the results of the doctors' poll. It was pointed out to the council that the City Planning Board had not yet made a recommendation. Wieland, who was present, told the council that his staff had studied the question during the past month and tended to favor Site D. After directing Wieland to secure a formal recommendation from the Planning Board, the City Council deferred its vote for a week. A few days later the County Board did likewise.

On August 19 Wieland briefly explained the staff's views to the Planning Board, which then voted unanimously to support the commission's decision. Wieland transmitted the result of the vote to the City Council. Meanwhile, the results of the doctors' poll were announced. To the chagrin of the Medical Society's leadership, Site D received 164 votes, Site B-1 received 147, and Site A (located adjacent to the present Ancker Hospital) received 70 votes. Close observers judged that approximately 90 per cent of the doctors practicing at Ancker Hospital had voted for Site B-1. If this was true, then almost no other doctors had voted for that site. The Medical Society did not bother to transmit the result of the poll to the City Council. The council learned of it through the newspaper.

At the next weekly meeting of the council on August 21, Wieland explained the ASPO criteria, and the council voted 5–1 in favor of Site D. The following November the Ancker Hospital Commission awarded the $1 million contract for design of the new hospital to Ellerbe and Company. By the fall of 1961, after more than a year of consultation with a Citizens' Planning Advisory Committee appointed by Delaney and chaired by Frank Rarig, Ellerbe's plans for the hospital were complete. It would have 600 beds on six floors in three circular towers. The hospital, a seven-story nurses' dormitory, and a three-story building for medical staff training were also planned for the site. On October 18, 1961 city officials broke ground and construction got under way.

In Retrospect

It was argued in the concluding section of Chapter I ("The Intercity Freeway") that generalist city planners had accepted the values of highway engineers, and in so doing had largely ignored other values which might have been thought worthy of serious consideration. In the Ancker Hospital dispute, on the other hand, generalist city planners actively took issue with a specialist adversary. Yet here again they seem to have selected values to emphasize in a rather casual manner. To make this point, it is unnecessary to pass judgment on whether the planners chose the "right" side of either dispute. The purpose of studying the planning process in detail is to shed light on whether they chose as they did for right and adequate reasons. Unless they did, it may well be that the "rightness" or "wrongness" of their eventual position was accidental.

St. Paul planners came to believe during the Ancker Hospital dispute that architect Ellerbe had acted dishonestly. Their suspicions had a surface plausibility, though "strategically" would have been a more appropriate word. First, Ellerbe never let on that he had made up his mind before the Commission hired him as its consultant, nor that he had had a hand in the formation of Harmon's Ancker Hospital Volunteer Committee. More important, he indicated on his scorecard that his primary criteria had been accessibility and freedom from nuisances. The planners knew that by these criteria Site D should have come out ahead.

Still, the planners might have looked beyond Ellerbe's actions and his scorecard to his fundamental arguments. Quite obviously, the architect's real concern was to create a contiguous medical center on Site B-1. He apparently believed that efficiency in medical practice was at stake, and that no other phalanx of considerations could outweigh this one. He also knew that efficiency in medical practice could be a controversial goal if its accomplishment required favoring two hospitals over the city's others. So he tried to demonstrate that he had based his recommendation on factors having rather little to do with the fact of proximity to Miller and St. Joseph's. He wanted to argue that even aside from the opportunity it provided to build a medical center, B-1 was by far the best site. Once opposition arose, he found it difficult to drop the pretense and admit that just one crucial argument favored B-1. So he defended B-1 against every attack, and eventually the Commission stopped paying attention to him.

Ellerbe's concept of the central objective in hospital site location had a good deal to recommend it. The ASPO criteria that the city planners presented were surely no more compelling. Yet the planners apparently believed that these criteria—applied without regard to a modifying statement that they might need alteration when the goal was to develop a medical center—could indeed suffice. They made no effort to inform themselves about the values at stake in the issue of whether or not to build a contiguous medical center. Nor did they ask any hospital specialist to advise them. Instead, they sought evidence that the title "medical center" had been applied to associations of noncontiguous hospitals. Finding this evidence, they assured the Commission that a medical center could develop in St. Paul even if Ancker were at Site D. They had made no effort to understand or evaluate the ways in which a contiguous medical center might differ from a noncontiguous one, or the reasons why St. Paul's hospitals had failed to form a medical center previously.

Even more significantly, neither Ellerbe nor the planners appear to have considered public opinion a significant datum. Both assumed that they could apply general criteria to physical facts and come up with "correct" recommendations. The planners did consider it unfair to favor two hospitals at the expense of others, but they made no effort to discover what personnel at the less favored hospitals thought. The doctors' poll result surprised them as much as anyone else. Administrators and doctors at these hospitals conceivably might have admitted that the medical advantages of B-1 outweighed the inconveniences that its selection would cause them personally. Their most relevant opinion, after all, was not what they selfishly preferred but what they thought a Commission entrusted with the public interest should do. Ancker Hospital Commission Chairman Delaney had a well-developed regard for appearances. Consequently, he neither made a quick judgment about the "fairness" of Site B-1 nor took a poll. He assumed that if the competitors of Miller and St. Joseph's felt strongly, after reflection, that B-1 should not be chosen, they would let him know. All he had to do was give them time. Under some circumstances, of course, he might have tried to persuade them that a given proposal merited their approval. In this case, however, he was having a hard enough time making up his own mind.

As for the religious issue, St. Paul's planners not only did not consider it; they were hardly aware that it existed. When informed by this writer that it had been a factor, they answered that they had heard vague rumors of its existence but had refused to listen. They considered the issue outside their sphere of concern. As their training certainly did not prepare them to deal with an issue of this kind, they were probably wise to take this position. It is mentioned here only to emphasize the extent to which they conceived themselves as technicians rather than generalists.

The leading members of the Ancker Hospital Commission took a broader approach to the site question than did the planners. They would have found it nearly impossible to defend their choice publicly, however, had the city planners not supplied them with technical arguments. At very least, the planners' support of Site D showed the public that Ellerbe's defense of B-1 rested on disputable premises. It may have done quite a bit more, of course, permitting sentiment against B-1 in some quarters to crystallize.

Finally, it is worth noting that the planners became involved only because the Housing and Redevelopment Authority had strategic problems of its own, and that their ultimate influence probably depended far more on Ellerbe's mistakes than on their own persuasive powers. Initially the Ancker Hospital Commission had not even considered asking the planners for advice. Nor had it urged Ellerbe to maintain liaison with them. Only after Ellerbe had come up with a proposal which, though it may have been the best possible, outraged the common sense of many laymen did the planners receive their chance. Even at that point, it was only because everyone had long since heard all of Ellerbe's arguments that the planners' analysis sounded so fresh and persuasive. Had Ellerbe talked to the planners initially, dealt with their arguments in his reports, and presented his own case with greater candor, he would no doubt have been more formidable in the end. At it was, his sheer self-confidence and prominent support might have carried a different set of commissioners with him before any opposition had a chance to take shape.

IV

A Plan for Central Minneapolis

The Problem

City planners generally spend most of their time gathering information, and many give little thought at the start of the planning process to the kinds of data needed to support the types of recommendations they hope to make. Consequently, they frequently borrow "standards" and "principles" from published works, with little regard to the data which they themselves have gathered. Some critical observers have suggested that to many planners fact-gathering is a ritual, designed to reassure laymen of the planners' competence rather than to help the planners in their work of conceiving and evaluating proposals.

The authors of the *Central Minneapolis Plan*[1] made a highly sophisticated effort to relate their research to their objectives, and they did not confine their research to the collection of easily ascertainable, tangible data. Rather, they extended their information-gathering efforts to include the search for politically acceptable planning goals. They divided their research effort into two parts. To carry out the first part, which dealt with physical and economic problems, they employed consultants. The consultants, who had had considerable opportunity to learn from past experience, were specialists in answering the kinds of questions which the planners

[1] *First report on the Central Minneapolis Plan* (City of Minneapolis Planning Commission: Central Minneapolis Series Number Eight, December 1959). This document is hereafter referred to as the *Central Minneapolis Plan*, or (in this chapter only) the *Plan*.

hired them to answer. They could not promise perfect predictions of future trends, but they offered a degree of probability on which shrewd businessmen commonly risked investment capital. The second part of the research effort, concerning community attitudes toward proposed planning goals, the Minneapolis planners carried out themselves.

Before the planners could begin their research, they believed that they had to answer a central question: Who could determine the appropriate goals and means of a plan for central Minneapolis? They found little guidance in the planning literature. Most planners throughout the country seemed to assume that all cities sought more or less the same goals, and that these were relatively well-known to their colleagues. Planners generally assumed, for example, that everyone (except a few profiteering investors, whose views should not count) would like to eradicate blight, traffic congestion, and inequality in the distribution of public services. In practice, of course, those planners who were anxious to succeed politically tempered their recommendations to avoid clashing with the better known preferences of powerful politicians and interest group leaders. In doing so, they often barred themselves from proposing any significant changes in the *status quo.*

In designing their strategy, Minneapolis planners sought clues from their political environment. They estimated that the city's population in 1959 was about 559,000, an increase since 1950 of 7 per cent. Minneapolis was a city of single-family homes. Its neighborhoods tended to be homogeneous and stable. Under 2.5 per cent of the population was Negro, and no nonwhite had ever been elected to public office. Slightly over 9 per cent of the population were foreign born; of these, almost half were Swedish or Norwegian. This was in accord with the patterns of earlier generations, in which larger proportions of the population had been first generation Americans. As a rule, politicians assumed that nationality was important in municipal elections, and therefore most of the leading candidates in city-wide elections had Scandinavian names.

The structure of the city government was determined by a 1920 city charter which provided for a weak mayor–strong council system with nonpartisan elections and a long ballot with forty-nine positions on it. The mayor and all thirteen aldermen were elected for two-year terms, the latter from wards.[2] The mayor had a staff of only two, aside from secretaries. He was empowered to veto ordinances, subject to overriding by a two-thirds council majority. With the council's consent, he appointed the chief of police and a majority of the members of five independent commissions. The latter served fixed terms and did not normally look to the mayor for leadership.[3] The council appointed the city attorney, the city engineer, the city clerk, and the city assessor. All other city officials were appointed, promoted, and disciplined under strict civil service rules. The Civil Service Commission, one of those appointed by the mayor, had a strong tradition of independence. It appointed and promoted under the rule of one, thus depriving operating officials of any discretion whatever in personnel matters. Moreover, it generally refused to give examinations unless it had what it considered a sufficient number of applications on file.[4]

Political party organization was extremely weak, and candidates for political office had no choice but to rely for aid almost solely on personal networks of friends and acquaintances. Once elected, they were immune from party discipline.[5] The political system,

[2] Prior to 1953 the terms of aldermen had been four years.

[3] On reading this, an alderman commented that most of the mayor's commission appointees served only three year terms and did cultivate the mayor's favor with an eye to reappointment. He admitted, however, that no recent mayor had striven for policy control of the independent commissions. In addition, he recalled that when a mayor of the late 1930's had proved ambitious in this direction, the City Council had simply refused to confirm any of his appointees. The result had been to perpetuate the incumbents in office until another mayor was elected.

[4] The only important exception to the merit system was an exaggerated system of veteran's preference. Any veteran who passed an examination automatically went to the top of the list. This had produced some unusual results over the years. One nonveteran thought sufficiently capable by two mayors to be appointed chief of police had never been able to rise above the rank of patrolman by civil service examination.

[5] This was a fairly recent development. From the 1930's until the mid-1950's, many councilmen had been subject to strict discipline by the Central Labor Union, to which nearly all of the city's labor unions belonged. In order to receive labor endorsement, candidates had had to sign written pledges committing them to accept Labor discipline. During the national reaction against the power of organized labor after World War II, the newspapers, supported by local conservative and "good government" organizations, had begun to make an issue of Labor dominance. The Central Labor Union itself had given

then, was characterized by extreme deconcentration of power. Legally, however, the City Council, with its combination of legislative and administrative authority, stood supreme. The only major limitations on its power were those on the power of the city government generally: namely, that the city charter assigned numerous important functions to independent commissions (some of them elected) and that it fairly narrowly circumscribed the city's taxing, spending, and substantive policy-making powers.

Within the council, members tended to divide along three axes. First, although they did not wear the usual party labels, they did go before the voters as Liberals and Independents. Elections of council officers were also along these lines. Liberals were generally supported by organized labor and the Democratic party. Independents were usually supported by business groups and "good government" organizations; the Republican party stayed out of local politics. The Liberals generally had a majority, but few votes on substantive issues reflected the Liberal-Independent division very closely. Second, the members divided (though not formally) into those who were highly satisfied with the existing city charter and the kinds of policies that had been produced under it, and those who desired thoroughgoing charter revision. The latter group rarely numbered more than two or three, but the division was significant because charter revision was a hot and "permanent" political issue in Minneapolis.[6] Finally, the members divided into

them a good deal of ammunition with which to work. For example, on one occasion it had induced the Council to fill a School Board vacancy by appointing a linoleum layer with an eighth-grade education. By 1957, open labor endorsement had become at best a dubious blessing in all but a few wards. See Charlotte Frank, "Politics in the Nonpartisan City," M.A. thesis, University of Chicago, 1958.

[6] The dominant charter reformers had long favored a strong mayor system. They were supported in this by the newspapers, "good government" organizations, and most business groups. The opponents of revision generally said that they were in favor of specific changes but not a wholesale redistribution of power. One leading councilman who favored the strong council–weak mayor system, for example, told this writer that he would favor a city manager system so long as the manager was appointed by and responsible to the Council rather than the mayor. He also said that he would strongly favor the introduction of some flexibility into the civil service system.

The proponents of a strong mayor system regularly managed to initiate a city-wide referendum on a proposed new charter every few years. To date, those interested almost exclusively in ward problems and those who also devoted a good deal of time and energy to city-wide problems. The latter group rarely numbered more than three or four; the others generally let them carry the burden of general policy determination so long as they did not seek to interfere with the overall pattern of ward-oriented politics and fiscal conservatism. The two, three, or four in this group at any time who were at the highly satisfied end of the second axis were thus the key elective officials in Minneapolis when it came to dealing with city-wide policy questions.

The Minneapolis planners judged that neither elective officials nor the general public could give them much help in defining

---

they had always lost. (The apparent futility of the cause led most business organizations to abandon it for inactivity during the charter referendum campaign of 1963.) Their primary opponents were the members of the City Council and the leaders of the Central Labor Union, who generally argued as follows: The "charter reform" movement is inspired and sustained by the newspapers, whose owners and editors wish to concentrate power in an official elected at-large. Candidates in at-large races cannot reach their constituents directly, so newspaper endorsement tends to be nearly all-important to them. Labor leaders and Liberal aldermen generally added that the newspapers were hostile to the Central Labor Union and favorable to the Republican party. Independent aldermen generally believed that the newspapers were favorable to "liberal intellectuals" rather than to Republicans. They noted that the newspapers had consistently supported Hubert Humphrey for mayor and then Senator, and Orville Freeman for Governor. The CLU, they said, preferred to keep its theory as simple as possible so as to avoid confusing its rank and file. When it found the newspapers allied to it in an election campaign, it took the position that the candidate was so outstanding that even the newspapers, despite their Republican bias, could not oppose him.

It should be noted that Minneapolis had two newspapers, the *Star* and the *Tribune*. Both were part of the Cowles chain and followed virtually identical editorial policies. They considered themselves independent (with a small "i") politically. Their local political orientation was toward "good government," which meant support for a strong mayor system, a city council elected at-large, and vigorous planning and urban renewal programs. Their primary bogey was the ward orientation of Minneapolis politics. In national politics, they were moderately conservative on economic issues and extremely liberal on international, civil liberties, and civil rights issues. Their favorite candidates appeared to be blue-ribbon liberal Republicans, but they generally preferred liberal Democrats to conservative Republicans. The characterizations in this paragraph are of course no more than the author's impressions, and they are offered as background only.

general planning goals. The city's politicians received many communications from their constituents, but nearly all were complaints of a highly specific nature, referring to unrepaired streets, dangerous intersections, inadequate garbage collection, and so on. Most of them inclined to doubt that their constituents desired major policy innovations; and many of them appeared to worry more about inadvertently committing acts that might alienate constituents than about positive goals.[7] They knew that incumbents rarely lost elections in Minneapolis as a result of doing too little; the few who lost were those who acted too much. For example, in recent years the councilman who proposed an open-occupancy ordinance, one who championed public housing and urban renewal, and several councilmen who acted favorably on labor union recommendations had all been defeated. Virtually all the city's councilmen made their living in politics; they simply could not afford to lose elections. An occasional mayor thought of his office as a stepping stone to something better, but while in office he had virtually no power to act positively.[8] The City Council usually deferred action on any issue until the private parties most concerned reached agreement, rendering council ratification uncontroversial. When some action could not be postponed, the City Council generally appointed committees of prominent men to formulate "nonpartisan" solutions.[9] For example, the council in 1953 had created the Capital Long Range Improvements Committee (CLIC), whose annual task was to recommend capital improvement priorities and city borrowing levels. Several leading

[7] On reading this, one leading councilman commented: "We do get specific complaints, but this is not the key to understanding the Council. We *have* shown that we can conceive and carry out plans. Consider, for example, the city's marvelous park system and its capital budgeting system. Let me add that while some councilmen may have the strong bias against innovation that you suggest, I can't afford to have that attitude in my ward."

[8] He did have his veto power, of course, in addition to administrative control of the Police Department and access to the news media.

[9] On reading this, a leading councilman commented that *all* American legislative bodies tried to avoid making controversial decisions. He noted that the Minneapolis City Council sometimes pressed groups engaged in controversy to resolve their differences, employing the *threat* of action to good advantage. He added that most mayors and governors employed blue-ribbon citizens' committees far more than did the City Council.

councilmen took part in the committee's work, but the council as a whole never modified its recommendations significantly.[10]

In view of this situation, Minneapolis planners judged that the city's politicians were unlikely to take the lead in shaping community planning goals, and that recommended planning goals would be ignored unless consensus regarding them evolved in the community. The problem was how to discover such a consensus or bring it into being.

St. Paul's planners had faced a similar problem as they developed their *Land Use Plan*.[11] They had considered two general methods of discovering community goals: public opinion polling and consultation with organized groups. They had rejected both. The primary arguments that they had advanced against polling were—and the Minneapolis planners agreed—the following: (1) the general public was unable to pass thoughtful, informed judgment on its own likely reactions to future states of affairs; (2) members of the public who answered polltakers tended to ignore their own prior approval if they later disliked proposals in execution; and (3) the essence of successful democracy was not the mere recording of answers to certified unbiased questions, but the willingness of representative leaders to judge the public interest, act boldly to achieve it, and assume personal responsibility for results.

Minneapolis and St. Paul planners differed, however, on the value of consultation. St. Paul's planners had maintained that they knew very well what programs of action would benefit the entire

[10] The one man staff of CLIC was W. Glen Wallace, who had served as chairman of the City Council Ways and Means Committee until his voluntary retirement from elective office in 1955. He had joined with Frank Moulton, the ranking minority member of the Ways and Means Committee, in persuading the Council to establish CLIC in 1953. Wallace and Moulton each considered the other the closest associate he had ever had on the Council, despite their different party affiliations. Both shared the conservative fiscal views which had been predominant in Minneapolis government since the early 1940's. They referred frequently to the city's Triple A municipal bond rating and its net debt of under 4 per cent of assessed valuation—a reduction from 9 per cent in 1942. (Assessed valuation was estimated to be about one-third of fair market value on a city-wide basis.) Many observers believed that Wallace and Moulton still dominated CLIC. They themselves tended to emphasize that CLIC had twenty-one members, some of them very strong-minded people.

[11] See above, Chap. II.

community, and that the groups with whom they could carry on continuing discussions had no claim to represent the community. Any consultation with them would consume great quantities of time and would probably result eventually in the planners having to "sell out" to partial views of the public interest. It was up to politicians, not civil servants, they reasoned, to compromise plans if the narrow demands of special interest groups had for political reasons to be satisfied. This is not to say, of course, that the St. Paul planners made no compromises in practice; it is only to set forth the reasons they gave for not consulting systematically with private interest groups and individuals.

Minneapolis Planning Director Lawrence Irvin and Assistant Director for Advanced Planning Rodney Engelen disagreed with these views. They did not see consultation as a serious threat to important values. The City Council requirement that consensus among the interested groups be achieved before it would authorize action insured that planners could hardly become dictators. Nor would planners administer their own proposals, so they had few means of paying political debts in the dark labyrinths of executive discretion. The political process already expressed the will of organized interest groups, for the most part, rather than that of the entire public. Planners were not the designers of the political process, and no one expected them to work to change it. Supporters of planning did hope, however, that planners might make the system work better. If they could not achieve planning goals at all except by working with allies, then they would work with allies. No other strategy made sense to them. Their allies would differ, of course, from one proposal to the next, but planners could never afford to choose allies casually. If they were to accomplish anything, they had always to think strategically. In practice this meant that in every proposal they should aim at a specific audience of potential allies. Each audience should be chosen largely for its capacity to bring proposals to fruition, without antagonizing too many other potential audiences.

To Irvin and Engelen, the question of alliance formation was not primarily one of "power." Planners, they believed, could not hope to bully anyone; at best, they might open the minds of their allies to new ways of doing things, to new conceptions of self-interest. Beyond the realm of ideas, a planning director could offer or withhold from these allies only the support of his agency, which had no legal power of its own and whose political capital consisted of little more than its reputation for devotion to the public good. Given this foundation, the planners thought it far more likely that their quest for modest achievement would fail than that they would become threats to important values. Irvin articulated the danger he faced: "You make a lot of enemies when you stir up the Indians, particularly if before your arrival everyone has come to identify quiescence with normality." He did not see, however, how his and Engelen's efforts could harm the city. They would deal with interest groups, but only to make the political process work more effectively for the public interest. In return for permitting the groups to modify the planners' ideas and priorities, they would try to educate the groups. They would serve the public interest as they saw it, more boldly and yet with more political sophistication than most planners had in the past.

There seemed little doubt, however, that the planners could provide crucial political support on occasion to segments of the community that would otherwise have failed. The fact that no articulate groups opposed a certain proposal before the City Council could not assure that the proposal was in the public interest. Conceivably, it might even harm the public interest in the long run just by strengthening the planners' allies in relation to other groups. For these reasons, Irvin and Engelen assumed that they were obligated to temper their alliance commitments in several ways. First, they intended never to become the "prisoners" of any single set of interests, but here they faced the problem of defining a "set"; organized groups might well be defined as a set vis-à-vis the unorganized or potentially organized groups. Second, they felt obligated to make their knowledge available to all interested citizens impartially. Third, they thought that, if asked by responsible officials, they should show how their techniques might serve other goals than those they personally favored. Finally, they considered themselves duty bound to list the significant disadvantages of their proposals for all to see, to mention alternatives, to acknowledge indecision, to act no more confidently concerning their conclusions than their convictions warranted, and to maintain a high degree of objectivity in an effort to get decisions on goals from community leaders.[12]

Irvin and Engelen believed that consultation could serve two objectives: that of enlightening them about the thoughts of those for whom they were planning, and that of winning support. They considered that these two objectives were related, that mutual understanding would tend to produce proposals that could win broad political support. At the same time, they did not conceive consultation as a way of educating themselves about what was "objectively" good for the city. Personally, they believed that most cities would do well to give planners wide leeway to apply most of the reputable planning principles and techniques. To be sure, they did recognize discussion and consent as important democratic values. As they perceived it, however, their serious practical problem was to determine which of the reputable techniques could be made politically palatable, and how. They recalled that even the St. Paul planners had taken care not to antagonize powerful interests; what was this, after all, but dealing with interest groups politically? The problem was that in dealing with them only implicitly, the St. Paul planners had neither educated nor won support.

This case study deals primarily with the ways in which Minneapolis planners tried to combine their search for facts, goals, and community support throughout the development of a major plan, and the difficulties that arose to complicate their task.

Minneapolis Seeks Planners and a Plan

In Minneapolis, as in many other cities, central business district property values reached speculative peaks in the 1920's to which they never returned later. Only after World War II, however, did many people begin to realize that downtown growth in periods of national prosperity was not inevitable. During the 1930's central area depression had seemed no more than part of a disaster that pervaded the entire country. After 1940, prosperity came with a rush, and for a few years downtown businessmen grew rich along with businessmen in other locations. After the first postwar decade (1945–1955), however, central area business activity lagged de-

[12] See Chap. VII for a discussion of the pressures on planners to neglect these obligations.

spite general prosperity. The level of dollar sales rose barely fast enough to keep up with inflation, while the amount of new construction was very limited. Minneapolis businessmen read that similar problems plagued downtowns throughout the country.

Toward the end of this period several events occurred which dramatized the apparent decline of the downtown area. First, General Mills, one of the largest national companies with central headquarters in Minneapolis, announced that it would build its new home office building beyond the city limits. Later, the Prudential Insurance Company and the American Hardware Mutual Insurance Company decided to erect new office buildings outside of the downtown area, although within the city. The officers of all three companies mentioned traffic congestion and the difficulty of assembling land as their most important reasons for abandoning the downtown area. Some observers doubted subsequently that these reasons had really been decisive, and suggested that the companies may have been responding to a fad of decentralization. Nevertheless, their decisions jolted many executives whose companies had substantial downtown investments.[13]

In 1955 Southdale, a mammoth, fully enclosed shopping center in the suburb of Edina, opened. The Twin Cities metropolitan area had never seen anything like it— nor had more than a very few other metropolitan areas. It combined free parking, protection from inclement weather, and exciting modern design with a variety of goods and services rivaling that of downtown Minneapolis itself. Southdale's two department stores, Dayton's and Donaldson's, were branches of the two largest stores in downtown Minneapolis, so their competition with downtown for business seemed unlikely to become cutthroat. The very fact that Dayton's and Donaldson's had found it necessary to enter into vigorous competition with themselves in the first place, however, dramatized the force of the suburban surge.

The passage of the Federal Aid Highway Act in 1956 aroused downtown businessmen still more than either of the above-mentioned developments. They hoped that the enormous

[13] The Prudential and American Hardware Mutual decisions were especially well publicized because both companies managed to purchase beautiful sites on park property from the city for their new buildings.

expenditure of the freeway program might provide a counterforce in favor of downtown. At first, they assumed that the freeway had been designed to provide maximal relief for downtown traffic congestion. Traffic congestion was, after all, often cited by defenders of the freeway program as the most serious threat to American central business districts. On inquiry, however, some businessmen reluctantly came to the conclusion that no one *knew* what effect the freeways would have on central business district traffic in Minneapolis. What, they asked, had city planners been doing all these years? One observer later described the situation as follows:

Previously, Minneapolis businessmen had only the vaguest idea of what city planning was. But they assumed that, whatever it was, someone was doing it. Now they realized that they had assumed far too much: the state Highway Department was going to spend a hundred million dollars or more within the city, and no one had bothered to evaluate the Department's plans from the point of view of local interests.

Minneapolis had had a planning commission since 1919. During the 1920's it had occupied a rather prominent place in city government. But the depression, the withdrawal of businessmen from civic activity after Minneapolis' famous strike of 1933–1934, and a change of planning directors brought an end to the period of prominence. Herman Olson, the planning engineer after 1929, did not believe in consultation or compromise; everyone agreed that he was a competent technician, but during the several decades of his tenure he alienated virtually every participant in the city's governmental system. By the postwar period, he had only one other professional planner under him. He never lost heart, however; he continued to issue reports and proposals right up to his "encouraged" retirement in 1955.

The first halting steps toward a revival of planning were taken after passage of the Federal Housing Act of 1949, with its Title I creating a new program of federally aided urban redevelopment. Several representatives of large downtown corporations, along with a few respected individuals who had long made civic activity their hobby, organized with the immediate objective of securing federal aid to help "clean up" the city's lower loop. The lower loop was a section between the central business district and the Mississippi River that had been the original downtown area of Minneapolis. The city's more substantial businessmen had started to abandon it before the turn of the century, and despite sporadic efforts to spur revival by constructing new buildings in the area,[14] it had gradually become known as the skid row of the Upper Midwest, a neighborhood of saloons, pawn shops, secondhand clothing stores, flophouses, and similar establishments.[15] Herman Olson, the editors of the local newspapers, and committees of local businessmen had occasionally suggested face-lifting jobs for the lower loop, but none of the proposals had appeared even remotely possible to achieve so long as the only potential sources of funds had been local.

Immediately after 1949, many downtown businessmen considered the concept of redevelopment "socialistic," and many local politicians considered the idea too unprecedented and controversial to touch. Thus, the lower loop redevelopment project did not get under way for half a dozen years.[16] The campaigns and battles that eventually produced it, however, taught a core of downtown businessmen the ways of local politics. Those most active in this period were generally associated with companies that owned prop-

[14] During the 1920's a syndicate of businessmen had built what is still the citys third largest hotel, the Nicollet. It later went through two receiverships. The federal government had erected post office buildings in 1914 and 1935. Before consenting to build in the latter year, federal officials had demanded that a block of brothels across the way be demolished and the land be used to create a small park.

[15] The general view of the inhabitants of the lower loop was that they were drunks and deadbeats. When redevelopment of the area reached an advanced stage, however, a survey was made to guide those responsible for relocation services. The survey showed that the lower loop was not primarily a skid row for transients after all. It was rather a neighborhood of retired single old men, most of them very poor but quite sober. The neighborhood had never constituted a significant crime problem.

[16] Even so, it did get under way several years before the arrival of Irvin and Engelen on the Minneapolis scene. As in nearly all other cities, the Housing and Redevelopment Authority was completely separate from the Planning Commission. This fact was to cause some frustration to Irvin and Engelen when they turned to downtown planning in 1958. Efforts by Engelen, in particular, to induce some rethinking of certain aspects of the physical layout of the project were rebuffed and caused some resentment. One alderman later declared that he had believed that Engelen was trying to undo commitments already made and placed beyond the realm of legitimate controversy.

erty within or adjoining the blighted area: most notably, the Nicollet Hotel, the Midland Bank, Powers department store, and (before it moved out) General Mills. Gradually, as more and more central area investors became aware of suburban competition, the active leadership base of the downtown civic community widened substantially. By the late 1950's the lower loop project itself was providing a spur in this direction, by challenging the existing core of the downtown area to brighten its image. It should be emphasized, however, that the expanding group of business civic leaders was not composed of corporation presidents. By all accounts, the major independent decision-makers of Minneapolis business and commerce were not yet sufficiently concerned to participate in civic affairs themselves. Most were, however, and this was a new development, willing to see a vice-president assigned to participate on company time and as company representative.

In August 1955 a group of these business civic leaders, representing nearly all the major companies of downtown Minneapolis, created the Downtown Council. They reasoned that the Chamber of Commerce, in which most of them were also active,[17] drew its membership from all over the metropolitan area. It had never represented downtown interests vigorously and probably never could. A separate organization was needed. The chamber itself, the Minneapolis Retailers Association, the Minneapolis Association of Building Owners and Managers, and the Citizens League of Minneapolis and Hennepin County (a leading good government organization, financed largely by business contributions) all agreed to give way to the newly created Downtown Council in the impending campaign for an ambitious rejuvenation of the downtown area.

The Downtown Council concentrated first on the lower loop project. Its leaders reputedly helped to arrange the replacement of A. C. Godward, the elderly Housing Authority director,[18] by a

[17] Gerald Moore, for example, who gave up his own position in business to become full-time director of the Downtown Council, had been president of the Chamber from 1952 to 1954.

[18] In the late 1920's Godward had combined the positions of planning engineer (the city's first), traffic engineer, engineer for the board of estimate, and financial consultant to the City Council. On his resignation in 1928, his jobs had been divided. During his tenure, however, he had authored the so-called Godward Plan for the city. Part of it had proposed that a cultural

"bright young man" who had directed St. Paul's Housing Authority. Under his direction, and with Downtown Council support, the project was to grow in concept until it embraced sixty-eight acres and entailed clearance of the entire "skid row" area. Within a short while, Downtown Council leaders also began to ask what effects the freeways would have on downtown Minneapolis. In 1956 they helped induce the Minneapolis City Council to retain George Barton and Associates, a consulting firm, to evaluate the Highway Department's proposed freeway-route locations and designs.[19]

Barton emphasized at the start that he had no way of knowing community goals, and therefore could not compare the freeways to other possible means of dealing with the transportation problems of Minneapolis. All he could do was evaluate the route locations and designs in terms of highway engineering objectives. He did, however, retain Frederick T. Aschman, a city planning consultant, to advise him on land-use relationships. In his report,[20] which appeared early the following year, he stated that ideally the freeways should connect directly with "super parking terminals" penetrating to within 600 or 800 feet of all downtown destinations. If the city had plans to build such terminals, the freeway ring around downtown should be moved closer to its center. On the other hand, if the city had no such plans, the freeways had to be far enough from downtown so that vehicles exiting from them could disperse to enter downtown on many streets. If all the traffic from any freeway interchange were to enter the downtown area on

---

center, mall, and public services area be created in the lower loop. The Godward Plan had stirred a good deal of opposition from groups likely to be adversely affected by it, and its supporters had abandoned it with the onset of the Great Depression.

[19] By the time the author did his interviewing, some disagreement existed as to how Barton had come to be retained. Hugo Erickson, who had been city engineer in 1956, recalled that he had been the man primarily responsible. He said that the City Council had been highly receptive because it had wished to forestall the possibility of serious controversy over the freeway route locations. Downtown Council leaders recalled, on the other hand, that they had very actively promoted the hiring of Barton. They thought that their efforts had probably been decisive.

[20] *The Freeways in Minneapolis,* an appraisal prepared for the City Council and the City Planning Commission by George Barton and Associates, of Evanston, Illinois, January 1957.

one street, the congestion would be intolerable. Barton believed that the freeways would benefit the city on balance (although he did not know its goals), but only if the city performed two great tasks: (1) formulated plans for harmonizing freeway development with the city's own street system and with other land uses; and (2) financed the collateral highway improvements, outside the city limits as well as within them, that would be needed over the next twenty years. The freeways represented a decision that public policy would henceforth accommodate the automobile. As the public responded to this decision, an increasing number of freeway routes would have to be built, more city streets between the freeway interchanges and common destinations would have to be improved, and more parking facilities would have to be provided.

Barton and Aschman convinced the Downtown Council and City Engineer Hugo Erickson that the task of harmonizing freeway development with economic needs was one for city planners. The council and Erickson then induced the City Council to appropriate funds for the Planning Commission to hire Aschman as a consultant on the general state of city planning in Minneapolis. He was to recommend ways of developing an adequate planning staff. Aschman produced a report in May 1957.[21] He noted that the City Planning Department had a budget barely adequate to support its work of zoning administration and map maintenance duties—$56,000 in 1956. At the moment, the Department did not even have a director; the office had been vacant for two years. Aschman believed that the main challenges to a new planning director would require that he possess great skill in coordination and conciliation as well as in technical planning. He therefore stressed the importance of hiring a planning director who could win the confidence of the City Council, the Planning Commission, city department heads, and the public. He also emphasized the need to increase the planning budget to a recommended $258,000.

Subsequently, Aschman served on a committee of civic leaders which, after advertising nationally for applications, selected the new planning director. The committee's choice was Lawrence

21 *The Function and Organization of City Planning in Minneapolis,* a Report to the Minneapolis City Planning Commission, May 1957.

Irvin, who reportedly had done excellent work as director of the Slum Clearance and Rehabilitation Commission in Columbus, Ohio. Previous to that he had served as Assistant Director of the Columbus Metropolitan Housing Authority. Irvin arrived for active duty on March 1, 1958. As of that date, he had three professional city planners under him and a first-year budget three times greater than the last budgets of the Herman Olson regime. Furthermore, since the Downtown Council had induced several prominent businessmen to accept membership on the Planning Commission, he started with a more weighty commission than Olson had ever enjoyed. The significance of the commission's composition was that it symbolized an expectation that city planning in Minneapolis would become important enough to warrant the close attention of important men. Among those who became members of the Planning Commission during this period were Arnett Leslie, retired president of the Leslie Paper Company and a member of the Minneapolis School Board (which he represented officially on the commission); Clifford Anderson, president of the Crown Iron Works Company; and Robert Boblett, a prominent realtor. Leslie became the commission's president.[22]

In sum, it may be said that Planning Director Irvin found a ready-made constituency waiting for him, and no outspoken enemies. He realized, however, that a good deal of resentment and antagonism remained in the city toward planning generally— largely because of Herman Olson's legacy of controversy and inept public relations.

Developing a Research Program

Although Irvin had virtually no staff when he assumed his duties as planning director in March 1958, he knew that the supporters of planning in Minneapolis might lose interest if he took too long to produce concrete proposals. Considering who had taken the initiative in reviving the Planning Commission and bringing him to Minneapolis, there seemed little doubt that he should first concentrate on planning for the downtown area.[23]

[22] In 1961 Leslie resigned from both the School Board and the Planning Commission to run successfully for the City Council from his ward.

[23] He did not intend to confine himself to downtown planning, however. In the event, within six months of his arrival studies were initiated preparatory

Furthermore, the downtown "problems" of which people were acutely aware were business problems.

As Irvin understood the situation, his most immediate task was to launch a study of the downtown economy. As he had a large budget and no staff, the obvious answer was to hire consultants. They could study while he spent his time assembling a staff. The Downtown Council was so anxious for work to begin that it offered $30,000 of its own funds to help finance consultant studies. On Irvin's recommendation, the Planning Commission eagerly accepted. It should be noted that even aside from the necessities of the moment, Irvin approved of the use of consultants by planning agencies. The planning staff itself, he believed, should consist of generalists; their expertness should be in drawing general conclusions from the work of many specialists. The more time planners were compelled to spend mastering the techniques of data collection, the less they would have for the intricacies of planning theory; yet, an understanding of planning was, above all, what their function required. It was difficult enough to master economic, aesthetic, and traffic control theory; urban geography; and other related fields. The time could not be spared to learn how to design market analyses and origin-destination surveys.

With the aid of planning consultant Aschman, Irvin and the Downtown Council developed a research program. They agreed that the predictions they most needed, if they were to plan intelligently, were of future market demand for downtown land and of future traffic demand on downtown street space. In addition, they hoped to improve their understanding of the reasons why businessmen sought downtown locations, and the ways in which cities could, without unduly increasing the exercise of public power, enhance the economic advantages of downtown locations. From the start, then, the focus of the planning effort was economic.[24]

To direct the traffic studies the Planning Commission hired the

---

to a new city-wide zoning ordinance, a new city-wide industrial land-use plan, and three specific neighborhood plans. Nonetheless, central area planning remained the planning staff's highest priority project during at least Irvin's first two years in Minneapolis.

[24] The remainder of this section, which runs to page 212, outlines the Central Area research design. Readers who skip it will have no difficulty following the rest of the narrative.

consulting firm of George Barton and Associates, which, it will be remembered, had been retained by the City Council in 1956 to evaluate the Highway Department's proposed freeway-route locations and designs, and which had originally recommended Aschman to the city. To conduct the market analysis, it employed the Real Estate Research Corporation (RERC) of Chicago, a firm that Irvin had found reliable and respected in Columbus. He also realized that RERC president Richard L. Nelson's father had been one of the early executive secretaries of the Minneapolis Real Estate Board, and that the local image of Nelson's firm was very favorable. Barton and Aschman had frequently associated with RERC in other cities, and Aschman and Nelson had co-authored a book.[25] All agreed that RERC should be retained.

Barton's 1957 freeway study had covered the entire city of Minneapolis. In his section on the freeway ring around downtown, he had concluded that he could not evaluate the Highway Department's design unless the city decided how it wanted to handle traffic exiting from the freeway, and how it proposed to use the land along each potential right-of-way. He had pointed out that there were definite advantages to having the freeway ring as close to the central core of activity as possible. On the other hand, impossible congestion would result if traffic poured from the freeway onto the congested streets near the core. Therefore, any proposal to move the freeway ring closer to the core would depend on local plans for major street and parking improvements near the interchanges. In his new studies he hoped to explore in greater detail the existing characteristics of downtown traffic movement.

For purposes of analysis, the City Planning Commission, aiming at the central business district and its environs, defined the central Minneapolis area as bounded by the freeway (in the Highway Department's proposed design) on three sides and by the Mississippi River on the fourth (see map, page 213). About two-fifths of this total area was devoted to industrial uses, one-fifth to residential and institutional uses, and two-fifths to commercial uses.

[25] Frederick T. Aschman and Richard L. Nelson, *Real Estate and City Planning* (Englewood Cliffs, N.J.: Prentice-Hall, 1957). In their preface the authors acknowledged specialized assistance from four individuals: one was Barton; a second, who specialized in zoning, was hired by the Minneapolis Planning Commission in 1958 to prepare a draft of a new zoning ordinance.

"Commercial" included office, financial, retail, entertainment, and hotel uses, along with the service establishments that commonly located close to them. The bulk of the downtown tax base, composed mostly of the largest downtown corporations which also provided the major support for planning, was concentrated in the area of commercial use. Irvin realized, of course, that commercial uses were generally thought of as the "characteristic" downtown uses, the ones that should be kept healthy if the downtown area was to retain its economic and cultural importance. Consequently, he agreed with the consultants that their analysis should focus primarily, though not exclusively, on the needs of central Minneapolis commercial establishments.

RERC confined its study to the four census tracts [26] within central Minneapolis containing the greatest concentration of commercial uses. All the major retail establishments, office buildings, and hotels were well within this area, which included on its fringes many lesser uses. The entire area, totaling 140 city blocks, was termed the "Central Commercial District" (CCD).

The Minnesota Highway Department already possessed detailed estimates of expected traffic on the freeways, so Barton was able to focus his forecasting efforts solely on city-street traffic. In September 1958 he directed a count of vehicular and pedestrian traffic volume on each approach to the central commercial district between 7 A.M. and 7 P.M. on a "typical" weekday.[27] The division of labor was, Irvin later recalled, in accord with his conception of broad participation in the planning process. Barton prescribed

---

[26] Census tracts were chosen as the unit of study to permit maximum comparability of the market analysis data with the U.S. census data.

[27] The day was a Wednesday—cool, clear, and free of major events. See *Central Minneapolis Cordon Count: 1958* (City of Minneapolis Planning Commission, Central Minneapolis Series Number One, January 1959).

The state Highway Department had traffic count data that had been collected monthly throughout a recent year on one of the approaches to downtown Minneapolis. These data were used to estimate seasonal variations for all of downtown. The City Engineer's Office maintained an automatic traffic-counting machine on another approach in August and September 1958, to provide data for estimating variations according to the day of the week. See *Central Minneapolis Master Station Count: 1958* (City of Minneapolis Planning Commission, Central Minneapolis Series Number Seven, July 1959).

the methods; the City Engineer's Office provided some counters and supervised the counting; private companies and organizations contributed most of the counter time—580 man hours. The firms that contributed were, as might have been expected, those with the largest investments in the downtown area. The major department stores, banks, public utilities, and property-owning syndicates were conspicuous. The Downtown Council organized and publicized the venture.[28]

Among other things, the cordon count revealed that 60 per cent of the people who entered the central commercial district during the peak hour came by automobile; 40 per cent entered by bus. Yet 90 per cent of the vehicles entering the CCD in the same hour were private automobiles and less than 2 per cent were buses. The balance were trucks and taxis.

In August and September 1958 the second part of the research program was undertaken. Pedestrian counts were made on typical weekdays at 68 mid-block stations in the core area.[29] The planners considered these data important because pedestrian volumes affected both the value of retail locations and the freedom with which streets could be widened to move traffic more quickly. It could be disastrous to widen streets—thereby narrowing sidewalks —if sidewalk pedestrian traffic was already congested. Moreover, downtown merchants and city planners believed that it was essential for central area walking to be made pleasant. Plans to increase the joys of walking were difficult to make wisely unless it was known where pedestrian traffic was congested.

Finally, Barton designed and the City Engineer's Office executed a parking survey of the central commercial district. The study consisted of four parts:

(1) Inventory of curb use in the central retail and office core—

28 It may be noted that, as of 1964, annual cordon counts were still being made. The arrangement, as it had become routinized, was as follows. Downtown corporations employed students to do the actual counting. The City Engineer's Office instructed the counters, supervised the counting, and analyzed and published the data.

29 As with the cordon count, the survey was designed by Barton and executed by the City Engineer's Office. The data were published as: *Pedestrian Count: 1958, Central Commercial Area* (City of Minneapolis Planning Commission, Central Minneapolis Planning Series Number Six, May 1959).

equivalent to all four sides of ten blocks. The type of vehicle, its length of stay, and the destination of its passenger or freight were recorded.

(2) Inventory of truck and service stops at curbs and in alleys within the core. The trucks were classified into thirteen types, according to their cargo.

(3) Off-street parking survey. A questionnaire dealing with trip purposes was administered to the drivers of all cars parked in a generous sample of the central commercial district's parking lots and ramps during the half-hour of maximum accumulation.

(4) Within the area of the cordon count survey, all automobiles parked at all curbs, in all off-street facilities, and in all alleys were counted during the half-hour of maximum accumulation.[30]

While Barton directed and the City Engineer's Office executed the four studies described above, RERC, financed by the Downtown Council, directed the city planning staff in collecting data for the CCD market analysis. Some RERC personnel had specialized in central area market analyses since 1946; they had more or less standardized their data needs, and were able to provide the planning staff with a veritable host of questionnaires to administer.

The collection of market analysis data was conducted in three phases. The first consisted of interviews with businessmen of the central commercial district. To assure their cooperation, meetings were held early in 1958 to explain the survey's purpose and to promise that certain data would be kept confidential. Between May and November 1958, planning staff members administered a four-part questionnaire provided by RERC. Parts I and II were for the owners and managers of buildings. Key questions dealt with the type, age, and use of each structure; parking facilities; typical numbers of daily visitors; ceiling heights; front setbacks; toilet facilities; and air conditioning. Parts III and IV were for all downtown businessmen, and dealt with the characteristics of individual establishments. An establishment was defined as "each separate commercial or industrial unit doing business." A restaurant, a newsstand, a law firm, and a department store each counted

[30] This material was presented in *Parking Survey: 1958, Central Commercial Area* (City of Minneapolis Planning Commission, Central Minneapolis Planning Series Number Four, April 1959).

as one establishment. The key data sought by Part III were each establishment's U.S. Census Standard Industrial Classification, its net usable floor space, its net sales floor space if a retail establishment, its number of employees, and its service area. Part IV consisted of specialized questions for the owners of specific types of establishment. There were separate sheets for the owners of office-buildings, theaters, hotels, warehouses, and parking lots.[31]

The second phase of data collection in the market analysis was designed to ascertain shopper motivation. Barton's pedestrian counts had established the numbers of pedestrians crossing mid-block points in the major retail and office core. RERC now designed a sample interview survey to learn their characteristics; planning staff personnel conducted the interviews. Interviewees were asked, among other things, their reason for being downtown, their mode of transportation to and from downtown, and their shopping plans, if any, for the day. The outlines of downtown shopper motivation had of course been studied in many cities previously. RERC's president had recently published a book in which he had discussed at length the findings of these studies.[32] The pedestrian interviews were intended to shed light on the extent to which Minneapolis fit the general theory.

Phase three aimed at determining the market for central area housing. A sample of 6,235 downtown employees completed a twenty-three-question form prepared by RERC. Key questions dealt with the location and characteristics of their present housing, the characteristics of other members of their households, their means of getting to work, their shopping habits, and their interest in living close to downtown if good housing at moderate prices was available.

The housing market study was financed separately from the rest of the market analysis, but it too provided an occasion for cooperation between the city's planning agencies and private business organizations. The Minneapolis Housing and Redevelopment Authority and the City Planning Commission collaborated in paying

---

[31] The data collected in answer to all four sets of questions were published as *Land and Space Use Survey, Central Commercial Area* (City of Minneapolis Planning Commission, Central Minneapolis Series Number Five, May 1959).

[32] Richard L. Nelson, *The Selection of Retail Locations* (New York: F. W. Dodge Corporation, 1958).

RERC's fee, on a two-thirds/one-third basis. The Downtown Council provided free office space to the consultant's staff during the survey, and the Minneapolis Retailers' Association secured the cooperation of downtown employers in distributing the employee questionnaire. This was all possible, of course, because the consultant had convinced the leading downtown retailers that their future economic health depended in significant part on the development of middle and upper income housing close to downtown.

The planning staff, without consultant aid, conducted one final inventory, of industrial land use, preparatory to writing the *Central Minneapolis Plan*. While far less detailed than the CCD studies, this survey at least enabled the planning staff to claim that in planning for downtown commerce and housing it was not totally ignorant of the problems of industry.

Upon completion of the entire research program, RERC announced that more economically relevant information was now known about central Minneapolis than about any other major downtown area in the United States.

The Research Findings [33]

During 1958 and 1959 the Planning Commission brought out no analyses, but it published almost all of Barton's data and RERC's space-use survey data in five handsome booklets. RERC, on the other hand, published no raw data but brought out two limited-edition, analytical reports in the early summer of 1959, entitled respectively *Economic Development Study of Downtown Minneapolis* and *Central Area Housing Market Analysis*.[34] Only the brief summaries of each, which listed conclusions without even the elementary reasoning behind them, were made available in larger quantities. By a peculiar twist, therefore, the raw data were available to everyone; the analyses, predictions, and recommenda-

[33] The following section, which runs to page 224, summarizes RERC's substantive findings, forecasts, and recommendations. Readers whose interests are purely political may wish to skip it. They will be able to follow the rest of the case narrative without difficulty.

[34] The dates of publication were June and July respectively. Twenty-five copies of each were printed. Barton published nothing, but RERC made some use of his findings in its *Economic Development Study*.

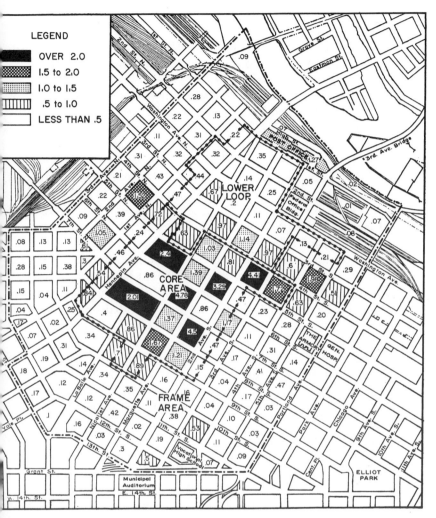

Map 3. Central Commercial District of Minneapolis, 1959, showing employment density by block (number of employees per one hundred square feet of land).

tions were available only to those interested enough to read them
in the offices of the few organizations and public agencies that had
copies.

RERC's *Economic Development Study* began with a historical
discussion. Central area problems had emerged similarly throughout the country, RERC wrote. Downtown areas originally grew
around the meeting places of main routes of travel and sources of
power. In Minneapolis the route was the Mississippi River; the
source of power was St. Anthony Falls, which at one time marked
the river's highest navigable point. Later, transportation routes
focused on downtown *because* it was the center of activity. The
person traveling from one outlying area to another generally had
to make streetcar connections downtown. Investors whose enterprises needed service areas of more than a few blocks radius, a
substantial labor pool, or high-quality transport service naturally
tended to locate downtown. Eventually, the central area's economic
leaders became the economic giants of the metropolitan area, and
their interest in preserving their investment became monumental.
In Minneapolis, as of 1958, this investment, though it involved
only 4 per cent of the city's land, still provided one-third of all
employment and tax revenue; a prima facie case surely existed
that the entire population had a stake in maintaining its value.

Until recently, downtown had been able to rely on necessity to
attract ever-increasing numbers of people. By the 1950's it could
no longer do so, and it was no longer as attractive to those with
free choice. There were many reasons for this change. The rise of
the automobile had eliminated the dependence of most people
on the route patterns of public transit. It had also created congestion on the approaches to downtown, and made shortages of
central area parking space important. Public transit vehicles, of
course, had not had to park downtown. Automobile transportation
had also produced urban sprawl, which in turn had made good
public transit service unprofitable. Many workers now preferred
driving to suburban plants, where they could park, to traveling
downtown. They had this alternative in large part because improvements in engineering technique over the past century had
made power for industry as cheap in outlying areas as downtown.
The telephone had made face-to-face contact less essential for
many businessmen. Shoppers had once come to the great center for

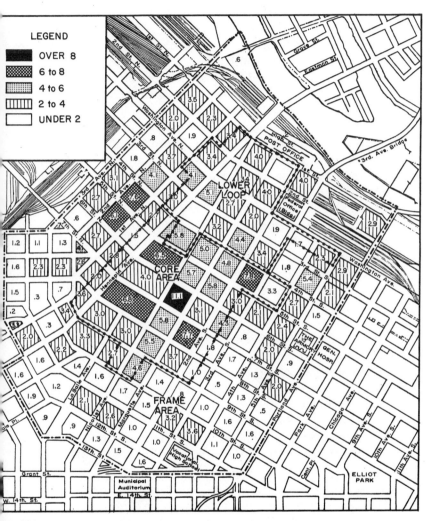

Map 4. Central Commercial District of Minneapolis, 1959, showing floor-area ratios by block (gross building area divided by total land area).

retail facilities to compare prices and quality; but the growth of standardized brand names and prices since the 1920's had drastically reduced the importance of this motive. Finally, central area land values had been so high, and land assembly so difficult, that many investors who had preferred downtown locations in theory had been led to choose outlying sites in practice.[35]

Central areas retained many sources of vigor, however. People liked to work, visit, and live near downtown because its concentration of activity excited them. Downtown employees, residents, and tourists provided an enormous core of customers; the unparalleled variety of enterprises that they could support attracted other people to the area for shopping and recreational purposes. Downtown retail establishments had lost business in recent years to outlying shopping centers, but there was no *necessity* for them to lose more; the inherent advantages of outlying commercial centers over the main center of the metropolitan area had already been exploited in full. By now the main center catered to its core customer groups mentioned above, plus people seeking unusual goods and services that the outlying centers with their smaller service areas could not provide. Conventioneers and tourists wanted to be in the vicinity of exciting places in which to shop, eat, sightsee, and attend cultural events. Many executives and professional people still needed the opportunity for close face-to-face contact, and in general the most convenient place to meet was the downtown area. Specialized services were most easily and quickly obtainable downtown. The number of workers who would still travel downtown at any given salary remained greater than the number who would travel to any other point; for those unable to commute by automobile, downtown remained the most accessible location outside their own neighborhoods, and many enjoyed working downtown because of

[35] A serious problem not mentioned in the report was that downtown property assessments had not in most cases been reduced as values had dropped after 1929. As of the early 1950's, assessments on a city-wide basis averaged about one-third of fair market value. Assessments of some core properties were over 100 per cent of fair market value. This was a serious deterrent to potential investors, particularly retailers—who had to consider the prospect of price competition with merchants located on outlying sites. By the early 1960's, it may be noted, this problem had abated somewhat due to a series of court decisions and subsequent revisions of policy by the City Assessor.

the other activities near at hand. Moreover, the cost of office space was not always higher downtown than in suburbs; it was surely higher per square foot, but employers were not required to provide parking space, eating facilities, landscaped surroundings, or the other frills of outlying locations. In sum, downtown remained very attractive to many people with a wide variety of purposes.

The greatest threats to downtown, RERC contended, were the difficulties that people had in gaining access to and circulating within the area. Clearly, no business complex could thrive if it were too hard or unpleasant to reach. The primary goal of any central area plan in the automobile age, consequently, had to be to facilitate "access." Since the ease of interchange between enterprises and types of activity was the primary source of downtown attractiveness, a second objective had to be to facilitate "circulation." The most efficient way to transport enormous numbers of people within such a small area was on foot; vehicles took up too much room and were too inflexible. Every effort, therefore, should be made to keep typical trip distances within downtown short—by encouraging entrepreneurs to expand vertically rather than horizontally and by controlling the physical arrangement of related enterprises—and to increase the attractiveness of pedestrian facilities.

Governments in this country, the RERC report went on, could not create strong downtowns by themselves. Most downtown enterprises were privately owned, and operated for profit. The "strength" of downtown, therefore, depended in the final analysis on private investment and consumer spending. The purpose of public action had to be to encourage these. No public plan for a central area could succeed unless businessmen participated by maintaining and improving the attractiveness of their facilities. If hotels lacked adequate convention space, conventioneers would be deterred, no matter how attractive the city. If prestige office space was unavailable, prestige firms with locational freedom would go elsewhere. If people with high incomes could not find attractive housing close to downtown, they would spend most of their money near where they did settle. Given American governmental forms and beliefs, certain economic forces at work against downtown could not be directly affected by public action. Other forces could be so affected. The goal of planning research should be to determine which forces could be countered and how best to counter them.

Government powers could not be increased, RERC assumed, and the tides of technological change could not be reversed. Investors could not be forced to put their money downtown if they considered outlying sites preferable. Zoning powers could not be used to prevent the availability—even within the city, let alone in the politically independent suburbs—of desirable outlying sites. Businessmen in outlying locations could not be prevented from competing with all their vigor against those of downtown. On the other hand, public officials and businessmen working together could do a great deal to improve the central area's competitive position. Travel to downtown could be made easier and more pleasant. The City Council could collaborate with federal authorities in securing a write-down in price on lands under the urban renewal program. Tourist, convention, and shopping facilities could be made more attractive and varied. Downtown businessmen could be reminded of advantages that they had come to take for granted.

Although RERC was employed to make land-use forecasts rather than to propose public policy recommendations, the firm endorsed the principles of land use and street functions set forth by the planning staff in their May 1959 publication, *Goals for Central Minneapolis* (see below), and made a number of specific proposals. The latter may be summarized briefly, as follows. The freeway would solve only part of the problem of "access" to Central Minneapolis; for it to be truly effective, drivers would have to be able to park within easy walking distance of their destinations, and to approach the parking facilities from the freeway via uncongested routes. Wherever possible, protection from weather extremes should be provided along the pedestrian routes from the parking terminals to common destinations. Within the central area, all activities should be arranged according to the amount of interchange desirable between them. As the ease of comparative shopping and combining visits to numerous kinds of stores on a single trip remained one of the important attractions of downtown, retail facilities particularly should be grouped. Only enterprises which concentrated great numbers of employees and other potential shoppers daily per acre of land should locate within walking distance of the major retail entertainment complex. The office complex was the most obvious candidate for this area, and certain types of office building should be grouped together within that complex.

RERC suggested three categories of office buildings: multiple occupancy, government, and special purpose. A special-purpose office building was defined as one in which the leading user occupied 85 per cent or more of the total floor area. One could not predict the needs of the tenants in multiple-occupancy buildings with any precision; it was safest to assume that most tenants who paid central area rents would require proximity to other office users. Many occupants of single-purpose buildings, however, could afford to locate several blocks away from the central office core in return for cheaper land. They and the city would benefit if they could obtain land at prices they could afford inside the central area, because the alternative was often a suburban location.

Minneapolis planners thought of the lower loop redevelopment area as the section most appropriate for special-purpose office construction. Its southern boundary was just two blocks from the central office core, and it adjoined the only large secondary core. The latter included City Hall, several federal government office buildings, the Grain Exchange, and the Telephone Company building. The blocks between the redevelopment area and the central core were suitable for future multiple-occupancy office construction.

Enterprises that concentrated few employees or visitors each day or that needed great volumes of truck delivery, it was reasoned, should be kept out of the central commercial district.

RERC had not had to study Central Minneapolis to explain this history or to recommend these policy objectives. The history, as RERC admitted, applied to downtowns throughout the country, and the policies were in the generally accepted public domain of planning thought. The ostensible purpose of the market analysis was to discover how much investment and consumer spending the city might attract by pursuing these policies with any given amount of vigor. Planners did not want to plan for either too much or too little growth; businessmen and politicians were likely not to care to commit great sums of money and effort to bring forth molehills.

The market analysis reports contained little on RERC's methods of estimating potential demand. Instead, they emphasized the enormous amounts of data about currently effective demand that had been collected. The omission was serious, but unavoidable; demand prediction was not a science. Every entrepreneur who considered investing in an enterprise had to consider whether his product was saleable, and RERC had served entrepreneurs in such situations for twenty-eight years. If a great deal of intuitive judgment was needed to move from the facts of current demand to estimates of future demand, RERC could at least claim that its personnel were experienced judges.

RERC president Nelson had discussed his organization's techniques for estimating demand in *The Selection of Retail Locations*.[36] There he had stated that RERC had no formulas, and counted this among its virtues. He explained that RERC had divided the broad question of how much demand could be expected into a large number of smaller questions. With experience, it had learned what data were most useful in answering each question. The large number of questions, he believed, increased the likelihood that unusual factors would be noticed. Some RERC analysts had become specialists at estimating economic demand, and were more expert than any amateur could be. RERC theorists hoped that errors made by those answering the many questions would tend to cancel out. They considered this outcome more probable statistically as the number of separate judgments was augmented.

Nelson emphasized that all predictions were unreliable. He urged entrepreneurs not to build for more than their conservatively estimated third- or fourth-year needs. If their volume rose faster than expected, the worst that could happen was that they would earn less than they might have. If they could not expand when the time was ripe, they might be better advised in any case to open a second store where a shrewd competitor might otherwise choose to locate. Nelson's position, in short, was that the only way to make money was to take risks and that consultants could only

[36] Chap. 13.

reduce risk, never eliminate it. (RERC did not write these disclaimers into its report on Central Minneapolis.)

RERC reported that retail sales space in Central Minneapolis was adequate and that no shortages were likely to develop in the foreseeable future. The former judgment was based on RERC's own estimates of the amount of space that each existing retail establishment *should have had* in order to do its current volume of business without overcrowding. These estimates, RERC claimed, were based on interviews with retailers in many cities about optimal space allocation. The prediction of future adequacy depended on the rough assumption that increases in efficiency would balance off projected increases in dollar sales. The sales increase projection depended in turn on a prediction of future employment levels. The employment prediction rested, in turn, on two other assumptions: (1) that the proportion of metropolitan area employment concentrated in Central Minneapolis would remain constant, and (2) that metropolitan area employment would continue to grow at its 1950–1957 rate. RERC noted that, in the present era, central area retail sales seldom increased at a greater rate than central area employment; other metropolitan area gains in buying power tended to benefit outlying shopping centers rather than downtown.

RERC estimated that no overall shortage of multiple-occupancy office space would exist upon completion of a large structure being erected as the report was written, noting that quite a few of the older office buildings already had high vacancy rates. At the same time, it judged that the need for *prestige* space in new buildings would increase slightly each year in the foreseeable future. Certain space users who might be attracted to the city could not settle for space in second-class buildings. RERC estimated that the city would be able to absorb about one large multiple-occupancy building—400,000 square feet of floor space—every five years. The market for new special-purpose office space, it believed, would be slightly larger if land near the core were available in large enough parcels and at moderate prices.

These estimates of the increase in demand for prestige space were based on a somewhat optimistic assumption: that no further decentralization—proportionately—would take place in the metropolitan area after the lower loop redevelopment area was cleared and became available for construction. Between 1947 and 1958 downtown office space had increased at a rate of 1 per cent a year, versus a rate of 100 per cent a year for the rest of Hennepin County. In terms of absolute growth, the outlying areas had done only twice as well as central Minneapolis—75,000 square feet added annually, versus 38,000 square feet.

RERC noted that in Minneapolis, as in most other large cities, no new hotels had been constructed since the 1920's.[37] The existing hotels faced a major handicap in their efforts to attract large conventions because, as a group, they had few meeting rooms large enough to handle more than 700 people. In addition, any city without a truly modern hotel had difficulty attracting conventions. The primary reasons for this were the following: (1) those who chose convention sites often thought that their own prestige required that they be quartered at such a hotel; (2) hotels built several decades ago were poorly equipped to handle commercial displays, which provided important revenues at many conventions; and (3) it was difficult to inspire local members of national organizations to urge that conventions be held in their home town if it had no prestige hotel. Despite these handicaps, Central Minneapolis hotels consistently maintained an average annual occupancy rate above the national average. RERC perceived an unmet demand for 1,300 to 1,500 new hotel rooms, and it expected demand to rise at a rate of 60 rooms per year to 1970. In addition, it believed that a new 600–1,000-room hotel with adequate meeting facilities for large conventions would generate so much new business that it could thrive without harming the older hotels or affecting the other unmet-demand estimates.

RERC's housing market estimates [38] rested on even less exposed reasoning than its other forecasts. On the basis of available construction cost figures, certain minimum rentals for apartments in new buildings were assumed: $95–$120 for efficiency apartments; $110–$150 for one-bedroom apartments, and so on, with luxury apartments running higher. It was also assumed that

[37] The Leamington Hotel, however, which was the city's second largest, had undergone conversion from a residential to a transient hotel in the mid-1950's at a cost of several million dollars. Its meeting-room facilities were currently the most extensive of any Minneapolis hotel.

[38] *Central Area Housing Market Analysis.*

households had to have certain minimum incomes before they could be considered in the market for new housing. The standards were the following: one- and two-person households, $5,000; three-person households, $6,000; four-person households, $7,500; households of five or more persons, $10,000. The consultant offered no justification for these figures, but did offer data on the basis of which close students of the Housing Market Analysis might evaluate its conclusions. The questionnaire distributed to downtown employees contained a series of questions dealing with their income and that of other members of their households. On the basis of the income standards, 49 per cent of the households studied qualified for new housing. One-fifth of the qualified householders said that they would be interested in central area apartments with pleasant surroundings and off-street parking space—if the price were right. RERC personnel guessed that about one-fourth of the qualified householders who said they were interested actually would move downtown if new housing at the assumed prices became available. The current effective demand from this source, on this assumption, was 1,818 households.[39]

From the other potential consumers of new downtown housing —corporations, University of Minnesota employees, retired people, widows—RERC came up with a current effective demand figure of 270 households, making a total current effective demand of 2,088 units. It said further that as prestige neighborhoods developed in the central area more and more people would want to live in them. The *Housing Market Analysis* predicted a doubling of effective demand, to 3,860 units, within four years, and another

[39] The figures were as follows:

All downtown employees	83,240
Survey sample size	6,235
All households	70,588
Qualified households	49 per cent of all households
Qualified interested households	10 per cent of all households
Current effective demand estimate	2.6 per cent of all households

According to the study, 578 apartment units had been constructed in central Minneapolis between 1945 and 1958. The vacancy rate in these buildings was currently about the same as for the city as a whole. RERC admitted that there was no current shortage, but said that demand could be spurred if good neighborhoods, rather than individual buildings or small groups of them, came into existence.

doubling to 7,815 units, by 1980 if a vigorous effort to bring such neighborhoods into being were made, RERC admitted that its estimates were based on rentals [that] are not directly related to current rental expenditures of the interested households." For example, two-thirds of the qualified interested households that currently rented paid less than $100 a month, the minimum price for an efficiency apartment in a new building. Less than 10 per cent of them currently occupied such small quarters. RERC's 1980 projection depended on an assumption that 50 per cent of the demand would be for apartments renting at $150 a month or more; only 6 per cent of the qualified, interested renter households studied currently paid that much.[40]

The Strategy of Presentation

RERC did caution that its forecasts were of potentials only. For these potentials to be realized, it noted, vigorous public action as well as private investment would be required in every case. RERC did not say, however, exactly how vigorous an effort would be needed to bring about each forecast result. Nor did it make clear the unreliability of the assumptions on which its estimates of potential depended. Businessmen and public officials were encouraged by these omissions to accept the estimates without analyzing the assumptions behind them or trying to define their significance. The forecasts were cited to this writer constantly in the course of his study, but no one, not even the planners, could answer questions about how the consultant had moved from data to prediction.

Even if the estimates of potential demand were based in large part on guesswork, however, their publication was unlikely to cause either political or economic trouble. The consultants were less likely to be subjected to hostile questioning than the city's

[40] It should be noted again that the total number of qualified interested renter households was nearly four times as great as the estimate of current effective demand. Moreover, it could be assumed that real incomes would rise substantially to 1980. On the other hand, RERC did not state that it expected the demand for new central area housing to come predominantly from the wealthier among the qualified interested households. It rather implied that it was impossible to forecast which households would move; it was only possible to make a rough forecast based on experience in other cities of the *proportion* of qualified interested households that would move under favorable conditions.

own planners would have been. If they were questioned, they could truthfully say that they sold experienced judgment, not mere technical skill. It sounded reasonable for consultants to argue that they would not, any more than other executives, be worth such high fees if their judgmental processes could be reduced to formulae. Planners could not make the same claims. They could not refer to personal studies of many other downtowns; they were not respected businessmen; and they did not command high fees. In any event, neither the Planning Commission nor the Housing Authority had any thought of trying to fill the entire projected demand at once. They were more interested in the idea that demand could be spurred by public action than in precise estimates of its potential size. They hoped only to win public support for proceeding gradually on the basis of cautious estimates of current demand.

The consultants' contribution, in short, was not to urge a specific level of public activity in any field, but rather to popularize within the governmental and business communities certain economic ideas that would probably have met far greater resistance coming from planners. Most of these ideas were familiar to planners all over the country, and some of them were put forward by St. Paul's planners at about the same time that the *Central Minneapolis Plan* was evolving.[41] But the consultants gave them a kind of legitimacy in Minneapolis that they had not enjoyed previously, and persuaded many downtown businessmen that some public regulation of private enterprise, together with comprehensive planning of public expenditures in the downtown area, could contribute materially to their own interests.

Minneapolis businessmen respected the consultants as highly successful businessmen like themselves. No one accused them of empire-building. Most people were impressed by their frequent references to other cities; the consultants made clear that these references were not to books but to their own files. The consultants did most of their business with private investors; no one doubted that they were devoted to the private enterprise system. No one identified them with local factions. RERC's frequent assurances that its point of view was strictly economic allayed suspicions of "do-goodism." The fact that the Downtown Council paid RERC's fee for the general market analysis, although not for the

41 For examples see above, Chap. II.

housing market analysis, probably assured skeptics in the business community that, in case RERC were manipulable by its employers, at least its employers were businessmen, not planners.

Furthermore, the consultants were expert in the arts of communication. Their reports were edited with the polish of prestige magazines and issued in limited editions clearly intended for elite readers. Their analyses of causal relationships were uncomplicated for the most part by qualifications and admissions of ignorance. Their tables nearly always clearly supported their text, and were easy for a layman to take in at a glance. In short, they appeared to write with the clear object of holding the attention and persuading hurried executives whose primary interests would be in conclusions rather than methodology, whose commitment to finishing the report as they started it would be slight, and who would have many other matters competing for their attention as they read.

Several Minneapolis planners (*not* including Planning Director Irvin) later commented wryly to the author that they thought most consultants, though very able, were "Madison Avenue types." Their motivation in saying this may have been envy, but their meaning was that the consultants tended to give priority to the arts of persuasion when these conflicted with the strictest requirements of candor. For their part, however, the consultants resented any implication that they were less devoted to the public interest than publicly employed planners. Consultant Aschman, for instance, commented that he did not think he had changed since leaving public employ—he had been Director of the Chicago Planning Commission—and that he always demanded freedom from his private clients to articulate the public interest as he saw it. He agreed that consultants, working in many cities, probably developed a more refined sense than that possessed by most public planning staff members of the sorts of presentation to which businessmen and high public officials would respond. They did understand the value of simplification. It is impossible to be complete when you are brief, he said, but he thought he spoke for all the consultants who had worked in Minneapolis when he said that they strove manfully to retain accuracy as they simplified.

The fact was, nonetheless, that the consulting business was highly competitive, and that consultants could expect many of their clients to distrust self-doubters. The consultants were highly sophisticated about public relations; they understood the need to sell both their ideas and themselves. Minneapolis' publicly employed planners, by contrast, tended to experience discomfort at the idea that they should "sell" anything. According to some, planners might ethically be aggressive in their efforts to win a hearing; but virtually all maintained emphatically that when given their chance they should only "explain" their point of view. They agreed that they could not just present facts; they had to interpret, predict, and propose. They could, however, explain scrupulously the flaws in available methods of forecasting and the arguments against their proposals.

It will be remembered that the planners had, however, published nearly all of the raw data from Barton's studies and RERC's space-use survey during 1958 and 1959 without any analyses or conclusions at all. Their hope had been that some public officials and private investors would find the data useful. Unfortunately, the only strategic value that these publications might have had would have been to persuade some people that the planners really were hard at work, and that, in view of the amount of research that had to be done preparatory to planning, they should not be too impatient for finished proposals to emerge from the planning process. The danger, apparently unrecognized, was that recipients of these unanalyzed data compilations might acquire the habit of consigning Planning Commission publications to their shelves of unreadable reference works.

The research for this case study was not conducted until 1960, after publication of the *Central Minneapolis Plan* (which was quite free of unanalyzed data), but at that time there was widespread agreement among businessmen and politicians that the planners were poor communicators. As one put it during an interview:

No, I haven't read the *Central Minneapolis Plan* or the series of reports leading up to it. Their publications come out with greater frequency and bulk than most magazines. How am I supposed to know which are important and which are not? You say that this one [the *Plan* itself] is the most important. Well, it also comes after all the others have tired my patience, and it alone is over an inch thick.

Some who had dipped into the *Plan* had found it too full of alternatives, qualifying phrases, and methodological explanations. "No

one has time to study this thing like a textbook," said one alderman; "when they get ready to say just what they want us to do, we
may have time to wonder whether we should do it." [42] A former
city editor of the *Minneapolis Tribune* commented that he had
always had trouble with reporters who wrote to impress their
colleagues rather than to communicate with the public. "Most
planners are very similar," he said. "They write as though they
were more anxious to impress other planners than to convince laymen. Consultants never make that mistake."

When informed of this criticism, several planners admitted that
it might be valid. They protested, however, that they had an obligation to inform their readers both about their full reasoning and
about the gaps in their ability to predict results of any course of
action. As it was, they had simplified and eliminated many arguments relating to their proposals that reasonable people might put
forth. They had prepared a presentation with slides explaining
their recommendations in the simplest form they could imagine,
and had presented it to numerous groups, including the City
Council. They had written a summary version of the *Plan.* Concerning the full version, its author said philosophically, "We are
damned if we conceal our methodology and doubts, and damned if
we don't." The conflict, to some extent, was between an ethic of
public candor and the requirements of effective salesmanship.

The criticism made of planner communication in Minneapolis
seemed particularly ironic because the *Central Minneapolis Plan,*
by comparison with similar plans elsewhere, was a remarkable
combination of clarity and honesty. It contained almost no jargon.
The function of each activity in the Central Area was analyzed in
terms no less simple than, and frequently identical with, those
used by the consultant in his limited edition reports. Each proposal put forth was defended with arguments that certainly were
not difficult to understand. Alternative proposals were analyzed in
straightforward fashion, and the reasons given why the planning
staff believed its own recommendations were the best. The plan-

---

[42] The same alderman commented that he thought the planners published
so much for strategic reasons. He suspected, he said, that they hoped to prevent laymen from being able to criticize their recommendations. The flaw in
the strategy, he concluded, was that the Council would not approve what it
did not understand.

ners stated most of their predictions as ranges, the poles of which depended on the alternate assumptions: (1) that the *Plan* would be effectuated with vigor, and (2) that it would be ignored. RERC had made a general covering statement that it assumed for the purpose of prediction that the city would move vigorously to carry out its recommendations. It had not stressed this point as much as the planning staff did, however, and none of its predictions were presented in range—or rounded—form. If the *Plan*'s 180 pages of single-spaced mimeographed text were not light reading, their subject was a large one. If the reader was presented with many statistics, arguments, and trend reports whose importance was impossible to gauge from the text, this was primarily because no one knew exactly how important they were. If the planners failed in some instances to separate the major argument in favor of a proposal from the lesser arguments, their error was hardly of crucial importance. Surely no consultant would have written the *Plan* as the planners did, but the planners did not consider this a valid criticism of their work.

Despite this latent tension, the planning staff benefited immeasurably from the consultants' work. The consultants could work in their own way without compromising the "virtue" of the planning staff, and they "sold" ideas that the planners did favor.

Goals for Central Minneapolis

Rodney Engelen joined the planning staff as assistant director for advanced planning in the late summer of 1958. He had worked previously for three and one-half years in St. Paul, first with the Planning Board and later with the Housing Authority, after obtaining his master's degree in city planning at Harvard University. Engelen had developed a reputation during his years in St. Paul as an extremely creative planner. While working with the Housing Authority, he had developed by his own account a strong taste for concrete accomplishment above career safety. Minneapolis Planning Director Irvin intended to free Engelen from routine administrative chores to permit his energies full play. Engelen's first assignment was to direct the preparation of a Central Minneapolis plan.

He did not pretend to be a market or traffic analyst, and although he judged that the consultants had collected more data than they could profitably use, he was well pleased with the consulting analyses he had to work from. He tentatively accepted the consultants' estimates of market demand and traffic volume growth, and turned his mind to goal determination.

Unlike the consultants, Engelen could not concentrate entirely on the economic function of downtown. He appreciated that a political decision had been made to plan first for the downtown area, but he wanted the goals for downtown to mesh with appropriate goals for the entire community. Furthermore, he did not want to assume goals without articulating them. He believed that the proper way to plan in a democracy was to win public understanding and acceptance of general goals before spending a great deal of time conceiving specifics. As a strategic matter, he felt that laymen presented with generalities and specifics at the same time would inevitably concentrate on the specifics. His step-by-step approach might force those who paid attention to learn the fundamentals before they passed judgment on specifics. This gradual education process might keep them from rejecting unfamiliar specific proposals out of hand when the final stages were reached.

In short, Engelen believed that the "classic" approach of moving deliberately from general goals to specific recommendations was both desirable and practical. He added, however, that it could have meaning only when certain characteristic city planning errors were avoided. He argued that goal statements, to be of much value, had to be clearly relevant to problems of which influential people were aware, and with which they had indicated the will to deal. The planner, he said, should neither pronounce platitudes, step out too far in front of community opinion, nor harp on problems that community leaders consciously preferred to ignore. Both he and Irvin agreed that the planner could not be a community conscience and at the same time secure sufficient support within the effective influence structure to accomplish plans.

Within the downtown area, business interests were dominant. Any plan would require their cooperation, both in winning City Council approval and in securing private investment where needed. If additional parking facilities were necessary, downtown businessmen would have to arrange private financing or face higher taxes to pay for them. If it was decided that the government should strictly regulate the use of downtown land, businessmen would have to be convinced that in this case public regulation directly benefited them. The problem, as Irvin and Engelen saw it, was to maintain the support of downtown interests while leading them to serve goals of broader than economic importance.

Upon surveying the downtown scene, Engelen became convinced that very important social values were involved in preserving the economic importance of downtown. Most of the city's able leaders worked downtown during the day; their proximity made it easy for them to get together to discuss civic as well as business problems. These men provided the energy to support most of the city's organized civic life. They provided the boards of directors of charitable and good government organizations, and they supported the city's symphony orchestra and also its bids for first-rate professional theater and sports. The proof that the downtown clustering of activity played its part was that virtually all of the city's most active civic leaders were associated with downtown firms. From a political point of view, it was also important that they be encouraged to live inside the city. Those who moved to the suburbs could no longer take part in the political life of the big city; and as politics in the suburbs seemed of minor importance, they tended to drift away from political participation entirely.

Nonpolitical values were also at stake. Downtown housing could provide a haven for those—single people, old people, artists, intellectuals—who might feel terribly alone in typical family neighborhoods. Downtown areas, because of their size and variety, were the traditional havens of nonconformity everywhere. Their size itself was a source of excitement to people, adding color to their lives and making possible the sustenance of business and cultural enterprises of the one-in-a-metropolitan-area variety. Downtown, furthermore, had melting-pot characteristics that outlying centers could seldom match. People of all classes rubbed shoulders on its streets and in its stores. People who came downtown for prosaic purposes tried out its variety without very strong initial motivations: they went to conferences, foreign restaurants, theatrical events, the main branch of the library; they probably lived richer lives than those who spent their days shuttling between home, the suburban shopping center, and the plant site chosen because land for parking was cheap.

Needless to say, these arguments did not conclusively show the need for a plan to strengthen the downtown area of Minneapolis. The business activities which greatly needed face-to-face contact would remain downtown whether or not plans were made, and at the very least, retail facilities would remain open to serve downtown employees. People might derive more happiness from working near their homes—saving many hours each week that as commuters they spent standing in buses or fighting downtown traffic—than from eating lunch in foreign restaurants. Cultural centers would probably spring up in one place or another to satisfy those who cared. Downtown was not really much of a melting pot; those who rubbed shoulders seldom spoke to each other. Nevertheless, the case in favor of downtown was strong, and Engelen accepted it.

In reality, Engelen did not intend to maximize these social values. On the contrary, he always emphasized economic values in his planning and in his discussions with civic leaders. But unlike the consultants, he developed a rationale for doing so. When he finally wrote the *Central Minneapolis Plan,* he emphasized in its first section the relationship between Central Minneapolis' economic, political, and cultural functions. He did so, as far as this writer was able to discern, not primarily for strategic reasons but because he considered it proper for public servants constantly to reiterate that their concern was the public, as opposed to any special, interest. At the higher levels of generalization, there seemed to be no conflict between economic and other likely goals for downtown. The others seemed naturally to flow from the economic. The rub was that most of the means likely to contribute to the economic objective would have important side-effects. The problem was to discover which of these means, together with its side-effects, might prove acceptable. Because the operators of large downtown firms took the greatest interest in downtown planning and were almost certain to feel the effects of any plan in their treasuries, "acceptable" inevitably meant, above all, "acceptable to them."

Nevertheless, Engelen tried to ignore political strategy in the first phase of goal formation within the planning staff. He wanted to be limited only by the imaginative powers of himself and his colleagues. This limitation was itself serious enough. The literature on central business district planning was sparse, although less so than on many other characteristic city planning activities. No very bold plans had ever been carried into effect so that their impact might be judged in practice. When all was said and done, planners and economic analysts had conceived only a few broad principles of downtown planning.

The first and most important was "economic compatibility of activities." According to this principle, certain activities benefited from proximity to other activities; that is, one or several activities drew people who, after they were in the area, spent money at neighboring establishments. Also, according to this line of reasoning, people who might not bother to visit any of the activities standing alone might decide to come if they could visit all in the same trip. Some enterprises depended for the lion's share of their business on customers drawn to their vicinity primarily for other purposes; it was desirable for these that the land around them should be occupied by uses "compatible" with them. Downtown department stores, for example, did the larger portion of their business with people who worked downtown; the stores had an interest, therefore, in concentrating as many employees as possible on nearby land. Similarly, many people who came downtown for recreation did some shopping while there; others visited the downtown area only because shopping and recreation could be combined there. Compatibility was a matter of degree. All other things being equal, it was desirable for the most compatible activities to be located next to each other, and in the most advantageous directions from each other. The problem of direction was almost as important as that of proximity for many customer-oriented businesses. If the employees of an office building generally walked west upon leaving it, presumably to their means of conveyance home, a drug store to the east of the building was likely to get much less business than a similar one to the west. It had been found that in shopping centers the smaller stores benefited substantially if shoppers had to walk past them to get from the parking lot to the center's department store or, in smaller centers, to the supermarket. The department store and supermarket had a great deal of independent drawing power; the smaller stores, particularly those selling standard brands at list prices, depended more on momentary impulse to draw people in. RERC president Nelson had devoted a large portion of his book to a discussion of which economic activities were compatible with each other, and to what extent.

The second major principle was "access." According to the theory of access, the inherent drawing power of any complex of activities could be offset by the fact that most people preferred to spend as little time traveling as possible, and they wished to travel in as pleasant a manner as possible, in order to accomplish any given purpose. Downtown facilities might possess far greater independent drawing power than any others in the typical large metropolitan area, but so long as trips to downtown remained characterized by great length (in terms of time) and petty annoyance (in the forms, e.g., of traffic congestion and shortages of parking space), no major improvement in downtown economic vitality was possible.

The principles of compatibility and access were consistent with the traditional concern of city planners for the spatial distribution of land uses, and with the traditional responsibility of government for handling traffic.

In October and November 1958 Engelen conducted several "bull sessions" with planning staff members to elicit ideas for translating these principles into clearly applicable goals for downtown. Planning consultant Aschman attended and took a leading part in one of these sessions. The other consultants contributed ideas in the course of discussions of their own research projects. Engelen found only two published pieces of writing in which city planners had tried to state relatively specific downtown goals in systematic fashion.[43]

One was a six-page, impressionistic analysis of downtown Baltimore by that city's planning director. He wrote that the primary causes of recent downtown decline were the routing of through

---

[43] After publication of the Minneapolis goals report, the Minneapolis planning staff secured two additional goal statements. One was produced by the Seattle Planning Commission. The other was Information Report Number 125 of the Planning Advisory Service of the American Society of Planning Officials, which quoted extensively from the Minneapolis goals report. The ASPO report stated that, because most of any downtown was privately owned, very few public investments in a downtown area could be justified unless they (1) stimulated private investment and (2) won business support. This thesis was stated as if it were not disputed within the profession.

traffic on downtown streets, the haphazard arrangement of activities within the downtown area, obsolescence of structures, lack of beauty, and conflicts between pedestrians and motorists. He urged that incompatible uses be kept from the shopping, financial, and government districts and that pedestrian movement within each district be encouraged by the exclusion of vehicular traffic. He said that parking garages should be built around the districts. Aside from this, he urged that the local portion of the interstate freeway program be accelerated to divert through traffic—70 per cent of all downtown traffic in Baltimore—from city streets.

The Chicago Central Area Committee, an organization financed by leading Chicago business firms, had published a more elaborate statement in 1958. The consultants who worked for Minneapolis had had a hand in its preparation, and it was of particular interest because its recommended goals for Chicago and the stated goals of the *Central Minneapolis Plan* were almost identical. The Committee had listed principles that should guide all planning for Chicago's downtown area. The most important of these were the following:

(*1*) *Compactness.* The downtown area and each grouping of compatible activities within it should be kept within as small a total area as possible. Keeping the distances on typical trips minimal benefited everyone, and traffic congestion was alleviated to the extent that people moved within downtown on foot rather than on wheels.

(*2*) *Peripheral Development.* The activities close to downtown should serve but not duplicate central business district activity. The most likely candidates were residential apartment districts and service or manufacturing activities closely related to the central business district activities.

(*3*) *Ring Roads.* A belt of high-quality thoroughfares or expressways should be built around downtown. The aims were to induce through travelers to avoid the central business district and CBD-destined motorists to enter downtown streets near their destinations. The shorter the distance a vehicle moved on downtown streets, the less it contributed to congestion.

(*4*) *Parking.* Parking facilities should be located for the most part on the peripheries of downtown. Downtown employees should be encouraged to park near public transit facilities far from downtown. (The latter recommendation was not incorporated into the *Central Minneapolis Plan.*)

(5) *Internal Circulation.* Better movement within the central business district should be the prime goal. Vehicular and pedestrian traffic should be separated, because each delays the other when both share the same right-of-way. That is, vehicles must stop when pedestrians cross the street, and vice versa. Separate lanes for buses should be provided; if public transit vehicles could offer swift transportation, more people would use them instead of automobiles. Truck loading should be removed from the public streets as much as possible.

The Minneapolis planning staff elaborated these goals, and in February 1959 published a "discussion draft" entitled *Goals for Central Minneapolis,* an eighteen-page exposition of their meaning and rationale. Roughly 400 copies were circulated to public officials, political and civic leaders, and citizens' organizations. *Goals for Central Minneapolis* focused on two sets of questions: (1) What should be the function of Central Minneapolis in the metropolitan area? And, with this in mind, what activities should be encouraged to locate in Central Minneapolis? (2) What goals relating to land-use arrangement, transportation, and appearance should the city strive toward in order to help Central Minneapolis most fully to perform its proper function?

Engelen's purpose in publishing this goal statement was to spur public discussion. As noted previously, he hoped that this discussion would educate public opinion leaders in economic and planning theory, and educate the planning staff about the limitations of community consensus. Arnett Leslie, President of the Planning Commission, noted in an introduction to *Goals for Central Minneapolis* (written by Engelen) four advantages of discussing goals before launching action programs:

1. [Goals] help to avoid confusion of basic issues with secondary questions of details and thus help to achieve clearer and more pointed discussions of each.

2. They can create a common ground of agreement which is so necessary when many individuals and groups are actually involved in preparing and achieving plans.

3. They can prepare the way for achievement by warding off un-

warranted, johnny-come-lately criticism when the time comes to put a plan into effect.

4. Goals give direction to those responsible for planning public facilities, enabling them to prepare plans in closer accord with community desires.

The goals report stood as a landmark in the plan's evolution because the planning staff did conscientiously try throughout the remainder of the planning process to evaluate all proposals in terms of it. The planning staff members had attempted very little consultation with businessmen prior to the publication of the plan, but they had invited Barton Associates, RERC, and Frederick Aschman to comment on their early versions of it. They had also expected that reactions to the published "discussion draft" would aid them to revise before they published a final version of *Goals for Central Minneapolis.*

In the event, RERC had offered few comments. (It was subsequently, however, to endorse the recommendations of *Goals for Central Minneapolis* in its published Central Area market analysis.) Aschman had sat in on one of the "bull sessions" at which staff ideas had been solicited, but he had not commented at any length on the written versions submitted to him. Only George Barton had submitted lengthy comments in writing, but these had not dealt directly with the points raised in *Goals for Central Minneapolis;* they had, rather, stated principles that Barton had thought worthy of consideration. The most important of these were the following:

1. Parking facilities should be concentrated around the core area, lest the typical walk from parking facilities to downtown destinations be longer than necessary.

2. Curb parking, when reserved for short errand stops, is a positive asset to downtown enterprise. Curb parking should therefore take precedence over traffic movement as a use of street space except when most of the moving vehicles have downtown destinations. Congestion caused by through travelers should be relieved by diverting them around downtown rather than by eliminating curb parking within downtown.

3. Buildings requiring frequent vehicle access should be on the peripheries of functional centers rather than within them. This is in accord with the principle that, insofar as possible, vehicles should be

kept outside of the functional centers. Many buildings that do not seem to require frequent vehicle access at first thought do in fact: for example, a medical arts building. This should be kept in mind.

4. All transportation terminals, including those for autmobiles, should be on the perimeter rather than in the heart of functional centers. Government should regulate the location and design of parking facilities.

5. All means except subsidization should be used to encourage travel by public transportation.[44]

Engelen felt disappointed that he had not had the benefit of expert criticism, but he was not particularly depressed. His primary fears were of political rather than "expert" criticisms, and he still expected to be able to consult with local civic leaders at length before making any detailed proposals public.

The main contribution the goals report made to clarifying the issues was that it dealt with matters of priority. Certainly, the general problems of priority set forth had been perceived by other observers at other times, but the Minneapolis planners did try to make explicit the conflicts that were involved. This took considerable imagination and entailed some risk; other members of their profession rarely made comparable efforts to render hard issues explicit. Engelen and Planning Director Irvin reasoned, however, that hard issues that had been glossed over in the early stages of planning would rise to haunt them later at the stage of implementation.

Engelen and Irvin recommended four areas of priority choices. The first choice was the following:

Activities and functions which do not create a net addition to the efficiency and effectiveness of the Region and City by being in Central Minneapolis, and which do not need a central location for their own survival, should not be encouraged to locate there. Economic forces and existing governmental practices already serve to enforce this policy on a crude basis. Future government actions, including zoning, should also be developed so as to further enforce and uphold it.

[44] Barton had stated in the same document that no form of transportation should be "artificially restrained or subsidized." Since he had made clear on numerous occasions that he favored public construction of freeways, public garages, and other devices to facilitate auto transportation, the main burden of this recommendation appeared to be that public transportation should not be subsidized.

Eight categories of activity which the planners thought should be encouraged to locate in Central Minneapolis were listed: (1) "administrative and headquarters offices of organizations"; (2) "financial institutions"; (3) "services which are so specialized or which require such expert knowledge that they can only be performed effectively at one or at most a few locations in the region"; (4) "cultural, recreational or educational activities" of the same type as (3); (5) "the display and marketing [although not necessarily storage] of merchandise for wholesale distribution"; (6) "the display and retailing of lines of merchandise which are highly specialized or which will serve to provide maximum opportunity for comparative shopping in all merchandise lines"; (7) routine services for those attracted to downtown by other activities; and (8) special events of city-wide or regional interest—political, cultural, athletic, religious, and others.

Second, it was proposed that functional centers might be arranged in the following manner:

(1) Those activities which are benefited by being clustered together but which do not necessarily benefit themselves or the area by having direct, close contact with most other activities could be concentrated in centers somewhat apart from other activities in the area. Such activities might include: hospitals, housing, certain manufacturing, etc.

(2) Those activities of a type which need to be close to each other and to other activities as well could be concentrated in groups of like kind and these groups, in turn, concentrated together in one main center. Such groups might include: women's speciality shops, theatres, professional offices, etc.

(3) Those activities of a type which do not need to be close to each other, but do need close contact with other activities, could be dispersed and closely intermingled with these other activities. Examples are: restaurants, personal services, drug and variety sales, etc.

The specificity of this statement highlighted the point, albeit not in so many words, that the compatibility-compactness concept of downtown arrangement implied the generous exercise of public power. RERC president Nelson and others who had written on compatibility theory had generally taken the shopping center as their model and assumed that the builder of the center could control all location decisions. However, no entire downtown was owned by a single man or small group; the principle of centralized location control in this context was radical, and Engelen realized that he should not take its acceptance for granted. He hoped that if principles were clearly drawn and widely discussed, they would be implemented as much through voluntary action as by controls. The planners listed their third choice as follows:

The most important movement *within* Central Minneapolis is the movement of people . . . the most efficient and effective way to move large numbers of people short distances is on foot. *Therefore, as a basic goal, special facilities and routes should be provided to make pedestrian movements as pleasant, convenient and rapid as possible. Wherever possible within centers of intense activity and heavy pedestrian movement, pedestrian movements should be given preference over other means of transportation.*

The fourth choice in the listing of priorities was the following:

In all matters of the design and location of physical features in or relating to Central Minneapolis, the effects of such features on the appearance of the area should be taken into account so as to create the most rewarding, stimulating and memorable environment possible. [Central Minneapolis] should be distinctive: those aspects which distinguish Central Minneapolis from non-central areas and from other cities should be nurtured and developed. It should have variety: consistent with other stated objectives, the layout and details of Central Minneapolis should be such as to make it as interesting, surprising, alive and varied as possible.

A number of specific illustrations of means by which each of these aesthetic goals might be approached were listed. The statement stressed, however, that appearance was not something to plan comprehensively in advance.

Engelen admitted that the line between fostering a public awareness of aesthetics and setting up a form of aesthetic tyranny was blurred. All he urged specifically was that the city consider aesthetic factors in making decisions within its generally accepted spheres. In practice, the planners proved quite prudent: in the *Plan,* as it emerged eight months after *Goals for Central Minneapolis,* they discussed all proposals from the standpoint of the economic contributions they might make to downtown. Still, the planners *said* that aesthetics had intrinsic value, and that there was cause to rejoice when proposals of economic merit had aesthetic merit as well. They emphasized, too, that as necessity played an ever-smaller role in drawing people downtown, aesthetic considerations had a greater relative importance in motivating them to do so. In mentioning aesthetic values, they remained within the traditional boundary of planner concern, but they risked appearing impractical nevertheless. They were emboldened to do so, perhaps, by the current fashion of pedestrian malls in downtown areas. The economic argument for malls was that their aesthetic novelty and inherent appeal attracted shoppers downtown who would otherwise visit outlying shopping centers. In recent decades businessmen had come to recognize the value of aesthetics in advertising and product display; there seemed a fair chance that they would perceive its relevance to the economic problems of all downtown.

The planning staff listed five questions in *Goals for Central Minneapolis* which it deferred for future analysis:

(1) Who should be responsible for undertaking various parts of the plan?

(2) What forms of public action or control should be employed to put the plan into effect?

(3) How should the costs of improvements and programs be met?

(4) What standards or levels of service should be sought after in the various facilities of the area?

(5) In what order should various improvement work be undertaken?

Planning Director Irvin sent a covering letter along with the draft goals report to all those who received copies of it, expressing his hope that all individuals and groups interested in the future of downtown would express their reactions before detailed planning work began in earnest. He received only four letters in reply—all were from organizational representatives. Three of the letters indicated that committees had considered the report: the fourth represented the views of an individual. The organizations were the Minneapolis Association of Building Owners and Managers, the Minneapolis Board of Realtors, the Citizen's League (a "good government" organization), and the Downtown Council.

The committee of the Minneapolis Association of Building Owners and Managers was the only one to endorse specific goals in its letter. It approved the ideas that types of traffic should be separated and that the downtown areas should be made more appealing aesthetically. In addition, it urged several major tax incentives for downtown property owners who improved their property, and offered some strategic advice: proposals should be confined to those not requiring referenda. This, in effect, would restrict consultation to the elite. The public generally rejected new ideas, the committee's chairman explained, and the best way to get things done was through "a few informed, responsible and affected individuals, acting within established procedures."

The executive vice-president of the Board of Realtors wrote that the goals seemed "consistent with sound planning principles" and likely to stimulate discussion. He cautioned that serious differences of opinion were likely to arise over implementation. The Citizens' League committee approved the planning goals in general terms, but urged the planners to stress that "the primary method for achieving the stated goals is through private enterprise and the free play of individual competitive forces. This should be stated clearly so as to avoid any inference that development and change in the downtown area are to be controlled by a detailed master plan prepared and enforced by the city government." The Downtown Council's letter of endorsement was also in general terms.

Irvin and Engelen judged that this response hardly justified any assumptions about actual community goals.[45] They perceived no alternative, however, but to turn to detailed planning. They decided to draw in a small number of men familiar with Minneapolis business and government as unpaid consultants on actual and potential community consensus. Neither Irvin nor Engelen knew exactly what to expect, but they hoped that this intensive consultation would permit them to plan with an informed awareness of the temper of some of the groups most likely to support or kill any planning proposal for downtown. Each of those whose aid the planners sought was affiliated with a major downtown enterprise; and each was assigned by that enterprise to spend a substantial

---

[45] On reading this, one Downtown Council leader commented that Irvin and Engelen should also have judged that their method of communication was faulty. For an elaboration of this view, see n. 46.

The final version of *Goals for Central Minneapolis* was published in May. It was identical to the "discussion draft."

portion of his time observing and participating in civic activities. These men were the following:

(1) Dan Upham, former city editor of the *Minneapolis Tribune,* who had withdrawn from his high-pressure job after a heart attack in 1957, and had been assigned to quiet coverage of civic activities. Practically every door in the city opened to him, but the background information he gathered seldom found its way into print. His job, apparently, was not to find immediately newsworthy stories, but to know what influential people around the city were thinking. Upham took a particular interest in public planning, however; the articles that did appear in the newspaper under his byline generally dealt with the activities of the state Highway and City Planning departments.

(2) Robert Fischer, a vice-president of the First National Bank of Minneapolis, a prime mover in the Downtown Council, and chairman of the council's Development Committee. The First National was one of the two major banks in Minneapolis.

(3) Waite Durfee of Baker Properties, Inc., the largest owner-operator of downtown quality property. Leslie Park, the president of Baker Properties, was the only figure at the "presidential level" in a leading corporation—Baker Properties was not one of the city's *largest* corporations, of course—to show close attention to the planning process as the Central Minneapolis plan developed. His company's stake in downtown property values was greater than that of any other. Furthermore, unlike many realtors, Park had no compunctions about working with city planners.

(4) Robert Boblett, a prominent realtor and member of the City Planning Commission.

(5) Gerald Moore, executive director of the Downtown Council. Moore was too busy with other matters during this period, particularly with efforts to attract major league athletic teams to Minneapolis, to devote much time to planning, but he was considered a key man in any downtown civic venture.

(6) George Dayton, executive vice-president of The Dayton Company, whose enterprises included the largest department store in Minneapolis, one of the largest in downtown St. Paul, and one of the two in Southdale. George Dayton was a cousin in the Dayton family, which included five brothers active in the business. Paul Albrecht, former secretary to a Republican governor of

Minnesota, joined the Dayton staff during the consultation period and was taken into the consultant group.

Engelen had reasons for inviting only businessmen (plus one newspaperman) to help him. The labor movement had no one specifically assigned to civic duties; no one could find out with whom planners might profitably consult. The Citizens' League of Minneapolis and Hennepin County wished to avoid duplicating the efforts of the Downtown Council; it derived much of its financial support from the same sources as the Council, and it was unlikely to oppose a plan that the business community favored. Moreover, the League worked through citizen committees, so there was no one with whom to consult on a regular basis. Actually, the League's point of view received some consideration by virtue of the fact that Engelen himself was an active member. Neither Irvin nor Engelen knew of any other organizations that might take an active interest in their downtown efforts. They would have been happy to include virtually any organization's representative who showed some interest. Engelen did intend to consult with public officials from other city departments, but this was simpler and far more routine than consultation with business and political leaders. This, at least, was what Engelen believed initially.

Goals for Central Minneapolis was issued publicly in May 1959. Early in June, Engelen sent five mimeographed memoranda to his "discussants." Each memorandum dealt with means of implementing the goals for Central Minneapolis and of presenting a finished plan to the public. Each was less than ten pages of single-spaced typing in length. Four of the discussants responded. Moore, executive director of the Downtown Council, simply praised the ideas Engelen had expressed. Fischer, vice president of the First National Bank, was brief and noncommittal. Durfee, of Baker Properties, offered some information about building plans in the downtown area, but made only one comment on Engelen's proposals: he wasn't yet convinced that the clustering of activities into "clean neat groupings" was desirable or obtainable. Upham, of the *Minneapolis Tribune,* wrote a long and detailed comment urging Engelen to consider the creation of a music center near the civic auditorium, and he offered detailed ideas about the ways this might be done. To win the interest of a great many people, he contended, projects should be initiated at the earliest possible date. He also warned Engelen that his proposal to discourage through traffic from entering the downtown area would have to be handled delicately. Upham said that he had mentioned this proposal to some very "smart" executives and found that they thought it was madness. The men with whom Engelen was consulting, Upham concluded, were not typical in their easy acceptance of planning ideas.

Within a few weeks, Engelen sent six more memoranda. Again the answers were brief. Durfee wrote only that he wondered whether it would be possible to interest people in a plan as complex as this one seemed likely to become. Fischer commented that he thought government expansion should be accommodated in privately owned buildings, so that cutbacks in the size of government would remain possible. For the rest, he promised vigorous Downtown Council support for the general objectives. Upham again responded with the longest reply. He corrected some factual errors that he had found, but commented on only one proposal. He warned Engelen that in his enthusiasm to exclude vehicles from downtown and to make walking more pleasant he must not expect people to walk *too* far. As the distances became greater, more and more people would avoid downtown, he believed.

A short time later Engelen issued several more memoranda. This time only Upham bothered to reply at all, and only briefly. When he and the others saw Engelen personally, they commented that his efforts to consult took too much of their time. Upham told this writer that he had had more time than any of the others, as his job was simply to keep informed, but that even he had finally had to abandon his efforts to evaluate the proposals that came rapid-fire from Engelen's mimeograph machine. Upham pointed out that these came on the heels of the RERC analyses, the traffic inventories of downtown, and the series of undigested data complications that the Planning Commission had published. To evaluate all this material independently had become a full-time task, and no one outside the planning staff could devote full time to it.[46]

[46] On reading this, Robert Fischer commented that Engelen had been naive to believe that busy executives would comment in writing on long mimeographed memoranda. He thought that Engelen could have communi-

Albrecht, the new addition to the Dayton Company staff, said that he preferred not to comment on planning proposals while they were in incipient form:

> I don't want to discourage the planners from developing their ideas, but I have no right to speak encouraging words, either. The truth of the matter is that The Dayton Company's top policy makers will not worry about any planning proposal until it is available full flown, with cost estimates. And I cannot bother them with my thoughts unless I can present pros and cons in rather precise terms. Even now [shortly after publication of the complete draft *Plan*] I can't begin to estimate how the downtown plan will affect Dayton's interests. So I have skimmed each planning publication and memorandum to keep informed, but I have not tried to understand them in enough depth to make my comments predictive of any final Dayton positions.

Meanwhile, Engelen had discovered that preparation of his various memoranda in sufficiently finished form for distribution to the discussants had consumed a great deal of his time. The task of editing these memoranda was further diverting him from the more important work of finishing the draft *Plan*. When Upham emerged as the lone commentator on the third set of memoranda, Engelen decided to write no more of them. During the remainder of his work on the *Plan,* he tested his current ideas on the discussants whenever he met them, but he made no systematic effort to consult.

Drafting the Plan

From mid-summer 1959 to the end of the year, Engelen devoted himself to the evaluation of specific action possibilities. Of course, he had not ignored the specifics up to this point. He had had to think of plausible applications of his goal statement to be sure that the goals themselves were technically and financially, even if not necessarily politically, feasible. The task of designing project proposals in detail, however, was far more time-consuming than the general analysis that had hitherto occupied him.

---

cated much more effectively by going out to talk to his discussants in their offices. Parenthetically, the author's experience with the case studies in this volume tended to support Fischer's view. Most of the subjects responded briefly or not at all to the drafts of the case studies mailed to them. All were willing to review them in detail, however, when an interviewer called on them.

The general methods of implementation had all been discussed at other times and places; the problem was to determine which of the many possibilities would prove best suited to conditions in Minneapolis. Engelen found it almost impossible, he later recalled, to obtain constructive criticism of his ideas.[47] The consultants to the Planning Commission were experts in research and in the articulation of general planning principles; they did not wish to assume any responsibility, even indirectly, for specific project proposals. This was especially so because the commission could not afford to pay them for detailed analyses of each possibility. City officialdom provided still less help. The City Engineer's Department, comparable to the Public Works Department in other city governments, was the agency with which contact was most essential. Its responsibility included most road and utility construction in the city and all traffic control. It was likely that when it came to action on these subjects, the City Council would accept the city engineer's estimates of cost, feasibility, and desirability, rather than those of the planners. Even aside from the obvious fact of traditional jurisdiction, the city engineer enjoyed numerous advantages over the planners. He was one of the three highest paid city officials. Along with the other two, he had been appointed by the City Council and had risen through the Minneapolis civil service system. Each had won promotion to his current post in large part by demonstrating an ability to get along with the City Council. The loyalty of all three to the Council was undoubted and exclusive; its loyalty to and confidence in them was hardly less impressive. The character of this alliance had persisted unchanged in its essentials for decades, despite frequent public attacks on it. Most prominent among the attackers were the local newspapers and good government groups. Their capacity to influence the electorate suffered from the united front that City Hall could always produce for public battles. As noted previously, these perennial adversaries engaged in frequent referenda campaigns on proposals to change the form of Minneapolis government itself from the "strong council" to the "strong mayor" type.

[47] On reading this, Robert Fischer emphasized again his opinion that Engelen had found it impossible to obtain constructive criticism, at least from the businessmen, only because of the method of communication that he was using.

During most of 1958—the Planning Department's first year of revival—cooperation with the City Engineer's Office was good. Hugo Erickson, the city engineer, assigned a staff person to work with the planning staff. In December, however, Erickson left the city government and was replaced by his assistant, Gordon Bodien. Shortly afterward, the liaison man withdrew from contact with the planners. The planners later recalled that this had seemed to be part of a general withdrawal from cooperation with them by the City Engineer's office. The liaison man himself later recalled that he had withdrawn because of the pressure of time and because he and his superiors believed that the planners' faulty handling of traffic issues would make their plan unworkable.[48]

Nonetheless, the Planning Commission supported Irvin in his view that land-use planning, particularly for downtown, could not be separated from at least general (as opposed to highly detailed) traffic planning. In its budget request for 1960, presented during the summer of 1959, the Commission requested $48,700 for "major streets planning." City Engineer Bodien publicly protested the implication that Minneapolis had no street plan. At a hearing before the City Council Ways and Means Committee at the end of August, he presented a map showing the city's arterial street system, which had evolved over the years. It consisted of streets officially designated as parts of the federal aid, county state aid, and city state aid street systems. He emphasized that additions to and subtractions from these aid systems were proposed periodically, as conditions changed, and that improvements of the streets in these systems were going on constantly. He stated that a radical reassessment of the major streets pattern was unnecessary, for the reason that "our street pattern is pretty well fixed by what's

[48] On reading this, City Engineer Bodien commented that he did not think the change in city engineers had been relevant to the withdrawal of the liaison man, who in any event had withdrawn on his own initiative. Erickson recalled, on the other hand, that while he and Bodien agreed on nearly everything, he thought that he would have maintained liaison. He said that he would have felt confident of his capacity to veto any unacceptable planning proposal in the area of traffic, and that he would have considered it important to remain informed and to nudge the planners toward practicality in their thinking. Bodien, in his recollection, emphasized that the planners were completely ignoring the liaison man's advice and that he felt the "liaison" had become waste of valuable staff time.

already here, by the shape of the land and by the state highway laws. Decisions about street improvements and traffic belong to the traffic engineers." He went on to say that while he considered the planning function a useful one, the particular planners who had made the proposal under discussion were new to the city and inclined to put forward unrealistic ideas. They had learned a variety of principles in school, he said, and they were anxious to apply them though they did not yet really understand local circumstances. When Irvin quoted the commissioner of the state Highway Department to the effect that the department did not know what Minneapolis wanted, Bodien vigorously denied it. Frank Moulton, considered by many observers to be the most influential member of the City Council, came to the city engineer's defense. He claimed that the Highway Department found it politically advantageous to build the rural portions of its various aid systems before the urban portions,[49] but that when pressed by urban officials and residents about the delays in constructing urban portions, Highway Department officials tended to cast the blame on local officials. Irvin, who should not have been in contact with the Highway Department in any event,[50] Moulton said, was simply passing on the department's propaganda. He went on to note that he was skeptical of long-range plans. To explain why, he cited a 1912 planning study published in 1917 which had predicted that Minneapolis would

[49] The causes of this phenomenon, according to Moulton, were the following. First, the Highway Department was under constant pressure from contractors and labor unions to build the rural portions first. The proportion of each highway dollar that went into construction as opposed to land acquisition was much higher in rural than in urban areas. Second, the engineers and many of their critics tended to measure accomplishment in terms of mileage completed. Many more miles could be completed for a given number of dollars in rural than in urban areas. Third, the engineers tended to prefer to let time cool political disputes, and controversies over highway location and design tended to be much hotter in urban than in rural areas.

[50] A 1953 City Council resolution had "exclusively empowered" the city engineer to negotiate for the city with the Highway Department. Irvin recalled, however, that a 1957 City Council resolution had instructed the newly enlarged city planning staff to "integrate freeway plans with the general city plan." He had not been negotiating with the Highway Department, he said, but he had continuously maintained liaison with it from the start of his tenure. He did not remember anyone having suggested previously that this violated City Council policy.

have a population of one million and a transportation network based on street cars in 1946.[51] Concluding, he said that the burden of proof should be on the planners. The City Council's primary financial adviser, Research Engineer Nathan Harris, stated that the planners' requests for more money seemed endless. Their bid for influence over major streets planning, he thought, indicated "time and thought by the planning staff in areas which may not be in accord with the policy, thinking, and programs of other agencies." He called for "an understanding, at the policy level, on the scope of the activities of the planning commission." In the end, the planners received one-third of what they had requested for major streets planning. They felt that they had failed doubly, in that they had failed to win their point and yet by trying they had intensified the antagonism of several leading city officials toward them.[52] Planning Director Irvin still thought that he had been right to run the risk of battle, however. The alternative, he said, had appeared to be the eventual exclusion of all traffic problems from his staff's recognized jurisdiction. He saw no way to plan comprehensively, especially for downtown, without considering traffic.[53]

[51] The study referred to was the famous 1917 *Plan of Minneapolis,* prepared by architect Edward H. Bennett. Bennett had previously served as Daniel Burnham's chief assistant in the preparation of the 1908 *Plan of Chicago.* The *Plan of Minneapolis* forecast a 1946 population of 1.5 million for the city and its suburbs, which it expected to be incorporated within the city as expansion took place. The 1950 population of Hennepin and Anoka counties, which included Minneapolis and nearly all the suburbs normally attributed to it (as opposed to St. Paul), was 712,000.

[52] On reading this, City Engineer Bodien commented that he for one had not been antagonized. He had disagreed with the planners and had made his views known, he said, but he had continued to work amiably with the planners in areas where they did have a genuine contribution to make: e.g., in the location of various public facilities.

[53] On reading this, Alderman Moulton agreed that half of Irvin's job was fighting for jurisdictional authority. He felt, however, that in this case Irvin had given insufficient weight to the Council's view of the planning role. The Council, he said, considered the planning function purely advisory and relied primarily on the city engineer for advice with regard to the workability of traffic proposals. Irvin had given the impression, Moulton thought, of wishing to relegate the city engineer to a ministerial role while the planners made all the policy decisions. The only realistic option for the planners in this case, he concluded, was to have worked closely with the city engineer and tried to

The planners still hoped that the city engineer might be induced to approve, or at least not to oppose, the *Central Minneapolis Plan*. Engelen, therefore, did not write a comprehensive street plan for downtown. He developed his conceptions of what the downtown street system should look like, and used them to evaluate his ideas for overall downtown design. No major project could be effectuated downtown, after all, that would not have important effects on traffic. The question that would be asked most frequently, with regard to traffic, was whether the downtown street system could handle the altered patterns of traffic that the *Plan*'s projects would cause to develop. Engelen had to be able to answer "yes." If the project proposals were adopted, the city engineer would *have* to adapt the street system to the new patterns. The danger was that he might argue against the entire plan on the grounds that the street system could not handle such patterns in the absence of prohibitively expensive improvements.

The first (and, in the event, only) complete version of the *Central Minneapolis Plan* was released as a working document for limited circulation in February 1960. Stamped across its cover in large letters were the words "Draft, for discussion only." The *Plan* was mimeographed, not printed. Planning Director Irvin wrote in his introduction:

This is a true rough draft; not only should conclusions and recommendations be considered tentative and subject to comment and revision, but the text, tables, etc. must be viewed in the light of the fact that they were (mostly) typed directly from freehand manuscript copy with little or no chance for significant editing or correcting.

Irvin did not ask the Planning Commission to approve the *Plan* draft but only to approve its circulation. He and Engelen emphasized that they still did not want people to begin taking sides. They hoped that some of the discussion they had so far been unable to spur would develop now that the whole rationale was set forth.

On the other hand, they told the Planning Commission that

---

persuade him that they were right. The planners, of course, thought that they had striven manfully to work with the city engineer. City Engineer Bodien recalled that they had incurred his displeasure by pressing constantly for commitments on ideas that he had considered unworkable.

they intended to consider their central recommendations final unless important new arguments were brought to light. They did not expect this to happen. During the *Plan*'s preparation, the planners had frequently briefed the commissioners and supplied them with presentations of material. On numerous occasions they had brought key commissioners in on discussions of issues. The commission now accepted Irvin's assessment of the *Plan*'s probable finality without protest.

Aside from introductions, tables of contents, maps, and illustrative sketches, the *Plan* consisted of 180 pages of single-spaced, typed text. The first 80 pages summarized the findings and recommendations of the consultant-directed research program. The next 30 pages dealt with goals, central concepts, and rationale. The final 70 pages discussed means by which the concepts in the *Plan* might be translated into reality, and tentatively proposed a few specific projects.

The planners' reasoning was clear, but the tone of the *Plan* was rambling. The facts and figures packed into the research summary were so voluminous, and the number of trends listed so great, as to overwhelm most readers. The pages in which possible means of effectuating the *Plan*'s major concepts were discussed were so full of alternatives and balanced presentations of pros and cons as to confuse hopelessly those who had not been overwhelmed before. Only the short chapter entitled "Proposed Concepts," which contained the *Plan*'s core, was presented as a closely reasoned and unequivocal case. Unfortunately, this chapter lay buried in the middle of the document, and few of the officials and civic leaders later interviewed had read it. In fact, few seemed to have read beyond the seven-page summary statement of the *Plan*.

The fact that the *Plan* was not widely read, however, did not mean that it was entirely ignored. Before discussing the attention that was paid to it, let us summarize its contents. Engelen deliberately emphasized concepts more than specific projects in the *Plan*. He hoped that whether or not his project recommendations won acceptance, a climate of opinion might be created in which the *Plan*'s concepts would eventually be implemented. He wrote the following:

Probably the most important parts of any plan are the overall or major concepts which underlie it. There are a wide variety of ways in which the details of any plan can be carried out but it is the overall concept which ties the details together, which provides a sense and a framework of order and which can, if it is sound, provide a continuity through time and change. Some examples of major concepts which have been successfully used in constructing features of Minneapolis are the "Grand Rounds" parkway system, the "Mall" at the University of Minnesota, and "belt-line" highways. . . . Some well known concepts which have been successfully applied in other cities are the Chicago lake-front improvement, the Cleveland Mall and Civic Center, New York's Rockefeller Center and the Cook County (Chicago) Forest Preserve System. . . . A concept can be conceived and then stamped into street and land use patterns over a period of many years and by many people who know nothing of its origins or reasons for being.[54]

The central concepts of the *Plan* were five: (1) bypass, ring route; (2) super grid, superblock; (3) freeway terminals; (4) pedestrian routes, specialized street use; and (5) center-subcenter clustering of activities. It may be noted that the first, second, and fourth concepts were all aspects of specialized street use, and that all five concepts had a great deal to do with the problems of access to and circulation within the central commercial district.

(*1*) *Bypass, ring route.* The ring or belt-line route was by this time an orthodox traffic engineering concept. The design for the freeway included almost a complete ring around the Minneapolis central area, but for reasons discussed previously (pages 203–204) this ring was many blocks from the core area. After the freeway was built, many drivers on short trips would still find their most direct route through the downtown area. The city engineer and the planning staff agreed that this through traffic should be deterred from using streets in the core of the central commercial district. By making a few relatively small improvements, it was possible to create an inner ring route composed of a pair of one-way city streets. Engelen hoped that the attractiveness of this route would reduce traffic volume in the core substantially.

[54] *Central Minneapolis Plan*, Chap. 5, p. 1. Engelen admitted, however, that "often, as in the case of gridiron streets, persons will blindly follow a concept even though it causes undue hardship and expense and destroys important values in the process." The people who do this are generally those "who know nothing of the concept's origins or reasons for being."

(2) *Super grid, superblock.* The *Plan* urged that in certain sections of the central district every second street should be withdrawn from its current role as a major traffic circulator. Each unit of land bounded by an arterial street would have sides twice as long as those of an existing city block, and therefore an area four times as great. Streets within each superblock would be developed for pedestrian use, for transit use, or to provide access to parking facilities.

The superblock scheme, Engelen wrote, would cut the number of intersections by more than half. With so many fewer intersections, turning movements would be reduced, far more effective timing of traffic signals would be possible, and the construction of special facilities on which pedestrians could cross without interrupting traffic would be much more feasible. To the extent that the superblocks incorporated existing functional centers, the greatest pedestrian volumes would move within them, out of conflict with traffic, rather than between them. As the centers developed their functional homogeneity in future years, this tendency would be accentuated. Engelen claimed that the streets remaining in general traffic use would be able to move as much traffic as the entire street system did currently. Upon being challenged, he noted that George Barton endorsed his estimate. The main benefits of the superblock were that it would permit investors to assemble large tracts of land for ambitious ventures, and would facilitate the development of plazas and other focal points in Central Minneapolis. Ideally, parking facilities, service-vehicle access points, and related features would face the arterial streets bordering each superblock, while store fronts, displays, and other attractive features would face the internal streets.

(3) *Freeway terminals.* This concept sprang from an argument that had become orthodox among traffic planners in recent years, namely, that the usefulness of highways depended as much on their relation to parking space as that of railroad tracks depended on their relation to stations. Barton, for example, had accepted the idea in his 1957 report, *The Freeways in Minneapolis.* In short, freeways could not by themselves make the typical trip downtown quick and pleasant; it was just as important that drivers should be able to park near—within two or three short blocks of—their de-

sired destinations, and not have to fight congestion on their way from the freeway to their parking space. The demand for parking space in Central Minneapolis was expected to increase by 65 to 100 per cent between 1960 and 1980.

This prediction had been made by Barton in mid-1959. There was some reason to believe that his estimate was too low. Barton had assumed that all through trips of five miles or more whose straight-line routes passed through the central area would be diverted from central area streets by the attractiveness of the freeway. He had also assumed that public transit patronage would remain constant. Barton had accepted Highway Department predictions of trip volume—overall and between given points—as the basis for his work. Pessimists noted that the Department had never been known to err on the high side in its forecasts. Even with these assumptions, Barton had found that traffic volume on central area streets would increase slightly over the two decades. The expected decrease in through traffic would be more than offset by the expected increase in traffic bound for downtown destinations. Therefore, the same volume of traffic would require up to twice as much parking space as it did currently.

Engelen wrote that unless parking terminals were built to intercept vehicles between the freeway exits and the core area, vehicles circulating on downtown streets would create serious traffic congestion problems long before 1980. If certain trends—the rise of downtown employment, the decline of public transportation, the sprawl of residential areas—proceeded more rapidly than the Department had conservatively assumed they would, the dimensions of the traffic problem would grow that much faster.

One solution might have been to discourage automobile use in the central area. Efforts might have been made to increase the cost of downtown parking, to reduce transit fares, to improve transit service, to provide parking lots near outlying bus terminals, etc. But those with whom Engelen spoke believed that Americans had become too attached to automobile travel to respond in large numbers to these inducements. The planners tended to agree. The freeway had been designed and sold on the theory that it would accommodate the trend toward increased automobile use; its cost could hardly be justified as a subsidy of fast bus transportation.

Moreover, to the extent that any proposal made central area driving less attractive, it would be likely to induce many people simply to shun downtown, thereby contributing to its decline.

As a first step toward a complete system of peripheral ramp garages around the core, the *Plan* proposed construction of a large facility on the southwest edge of the core, at a point roughly equidistant from the two interchanges expected, on completion of the freeway, to unload two-thirds of Central Minneapolis' rush-hour traffic each morning. Unfortunately, the few feasible sites—those not presently covered by high-quality, high-density structures, yet within several blocks of the core's center—faced the only streets suitable for the near-in ring system. These streets were already being used virtually to capacity; within ten years they might prove inadequate for their ring-route function alone. Surely their usefulness as traffic carriers would be virtually destroyed if at peak hours thousands of vehicles had to enter them from, or leave them to, ramp garages.

The *Plan*, therefore, went on to propose construction of an underground expressway from the two freeway interchanges to the proposed parking facility. Engelen claimed that the expressway could be designed to absorb the great rush hour volumes so long as it had no other function. Barton had agreed with this view. In his 1957 report he had written that ideally traffic should never enter the surface street system in its movement from freeway to parking terminal. Construction of the peripheral terminals, he wrote, should be accompanied by destruction of the parking facilities currently interspersed throughout the downtown area.

Engelen had more modest hopes. He believed that the rate structures at facilities within the core might be modified to ensure their use almost exclusively by motorists having short errands. The difficulty was that such a rate structure would reduce the return from these facilities to their owners. Consequently, the existing rate structure favored long-term parkers. It was possible, however, that in the future, as more self-service ramps came into operation, this might change.

Engelen believed that unless the parking terminal concept, together with its corollary of connecting garages to the freeway by expressway, were implemented, the rest of the *Plan* could contribute little to downtown economic strength. No matter what else was done, downtown growth would be severely stunted for lack of street capacity to handle the traffic that, if the concept were implemented, would never enter the surface street system in the first place.

(4) Pedestrian routes. "Shopping is a recreation," Engelen wrote, and the ability of downtown to attract shoppers from outlying centers would depend in large part on downtown's unique features. "Facilities," he added, "and the activities which will attract an interest able to make a substantial difference in the drawing power of Downtown cannot be provided with improvements involving only minimum or modest change." Elsewhere, he contended that programs of aesthetic improvement in the downtown area should give first priority to projects which *by themselves* were sufficiently "dramatic" to draw substantial numbers of people downtown. The *Plan* urged creation of a ten-block-long pedestrian mall on Nicollet Avenue, Central Minneapolis' major shopping street. It also recommended that pedestrians be given first priority on several streets providing direct routes from other functional centers and from peripheral parking facilities to Nicollet Avenue. On these, sidewalks would be widened, weather protection might be provided, and other amenities could follow in time. The *Plan* also included general discussions of other ways in which downtown might be made more attractive to pedestrians, from improving street signs to creating second-level walks.

Irvin and Engelen conceived the mall to be the project, of all those in the *Plan,* most likely to come to fruition. The expense of doing a good job was substantial, but certainly not prohibitive. Its glamour and its renown as the latest fashion might appeal to downtown "boosters." Of course, some critics might charge the planners with being "faddists," [55] but Engelen felt confident that the mall

[55] See Victor Gruen, "Save Urbia for the New Urbanites," *Journal of the American Institute of Architects* (February 1960), pp. 35–38. Gruen, a consultant, was himself generally considered the American who had done the most to popularize the mall idea. He wrote frankly that every one of his firm's central area plans had included three concepts: (1) the mall, and (2) the ring road, with (3) directly adjoining terminal facilities. Nevertheless, he wrote: "Frankly, we are concerned about [the malls]. We believe that not only will they be ineffective after the first excitement over the unusual sight of grass and bushes on a downtown street has died down, but they may prove downright dangerous to long-range overall planning efforts." The reason, he added, was

would continue to benefit downtown even after its novelty effect wore off. The mall idea fitted few cities so well as Minneapolis, he said, because 90 per cent of the central commercial district's primary shoppers' goods stores fronted on Nicollet Avenue, including every department store. (RERC, in its *Economic Development Study*, had introduced the term "primary shoppers' goods store" and defined it to include all retail stores except eating and drinking establishments, drug stores, barber and beauty shops, tailors, and similar establishments.) The city's largest office buildings were all within a block or two of it. The central area's six blocks with heaviest pedestrian volumes were a four-block span on Nicollet Avenue and the two blocks perpendicular to this span on either side at its midpoint. "A block" was here used to mean the sidewalks on both sides of a street for the length of one side of a four-sided city block. Twelve-hour pedestrian volumes on these six blocks averaged over thirty thousand. No other block in the city had a volume as high as twenty-three thousand.[56]

(5) *Center-subcenter.* The principle that economically compatible activities should cluster together was one of the guiding principles of the *Plan,* as previously discussed in this narrative. Engelen proposed that this principle provide "the basis for organizing and locating land uses and parking, routing traffic, and laying out pedestrian routes." A twenty-two-block area containing the highest central commercial district employment densities, officially designated the core, together with those parts of the lower loop redevelopment area intended for office use, would be the main center. The functional clusters within it would be the subcenters. Engelen wrote that their boundaries should coincide with superblock boundaries, so as to keep the greatest pedestrian volumes within the superblocks. Whereas RERC had mentioned only the economic values of compatibility clustering, Engelen spoke of less tangible values as well. The articulation of centers would, he hoped,

---

that those malls that come into being invariably "are spatially limited, poorly executed, promotional measures based on a complete misunderstanding of the whole problem. They are the direct outcome of the desire which most downtown interests share to do quickly and cheaply something spectacular and to rely on patent medicines rather than a thorough treatment."

[56] The data were from *Pedestrian Count: 1958.*

provide a basis for creating special designs . . . which would add to the distinctiveness of Central Minneapolis and tailor each area more closely to its particular use. This organization would help people find their way about [the whole area] and would provide a sense of order in an environment which is complex and often confusing.

Most downtown businessmen of any stature understood the clustering concept, and agreed that certain types of activity should be excluded from downtown. The question at issue was how far to go in forcing compatible enterprises to concentrate. During this period George Kranenberg, a consultant, prepared a provisional outline of a new zoning ordinance for the city. He proposed the creation of three zones within the central commercial district: retail, service, and commercial; and said that the planning staff should decide which parcels of land should fall within each category. Planning Director Irvin, noting that the City Council had rejected proposed zoning ordinances in 1948 and 1956 because of neighborhood protests, decided to draw maps for each neighborhood at meetings with its own residents and businessmen. The planning staff would, of course, come to each meeting prepared with recommendations and reasons. After hearing these, the citizens who came to each meeting would direct the drawing of the map to suit themselves. No one quite knew how the planners would resolve conflicts among those who attended any meeting, but Irvin's strategy left the way open for central area business interests to draw the map for downtown.

Aside from drawing the maps, the most delicate part of central area zoning was the setting of floor-area ratios. The floor-area ratio was the relationship between the amount of floor space inside a building and the size of the lot upon which it was situated. In the early years of zoning, ordinances had merely stated maximum building heights. Experience had soon demonstrated that height regulations induced speculative builders—those to whom a building was purely a profit-making venture—to build on every square foot of their lots. The result was crowded, undistinguished, uniform architecture. In time, the floor-area ratio had been introduced to give architects greater freedom and to encourage them to provide more open space. If the permitted floor-area ratio on a lot were three, a builder might construct a three-story building on the whole lot, a six-story building on half the lot, a twelve-story building on one-quarter of the lot, etc. The planners hoped that floor-area ratio regulation could be used to maintain the central commercial district's compactness, and therefore proposed a basic floor-area ratio of twelve—ramp parking being permitted in addition. This ratio, the planners noted, was slightly higher than that of Rockefeller Center in New York City. Using it, all of the city's projected increase in office space needs to 1980 would fit on two city blocks. The projected rate itself—RERC's prediction—was rather optimistic, being three times the 1947–1958 rate. The 1947–1958 rate, as noted previously, had been 38,000 square feet annually. The projected 1960–1980 rate was 117,500 square feet annually.

Beyond the basic floor-area ratio, the planners proposed an elaborate array of "bonus" inducements. Simple floor-area regulation had elsewhere proved unable to cure the problem of monotony. If the permitted floor-area ratio were three, and it cost less (per square foot of eventual floor space) to build a three-story structure than anything higher, most speculative builders would build three-story buildings covering their entire lots. The "bonus" technique increased the permissible floor area ratio for builders who took steps considered desirable. Therefore, the floor-area ratio could be increased by a given amount when the builder set back his building, created an open plaza, or provided a covered walkway for pedestrians. Then he could offset his increased costs by concentrating more rentable floor space on his parcel of land. The problem was to gear the bonuses to the economics of construction. A bonus offered little incentive unless builders thought, they could reap profits from taking it. If the basic permitted ratio, without bonuses, was high enough to satisfy a builder, he did not have much reason to take bonuses. Similarly, if a specific bonus was too high, no builder would take any other. Since the primary purpose of providing bonuses was to encourage architectural variety, planners hoped that each bonus would prove attractive to *some* builders, and that many builders would take advantage of *several* bonus offers.

The builder in Minneapolis who took advantage of all of the bonuses would be able to fill the central area's projected space need to 1980 on one city block, with a floor-area ratio higher than that of the Empire State Building. Engelen himself feared that a basic floor-area ratio of twelve might prove too high to encourage the taking of bonuses. If so, variety might depend as it had in the past on the desire of "name" corporate builders for prestige construction.

Shortly after the draft of the *Central Minneapolis Plan* was issued, the planning staff published its plan for the Loring Park neighborhood.[57] This was certainly a part of the overall downtown plan. RERC's *Housing Market Analysis,* it will be remembered, had stressed the importance of middle- and upper-income Central Area residents to the downtown economy. The Loring Park Plan proposed that vigorous code enforcement and, if possible, urban renewal be used to weed out the neighhorhood's most run-down structures, and to force the owners of other structures to improve them. It also proposed elimination of several streets, development of "pedestrian parkways" and a neighborhood shopping center, and construction of a low-rent housing project for the aged. The pedestrian parkway was to be "a landscaped walkway given special design considerations to stand out as a major pedestrian facility to provide movement within the neighborhood. This would be a positive way to tie the various 'pockets' of the neighborhood together by providing an opportunity for pleasant and safe pedestrian movement between them." The term "pockets" referred to the fact that the neighborhood was already divided by two arterial streets in a north-south direction, and would be divided by the freeway in an east-west direction. The *Plan* added: "In concept the parkway is envisaged as at times passing through the interior of blocks, at times being no more than a specially emphasized sidewalk."

The planning staff proposed to make the best of a bad situation by encouraging apartment house construction along the proposed freeway route through the neighborhood. According to the *Plan,* "use could be made of the openness provided by the Freeway to create a landscaped vista." The *Plan* also urged new housing construction near the thirty-six-acre park from which the neighborhood took its name. The new housing in the area was all to be

[57] *Comprehensive Planning for the Loring Park Neighborhood* (City of Minneapolis Planning Commission: Neighborhood Series Number Six, December 1959). Despite its official date, it did not become available until February 1960.

multifamily and designed primarily for childless people. The function of the neighborhood, the planners wrote, was to provide near-in residences for downtown employees and others who typically provided the market for downtown housing. Children had great space needs, and the purpose of Loring Park planning was to concentrate a great number of people in a small space within walking distance of downtown. Moreover, an important objective was to attract people with substantial buying power into the neighborhood, and few wealthy people with children chose central area residences. Aside from wealthy people, those best able to afford new housing were childless working people.

The planners hoped that their urban renewal "package" would create a climate of investor confidence in the neighborhood. No single investor could revive the neighborhood by his own action; consequently, few were likely to risk capital until convinced that the neighborhood's future was secure. A firm public commitment could begin the process of persuasion. Then, it was hoped, Downtown Council members might complete it by exerting themselves to ensure that private capital would come forth.

Before concluding this section on the *Plan*'s contents, a few words seem called for on its omissions. These were, it should be noted, extremely easy to justify if one assumed that planners should limit themselves to problems that they believed the political system was equipped to handle. If one assumed, however, that plans should be evaluated from the standpoint of the overall public interest, they were likely to appear highly arbitrary. However that may have been, the *Plan*'s omissions clearly distorted the balance of its analysis in such a way as to favor the implementation of its contents.

One crucial omission concerned the relation of Central Minneapolis planning to the housing problems of low income people. According to the *Plan,* some 19,000 dwelling units needed to be cleared from within or near Central Minneapolis to make way for public projects, including the interstate freeway. If all 19,000 units were cleared, approximately 60,000 people—one-eighth of the city's population—would be displaced. In support of their recommendation, the planners wrote: "While this [clearance] will do nothing positive to improve or enlarge the housing supply, it will eliminate much obsolescence and will radically alter the appearance of some housing areas." They said nothing about the effect that this wholesale demolition would have on the rents poor people would have to pay in Minneapolis.[58] At the time they wrote this recommendation, the planners had predicted that the 1960 census would show a decennial increase of 8 per cent in Minneapolis population. When the census report appeared several months after the draft of the *Plan*, it revealed instead an 8 per cent decline. The latter figure provided some justification for thinking that a large clearance program could begin without creating a major low-rent housing shortage. This was, from the planners' point of view, a fortuitous accident.

Second, the *Plan* omitted the subject of costs. The primary reason for this was that the planners did not want to frighten off potential supporters before they had read the *Plan*. In fact, the planners believed that the level of public investment the *Plan* would require would prove no greater—though the absolute dollar figures would sound high—than the city would probably end up spending anyway. They were merely proposing, they said, that the city plan its investments as carefully as large corporations commonly planned theirs. The decision had already been made before

[58] On reading this sentence, Robert Fischer commented that he did not consider relocation one of the functions of a central area plan. The function of a central area plan, he said, was to develop the best land-use pattern for the economy of the central area. He recalled that he had taken a similar position during the formative stages of the lower loop project. The lower loop had contained a large number of liquor stores. The number of liquor licenses in the city, and the portions of the city in which they might locate, had been fixed for several generations. Thus, each license represented a large investment. Some people had said that the lower loop project could never get off the ground unless the problem of relocating the liquor licenses were resolved first. Fischer and others had contended successfully that the licensees would just have to take care of themselves. In the event, when the project had reached an advanced stage, the licensees had organized themselves and won the support of even "good government" organizations and the clergy for a major expansion of the boundaries within which liquor licenses might be located. They had succeeded in having the city charter amended by referendum. The referendum had revealed such strong opposition in many neighborhoods, however, that the City Council never had gotten around to relocating most of the lower loop licenses. The lower loop project had never faltered, however. For a more detailed account of the liquor license referendum, see below, Chap. VIII, p. 371.

their arrival, they noted, to adjust Central Minneapolis to the automobile age. On the whole they approved of this decision. Given the nature of American social and economic life in the current era, they believed, adjustment to the automobile was essential to the economic strength of downtown, and a strong downtown was essential to the vitality of Minneapolis. Nowhere in the *Plan,* however, did the planners explore matters of degree. That is, they did not explore the problems raised by the fact that this adjustment might commit the city to expend enormous sums of public money, which might alternatively help to support other public services. The planners knew that the adjustments could not consist simply of the freeway plus one enormous distributor garage, one underground expressway, and one inner-ring route. They estimated that within a few years the city would have to build several additional freeway radii, whether or not the federal government offered to finance them. The interstate freeway, moreover, was scheduled to lie on only three sides of the central area; the city would surely have to build a connecting link to complete the circle before long.[59] The *Plan* recommendation of a distributor garage south of the core would have to be supplemented, in the planners' view, by others to the north, east, and west. Unless expressways connected them to the freeway, the whole effort might prove in vain.

The planners believed that the city should undertake these expenditures as investments, which would more than pay for themselves by increasing local tax revenues. They did not argue that Central Minneapolis would decline absolutely without a plan. At the time the *Central Minneapolis Plan* came out, the freeways had not been built and no other major projects in the automobile adjustment process had even been widely discussed. Yet the planners and their consultants had found Central Minneapolis in remarkably good health. Except within the core itself, traffic moved smoothly almost all the time. During a bus drivers' strike in December 1959, traffic had continued to move well despite a 50 per cent increase in traffic volume. The relatively inexpensive secret of success during the strike period, according to the city engineer, had been assignment of additional patrolmen to traffic detail.

[59] By 1962 the Minnesota Highway Department had released traffic projections resulting from the 1958 Twin Cities Origin–Destination Survey (see above, Chap. I) which indicated that by 1980 seven new freeways would be required in Minneapolis.

The planners' central argument was that private investment was being severely retarded by doubt about the future of downtown, and particularly of downtown parking. A large portion of the downtown parking spaces currently available were "temporary." They lay on block after block of vacant lots waiting for more profitable investment opportunities. The planners believed that potential investors were deterred by the possibility of severe parking (and related congestion) problems in the future, and that this would cost the city dearly unless firm policies were developed to encourage the development of "permanent" parking facilities. There was no way of telling whether the planners were correct. Most of the nonplanners interviewed for this study were to find their reasoning plausible, but to contend that only small amounts of investment were at stake. They were to note that large investors could assure their own parking supply, and that the city government had neither sufficient financial power nor legal power to have a major impact on economic trends. It had to compete with other cities and with suburbs in the matters of tax rates and services offered—to all citizens, not only those particularly interested in downtown. Their inclination was to be to wait for detailed cost-benefit studies before committing themselves to anything. In the event, the planners' immediate problem was to be to spur sufficient interest so that the detailed studies would be financed.

By way of concluding this section, a word may be said about the popularity of central area planning throughout the nation in the late 1950's and early 1960's.[60] Central area planning commended itself strongly to planners, politicians, and civic leaders for a vari-

---

[60] Clyde Browning has written: "A decade ago relatively little mention was made to central business districts in the popular, planning, or scholarly literature. The rush to the suburbs and the rise of the planned shopping centers prompted popular, professional, and public concern. Today the emphasis has undergone a radical transformation. One of the hottest topics in urban research revolves around the problems and prospects of central business districts. Indeed, the topic has become a virtual fad. Planning agencies have rushed to study their CBD's and businessmen's downtown organizations have been formed all over the country. From New York City to Podunk, central business districts and their problems are receiving top priority" ("Recent Studies of Central Business Districts," *American Institute of Planners Journal*, XXVII, No. 1 [February 1961], 82). The same article singles out *Goals for Central Minneapolis* as "an extremely thoughtful presentation of a subject often quickly glossed over" (p. 86).

ety of reasons. It attracted the support of highly articulate segments of the community, especially businessmen stirred to action
by the economic impact of urban sprawl. It stirred little opposition, probably because it did not involve much tampering with
relations among social groups; that is, central area planners did
not have to determine who should live near whom, who should go
to school with whom, and similar relationships. But when central
area planners recommended enormously expensive projects,
which, if implemented, promised to tie up the capital improvement energies of their cities for many years, there was reason to ask
whether central area planning really had a positive impact on the
quality of urban living commensurate with its cost. Planners may
have had reason to answer that their cities were going to spend
comparable sums on adjustment of their downtowns to the automobile age regardless of whether they planned, but this did not
have to deter outsiders from questioning the value of the whole
expensive adjustment process.

There seemed little reason to believe, for instance, that the
important cultural benefits of urban living depended on the continuing preeminence of downtown, at least in a city like Minneapolis. The *Central Minneapolis Plan* itself contained the statement that

cultural activities (including religion) do not occupy a large amount of
land in Central Minneapolis nor are they concentrated in the area as
they are in the central areas of some cities. For example, the Minneapolis Art Institute and the Hennepin County Historical Society are
located almost two miles away from the Core. The University [of
Minnesota] houses virtually all of the musical and many of the dramatic and cultural events which, in many cities, occur immediately
within the central area. Practically no outdoor events, such as summer
concerts or athletic competitions, are held in the area. And museums,
markets, or other features which would recall the cultural heritage of
the region are virtually non-existent.

The central area did contain the public library main branch, a
number of specialized private schools—music, art, bible, and
business—and some fine eating establishments. But the University
library, the city's distinguished educational institutions and museums, and many of its best eating places lay outside the area. The
symphony orchestra played at the University, not downtown.

Foreign-language films played regularly at several outlying cinemas, but at none downtown. Beginning in 1962 the city was to have a nationally famous repertory theater company; it too would be based outside of downtown. Central Minneapolis certainly did provide excitement in its variety to the people who assembled there each day, but they paid the prices of commuting and congestion. If, as the planners maintained, few of them enjoyed the central area's glamour enough to use public transportation to reach it, perhaps they were also lukewarm about using tax dollars to strengthen it. It was impossible to know how much the strengthening of downtown meant to them, or to other taxpayers who rarely went downtown. The issue had to be for the political process to decide, regardless of how strongly planners themselves might feel.

The City Receives the Plan

Early in March 1960 the planners sent copies of the *Central Minneapolis Plan* to ninety-six political and civic leaders, public officials, and businessmen. During the following several months, Irvin and Engelen made oral presentations to the City Council and to various civic groups, but there was a continuing absence of any evidence that many people had read the entire *Plan*. There were many, however, who had acquired some understanding of, and had formulated opinions about, its central concepts.

City councilmen tended toward hostility and indifference in their discussions of the *Plan*. Some of them expressed resentment that Irvin and Engelen had, in their view, regularly bypassed them during the planning process in favor of recruiting support from nongovernmental groups. Frank Moulton, generally considered the Council's most influential member, articulated a typical view when he said that planners were unwilling to accept their place in the scheme of things. They preferred to propagandize and lobby, he said, to bring pressure to bear on the City Council to revise the scheme. He did not expect them to succeed. The specific questions about the *Plan* that interested most of the councilmen were (1) whether unanimous support for any of these new ideas could be secured, and (2) whether their implementation would cost the taxpayers much money.[61] They considered it highly probable

[61] On reading this, Moulton commented that the questions that interested him were slightly different. They were: (1) whether enough support for any

that the answers to both questions would prove politically un-
palatable. For this reason they tended to agree with Moulton's
description of the *Plan* as "ivory tower staff work," and with his
more detailed indictment of the *Plan,* which ran as follows:

> The *Plan* is so long and complicated that no one can understand it
> except the planners. Moreover, the planners maintain that the parts of
> their plan are interdependent. Well, if they really have to get all they
> request before they will think they have gotten anything worthwhile,
> maybe we should ignore them entirely. No one knows today just who in
> the community will oppose any specific project, but each is certain to
> have its opponents. In addition, some of their proposals are probably
> illegal under the present charter.[62] So the planners are likely to end up
> with a hodge-podge selection of their proposals if they end up with any-
> thing. Even if they think the hodge-podge worthwhile, they will have
> to work many years to overcome fixed prejudices against new ideas.
> They will have to learn, as I have had to learn, infinite patience.

Each alderman interviewed took the position that since any
final decisions on the *Plan* proposals were years away, the Council

---

proposal could be generated so that its implementation would not mean
political suicide for sitting councilmen, and (2) whether any of the spending
proposals would prove clearly worth their cost.

[62] On reading this in 1964, Moulton commented that planners tended to
consider lawyers "dumb bunnies" who did not understand community needs.
It rarely occurred to them, he said, that *they* might be wrong, that there might
be something to be said in favor of a nation of law. Moulton was particularly
concerned about the principle of zoning, because the city had adopted a new
zoning ordinance in 1963 that was just beginning to be tested in the courts.
Moreover, the local newspapers were carrying on an editorial campaign against
piecemeal amendment of the new zoning ordinance by the City Council.
Moulton argued that the United States had been built on the notion of individual rights, including property rights, and that a zoning ordinance which
seriously reduced the sale value of a man's property deserved to be amended or
declared unconstitutional. State courts all over the country were declaring
zoning provisions unconstitutional on this basis, he said, and all the planners
knew how to do was to condemn the courts. The consequence was that they
were undermining their political position. They had sold communities like
Minneapolis on the general idea of planning, but each time they treated
a property owner as if he were antisocial for wanting to protect his investment
they created a bitter enemy. The army of enemies was growing rapidly in
numbers and power, he believed. Moulton added that he thought "sound"
planning would have a genuine contribution to make, but that Minneapolis
had never had such planning. (Parenthetically, Moulton had helped enact the
new zoning ordinance in 1963.)

had no need to hurry in starting to review the *Plan* formally. The predominant view was that the *Plan* should be viewed as at best a trial balloon. The councilmen emphasized that they were busy men and had to concentrate their time on "serious" proposals; i.e., those which had important backing and which were being put to the Council for firm decision. No member of the Council expressed interest in taking part in the public discussions from which consensus on particular proposals might emerge. On the contrary, the predominant mood was one of mild annoyance at having been handed a document which demanded some attention but which did not appear capable of being put to use.[63]

Neither the whole Council nor any of its committees intended to consider the *Plan* or any of its parts in the foreseeable future. The councilmen expected that, if the *Plan* proved to have any workable parts, eventually some private groups would draft specific ordinance proposals and ask aldermen to introduce them; then the Council would evaluate each proposal "on its merits." The aldermen thought that a prerequisite for the passage of any proposal affecting downtown would be consensus in its favor among downtown businessmen, but they stressed that the Council would not unquestioningly ratify agreements arrived at by the downtown business community. Their own constituents had a great aversion to tax increases, they noted, and innumerable groups contested for every one of the few dollars the Council was free to allocate. Clearly, they pointed out, the supporters of Central Minneapolis projects would never persuade every partisan of other potential expenditures to forebear.

Summing up, then, it may be said that the Council took a "hands-off" attitude toward the *Plan*. The mayor did likewise.

---

[63] On reading this, Moulton commented that in his view the situation was that the councilmen did not understand the *Plan* in any detail, that they were deluged with information to the effect that particular aspects of the *Plan* were unworkable, and that they did not want to attack the *Plan* publicly because they still hoped that it would evolve, at least in part, into something workable. He added that he wished the planners would recognize that public affairs move by evolution, not revolution. He thought that by writing plans composed of "dreamboat" proposals the planners inspired opposition needlessly and failed even to educate. They also stirred doubt in the City Council, he said, about the justification for continuing to appropriate tax dollars for planning.

Asked to grant his permission for the planning staff to circulate the draft *Plan,* he gave it without comment. Thereafter, he gave no indication that he knew of the *Plan*'s existence.

The city's engineers had not read the bulky *Plan,* but various of them had attended a total of dozens of meetings with the planners during its evolution and had discussed most of its features with the planners. They felt that they understood the *Plan*'s essentials. Most of these they opposed. They did not formalize their opposition by committing it to paper, but they expressed their views orally at meetings with the planners, other city officials, Downtown Council representatives, and the consultants. Consequently, their opinions soon became known throughout the City Hall and Downtown Council "communities."

They agreed wholeheartedly with only one proposal in the *Plan*—the construction of an "inner ring route." But they emphasized that this project had been on their agenda for some years, that George Barton had endorsed it in his 1957 freeways report, and that the City Engineer's Office had started work on it before the *Plan* appeared. Engelen agreed that this proposal, along with most of the others in the *Plan,* had been discussed for some time, but he doubted that the engineers would have done much about it in the absence of prodding. Needless to say, the engineers considered Engelen mistaken.

With respect to the superblock system, the engineers contended that you simply could not take half the downtown streets out of general traffic service and still move traffic smoothly. They denied that the greater spacing of traffic lights would enable traffic to move much faster on the streets bounding superblocks, because during rush hours the technique used already was to move each batch of vehicles five blocks at a time. That is, five traffic lights changed simultaneously; they remained green long enough for traffic to move past them all. This technique, they claimed, was better than that of "staggering" lights because closely packed groups of vechicles—the rush hour norm—started up at widely varying speeds. It was impossible to know what speed to assume for a stagger system. The effective unit of movement, therefore, was already five city blocks, rather than the two blocks contained in the *Plan*'s superblock system. The engineers went on to say that turning movements could be reduced—another *Plan* objective—by simple prohibition. That is, there was no need to remove streets from service. They added that the city already had an elaborate one-way street pattern, and that in their view turning movements off one-way streets did not create serious problems.

Another point of dispute was whether the city should set aside special transit streets and pedestrian facilities. The engineers argued that it was preferable to spread buses more thinly over the street system, giving them special lanes, as the city was doing already. Different bus lines required different amounts of time for loading, they said; if all the buses were routed on a few streets, those with light loading requirements would pile up behind those with heavy loading needs. In short, they concluded, there was no way to reduce congestion by eliminating streets. They applied similar reasoning to proposals to widen sidewalks to improve pedestrian facilities. The end result of all actions which reduced the carrying capacity of the street system, they thought, would be to make it more difficult for people to come downtown. This would deter more potential investors and shoppers, they concluded, than pleasant pedestrian facilities would attract.

Planning Director Irvin disagreed on all counts. With regard to transit streets, he said, the only street on which bus movements were currently near saturation was Hennepin Avenue. Therefore, in Irvin's judgment, the engineers had knocked down a straw man. He still believed firmly that concentration of bus traffic on fewer streets to free others for rapid automobile movement would prove both workable and highly beneficial. He added that the city's existing "special" bus lanes added very little to mass transit efficiency. The lanes were not exclusive; they were designated only by signs. Drivers making right turns and those discharging passengers constantly violated them. With regard to the value of pedestrian facilities, he stuck by the reasoning of the *Plan*, as outlined earlier.

The engineers agreed that serious problems would arise unless peripheral parking terminals were built, and that if access to them were possible only on surface streets the congestion might become unmanageable. But they emphasized the difficulties of building an expressway through the central area's subsurface, a region already filled to overflow with telephone, gas, water, sewer, electric power, and various other lines. The expense of this one project, they argued, would be so great as to compel the city to forego all other capital improvement projects for several years. At the same time, high-rise ramp garages without an expressway would solve nothing. They would empty so many automobiles into such small areas as to create chaos. (The planners, of course, agreed with the engineers on this point.) They recalled that years ago their staff had drawn up a plan for low-rise ramp facilities all around the core. Although construction during the intervening years had eliminated the possibility of effectuating the plan, they still felt that low-rise structures emptying onto surface streets were the only practical possibility.

Engelen maintained privately that the high-rise facility with underground expressways could be built without public financing. The project was so essential to the future value of downtown investments that downtown corporations might join to finance it initially.[64] They might only have to guarantee a bank loan if studies showed that parker charges could pay it off. The engineers remained skeptical; they pointed out that until now downtown firms had preferred to reap the immediate benefits of building ramp garages adjacent to their own places of business. Almost all of the large enterprises had already invested heavily, or announced plans to do so, in their own facilities. Engelen hoped they might still realize the economic benefits to be gained from supplementing their own facilities with peripheral garages.

The engineers opposed the mall concept. Nicollet Avenue, they argued, was needed to carry traffic. They advanced three main contentions: (1) the overall attractiveness of downtown would not be increased if the mall caused congestion on adjoining streets, which was likely; (2) after the initial novelty effect wore off, the mall would draw very few shoppers to the downtown area; and (3) transit passengers on Nicollet Avenue could already exit directly in front of the retail stores they wished to visit; this con-

[64] He added that an important precedent already existed. The largest owner of downtown ramp parking facilities in Minneapolis was Downtown Auto Parks, Inc., a company founded by a group of downtown corporations in 1950. The founding corporations had purchased stock in Downtown Auto Parks and thereafter assigned representatives to serve on its Board of Directors. Unfortunately (from the planners' viewpoint), Downtown Auto Parks made its investment decisions on purely economic grounds, and had judged that the highest profits were to be made by locating as close to major generators of traffic as possible.

venience probably attracted more shoppers already than the mall could attract potentially.

Speaking of the *Plan* as a whole, the engineers' articulate views could be summarized as follows:

We are open-minded toward any new ideas the planners can offer us, but someone has to reconcile their praiseworthy abstract concepts with our traffic, budgetary, and construction problems. The two crucial things to keep in mind are: (a) that the planners are very new to Minneapolis, and (b) that the city's experienced engineers have a deep understanding of the city's traffic patterns and of the possible ways of servicing them.

We try for the most part, it is true, to propose incremental rather than radical changes. Radical proposals generally create terrific political and financial problems. Their enormous expense is difficult to justify, because the city's entire capital improvements budget is very limited and it must be split many ways. Furthermore there are always a great many people hurt by any large proposal. Land must be taken, and no one is quite able to say when the owners have been paid "fair" prices; the alteration of traffic patterns always hurts some people who have devoted time and money to adjusting to the present patterns; and so on.

If the city really decided to handle traffic adequately, it could spend all of its tax revenues on this purpose, to the neglect of everything else. The first peripheral ramp garage and underground expressway, for instance, would not begin to solve all of the city's difficult traffic problems, but they would cost more than we spend adjusting the city's street system incrementally over several years.

Irvin and Engelen, on the other hand, thought that the engineers' predilection for gradual adjustment equaled in the existing context a tendency to make big decisions by the aggregation of numerous little decisions without ever posing general issues for public discussion. They believed that incrementalism had a variety of hidden costs. For example, it tended to produce "traffic blight," a condition characterized by narrow sidewalks, difficulty of land assembly and property access, high levels of noise and danger, and similar problems. "Traffic blight" caused property values to deteriorate and the city as a whole to become less attractive. The engineers did not find these criticisms persuasive. They insisted that their own judgments were rooted in long experience and depended on views about the correct system of priorities for distributing a severely limited total of resources available to the city for street and highway improvement.[65]

It may be noted that the city councilmen and the city's engineers both emphasized cost considerations in their evaluation of the *Plan,* despite the planners' strategy of trying to keep cost out of the discussion until a later phase. One conservative councilman maintained that he would never bother to read the *Plan* until someone wrote an evaluation of each project in relation to the city's budgetary problems: "Anyone can think up fine projects if he doesn't have to worry about cost," he scoffed. From the planners' point of view, he was wrong. It was extremely difficult to conceive intergrated solutions to complex problems.

The business community reacted to the *Plan* more slowly and with greater sympathy than the professionals in City Hall. It expected little help from City Hall in the tasks of evaluating the *Plan* and shaping a measure of consensus; neither did it expect obstruction from City Hall once these tasks were completed. Shortly after circulation of the *Plan* got under way, the Nicollet Avenue Subcommittee of the Downtown Council's Development Committee retained Frederick Aschman, who had merged his firm with George Barton's early in 1960 to form Barton-Aschman Associates. Aschman's task was to evaluate possible Nicollet Avenue improvements. A month later the council formed a special committee of its

[65] On reading this, Robert Fischer commented that the planners had exasperated him by never producing cost-benefit analyses to "prove" their case against incrementalism. He recalled that he had served in the early 1950's on a committee charged with advising the directors of the First National Bank on whether to remodel their old building or construct a new one. The committee had produced cost-benefit studies to demonstrate that construction of a new building would be more profitable in the long run. In the event, the First National Bank had constructed a twenty-eight-story skyscraper with a large pedestrian plaza in front of it that was still, as of 1964, the most striking building in the core. Planning Director Irvin noted that he had chosen not to make a public issue of "incrementalism" because it would have involved a more direct clash with the city engineer than he had desired. The debate on incrementalism reported in these pages had been carried on in private, not public, conversations. Fischer believed that Irvin had been right in challenging the city engineer on the "major streets planning" issue and should have taken the additional risk of making explicit the fact that the real issue was that of incremental vs. comprehensive traffic planning; he should then have "proven" his case with irrefutable facts and figures.

members to evaluate the *Plan* as a whole. Observers agreed that the committee had been chosen primarily for its working ability rather than its "power" to impose a solution on downtown. Only a group composed of the presidents of the largest central area corporations could have done the latter. But the present council committee did have considerable stature. There seemed every reason to believe that it would be able to spotlight those recommendations on which all downtown interests were likely to be able to unite. Moreover, it could formulate, with consultant assistance, tentative downtown viewpoints on matters of controversy between the City Engineer's Office and the Planning Commission.

Three members of the committee—which became known as the Nelson committee, after its chairman—did head the firms with which they were affiliated. Chairman Walter Nelson was president of the Eberhardt Company, a large mortgage banking firm, but by no means one of the city's largest corporations. Nelson personally was held in great esteem throughout the business community. Leslie Park, president of Baker Properties, Inc., was clearly the city's leading real estate man. As previously mentioned, his company was the foremost owner-operator of downtown quality property, and he had taken a deep interest in planning for years. He had been one of the Downtown Council's founders, and its president one year. Roy Larsen was president of the Twin City Federal Savings and Loan Association. The Association had not previously shown much interest in planning, and Larsen was not considered particularly influential as an individual.

The remaining four members were vice-presidents. The most influential by reputation was Joyce Swan, executive vice-president of the *Star* and the *Tribune*. Swan managed the newspapers' day-to-day operations, and in 1961 was to become their publisher. He was not primarily a professional discussant, but the *Star* and *Tribune* took a strong interest in civic projects and Swan often represented them. Like Park, he was a founder and former president of the Downtown Council. Robert Cerny, vice-president of the architectural firm of Thorshov and Cerny, had been a prime mover in the early phases of lower loop redevelopment and was a charter member of the Downtown Council's Board of Directors. Although he did not speak for any particular downtown interest, his professional advice carried substantial weight in many quarters. Lester Eck was a vice-president of the Minneapolis Gas Company. He was not considered very influential personally, nor had the Gas Company hitherto taken an interest in planning. Dayton, it will be remembered, had been on Engelen's "consultant" list.

Three men served as ex officio members of the Nelson committee. They were Henry Rutledge, current president of the Council; Gerald Moore, its executive director; and Robert Fischer, the chairman of its Development Committee. Rutledge was executive vice-president of the Northwestern National Bank. Fischer and Moore, we have already noted, were members of Engelen's "consultant" group. An interesting sidelight on the *Plan*'s assertion that people who moved out of the city tended to become inactive in civic affairs was the fact that nine of the ten committee members, including those in an ex officio capacity, lived outside of the city limits. All of them, of course, worked downtown.

While the Nelson committee was being organized, the Downtown Council sponsored an afternoon-evening "seminar" at a leading downtown hotel. Several hundred downtown executives attended, and speakers were imported from outside the city—General Otto Nelson of the New York Life Insurance Company; Kenneth Zweiner of the Harris Trust and Savings Bank of Chicago, who was chairman of the Chicago Central Area Committee; and Herman Finer, professor of political science at the University of Chicago. Three local executives who spoke briefly were Donald Dayton, president of the Dayton Company, Walter Nelson, and Henry Rutledge. The imported speakers discussed the benefits of planning in general terms, and ways in which businessmen had helped in other cities to effectuate plans. Downtown Council leaders said that the meeting was intended simply to put the business community on notice that a plan existed, and that planning had become respectable. No one said anything specific about the *Central Minneapolis Plan* or about anything else for that matter. Nonetheless, the small sample of businessmen in attendance who were interviewed seemed to understand the underlying idea of the "seminar": to make clear that downtown planning had become respectable.

The foregoing activities were concerned with the evaluation of the plan for Central Minneapolis generally. Meanwhile, consultant Aschman worked on the Nicollet Avenue study. In June 1960 he completed his report on potential Nicollet Avenue improvements for the Nicollet Avenue Subcommittee of the Downtown Council Development Committee.[66] The members of the subcommittee, representing every leading Nicollet Avenue retailer and prospective owner, expected to use Aschman's report in discussing prosperity treatment of the Avenue with top management in their own companies and with the owners of small businesses located on it.

The consultant explained that, in addition to containing 90 per cent of the central commercial district's primary shoppers' goods stores, Nicollet Avenue carried less traffic than any street parallel to it. It carried one-sixth as much bus traffic as its adjoining parallel street, and just one thousand vehicles *in toto*, including twenty-five buses, during the peak hour. The only buildings on it requiring vehicular access were at corners and could be reached from the cross streets. In short, the report bore out Engelen's assertion that Nicollet Avenue could easily and profitably be altered to improve pedestrian amenities.

Aschman listed five possible treatments: (1) a continous surface mall shutting off traffic *across* as well as *on* Nicollet Avenue; (2) a series of plazas or surface malls interrupted at each street intersection; (3) a modified street, with widened sidewalks, curbside landscaping, and similar arrangements; (4) a transit street, closed to all vehicles except city buses, and with much wider sidewalks then at present; and (5) underground or elevated concourses connecting the four corners at street intersections. The first four possibilities were alternatives; the fifth, however, was compatible with the "series of plazas," "modified street," and "transit street" concepts. The mall proposal, of course, would eliminate intersections altogether.

Aschman indicated that he had evaluated each possibility on the basis of fifteen criteria. In fact, however, it was clear that each possibility stood or fell on the basis of one or a few considerations. The continuous mall concept was clearly unfeasible because it involved blocking all crosstown traffic for the mall's length. Every-

[66] *Nicollet Avenue Study: Principles and Techniques for Retail Street Improvement,* prepared for the Downtown Council of Minneapolis, Minnesota, by Barton-Aschman Associates of Evanston, Illinois, June 1960.

one agreed that traffic chaos would ensue. The modified street concept was potentially useful but hardly dramatic. Its actual effectiveness would depend almost entirely "on the excellence and ingenuity of architectural design." The "series of plazas" concept, which was what Engelen had meant when he used the word "mall," offered almost the full attractiveness to pedestrians of a continuous mall, and threatened no serious traffic disruption. The "transit street" would be less attractive because of noise and fumes, and would make crossing Nicollet Avenue to shop a little more hazardous, but it had several distinct advantages over the plaza. It opened the way for buses to bring shoppers directly in front of Nicollet Avenue stores, an important factor during the long, cold Minneapolis winters. It made possible inauguration of a "no fare" plan for bus rides on Nicollet Avenue, which would link the shopping area with parking facilities to the south and the lower loop to the north.

Aschman suggested that a combination of either the plazas or transit streets with intersectional concourses would be more dramatic than either would be separately. The concourses promised both protection from the weather and freedom from the hazards of street crossing. They could easily be designed to link the four major downtown department stores, thereby solidifying their position as the main shopping attraction of the area, but perhaps weakening the position of their lesser competitors. Unfortunately, each concourse would cost five times as much as a block of plaza or transit way. Aschman estimated that each elevated concourse would cost $250,000. Subsurface concourses would cost about $100,000 more. Each block of plaza would cost about $45,000. The cost of each block of transit way would be about $50,000. Streets could be "modified" for about $15,000 per block. These estimates did not include the costs of new design features—pools, canopies, screens, display structures, and so on.

Aschman informed the Nicollet Avenue Subcommittee orally that he and George Barton both favored the transit-street alternative; the members of the subcommittee inclined to agree, but decided to withhold any formal recommendation for diplomatic reasons. They wanted to let others arrive at their own conclusions from Aschman's report. They were unanimous, however, in agreeing that their own top managements were in a mood to "do something" along planning lines and that Nicollet Avenue improvements were the things most likely to get done. They estimated that within a year or two the leading firms would agree on a "series of plazas" or "transit way" treatment, and would start trying to convince the owners of small businesses along the Avenue.

The subcommittee members saw several obstacles. First, the small-business owners on Nicollet, as elsewhere, tended to be suspicious of the large corporations and had no time of their own for civic affairs. It would be difficult to induce them to believe that nothing was being hidden from them, and then to get them to think about Aschman's reasoning. The process might take several years. Owners of property on other downtown avenues might prove even more recalcitrant, and not without reason. For Aschman seemed to admit that if Nicollet Avenue were made more attractive it would draw pedestrians from other downtown streets. If Nicollet were made a transit way, additional bus traffic would be routed on it, and more transit patrons would find its stores the most convenient to use. Whether or not these were "problems" was a matter of opinion. Aschman wrote that while "consideration should be given to the effect of Nicollet Avenue improvement upon the immediate welfare of shoppers' goods stores off the Avenue . . . it should be a long-term objective to locate as many of such enterprises as possible in such proximity of the Avenue as to gain for them the benefits of generation by the compact, attractive prime district." The representatives of Nicollet Avenue corporations, and some corporations whose interests pervaded all of downtown, felt that its improvement would benefit all of Central Mineapolis in the long run. But they did not know how many entrepreneurs on other avenues would be willing to take distasteful medicine in the short run. The opposition would probably prove insignificant if Nicollet Avenue businessmen could achieve unanimity and organize the project themselves. If, on the other hand, they had to ask the City Council to concoct an assessment formula, or to contribute money from general tax revenues, the project would have rough going. Even while taking this into consideration, however, Downtown Council leaders expressed confidence that the plaza or transit treatment would come into operation within three to five years.

(As it happened, the City Council authorized detailed engineering studies leading to construction of a transit street in May 1964. The studies and construction were to be financed by special assessment of the affected property owners. The assessment formula was one worked out by the property owners themselves.)

Let us now return to the reception of the *Plan* as a whole. During the spring and summer of 1960, the Nelson committee began slowly to educate itself about the economic rationale of the *Plan*. It met with the city planning staff, the city engineer's staff, president Nelson of RERC, Aschman, and Barton. Committee members indicated that they would first try to determine the soundness of the *Plan*'s concepts, and only later begin to worry about problems of implementation. As a first step, they hoped to isolate the areas of agreement among city planners, city engineers, and their own consultants. The consultants were of crucial importance, because the committee had confidence in their capacity and in the purity of their business orientation. Committee members judged that concepts which fell within the area of technical agreement would come to fruition in time, though many years of patient discussion might be necessary in some cases, especially in those involving cooperative action. After coming to understand the areas of agreement, committee members said, they would move on to those of controversy and uncertainty. They expected that the committee would ask the consultants who had been employed in the preparation of the *Plan* to analyze the crucial points of difference between the city planners and city engineers. They had no idea when the committee would reach the point of formulating its own positions on controversial issues.

(In the event, the committee completed the first and simplest part of its work on November 21, 1960, when it agreed unanimously to endorse the *Plan*'s general principles and concepts. The committee never met again, apparently for no more substantial reason than that its senior members were too busy. When I returned to Minneapolis several years later, Downtown Council leaders remembered only that great things had been expected of the Nelson committee, but that it had never seemed to get off the ground.)

During the summer of 1960 a number of prominent men in the Downtown Council consented to my request for their assessment of the *Plan*'s likely impact. With surprising unanimity they replied that the *Plan*'s effect, except on Nicollet Avenue, would be difficult to perceive for many years. They emphasized that the *Plan* was a dream, an ideal, and that it would be erroneous to think that success consisted of accomplishing projects just like those outlined in the *Plan*. Better, perhaps, than the planning staff had hoped they would, these businessmen accepted the doctrine that concepts were what mattered, not details. They expected the major concepts articulated in the *Plan* to be adhered to rather closely, and while they expected the *Plan*'s specific proposed means of implementation to be compromised severely, this did not upset them at all.

Their views may be illustrated with reference to the peripheral parking concept. They thought that it would win general approval and be encouraged by zoning regulations. Most of them did not think, however, that any properties should be zoned for parking only. This seemed too severe a restriction on the options available to property owners. Nor did they think that all parking facilities should be confined to the periphery.[67] They emphasized their belief that downtown would lose a great deal of business if everyone who had a short errand had to park on the periphery and walk several blocks to his destination. Furthermore, they believed that high-level executives would be deterred from locating their offices downtown if they thought that they were to be denied parking space close to their desks. Those already in the central area would vigorously oppose any rigid regulation. As a matter of principle, the businessmen doubted that the market should be stifled; they believed that those willing to pay for core parking should be permitted to have it—except on Nicollet Avenue.[68]

[67] The *Plan* had not proposed that *all* parking be eliminated from within the core. It had proposed that all major parking terminals should be located on the periphery, and that parking within the core should be held by regulation to levels that could easily be accommodated on internal streets. The difference with the businessmen was over emphasis rather than principle.

[68] Some of the planners believed that core parkers should be charged in some way for the street congestion to which they contributed as well as for the parking services they consumed. Few of the businessmen considered this desirable or feasible. President Leslie Park of Baker Properties, however, suggested that the traditional policy of giving parking facilities low property-tax assessments should be ended. He thought that the assessor had an obligation to keep the pressure on each core-property owner to develop his property to its most profitable potential use.

They confidently judged that the city would never finance gigantic ramp garages or underground expressways from the freeway to them. They said that the city could not, and should not, abandon all its other obligations for years to invest in an enormous parking-facility project. In addition, the operators of private parking facilities took a dim view of government-subsidized competition. Other businessmen inclined to support them, again on principle. The private operators, in fact, denied that any shortage of parking facilities existed. They admitted that occasionally at midday it became difficult to find a lot that was not full, but the city's own 1958 parking survey revealed that at the half-hour of peak accumulation on a typical weekday the central commercial area's facilities were only 80 per cent full. In any event, the operators measured "adequacy" on a scale of profit. Few considered their present return on investment abnormally high.

Virtually all downtown leaders admitted, of course, that when the freeway came into operation, large facilities designed to provide all-day parking at reasonable rates would be needed. But they believed that investors would rush in to meet the demand. In order to charge prices that the average commuter was willing to pay, most would have to build on the core's periphery, even in the absence of zoning regulations. But unless the federal government came up with a new grant program, the underground expressways would not be built. In their absence, the parking ramps would have to be more widely dispersed and less monumental than those conceived by Engelen.

Everyone expressed conviction that a new zoning ordinance would be passed within five or ten years, and that it would incorporate the principles of compactness and economic clustering. No one doubted, however, that the intensive zone would be defined broadly enough to include all land that might conceivably come into intensive CBD-type use. All agreed as well that the ordinance would have to include a "grandfather clause" insuring the owners of older buildings that they would be permitted to remodel and expand at will. Most of those interviewed agreed, finally, that the floor-area ratios enacted would not place significant restrictions on any builders.

With regard to land-use regulation, the general view was that large investors would have appreciated the economic benefits of compactness and clustering even without the *Plan*. They had no fear, therefore, that a tough zoning ordinance would deter any significant amount of investment in the downtown. They added that if the ordinance ever threatened to block any project that a substantial number of downtown businessmen considered "good for downtown," the ordinance would be quickly amended. They generally noted that they considered this wise; the ordinance should not be a straitjacket, but should leave the way open for evaluation of particular proposed projects "on their merits." With regard to height, bulk, and design regulation, most were relatively indifferent. Several pointed out that the floor-area ratios proposed in the zoning draft would not have affected any building of recent decades. There had not been a truly speculative office building constructed in Minneapolis for forty years. Leslie Park, and some others highly sympathetic to planning in general, opposed floor-area ratio and design regulation on principle. They noted that the object of floor-area ratio regulation was variety and that the object of design regulation was good taste. They considered both of these objects impossible to measure objectively and insufficient to justify limiting the freedom of property owners. When confronted with the planner defense that sunlight penetration, air circulation, and ease of pedestrian movement were also at stake, they pointed out that the planners had no standards of adequacy for determining the proper balance between compactness and spaciousness. They said that in their opinion the denizens of downtown Minneapolis were *not* starved for sunlight, fresh air, or walking space.[69]

(In the event, the City Council enacted a new zoning ordinance for the city in May 1963. Its downtown portions closely reflected the business community's views as reported in the two preceding paragraphs. Its basic floor-area ratio for the core was fourteen, rather than the twelve originally recommended in the *Plan*.)

[69] Park added that he thought compactness was by far the more important ideal for downtown. You could only have the amenities of interior arcades, covered second-level walkways, great variety, and so on, where great numbers of people congregated daily. The automobile put everyone close to open space in his daily life. The important thing downtown was to provide something different. He did not object to planners trying to *persuade* developers to share their conceptions of good taste, but he did not think public *power* should be available to further this end.

On the whole, the businessmen inclined to optimism, noting that the Minneapolis central core, according to the planners' own testimony, had developed in remarkably fine fashion through the normal operation of economic forces. And so it went with the entire *Plan*. No one expected a great deal of public activity, but everyone expected the major concepts in the *Plan* to be realized gradually.

Downtown Council leaders spoke as though the *Plan* were a consulting report of their own use. They expected no initiative from public bodies in implementing it. They seemed untroubled by the thought that they would have to evaluate the *Plan* and "sell" any aspects of it that they considered worthwhile without much help from other sources. Perhaps because of this, none seemed to sense the *Plan* as in any way a threat. They insisted simultaneously that economic rather than political forces would dictate the future of downtown and that the *Plan* would prove a useful tool. They appeared to mean that they intended to use it as they typically used consulting reports—to illuminate the concrete meaning of self-interest. The Downtown Council had taken shape as part of a continuing educational process, in which more companies, and more important people within them, were searching for common interests with each other. Eventually, the professional discussants felt, top management would realize that something important was going on and would assume leadership of the Downtown Council. When that happened, they said, the Downtown Council would be able to serve as an effective regulator of central area development.

This was a rather long and problematic view, however. In the short run, most of the businessmen believed, the *Plan*'s most perceptible effects were likely to be on public facility management. Two examples were frequently cited. First, the Nelson committee intended to have consultants evaluate the whole controversy between the city planners and the city engineers over specialized street use. Had the planners not articulated this controversy, the businessmen noted, it might have gone unrecognized for many years.[70] Second, the recommendations of the city planners and consultants seemed likely to have an immediate impact on a large

[70] In the event, the Nelson committee never got around to considering the controversy.

project, that of expanding the civic auditorium. The auditorium was located several blocks south of the major convention hotels, which were themselves at the southern edge of the core area. Auditorium expansion had for some years ranked high on the city's capital improvement agenda, but those interested in it had taken for granted that the direction of expansion would be south. Supported by the consultants, Engelen, beginning in 1959, had challenged the reasoning behind this assumption. Citing the principle of compactness, he had contended that the direction of expansion should be north, toward the major hotels and the downtown shopping district. Alongside this, he had maintained, the primary argument in favor of southerly expansion—low land-cost—was trivial. Expansion to the north would place the auditorium closer to downtown hotels, restaurants, and stores. It would thus encourage people attending events at the auditorium to spend money downtown. Moreover, it would improve the central area's appearance; a magnificent opportunity would be lost if the new facilities were constructed on the side of the auditorium that few people saw. By mid-1960 it seemed highly probable that Engelen's view would prevail; he had definitely persuaded the leading members of the Downtown Council.[71]

In Retrospect

At least in the immediate sense, the planners' efforts to consult during the Central Minneapolis planning process failed. Yet, to a surprising degree, they achieved their objective of working within the most relevant framework of power. This was true even though the City Council had little to do with the *Plan,* and the mayor al-

---

[71] In 1961, however, the business leaders acquiesced as the city officially endorsed the concept of southerly expansion. According to reports reaching the writer, the leaders of the Downtown Council had continued to favor northerly expansion, but they had compromised in the face of adamant opposition from the city councilman who represented the downtown ward. Northerly expansion would have required the closing of one street, and as a matter of principle he voted against all proposed street vacations. His argument was that one could not solve traffic problems by closing streets. His primary constituency, the small property owners and merchants of the downtown and its immediate environs, tended to support this position. The Council as a whole treated street vacations as matters to be handled by each alderman in his own ward.

most nothing. Planning Director Irvin correctly perceived that the City Council and mayor would normally ratify proposals for downtown behind which downtown businessmen united so long as they did not require substantial expenditure by the city. The reason was not that central area businessmen possessed great power, but that no other interest groups were likely to challenge them on downtown affairs. The best available focus of downtown business power was the Downtown Council. Irvin and Engelen convinced the Downtown Council's leaders that the objectives of the *Plan* were business objectives. They did this by justifying each recommendation of the *Plan* in economic terms, and by employing the Downtown Council's own consultants to help develop the *Plan's* economic rationale. When the council subsequently asked its consultants for aid in evaluating the *Plan,* they were hardly in a position to be hypercritical.

The planners denied that they themselves had been co-opted. They judged that in focusing on economic issues they were simply dealing with a strategic factor. The crucial cultural functions of downtown seemed to follow directly from its economic strength. If their approach produced other dividends as well, they saw no reason to complain. The most important of these dividends were (1) that their approach provided the *Plan* discussion with a focus for disciplined, and therefore highly persuasive, reasoning, and (2) that it rendered more likely the possibility that private expenditure to effectuate the *Plan* might obviate the need for public spending. They believed that the latter fact was particularly important. Every organized interest in the city competed for public revenues, and the electorate regularly demonstrated its disapproval of tax increases. Downtown businessmen themselves preferred to think of the execution of the *Plan* as primarily a nongovernmental function. As a practical matter, they recognized that only if *they* executed the *Plan* could they be certain that proposals were evaluated on grounds of which they approved. As a matter of principle, they thought it was best, when feasible, for government to permit citizens to solve their own problems. This method, they believed, minimized bureaucratic regulation, and prevented any set of officials from imposing its own ideas of desirability without fully convincing those who had to live with them.

When businessmen accepted responsibility for executing the *Plan* they did not of course mean to imply that any existing institution could perform the task on its own authority. Instead, they professed to consider the *Plan* a working paper for use in a slow-moving, never-ending civic discussion.[72] They did not expect any immediate visible results. They maintained that two features of downtown civic life were indispensable to an understanding of it and unchangeable over the short run: (1) every corporation negotiated as a sovereign power, and (2) the individuals who negotiated *for* the corporations seldom possessed authority to make important concessions or commitments.

Downtown civic leaders said that they had learned from experience to think in terms of mood rather than decision. The emergence of the Downtown Council itself, they held, was hard to explain except as a local manifestation of a national mood among businessmen. The discussants who first personified this mood in Minneapolis had had to shed their notions of decisiveness, and to learn the arts of patient, indirect, good-humored negotiation. Over a period of time, the mood seemed to become contagious; more and more firms were assigning people to work with the Downtown Council. Now that a continuing discussion had begun, consensus on ways and means of handling downtown problems might begin to evolve. The presidents of the large corporations, however, were not yet ready to take time from administering their business affairs to participate in long-drawn-out negotiations, and they instinctively shied away from the idea of committing money to projects they would not control.

Those vice presidents who did take part in civic affairs therefore inclined to discount grandiose recommendations. They judged that the city government would not finance them, and they could not envision their own corporations working out the details of

[72] For this reason, they were inclined to consider the opening sentence of this section inaccurate. They were less concerned about consultation during the preparation of the *Plan* than about consultation during the preparation of actual projects that might flow from the *Plan*. The important thing to them was that the business community retained confidence in the planners and intended to consider the more practical parts of the *Plan* seriously. By the standards of 1952 or 1953, they noted, this was very substantial success indeed, and it was certainly related to the planners' efforts to win the trust of the business community.

joint multimillion dollar projects. On minor matters, like Nicollet Avenue treatment, subordinate personnel like themselves might be permitted to work out agreements because only insignificant sums were needed for financing; top management would have little reason to quibble over assessment details. If the economic rationale for action were convincing, only owners of small businesses would require much persuasion. But the discussants believed that two other types of recommendation were the ones *most* likely to come to fruition quickly. The first involved recommendations that individual investors might effectuate while pursuing their own interest. For example, private investors would probably provide sufficient parking facilities, though with fewer accessory refinements than the planners contemplated. It seemed probable, of course, that such developments would have taken place even in the absence of a plan, but the discussants did not worry about that. The second type comprised recommendations that fell within long-accepted spheres of government responsibility: traffic control, management of the civic auditorium, zoning, urban renewal, and so on. The ideal proposal in this category would cost the city government little or nothing, appeal to everyone interested in it, attract federal funds to the city, and promise to increase future local tax revenues.[73] Politicians had no reason to block such projects, and a good deal of incentive to facilitate their implementation, so as to be able at election time to cite them as local government accomplishments.[74] The lower loop project had approached this ideal; the few thousand people affected adversely by it had been politically insignificant and inarticulate.

[73] On reading this, Robert Fischer commented that while each of the positive factors listed was certainly important, he did not think that the leaders of the Downtown Council had thought consciously about trying to combine all of them in specific projects. They had rather looked first for worthwhile projects, he said, and then turned their attention to means of implementing them.

[74] Several of those interviewed suggested that the city's professional discussants also had a good deal of incentive to press them, in order to have some tangible accomplishment to show for their civic activity. Robert Fischer probably spoke for most of the discussants, however, when he denied that he had ever thought in these terms or that he had ever heard others speak in these terms. There was of course a natural desire for accomplishment, he stated, but it had never become either uncritical or unduly enthusiastic. Nor had it reflected any desire to impress top management cheaply.

Similarly, the *Plan* called for urban renewal activity in the residential neighborhoods near downtown. Downtown Council leaders appeared fully alive to the benefits their companies would reap if high- and middle-income people could be attracted in significant numbers to central area housing. They thought that the Downtown Council would vigorously support federally aided urban renewal activity in Central Minneapolis residential neighborhoods, but that progress would necessarily be slow. It took a long time to formulate and carry out a renewal project; the first efforts would have to be on a small scale, because no one knew how enthusiastically investors or potential residents would respond. Presumably, however, leading downtown businessmen would do what they could to encourage potential investors, and to ease their financing problems.

City planners found the businessmen's attitude difficult to accept. Having devoted two years to the formulation of the *Plan*, they tended to think of it as a coherent whole, every part of which was essential to the rest. They had envisioned a massive cooperative effort—government and business working together—in which, within a few years, the great things that needed doing would be done. They found it hard to conceive of their *Plan* as a mere working paper in a long educational process, which had begun before the *Plan* appeared and might go on for many years without a great deal of regard for its existence. During the first months after circulation of the draft *Plan*, planners saw most clearly that the city engineer had disparaged their ideas and that downtown businessmen were preparing to react at a maddeningly slow pace—again, Nicollet Avenue was the exception. According to every indication, neither public officials *nor* businessmen intended to spend much money to accomplish the objectives of the *Plan*. No downtown businessmen seemed anxious to subject themselves to public regulation. Downtown Council leaders, the staunchest supporters of planning, spoke of permitting the major concepts of the *Plan* to work themselves out through the inevitable movements of private capital in search of profit. Not surprisingly, the planners doubted sorrowfully and prematurely whether their work would have any significant independent influence. No one had prepared them to wait ten or fifteen years before attempting a tentative answer.

Postscript

The author returned briefly to Minneapolis in June 1964. Whether the *Central Minneapolis Plan* had proved a success to that point depended on one's perspectives and expectations.

The only important public project directly traceable to the *Plan* was the Nicollet Avenue transit street, which was expected to come into operation in September 1965. In addition, the city zoning ordinance enacted in May 1963 had adhered closely to the land-use principles for downtown articulated in the *Plan*. The Downtown Council and the City Council had refused to act on the planners' proposal that some peripheral land should be zoned for parking alone, but the area zoned for central business district uses was compact enough to please the planners.

Public and private construction in recent years, aside from the auditorium expansion, had generally tended to accentuate the compactness of the core area. The auditorium expansion itself, while it detracted somewhat from compactness, was expected substantially to increase the attractiveness of Minneapolis to conventions. Moreover, downtown Minneapolis had experienced a building boom in recent years. In the opinion of Downtown Council leaders, the lower loop project—taken together with general prosperity and a continuing intensification of competition from the suburbs—had spurred investors with a stake in the other end of downtown (the core) to rejuvenate their own properties. The process had begun about 1956 or 1957, but most of the construction stemming from it had occurred after 1959. The first great project had been the 20-million-dollar, 28-story, First National Bank Building, completed in 1960. The boom had begun to taper off with the completion of Baker Properties' 20-million-dollar Northstar Center in 1963. Northstar Center combined stores at ground level, interior parking facilities for 1,000 cars, 610,000 square feet of office space (477,000 of them new), 180 hotel rooms, and several restaurants.[75] These were the most dramatic additions

[75] It may be noted that Northstar Center was connected by covered second-level walkways to two adjoining blocks. One of these blocks included Donaldson's department store and the Northwestern National Bank building; the other was a block of internally connected office buildings known as the Baker Block. The planners did not claim that they had had anything to do

to the core, but a number of lesser structures had also been built, and numerous important additions to existing buildings had taken place. The Downtown Council estimated that $129.1 million had been spent on construction in the Central Area between 1960 and 1963, as compared with $24.4 million in the previous four-year period.[76]

The most significant expansion relative to the magnitude of previously existing facilities was in the hotel and motel category. The Central Area's supply of Class A and B hotel and motel

---

with the decision by Baker Properties to build Northstar Center, but they did note that it added substantially to the compactness of the core. They also noted that the *Plan* had pointed to the corner of Marquette Avenue and Seventh Street as the most likely site for the development of second-level walkways. The three blocks connected by the Baker Properties walkways all had corners at Marquette and Seventh. One point about Northstar Center that the planners chose not to emphasize was that the development of so much parking space in the middle of the core violated a central principle of the *Plan*.

Gerald Moore noted that he thought there was a real possibility that within several years the entire core would be connected by privately developed interior arcades, second-level walkways, and tunnels. The cold Minneapolis climate made these highly desirable, particularly with Southdale existing in the same metropolitan area. He thought that most of the arcades and tunnels were already in existence, and that a fairly modest investment in new connecting links (mainly second-level walkways) would make possible exploitation of the whole chain. He believed that quite a few downtown businessmen were aware of the value of such a development, and that its realization in the foreseeable future was a very real possibility. It seemed likely that the discussion of planning principles that had been going on in Minneapolis for six or seven years by this time had contributed significantly to the perception of this opportunity.

[76] These totals were compiled by the author from data on the individual projects supplied by the Downtown Council. Each project had already been categorized by the Council according to its completion date. This factor undoubtedly led to some underestimate of the actual amount of construction work going on just prior to 1960. On the other hand, where projects were listed as having been completed over several-year periods, their costs were arbitrarily divided equally among the years involved. *This* factor probably led to an *over*estimate of the amount of 1956–1959 construction. It is impossible to say whether the two factors cancelled each other out, but they did tend in that direction. Finally, it should be noted that public street construction projects were omitted from these calculations. All other known projects were included.

rooms had been 3,810 in 1958. That figure had grown by 50 per cent at the end of 1963. The *Plan's* total recommended expansion to 1970 had already taken place—with one important exception, to be discussed below. Several of the new facilities were quite striking. The Sheraton Corporation of America had built a 385-room hotel in the Lower Loop. At the other end of downtown, a new 350-room hotel—the Capp-Towers—had been constructed. The city's second and fourth largest hotels, the Leamington and the Radisson, had each added 200 rooms since 1960.[77] The hotel portion of Northstar Center had been constructed. And five new motels, with a total of 611 rooms, had opened on sites within a few minutes of the core. The exception to this bright picture was that no new headquarters hotel had come into being. It will be remembered that RERC had perceived a need for a new hotel having 600–1,000 rooms and more elaborate facilities for meetings than any of the city's existing hotels had. It had believed that such a hotel could generate enough new convention business for the city that it could thrive without hurting the other hotels. Development of such a hotel in the near future appeared unlikely, because the consensus among informed observers was that the city currently had too many hotel and motel rooms. It was believed that demand would require several years at least to catch up with the existing supply.[78]

Whether the *Plan* had been a significant cause of the hotel and motel construction boom was impossible to say. Those who doubted that it had been noted the following points. First, roughly half the expansion that had taken place had already been announced when RERC was writing its report. Second, the Minneapolis hotel and motel construction boom was part of a national spurt of downtown hotel construction which had gotten under way in the late 1950's after three decades of inactivity. And third, the expansion had been excessive, disregarding the *Plan's*

[77] After the additions, they were the city's second and *third* largest hotels.
[78] RERC had estimated a 1970 demand for 2,400–2,600 new hotel and motel rooms assuming construction of the new headquarters hotel. It had expected the market to be expanding at a rate of 60 rooms per year during the 1960's. By the end of 1963, a total of 1,924 new rooms had been completed—in the absence of construction of the new headquarters hotel. No further projects were on the horizon.

estimate of the limits of potential demand until the possibility of oversupply had been realized. The planners did believe, however, that going through the process of making demand projections and publicizing them had probably increased the amount of hotel investment that had taken place. They also emphasized that any overbuilding that had taken place was quite minor. Most of the Downtown Council leaders interviewed tended to agree with the planners on both counts.

The portions of the *Plan* dealing with traffic and parking had been ignored almost entirely. The superblock concept was not a live issue. The idea of the 10th Street distributor garage with an expressway connecting it to the freeway had never been taken seriously. Parking facilities had continued to develop on the peripheries of downtown, as they had prior to the start of work on the *Plan,* but the greatest expansion of parking facilities had taken place right in the heart of the core.[79] The primary reason for this appeared to be that the parking consultant used by most of the large downtown companies disagreed with the *Plan*'s parking recommendations. The consultant was National Garages, Inc., of Detroit, personified in its relations with Minneapolis by one of its partners, George Devlin.[80] Devlin advised that today's consumers and executives demanded comfort and were willing to pay for it. He told retailers that they could not afford to forego building adjacent parking facilities so long as their central area and suburban competitors had them. He expressed the general philosophy that executives willing to pay for all day parking should have it. He did not believe that any parkers should be subsidized (even those shopping at a department store which owned the parking facility they were using), but he did believe that the market could be trusted to distribute parking facilities wisely. To those interested in parking as a business in itself, Devlin advised that economic studies conducted by National Ga-

[79] Between 1960 and 1963, nearly 3,600 ramp parking spaces came into operation. Another 800 were scheduled to come into operation in 1965. All were in the core. There had been a *total* of 2,400 in operation at the end of 1959.

[80] National Garages also designed, engineered, and operated parking facilities. It had performed all of these services at one time or another for most of the large downtown companies, and it continued to be by far the largest operator of parking facilities in Minneapolis.

rages in Minneapolis had shown that the most consistent and the highest returns on parking investments were consistently obtained in the heart of the core, as close to the major generators of core-bound traffic as possible. With very few exceptions, downtown businessmen found Devlin's philosophy congenial and his reasoning persuasive. In this situation, the *Plan*'s recommendations with regard to parking had been all but forgotten. Planning Director Irvin noted that if he had it to do over again he would employ Devlin as the Planning Commission's consultant and work out the *Plan*'s parking recommendations in cooperation with him.

To the extent that the *Plan* had been successful, the reason appeared to be that the process of discussion surrounding it had influenced the thinking of downtown businessmen. Even the Nicollet Avenue transit street could be viewed as essentially a private investment, because the affected property owners had worked out the consensus which had made it possible, and they were to finance it by special assessment. Moreover, the City Council had insisted on a provision in the ordinance authorizing the transit street to the effect that if the innovation proved unworkable, Nicollet Avenue property owners would be assessed again for restoring the street to its original condition. Similarly, the zoning provisions for downtown had been acceptable to the City Council primarily because the downtown business community had backed them. It was impossible to determine whether the numerous private investors who had contributed to the implementation of the *Plan*'s concepts in the years since 1960 had been influenced by the *Plan*. It was possible to argue that their own consultants and the consultants employed by the planners and the Downtown Council had articulated the same economic principles. In point of fact, the consultants were the same in many instances. On the other hand, the planners tended to believe that they had performed an important catalytic role in organizing the coherent discussion of downtown's economic future, and that they had probably influenced the thinking of the consultants—and, through them, of the business community—as much as the consultants had influenced theirs. The outsider had no way of judging.

The planning function itself appeared somewhat less healthy than it had in 1960. If federal aid funds were discounted, the planning budget had declined by about one-sixth (and stood at about two-thirds the level that Aschman had recommended in 1957). A budget cut in 1963 had forced the Planning Department to let nearly half of its junior staff go. A number of other positions were currently unfilled due to lack of suitable candidates for them, and some observers feared that the City Council might eliminate a couple of them at budget time. (It was always attractive to eliminate vacant positions.) There had been some resurgence of right wing extremism in Minneapolis during the previous year or so, as there had been elsewhere in the country. Some right-wingers had questioned the desirability of city planning in principle, and several had publicly associated the concept of zoning with "socialism." During the brief period of the author's visit to the city, the *Minneapolis Tribune* cited the downtown ward's alderman to the effect that he opposed zoning because: "Nobody should tell a man how to invest his money." It cited the assistant city attorney charged with handling zoning matters for the city as having said: "Houston is the fastest-growing city in the country and the only one of its size without zoning." [81] The City Council as a whole had not indicated that it was moving toward extreme laissez-faire or antiplanning views, but it had shown its disfavor toward the planners in a number of ways. The most obvious way had been budget-cutting. Another had been to revise pay categories so that planners at various ranks received less pay than engineers at comparable ranks. All informed observers agreed that the leading councilmen had come vigorously to resent the outside connections of the planning staff, and that planning activity was sustained mainly by the support of the Downtown Council. To a lesser extent, numerous neighborhood organizations of property owners spread throughout the city also provided important support.

On the other hand, Downtown Council leaders still spoke in extremely friendly terms of the planning function and of Irvin personally.[82] They believed that he had had no choice but to fight

[81] Both quotes appeared on June 21, 1964, p. 10. The alderman in question was one of only two who had voted against the zoning ordinance on its final passage in May 1963. He was the same alderman who had insisted in 1961 that auditorium expansion be in a southerly direction. Parenthetically, the other alderman who had voted against the zoning ordinance was the City Council's designated representative on the Planning Commission.

[82] Rodney Engelen had resigned to take a position with Barton-Aschman Associates in the fall of 1960. He had become *persona non grata* at City Hall

the battles that had made him enemies in City Hall, and they thought that the planning function could still produce results when it had the support of the groups its proposals were likely to affect. If federal aid programs were counted, the planning budget had risen substantially since 1958. The pace of planning activity, therefore, had certainly not slowed down. The planners believed that their ideas were gradually penetrating (though the source of the ideas was not always recognized) many corners of the city's economic and political life, and that the new city zoning ordinance alone was worth more than the cost of their activity in the previous five or six years. Whether the planning function would have looked more vigorous had Planning Director Irvin chosen in 1958 to strive primarily for City Hall approval, it was impossible to say.

---

before leaving by working openly for charter reform in the referendum campaign of that year. On his departure, the City Council had abolished the position of Assistant Director for Advanced Planning. No comparably well-paid position had ever been created to take its place.

PART TWO

V

The Goals of

Comprehensive Planning

The Ideal of Comprehensive Planning

Those who consider themselves comprehensive planners typically claim that their most important functions are (1) to create a master plan to guide the deliberations of specialist planners, (2) to evaluate the proposals of specialist planners in the light of the master plan, and (3) to coordinate the planning of specialist agencies so as to ensure that their proposals reinforce each other to further the public interest. Each of these functions requires for ideal performance that the comprehensive planners (a) understand the overall public interest, at least in connection with the subject matter of their plans, and (b) that they possess causal knowledge which enables them to gauge the approximate net effect of proposed actions on the public interest.

This chapter is concerned with some ways in which city planners have approached the former of these two requirements, which—contrary to most students of planning—I consider the more interesting one. If comprehensive planners deal with a great many more areas of public policies than specialists, their factual and causal knowledge in each area is bound to appear shallow—at least by comparison with that of the specialists in it.[1] Hence their claims to comprehensiveness, if they are to be persuasive, must refer primarily to a special knowledge of the public interest. ✳

Every government planner of integrity, no matter how specialized, must be guided by some conception of the public interest.

[1] This theme will be taken up again in Chap. VIII.

And since plans are proposals of concerted action to achieve goals, each must express his conception as a goal or series of goals for his community. He will probably conceive these goals, of course, as constantly shifting rather than highly stable, as always intermediate rather than final, and as more in the nature of criteria than of concrete destinations. Community goal conceptions are likely to have these characteristics because of the limitations on collective human foresight and imagination. Nonetheless it is impossible to plan without some sense of community goals, call them what you will.[2] Moreover, for the planning process in any community to be

[2] A few planners, mainly in the universities, have recently come to doubt this. They are taken with Herbert Simon's model of "satisficing" administrative man, which I believe they fail to understand thoroughly. Several have suggested to me that this model shows up all talk about the need for planning goals as irrelevant. The satisficing model is set forth in Herbert Simon and James G. March, *Organizations* (New York: John Wiley and Sons, 1958), esp. pp. 140–141, 163, 175; Herbert Simon, *Models of Man* (New York: John Wiley and Sons, 1957), Chaps. 10, 14, 16; and Herbert Simon, "Theories of Decision-Making in Economics and Behavioral Science," *American Economic Review*, LXIX, No. 2 (June 1959), p. 253–283.

According to Simon, most theorists until recently accepted the model of "maximizing" (economic) man. Maximizing man was assumed to have all the alternatives that he needed before him and to be able to rank them all with reference to the desirability of their consequences. His ranking ability rested on his possession of a "utility function," which amounted to his values or goals. For purposes of simplicity, I am leaving out here the issue of his ability to forecast consequences. Let us deal in this discussion only with the evaluation of foreseeable consequences.

Satisficing (administrative) man, on the other hand, is moved by stimuli ("e.g.," writes Simon, "a customer order or a fire gong") to search for alternatives. When he finds one that is "good enough," he intelligently avoids spending time, energy, and resources on further search.

Simon himself tends to be indifferent to high-level goal determining processes, so it is understandable that some planners should have concluded that satisficing man does not need goals. According to their interpretation, the determinants of satisficing man's choices are largely, perhaps mainly, subconscious. He knows that in any case most of the consequences of any choice are incomparable on any single operational scale of value. Consequently, being a practical man rather than a utopian intellectual, he reconciles himself to the fact that his choices are bound to be essentially intuitive. From the standpoint of an outsider, the evidence that an alternative is satisfactory is bound to be no more than that it has been chosen.

The above is a misinterpretation of Simon. In his sustained discussions of satisficing Simon always makes clear that one can only speak of an alternative's

democratic—and I assume in these pages that it should be—the goals must win approval from a democratic political process; they must not be goals simply prescribed for the community by planners.

In this chapter we shall examine a few of the difficulties that face planners as they strive to determine community goals democratically. In the next two chapters we shall deal with the difficulties they face as they try to concert action.

Implications of the Ideal

The comprehensive planner must assume that his community's various collective goals can somehow be measured at least roughly as to importance and welded into a single hierarchy of community

---

being satisfactory if it meets standards set prior to its selection. Standards, however, are neither more nor less than goals. If they are not ultimate goals, they must ultimately be evaluated on the basis of their relation to ultimate goals. The very notion of formulating precise standards of adequacy at the beginning of a search for alternatives is, it strikes me, a more literal application of means-ends language than is normally feasible at the higher levels of politics and administration. The processes of balancing ideals, estimates of feasibility, and probable costs of further search are generally far more subtle than this language suggests. The phrase that Chester Barnard frequently used, "successive approximations," seems more appropriate here. This does not mean, however, that general discussions of goals and priorities can be dispensed with in any meaningful planning exercise.

More generally, it may be noted that the satisficing model, even correctly understood, hardly represents a major advance in our understanding of human psychology. The maximizing model has long been recognized as an ideal type, a useful measuring rod against which to compare optimal aspirations with achievements, rather than as a descriptive model of human choice. It has been most useful in economics, where it has been feasible to hypothesize a single substantive goal for actors other than ultimate consumers. Use of the satisficing model, on the other hand, requires that we have substantive knowledge of such variables as the values of actors, the costs of search, and the obstacles to implementation of particular proposals. Unless observers have such knowledge, the satisficing model approaches the conception of it held by the planners mentioned above. It tells us nothing about why any particular actor considered any particular standard "good enough."

One other point worth stressing is that Simon's actors typically assess values, and consequently the significance of obstacles and costs, in purely subjective fashion. Consequently, Simon's theories are essentially theories of irresponsible choice. This may not seem terribly significant when decision-makers are

objectives. In addition, he must argue that technicians like himself can prescribe courses of action to achieve these objectives without great distortion or harmful side-effects of a magnitude sufficient to outweigh the gains achieved through planning. We may conceive a continuum of faith in the feasibility and desirability of comprehensive planning. The "ideal type" defender of comprehensive planning would contend that a serious effort should be made to plan in detail the future evolution of all important economic and

---

choosing for themselves alone—as in the market—or for hierarchical organizations that have no pretensions of democracy or of responsibility to nonmembers. Such theories make both criticism and justification of choices on the basis of value considerations impossible, however, and this does matter in a democratic polity.

In *Organizations* Simon and March discuss the satisficing model in their chapter entitled "Cognitive Limits on Rationality." By contrast, my concern is with social and political obstacles to rationality. My purpose in these pages is political, not psychological, analysis. The approach taken here is that of the politician or citizen confronted with conflicting expert arguments, and anxious to decide wisely. Either may decide whimsically in the end, but it seems both nihilistic and paralyzing to assume in the beginning that no more is possible. It is also untrue, except in a number of rather obvious senses. The goodness of ultimate goals may not be demonstrable, but they are generally not the controversial ones. All the others can be analyzed and compared in terms of the consequences, unintended as well as intended, likely to flow from pursuing them. Simon specifically admits this, but he relegates scholarly consideration of such analyses and comparisons to the Siberia of "philosophy." His followers, whether "practical men" or self-conscious "scientists," are thus led to ignore these matters. I consider this unfortunate. (This viewpoint is elaborated in my introduction to a forthcoming reader that I have edited, entitled *The Politics of American Public Administration* [New York: Dodd, Mead & Co., 1966].)

Moreover, most planners themselves consider it essential for them to be able to demonstrate the nonarbitrary nature of their recommendations. I believe that Paul Davidoff and Thomas Reiner, in their recent article, "A Choice Theory of Planning," have articulated a major preoccupation of the profession in writing: "We are concerned with the problem, so trenchantly posed by Haar, that a major task confronting the planner is to see that he acts in a nonarbitrary manner, administratively as well as conceptually. We develop in these pages a theory of nonarbitrary planning." (*Journal of the American Institute of Planners*, XXVIII, No. 2 [May 1962], 103–115. The quotation is at p. 103. The piece by Charles Haar referred to is: "The Master Plan: An Inquiry in Dialogue Form," *Journal of the American Institute of Planners*, XXV, No. 3 [August 1959], 133–142.) It is clearly impossible to plan nonarbitrarily without knowledge of the proper goals for the planning endeavor.

social patterns. Others would limit their support to the planning-in-general-outline of change in particular strategic variables.

Those who contend that comprehensive planning should play a large role in the future evolution of societies must argue that the common interests of society's members are their most important interests and constitute a large proportion of all their interests. They must assert that conflicts of interest in society are illusory, that they are about minor matters, or that they can be foreseen and resolved in advance by just arbiters (planners) who understand the total interests of all parties. Those who claim that comprehensive planning should play a large part in the future evolution of any particular economic or societal feature have to assume similar propositions with regard to conflicts of interest likely to arise in connection with it.

To the extent, then, that comprehensive planning is possible, the correct law for a society is something to be discovered, rather than willed, by public officials. The role of the politician who ignores consistency or obstructs grand schemes to placate interest groups is hard to defend. So is the concept of majority will, and the idea that party conflict is desirable. It is in this sense that the claims of planners often seem to be in conflict with those of politicians. Both claim a unique ability to judge the overall public interest. The politician's claim rests on his popular election, his knowledge of the community, his sensitivity to human needs, and his personal wisdom. The planner's claim is one of professionalism and research. If it seems somewhat devoid of human warmth, it also sounds more authoritative, more precise, more modern. As will be seen shortly, I have no wish to imply that city planners and politicians must (or, indeed, invariably do) defend their work on the basis of conflicting assumptions. It may well be that the capacities of planners and politicians are, for many purposes, suited to complement each other. Here we are not discussing everything that men called planners do, but rather some implications of the concept "comprehensiveness" in planning.

Few sophisticated American defenders of planning, certainly, believe that any group of planners can achieve a total comprehensiveness of perspective on any issue. Many do believe, however, that professional planners can come closer to achieving it on numerous vital issues than other participants in the urban decision process. The primary purpose of this chapter is to explore the theoretical foundations of this belief. It should be noted, however, that the explicit claims of practicing planners often seem to suggest that a fair approximation of genuine comprehensiveness is currently attainable. The case studies in this volume provide a number of illustrations.

Case Study Illustrations

In his introduction to the *St. Paul Land Use Plan,* for example Herbert Weiland, the St. Paul planning director, described his conception of the planning function in these words:

> The total city planning process, of which land-use planning is but one part, involves a continuing program of deriving, organizing, and presenting a comprehensive plan for the development and renewal of [the city] . . . The plans must be economically feasible, and must promote the common good, and at the same time [must] preserve the rights and interests of the individual.

Long discussions with every planner involved in the preparation of the St. Paul plan persuaded me that these words were meant literally. City planning was comprehensive and for the common good, not for any lesser objectives.

Several members of the St. Paul planning staff were highly critical of C. David Loeks, Weiland's predecessor, for having offered advice freely to operating agencies without first developing a comprehensive plan. Loeks himself, however, had also conceived his responsibilities broadly, though he had not considered the time ripe for explicitly comprehensive planning during most of his tenure. He had written in the Planning Board's 1957 publication, *The Proposed Freeways for St. Paul,* for example, that while others had considered the cost of freeways and their effect on traffic, the Planning Board had "special responsibilities posed by virtue of its function and status as an advisory representative citizen's group concerned with the development of all facets of the community's life." [3]

In considering the development of Ancker Hospital, politicians turned finally to city planners to interpret the overall public in-

[3] *The Proposed Freeways for St. Paul,* Community Plan Report 4, June 1957, p. 30.

terest. First the city planners in the St. Paul Housing and Redevelopment Authority, and eventually those in the City Planning Bureau as well, accepted the challenge with confidence. When interviewed, both groups of planners stated without hesitation that they were better equipped to interpret the public interest than the consultant hospital architect, whose primary concern was how best to build a hospital. They believed that because their perspective was broader, their recommendation was highly likely to be wiser, or more rational.[4]

In formulating the *Central Minneapolis Plan,* Rodney Engelen, with the full support of Planning Director Irvin, cast his arguments in the broadest possible terms. The operational goal of the *Plan* was clearly a limited one: economic growth. Engelen, however, felt that he had to justify the goal itself. He stressed the functions of downtown as bearer of culture, disseminator of news and ideas, haven for unique activities, supplier of taxes to support all public services, and so on. When interviewed, he emphasized that his concern was to enrich the lives of all citizens, not to line the pockets of downtown businessmen. It was merely fortuitous, he believed, that in this case the interests of property owners and those of society coincided. He realized that on many subjects this coincidence did not exist, or was not perceived, and that in such cases the political implementation of the public interest might be impossible.

Engelen admitted freely that no plan or evaluation could be entirely comprehensive, as did all the planners interviewed for this study when pressed. His (and their) disclaimer was perfunctory, however, as if only a minor detail were at stake. Engelen wrote, for

[4] Planners tend to use the words "rational" and "wise" interchangeably in evaluating public choices. This is in accord with the usage of natural law philosophers, but not with that of contemporary economic and social theorists. For the latter, the term "rational" refers to the efficiency of means where ends are known. "Wisdom" refers to deep understanding and the ability to make what are considered "good" judgments on complex human issues, when goals and efficient means are not generally known.

Consequently, the planners use of the word "rational" in the classic sense to defend their distinctly modern "expert" recommendations makes for some confusion of thought. This confusion has a political function, however. It conveys the impression that expert logic or technique can produce "good" decisions on complex human issues.

example, that the *Central Minneapolis Plan* could not truly be termed comprehensive because "there are and will always be elements—new aspects—yet to be studied and yet to be decided upon." He thus rejected a conception of comprehensiveness that I have suggested is useless: i.e., that the comprehensive plan should deal with everything. In short, he admitted that the object of any decision is necessarily limited, at very least in time, but he preserved the implication that the planner's approach—i.e., his goal orientation—to the object may be comprehensive.

The Search for Planning Goals

All Twin Cities planners agreed that community goals could in the final analysis be discovered only through public discussion. Planners might propose alternative articulations, but goal statements could have no claim to represent community thought unless the community or its legitimate representatives ratified them after serious discussion and deliberation. In theory the primary problem was to guide the discussion and to decide when it had gone on long enough. The primary problem in practice, it developed, was to get a discussion going.

St. Paul's planners hoped, for example, that vigorous discussion would follow publication of their *Land Use Plan*. No one showed any interest in discussing it, however. The reason seemed to be that the *Plan*'s stated goals were too general. No one knew how the application of these goals would affect him in practice. Those who were not completely uninterested in the *Plan* had learned long ago to be suspicious of high-sounding generalities. The planners had not succeeded in showing opinion leaders the relationship between the *Plan*'s stated general goals and its great mass of "standards," or more specific goals. As a result, nonplanners decided with uncoordinated unanimity to ignore the *Plan* until someone proposed specific applications of it. Only at this point, they felt, would there by anything comprehensible—whether or not comprehensive—to argue about.

Minneapolis planners argued that the St. Paul planners' premises were wrong, and would have been wrong even if discussion of their plan had developed. For a discussion truly to influence the planning process, they said, it had to begin before detailed planning got under way. In their view, no one could effectively interpolate changes into a plan after it was complete without upsetting its internal harmony. If one of the goals of a plan were changed, then in theory every specific recommendation should be altered to some extent. No one had the time or intellectual energy to do this when a plan had already taken definite shape, however. The crucial phase in the evolution of any plan, then, was the development of its first draft. Goals should be determined before this phase moved far along.

Minneapolis planners themselves tried to obtain approval for planning goals before developing their central area plan. They decided at the start that they needed a goal statement which would be both "operational" and acceptable to all "reasonable" citizens of the city. By "operational," they meant that progress toward the goal could be objectively measured, and that the broad costs, both tangible and spiritual, of striving toward it could be foreseen. Comprehensive goals, they judged, could not be operational. Therefore, reasonable men could not pass on them intelligently. It followed that goals could win intelligent public approval only if they were partial. The question was: *how* partial? Perhaps it was possible to articulate, and plan to achieve, highly general goals even if not truly comprehensive ones.

They endeavored to bring about a public discussion of essential goal options before preparing the detailed plan. Fortunately, planners and planning consultants throughout the nation had applied themselves to downtown problems in recent years, and had developed a more or less integrated theory explaining characteristic downtown problems. Consequently, Minneapolis planners were able to present their preferred goals with tightly reasoned arguments behind them. The parts were related and mutually reinforcing. The man of affairs with a limited amount of time could quickly grasp the objectives and the main lines of reasoning on which the recommendations were based. The most general operational goal that the planners proposed was "the economic growth of downtown." They recognized that this goal was itself deceptive, however, in that although it sounded noncontroversial the steps necessary to its accomplishment could not keep from being controversial. In their publications on downtown planning goals, therefore, they chose to emphasize what they termed "design goals." These were in fact *types* of projects—rather than project proposals

for specific streets and blocks in Minneapolis—that had been tried
in other cities. The planners tried to explain the relationship between these types of proposals and the economic problems facing
urban downtowns in the current period. It was possible to discuss
the types of dislocation that might be expected, and so on, without
bringing in specific project proposals. The discussion was really a
model of comprehensible argument in favor of middle-range (i.e.,
operational but still general) planning goals. I strongly doubt that
existing theory was sufficiently developed to support comparable
justifications of goal recommendations in any other area of city
planning activity.[5]

Even in this area, however, the specific financial costs and unintended side-effects that would arise on application in Minneapolis
were difficult to foresee. Any intelligent discussion of planning
goals had to take these (or their unpredictability) into account.
For the discussion to be fully useful, the planners judged, its participants had to be willing to inform themselves about planning
detail at some significant expenditure of time and effort. The
discussion had to continue throughout the planning process,
which itself would have peaks of activity but no final termination.
Since the overall goal was partial, the discussants had to be urged
to consider the full complexity of its side-effects. This they could
not do if they confined themselves to examination of the central
economic reasoning behind the "design goals."

The first problem was how to find discussants. The comprehensive planner's search is more complicated than that of any specialist. He cannot be satisfied to consult a narrow constituency.
Presumably he should understand every important goal of each of
society's members. If he must deal with groups rather than individuals he should not limit himself to constellations of interest
that maintain permanent formal organizations. But the planners
knew of no way to approach the city's "potential" groups. These

[5] A major reason for this was probably that in no urban section but downtown did simple economic goals appear entirely plausible. Outside the United
States, planners rarely considered them so even for downtown. See, for example, the British Town and Country Planning Association's analysis of central London problems: *The Paper Economy* (London: Town and Country
Planning Association, 1962).

would not become actual groups unless some immediate threats activated their potential members; some potential groupings of interests that the observer might identify would not become actual even then. Even those in the first category, however, had no leaders to speak for them. The abstract discussion of goals could seldom seem sufficiently immediate to spur them to organize and choose representatives. It seemed that in no other public endeavor than general goal determination was the disproportion greater between the number of groups that *might* reasonably become involved and the number that *would*.

The planners soon found that they could carry on a continuing discussion only with men whose jobs required them to spend time on the study and discussion of civic affairs. Only a few organizations in the city had such men on their payrolls. All of these fit into a few categories. Most were large downtown business firms or organizations of businessmen. A few good government groups (supported mainly by the contributions of businesses or businessmen) had representatives who took an interest in city planning, but for the most part they were in the same position as planners: they could talk abstractly about the public interest but they could not claim any special qualifications to represent particular interests. The other permanent organizations in the city did not bother to have representatives spending the bulk of their time observing civic affairs. Each had a few continuing interests (racial issues, taxes, city hiring policy, etc.) and became politically active only when immediate threats to these arose.

Making the best of this situation, the planners tried to carry on a discussion of goals with the professional "civic affairs" representatives of downtown business. These professional discussants, however, lacked the power to commit their firms to anything; consequently, as the discussion became more specific they became more and more noncommittal. The businessmen who had the power to commit their firms to specific courses of action had neither the time nor interest to engage in almost endless discussion with the city planners. In a short while, even the professional discussants found that they had no time to study each tentative planning formulation with care. Thus, a major difficulty was revealed. Even had the planners been able to handle all the complexity of life, they would not have found laymen willing or able to evaluate their work.[6]

If it can be so difficult to spur well-informed discussion even of such limited goals as those of the *Central Minneapolis Plan,* the question necessarily arises: what should be considered an adequate discussion of planning goals? Was the discussion in this case adequate although its only participants were businessmen whose interest in the discussion was mild and who were concerned only with direct economic costs and consequences? One might say that it was, because other groups could have entered the discussion to raise additional points had they wished. I did not find any elected officials in Minneapolis, however, who accepted this reasoning. Most were rather inarticulate about their objections, but a few were able to state their views quite precisely.

Downtown businesses are, according to these objectors, "organizations in being." Their owners are accustomed to watching the civic scene and searching for issues likely to affect their interests. They enter the discussion of any proposal at a very early stage and understand its potential impact on their interests relatively early. Other members of the public, however, tend to became aware that something is afoot and then to conceptualize their interests more slowly. After the perception begins to dawn, most take quite some time to organize. The range in the amount of time, and in the degree of immediacy of a threat or opportunity, that it takes to move different types of people with potential interest in a

[6] From their viewpoint as political administrators, on the other hand, Minneapolis planners and their consultants won a major, and far from inevitable, victory in persuading the professional discussants that the general lines of economic reasoning in the *Central Minneapolis Plan* were valid, and that a plan based on them would quite probably benefit downtown business. After all, even the contribution of a plan to economic growth—let alone to the public interest—was impossible to predict and difficult to identify after the fact. Trend changes after specific actions were taken were possible to measure, but no one could prove that the actions studied had caused the result. Only comparative analysis of many cities could begin to test the efficacy of particular methods, and reliable comparative data were rare.

Still, the arguments of city planners in their role as economic planners had a hard-headed quality seldom present in their other work. They wrote as though from having defined their goal clearly they could identify the major bars to progress toward it without much trouble. Knowing the enemy, they could conceive tightly reasoned, even if untested, lines of attack.

proposal to the threshold of organizational expression is enormous. Government never moves slowly enough or poses issues clearly enough to give everyone his say. It is fair to assume, however, that only when government moves at a snail's pace and deals with issues of rather direct and immediate impact can a significant proportion of the great multitude of interests express themselves. Therefore, comprehensive democratic planning is virtually impossible. No legislature or committee of interest group leaders can rationally evaluate a statement of comprehensive goals. Its members cannot, in the absence of specific project proposals and citizen reactions to them, predict how the countless measures needed to accomplish the goals will affect the overall quality of community life or the interests of their own constituents and organizations. Consequently, they are likely to prefer operating on levels where comprehension and prediction are most feasible, even if this means fragmenting policy choices rather than integrating them. In practice, this means that they will rarely commit themselves to let general and long-range goal statements guide their consideration of lower-level alternatives.

There are no doubt many local politicians in America who would not find the preceding argument a compelling one. In localities lacking a coherent "power elite" firmly committed to a plan, however, it has a high degree of plausibility as a prescription for political survival. Its specific dictates are bound to be, at a minimum, a "project" rather than a "general planning" orientation and a disinclination to deal with controversial issues.

Systematic Criticisms of the Comprehensive Planning Ideal

The crucial assumptions of those who claim that comprehensive democratic planning is possible and desirable have of course been challenged more systematically than this. Martin Meyerson argued in a 1954 article that the major attacks could be divided into two types.[7] The first is that planning limits the range of individual choice by imposing centrally made decisions. The second is that planning requires "vastly more knowledge . . . about a huge

[7] "Research and City Planning," *Journal of the American Institute of Planners*, XX, No. 4 (Autumn 1954), 201–205.

variety of factors" than can be obtained or grasped by any individual or closely integrated group. Meyerson asserted that the few who had tried to answer these criticisms had been more successful in answering the first than the second. They had answered the first by saying that freedom is opportunity, not just the absence of restraint; and that planning agencies are created because people sense a failure of the market and of politics to satisfy their desires. As for the second question: unfortunately, wrote Meyerson, "we all know" that the assertion that planning can provide a rational basis for substantive policy decisions is just a goal today. The danger, he went on, is that planners will become content for it to remain a goal. He left the problem with a call for research.

It is questionable, however, whether planners have answered even the first objection successfully. Though it is certainly true that freedom consists of opportunity as well as the absence of restraint, there is little agreement as to whether planning to date has anywhere in the world produced more opportunity *in toto* than restraint. Only "commonsense" estimates are possible, as any more precise balance sheet would have to be based on determinations of the significance of particular opportunities and restraints. Neither the philosophic (assuming values to be objective) nor the scientific (assuming them to be subjective) foundations for such determinations exist. Second, the fact that people sense a failure of the market and the political process to meet their needs hardly forces one to conclude that they are better satisfied with the planning process. A reading of American city planning publications, not to mention conversations with numerous practicing planners, reveals a preoccupation among city planners with the failure of their work to win popular approval. Moreover, the winning of popular approval would itself prove very little. Planners themselves do not hesitate to bemoan the unwisdom of many popular governmental programs. They emphasize that the public must be educated by its leaders to favor comprehensive planning. They admit that the unguided public is likely to prefer an alderman who does petty favors for constituents to one who studies the city's overall needs.

Those who have made this first objection to comprehensive planning have generally emphasized that ambitious plans can only be realized through the generous exercise of public power. They have contended that every grant of power to government increases the chance of its abuse, increases the pervading influence of bureaucracy and red tape in the lives of citizens, decreases the self-reliance of citizens, and, as the habit of delegating tasks to government becomes prevalent, undermines their healthy suspicion of those who wield power. They have said that those charged with taking a comprehensive view of political problems are necessarily charged with safeguarding the complex requisites of the social and political system entrusted to their care. In the case of American society, this means a system in which the rights of individuals to wide spheres of personal freedom are recognized.

If the planner is truly to think comprehensively, in this view, he must consider not only the goals of society, but also the framework within which these goals can be pursued. If all proposals to enlarge governmental power threaten the framework of individual liberty to some degree, the planner must share society's initial bias against them. Those who oppose planning have generally asserted that planners have a professional bias in favor of bigger and bigger government, less and less subject to pressures from interest groups. Planners, they say, are in the business of creating new proposals which call for governmental activity. The planner's own interest is in the success of his plans: that is, in additional governmental activity *ad infinitum*. Most grants of power to government are long-term ones, because the electoral process is ponderous and inflexible. To reverse a major decision once ratified is extremely difficult, though it happens occasionally, as with Prohibition. The general pattern is for public interest to focus on an issue for a short while, and then move on. The planner's bias in favor of ever-larger government should therefore disqualify him from evaluating either his own proposals or those of others. Demands for public action in modern society are so numerous that only by subjecting each to the most searching criticism, based on an initial negative bias, can the trend toward concentration of power (which admittedly cannot be stopped) be slowed to a moderate rate. When government must act to deal with some pressing issue, every effort should be made to define the problem narrowly and to deal with it specifically. The approach should be one of dealing with bottlenecks, not planning the whole production line. In other words, it should be piecemeal, not comprehensive.

If these are some of the views intelligent people still can hold regarding the issue that Meyerson says planning defenders have dealt with rather successfully, we may expect to have considerable difficulty in dealing with the one he says planners have been unable to handle. In part the problem is, as Meyerson says, the inability of planners to know about the interrelations of a huge variety of factors. But every profession deals with matters of incredible complexity. No profession can bring order to the mass of facts until it knows what it hopes to accomplish. From its goals, the members of a profession can derive criteria for judging the importance of facts. Using these criteria, they can develop theories about which consequences of specific types of proposals are the most important to control. The next step is to develop techniques for controlling these consequences. All specialists have lists of techniques for dealing with the characteristic problems they encounter. Planners too have some when they act as specialists. The floor-area ratio, for example, is a characteristic device used to resolve an aesthetic problem: the fact that rigid height and bulk building regulations yield unvaried architectural patterns.

This need for criteria, however, returns comprehensive planners to their basic problem. To develop theories about what they should know when creating comprehensive plans or evaluating specialist plans comprehensively, they need to know society's goals. Unless society has goals that can be discovered and applied, the task of theory building cannot begin. The difficulty of dealing with factual complexity will always seem insuperable, though the truly insuperable difficulty may be that of defining the aims of the theory-building endeavor. The market and political bargaining processes depend on the assumptions that only individuals have goals,[8] that these normally conflict, and that the mysteries of bargaining yield the best results possible for men. The planner cannot rely on a hypothetical invisible hand; he must validate his claim to arbitrate, whereas the bargainer must only validate his claim to negotiate. Planners cannot claim to arbitrate on the basis of their own views of the public interest. If there are important conflicts of interest in a society that cannot be resolved to the advantage of all parties, then planners require the guidance of a

[8] Readers will note that I say the political *bargaining* process depends on this assumption, not the political *discussion* process.

strong political arbitrator. The alternative is a conception that essential harmony underlies all apparent clashes of interest.

The view that clashes of interest are only apparent has always appealed to one element of the American intellect. It is assumed by most conservative defenders of laissez-faire no less than by progressive attackers of "politics." Marver Bernstein reminds us, for example, that almost all American movements for regulatory legislation have had to adjust their arguments to this conception. In order to have any chance of success, they have had to protest their general disapproval of public action, even while saying that in this particular case it was needed to stop flagrant abuses by a few unscrupulous individuals. The ostensible purpose, always, has had to be restoration of the natural harmony of interests.[9] We may conceive a progression of steps in "natural harmony" thinking from support of laissez-faire, to regulation of specific abuses, to comprehensive planning. Laissez-faire theorists, of course assume that the interests of mankind are best served with no conscious coordination of effort. Theorists of regulation assume that just as healthy human organisms often require treatment for specific ills, so with healthy economic and social systems. The next step is to say that social and economic systems are not very good self-regulators, but rather require constant, carefully planned direction and care if they are to perform adequately. In this view, suitable to an age which accepts positive government, nature provides the common ends but human intelligence and elaborately coordinated effort are required to choose and implement the proper means of achieving them.

Those who reject comprehensive planning meet this reasoning in a variety of ways. Let us consider two of those which seem most plausible.

First, many writers, including the authors of *The Federalist*, have contended that conflict of interest is an invariable feature of all societies, and that the worst conflicts of interest are between those who manipulate governmental power and those who do not. By this view, whenever all those who possess governmental power are able, let alone encouraged, to synthesize their interests into a comprehensive goal, the rest of society had better watch out. A

[9] Marver Bernstein, *Regulating Business by Independent Commission* (Princeton: Princeton University Press, 1955), Chaps. 1, 2.

corollary of this position is that the few goals shared by all the members of society are not the goals most important to individuals. Thus, the primary function of government should be to provide an ordered framework in which civilization can prosper. The framework may be indispensable, because freedom is meaningful only within civilized society, but from the individual's viewpoint it is still only a precondition, not a preeminent goal in itself. Except during moments of supreme crisis for a society, in this view, the normal thing is for its members to differ, for each to want to seek happiness in his own way with a minimum of organized societal interference. This argument leads naturally into the argument against planning outlined above on pages 312–313.

Second, there are those who say that even if human interests harmonize and "big government" must be tolerated in modern life, the goal of comprehensiveness in decision-making should be viewed with the utmost suspicion. These critics do not, any more than those whose views are outlined above, recommend the banishment of intelligence from the handling of human affairs. They say only that the ways of the world are often contrary to logic. Logically, the wisest decisions should be those made at the highest level, where the widest range of arguments can be considered. But in fact, because the human mind can grasp only a limited number of considerations at any time, decision-makers at the highest level can act only by drastically over-simplifying their choice problems. According to this view, any comprehensive scheme is a Procrustes bed. The decision-maker does better to recognize the unforeseen and the unique in every situation without rigid preconceptions. He can, when "other things are equal," endeavor to harmonize each day's decisions with those taken previously, but he should recognize that other things often are *not* equal. What is lost in administrative unity when the piecemeal approach is employed is made up in superior contact with public opinion and the special needs of each situation.

The greatest virtue of the piecemeal approach, in this view, is that it poses a large number of policy questions. The comprehensive approach implies that politicians need only approve general policy statements periodically, leaving the rest to be deduced by experts. Politicians not unnaturally react to this idea with hostility. They recognize that if they are to be the actual deciders of policy, they must exercise their influence continuously, at levels of generality sufficiently low so that their decisions may affect the matters of interest to their constituents. They may forego interference with administration below certain levels of generality, but they must never let administrators persuade them to set the cutoff point too high. The question of where it should be is always debatable, of course. Highway engineers tend to think that the setting of highway routes should be a technical endeavor. Others, including city planners, often complain that highway engineers are inclined to handle the side-effects of route location—which may be as important as the intended effects—as peripheral matters. In a democracy, the administrators can advise but they cannot determine finally which side-effects are too important for them to handle themselves, or to ignore.

Pressure groups have a similar interest to politicians in the piecemeal approach. Their members typically are interested in direct and immediate consequences to themselves, not in the overall public interest. It is a value of the piecemeal approach that interest groups can deal with questions their members care about. They need not feel that by the time their members become aware of any threat or opportunity the issue will have been foreclosed by prior community approval of generalities. Interest groups depend for their survival on issues which move their members and on at least occasional partial successes.[10] A vigorous public opinion in turn cannot survive without vigorous interest groups, whose leaders articulate issues, command attention in the mass media, and assure supporters in dissent that they are not alone. In the absence of strong evidence to the contrary in any particular society, therefore, it should be assumed that whatever saps the vigor of interest groups saps the vigor of democracy. The ideal of comprehensive planning seems ultimately antagonistic to the level of group conflict which typically characterizes stable democratic societies. It casts doubt on the very value of public discussion, at least after the

[10] Not all interest groups need *political* successes, of course, because not all are primarily political in their orientation. Business firms, labor unions, and churches, for example, can retain their memberships without engaging in politics. They tend to retreat from politics, however, and thus to disappear as *politically significant* interest groups, when their members perceive public discussion as invariably fruitless.

stage of determining general goals. If a group of planners can comprehend the overall public interest, then any challenge to their specific proposals must be attributable either to their own incompetence or lack of integrity, or to the selfishness and shortsightedness of their critics. Faced with such polar explanations, those who take the side of the planners are apt to conclude that competition among parties and interest groups is alien to the public interest. Dictators frequently employ this very logic to defend their systems.

Defenders of planning may meet these criticisms in part by saying that they do not rely on the idea of a comprehensive harmony of human interests. They may contend merely that maintenance of a framework in which civilization can flourish is an enormous task, requiring all of man's ingenuity and foresight. Pressure groups are currently so vigorous, they may continue, and comprehensive planning is so weak, that concern for maintaining the divisive forces in our society at adequate strength is misplaced. Even if ideal comprehensive planning is impossible and in theory "big government" threatens democracy, they may conclude, democratic societies must strive toward the first and tolerate large doses of the second if they are to meet the challenge of modern welfare expectations and rapid technological change. This argument is highly plausible, but here as elsewhere serious debates center around location of the cutoff points, and planners suffer from lack of a theory to justify their positions in these debates.

To critics of planning there is an essential difference between public actions to meet crisis threats to crucial societal values and actions to ameliorate the effects of every societal dislocation. The passionate proponents of economic reform in the 1930's and of foreign aid in the postwar decade were able to argue that American democracy was in clear and mortal peril. Proponents of strong public action to bring about desegregation in the 1960's can cite highly serious injustices and threats to domestic tranquility as the justifications for intervention. Few defenders of city planning cite such serious or immediate crises. They say instead that planning is desirable to help minimize the pains of adaptation to change, and to develop cities in which everyone's opportunity for fulfillment will be enhanced. They generally fail, however, to confront certain obvious questions squarely. How, for example, should one judge whether the alleviation of a specific social pain warrants the amount of growth in governmental power over the lives of individuals which it will require? Is it possible to achieve a high level of intelligent consensus about the substance of personal fulfillment, and the kinds of environment most conducive to it? The final judge of proposed answers to such questions must be the political process. And here is where planners' troubles have usually begun.

Political Restraints
on the Goal Development Process

Speaking broadly, there are two ways to win political acceptance for new ideas in a stable democratic system. The first is to challenge the theoretical foundations of popular beliefs with which they conflict. This way is slow at best. Moreover, it requires a highly persuasive theory. Such theories are never easily come by, nor, if they challenge older persuasive theories, do they win acceptance quickly. In the United States, the other theories with which a throughgoing defense of comprehensive planning would have to contend are not even perceived as theories, but rather as part of the American tradition. Perhaps in consequence, American planners have generally eschewed full-scale defense of social planning, preferring to conciliate the powerful reasoning of American conservatism rather than to challenge it directly. The only theoretical defense of public planning which planners have frequently asserted has been based on a conception of planning as businesslike foresight. The simple theories required to defend this idea of planning have won fairly easy political acceptance, but they have not dealt with the inevitable political and social implications of serious efforts to plan generally or comprehensively. It has remained necessary, therefore, to deal with these implications *ad hoc* when such efforts have been made.

One way, then, to win political acceptance for new ideas is to challenge the theoretical foundations of older ideas with which they conflict. The other way is to adapt one's own arguments and objectives to the beliefs, attitudes, and political customs already prevalent. The latter way is more likely to yield immediate results, and it minimizes the risk that no results at all will be produced. American planners almost invariably have chosen it, no doubt in part because they are influenced even more by American culture than by international planning theory. It has certainly contributed to the political security of planners and the planning function. It has perhaps obscured, however, the problem of maintaining a clear professional viewpoint.

There is no need to search far for an explanation. It is extremely difficult for any agency whose explicit function is to propose new ideas to avoid coming into frequent conflict with established ways of thinking and doing things. Even if general strategy is articulated in the most conventional possible terms, this tactical dilemma is bound to remain. With respect to planning, it is bound to be most apparent when the planning is general and community goals must be determined. Given the importance of such a determination—if it is in fact to provide a guide for future public action—and the infinite varieties of emphasis possible, one would expect that the officials making it would run the risk of offending everyone. Even if they are oblivious of their own safety, the problem of winning political approval for their proposed goal statements remains.

Two methods of dealing with this problem at the level of general goals may be outlined.[11] The first is to state goals on which all reasonable men can agree. Unfortunately, goals of this type tend not to provide any basis for evaluating concrete alternatives. Thus, the St. Paul *Land Use Plan* stated as its most general goal the "evolution of St. Paul as a better place to live and work," and the *Plan* constantly justified its more specific proposals in terms of increasing "liveability." The second alternative is to propose somewhat more controversial goals in the expectation that the community's elective policy-makers will consider, if necessary amend, and ultimately approve them. Conceivably, planners might offer elected officials several choices of goals in each area of concern, though to the extent that they did so they would reduce the possibility of all the goals finally chosen being consistent with each other. Inconsistency might be turned to positive advantage, however. Part of using this approach successfully would be to deal in "packages," so that those in the minority when one goal was approved might hope to be in the majority when others were. The

[11] It is dealt with generally at the level of means in Chap. VI.

objective, of course, would be to win all or almost all reasonable politicians to support of the package.

This method is tried frequently in the American system, but it seldom succeeds where the package is a set of general goals. Part of the reason, we have seen, is that many "reasonable" politicians in the system oppose general planning and the articulation of general goals on principle. Even more important is the fact that American politicians typically depend on public discussion to inform them of the interest and values affected by any proposal. If planners cannot spur adequate discussion of their goal statements, politicians cannot, and know they cannot, make informed choices among them. Even when discussion is achieved, the dictates of prudence and democratic ethics impel politicians to wait for consensus to form before acting. The upshot is that very few proposals emerge as law from American legislative processes until and unless the vast majority of articulate groups interested in them favors some version of them. In the case of novel proposals, virtual unanimity seems generally to be required unless the need for decision is seen by the vast majority to be inescapable.[12]

12 The phrases "vast majority" and "virtual unanimity" must be taken to mean proportions of those interested in each issue. Charles Merriam wrote thirty-five years ago in his classic description of Chicago politics that while virtually any group in the city could veto proposals affecting it, even the weakest group could get its proposals approved if no other group rose to object (*Chicago: A More Intimate View* [Chicago: University of Chicago Press, 1929]). Edward Banfield reports that Chicago's political system, run by the most powerful machine in the nation, operates still in roughly the same manner (*Political Influence* [New York: The Free Press of Glencoe, 1961]). According to Banfield, the "bosses" have few or no policy objectives of their own, and therefore decide issues in response to the electoral interests of their organization (i.e., the "machine"). They seem to accept the view that electoral benefits are probable only when what we have termed the "vast majority" and "virtual unanimity" rules are followed, and when ample time is given potential interests to recognize their concern and express it.

No political machines operated in either of the two cities I studied, but the professional politicians who ran each acted similarly to the Chicago "bosses" in committing their prestige and influence.

Some members of the planning profession have themselves publicly approved the politicians' instinct. The President of the American Institute of Planners wrote in 1955, for example, that at a minimum policies adopted by government should be acceptable on a voluntary basis to 80 or 90 per cent

In the national sphere, these "rules" may be waived when survival seems to be the stake. In most areas of urban life, however, people with money can escape the worst consequences of any change. Thus, Scott Greer has characterized the American city as one of "limited liability" from the viewpoint of the individual.[13] To illustrate: if a middle-class neighborhood becomes a slum, the original residents can move out, and though this has a price it is generally easier and cheaper than fighting the trend. So long as the general standard of living is rising, most of the newcomers are taking a step upward; they are likely to be apathetic toward efforts to resist the transition, and positively hostile to programs which might "improve" the neighborhood's prospects sufficiently to drive rents up. The immediate threats in urban life, then, are of individual dislocation rather than of societal survival, or even decline.

Politicians in American society occasionally alert their constituents to specific ills and dangers, and champion specific programs for dealing with them. It has recently become fashionable, moreover, for some politicians to conduct well-publicized quests for consensual, nonoperational general goals. It is a rare politician indeed, however, who leads his constituents in formulating positive operational social goals. The quest itself would be likely to stir antagonism among those who did not believe societies should have positive goals, and it would almost certainly stir new demands against the politician's limited resources. Moreover, those few citizens who long for positive planning rarely approach unanimity in any meaningful detail on what its substance should be. The obstacles to positive political leadership are such that even those who emphasize the potential educative role of the American Presidency usually admit that the President can be effective only so long as he confines his efforts to a very few widely perceived social ills and foreign dangers. The President who obtains authority to set up general planning agencies in moments of national crisis is

---

of the public (John T. Howard, "The Planner in a Democratic Society—A Credo," *Journal of the American Institute of Planners*, XXI, No. 3 [Spring-Summer 1955], 62–65). If he meant, which I doubt he did, that it was all right for 10 or 20 per cent to be strongly opposed, he was a radical by the standards of most local politicians.

[13] *The Emerging City* (New York: The Free Press of Glencoe, 1962).

likely, once the crisis begins to abate, to see them scuttled by Congress while he himself is charged with Caesarism. Consider the fate of the National Resources Planning Board, abolished by Congress in 1943 though its functions had been advisory only and it had carefully avoided direct confrontations with other agencies.[14] The incomparably more significant Office of War Mobilization and Reconversion achieved immense powers of coordination in the course of its brief life, but only during total war and at the expense of adopting a highly judicialized bottleneck—as opposed to policy-oriented comprehensive—planning approach.[15] The Bureau of the Budget has nurtured its far more limited influence similarly. Few chief executives at the local level have formal powers comparable to those of the President in his, and of course none have comparable prestige.[16] In general, the American distrust of executive power has found more forceful legal expression at the local level than at the national, perhaps because of the need for foreign and military policies nationally, and because opponents of executive power since the brief Federalist interregnum have found the constitution which it produced too difficult to change.

The opponents of planning have recognized the difference by focusing their attention on national rather than local planning efforts. Businessmen have been the primary patrons of the urban planning movement in America since its beginnings. As the planning movement has matured, moreover, fewer and fewer large property owners and executives have seen anything ironical about their providing the primary base of political support for local land-use planning while continuing bitterly to oppose anything remotely resembling national economic planning. The major reason

[14] See Edward H. Hobbs, *Behind the President* (Washington, D.C.: Public Affairs Press, 1954), Chap. 3; A. E. Holmans, *United States Fiscal Policy 1945–1959* (London: Oxford University Press, 1961), pp. 33–36; and Charles E. Merriam, "The National Resources Planning Board: A Chapter in American Planning Experience," *American Political Science Review*, XXXVIII, No. 6 (December 1944), 1075–1088.

[15] See Herman Somers, *Presidential Agency* (Cambridge: Harvard University Press, 1950), Chap. 2; and V. O. Key, Jr., "The Reconversion Phase of Demobilization," *American Political Science Review*, XXXVIII, No. 6 (December 1944), 1137–1153.

[16] Both of the Twin Cities had very "weak" mayors, even by local standards.

for the survival of this apparent inconsistency has probably been that leaders of property-oriented groups have lacked confidence that they could control planning at the federal level under the President. If this view is correct, the critics have spared local planning from their attacks just *because* local politicians have had insufficient power to defy the veto groups of their political system. This theme is elaborated in Chapter VII.

The Ideal of Middle-Range Planning

The point has been made in previous sections that truly comprehensive goals tend not to provide any basis for evaluating concrete alternatives. It is thus difficult to stir political interest in them and impossible to plan rationally in their service. Recognizing this, at least implicitly, many contemporary planners claim to practice middle-range planning—which they define as planning for the achievement of goals that are general, but still operational. It is not very fruitful to strive for greater definitional precision than this, because the image is one of balance between the contradictory ideals of comprehensiveness and specialization. Experienced planners have a "feel" for the conception, however, and explain it to neophytes by citing illustrations. For our purpose, the *Central Minneapolis Plan* may be cited as clearly falling in the "middle range."

The middle-range planning ideal has much to recommend it, despite its imprecision. It permits the promise of meaningful political discussion and approval of planning goals, even if the achievement may in practice be highly elusive. In addition, criticisms of comprehensive planning rooted in liberal democratic theory are much less forceful when applied to middle-range planning. From the viewpoint of the general planner, however, the middle-range planning ideal has one crucial flaw. It provides no basis for the planner to claim to understand the overall public interest. Men who plan to achieve operational—even though relatively general—goals are specialist, not comprehensive, planners. Consequently, they have no obvious theoretical basis for claiming to know better than other specialists how far each specialist goal should be pursued, and with what priority.

Specialization vs. Comprehensiveness:
The Uneasy Balance

The case for efforts at genuinely comprehensive planning has generally rested heavily on the thought that planners can resolve conflicts among goals in expert fashion. If they cannot, if they can only articulate specialist goals, then elected officials would seem required to act as the comprehensive arbiters of conflict. If it is assumed that arbiters operate most successfully when all important considerations are presented vigorously to them, one might argue reasonably that each important cluster of operational goals should be defended by a separate agency. Philip Selznick, for instance, has contended that leaders who wish to maximize their influence should structure their organizations so that the lines of jurisdiction dividing subunits are those along which important issues are likely to arise. His reasoning is that if issues arise within subunits they are likely to be decided by the subunit head, without the chief executive becoming aware of them. It is when subunits themselves come into conflict that arbiters at the next higher level are most likely to learn of issues.[17] Delegation of overall authority to arbitrate, in this view, even within the framework of highly general goal statements, is bound to transfer the substance of power from the delegator to the delegatee. If the delegator retains appellate jurisdiction he may dilute this effect. The more that he is committed to uphold the comprehensive policy vision of the delegatee, however, the less he will be able to do so. In trying to persuade politicians to make this delegation and to commit themselves to comprehensive policy visions, defenders of comprehensive planning must contend that the politicians will further the welfare of their constituents by doing so. To the extent that planning agencies lack truly comprehensive perspectives, this contention becomes less and less plausible.

Beyond this, even in pursuit of their own specialist goals, planners operate in a world of whole objects, not of analytical aspects. They cannot conceive means that will further the operational goals of primary interest to them without affecting innumerable others in uncontrolled fashion. Sophisticated planners

[17] Philip Selznick, *Leadership in Administration* (Evanston: Row, Peterson, and Company, 1957).

recognize this, and try not to serve their stated goals exclusively. The operational goal of the *Central Minneapolis Plan,* for example, was downtown economic growth. Its authors realized, however, that they could not reasonably ignore other goals. They wrote and spoke as though the cultural, political, spiritual, recreational, and other functions of downtown could never conflict with each other or with the economic function. In practice, they were saved by their common sense; they did not press their pursuit of economic goals sufficiently far to spur public awareness of potential serious conflicts. Conceivably, they might have listed all the significant operational goals they hoped to serve, but they would still have been left with the problem of balancing them. In short, every concrete object of planner attention is a miniature of the whole. The important analytical problems that arise in planning for an entire urban area arise in planning any section of it.[18] Perhaps the only escape is frankly to adopt a specialist orientation, even while remaining willing to adjust specific proposals as highly distasteful side-effects become apparent. It may still be plausible to maintain, however, that planners are custodians of values that somehow deserve to take precedence over the values propounded by other specialists. Let us consider the most persuasive lines of reasoning frequently advanced in support of this view.

One of the simplest was stated by Allison Dunham in a well-known article several years ago.[19] He claimed to have found after a survey of the planning literature that planners almost invariably believed that, at the very least, they were the officials best qualified to evaluate site proposals for every kind of facility. They based their position on the premise that planners were experts in the impacts of land uses on each other. The argument, in other words, was not that planners were "wiser" than operating agency officials, but that on certain types of issues their specialty deserved first place in the pecking order of specialities.

Two queries come immediately to mind. First, are the impacts

[18] The more limited objects (e.g., neighborhoods instead of whole cities) do present somewhat different, if not lesser, problems to the comprehensive planner. Cause and effect are easier to trace on the small scene, and important differences of interest are likely to be fewer. On the other hand, if planners emphasize the common interest of each homogeneous unit, they may well accentuate the differences between units.

[19] "A Legal and Economic Basis for City Planning," *Columbia Law Review,* LVIII (May 1958), 650–671.

of uses on each other regularly more important in site decisions than the intended purposes of each use? Second, can locational problems be separated meaningfully from all other problems? For illustrative purposes, consider a central issue of the Ancker Hospital site controversy: how should the potential health benefits of a contiguous medical center be balanced against the traffic congestion it would produce? Was it possible to say in the abstract which variable deserved greater weight? Was traffic congestion more a locational problem than building the medical center? The proponents of the medical center, it will be recalled, said that it could come into being only if Ancker Hospital were built on the one available site adjacent to the city's two largest existing hospitals. The only way to argue that planners should normally be given the benefit of the doubt in disputes of this kind is to say, as Dunham did, that specialists think of the needs of their constituents, while planners think of the impact of specialist proposals on others. In this case, the constituents were sick people and hospital staff personnel, while the "others" included many of the same people, but in their other capacities—as drivers and investors, for instance. The key question is whether the "others" should have had any more presumptive right to prevail than the recognized constituents.[20]

Another objection to this definition of planner competence is that it provides only the haziest indication of the legitimate jurisdiction of planners and of government. Just what is a locational decision? It is hardly enough to say, as planners generally have, that locational decisions are those that have an impact on surrounding property or people. Almost anything I do to my property affects my neighbor in some way. For instance, if I rent out rooms in my one-family home, I have changed the use of my land and therefore made a locational decision, by a common planner definition. Should government therefore control everything, as it

[20] This distinction recalls John Dewey's definition of the public interest (in *The Public and Its Problems* [New York: Henry Holt and Co., 1927]) as the interest in a decision of all those not directly party to it. Critics have pointed out that the parties to the decision have some claim to be considered part of the public too, in most cases the most clearly affected part. Those who dispute over definitions of the public interest are not mere academic quibblers. The phrase "public interest" has inescapable normative, and therefore political, significance. Those whose interest is opposed to it by a proposed definition therefore have ample reason to quibble.

already controls my right to rent out rooms? Planners deny that it
should, but they have rarely asked where the cutoff point should
be. They have typically been satisfied to say that government
should intervene only in cases of "substantial" harm, and that
common sense will prevail in interpreting the word "substantial."
They may be right, but this formulation gives the citizen no theoretical guidance as to whose common sense should prevail in cases
of disagreement between other decision-makers and planners.

A second persuasive line of reasoning to support the view that
planners should generally prevail in such disputes is that they
alone among city officials spend their days analyzing city problems
from an overall point of view. Operating agency officials cannot
rise above their day-to-day administrative chores, and in any event
their perspectives are conditioned by the narrow responsibilities of their departments. Even politicians typically devote most of
their time to maintaining contacts with, and to performing errand
boy services for, their constituents. In dealing with legislative
proposals, they generally focus on details of immediate interest to
vocal groups rather than on the overall picture. In most cities,
moreover, councilmen are elected from wards; in many they work
only part time at their jobs; and in some each councilman heads a
city department. Only planners can devote all their time to
thought about city problems at the most general level.

The most obvious criticism of this position is that freedom from
operating responsibility may not be the best condition in which to
make high-level decisions. Some prominent decision-makers have
argued that it is a poor one. Winston Churchill, for example, has
written that Stafford Cripps became restive and hypercritical of his
colleagues while serving as parlimentary whip during World War
II. What he needed, according to Churchill's diagnosis, was responsibility which would absorb his energies and give him a sense
of the concrete issues. Those who are free from operating responsibility, concluded Churchill, tend to develop an unhelpful
watchdog mentality. It is unhelpful because they usually think too
abstractly to be cogent critics of complex choices among policies.[21] Similarly, Chester Barnard has written that study and

[21] *The Second World War,* Vol. IV: *The Hinge of Fate* (Boston: Houghton-
Mifflin Co., 1950), p. 560.

Churchill was not arguing against the making of large decisions by gen-

reflectiveness without operating responsibility tend to lead to the treatment of things by aspects rather than wholes, to a disregard of factors which cannot be expressed precisely, and to an underestimation of the need for artistry in making concrete decisions. Because so many crucial factors cannot find expression in words, Barnard concluded, the interdependencies of social life can only be grasped intuitively. Only men of long and responsible experience are likely to acquire very much of this intuitive grasp, and therefore only such men—who will also grasp the supreme difficulty of planning in this "world of unknowns"—are qualified to plan.[22] This is unquestionably a rather mystical position, but for all that it is no less a respectable and forceful one.

Barnard and Churchill agree, then, that freedom from responsibility for operating decisions is anything but fit training for planning.[23] Those who accept their view are likely to believe that

eralists, of course. He himself was Prime Minister. Nor was he criticizing the British practice of concentrating authority within the civil service in the hands of generalists. Several points may be noted. The generalists in a British ministry exercise all formal power of decision not exercised by the minister himself. They bear responsibility as well for deciding which issues, and which specialist analyses of them, are important enough for the minister to consider. The elite corps of the generalists, the Administrative Class, are expected on entry only to think, write, and speak clearly, and to have done well in their subjects of undergraduate concentration. Any subject will do, although subjects fit for "gentlemen" (i.e., men devoted to culture rather than to making a living), notably the classics, have traditionally predominated. British administrators have no formal technical training for their work at all. They are platonic rather than functional leaders, but matured on responsibility rather than study. Those at the higher levels are notably unsympathetic to the ideal of general planning. They take well-known pride in deciding "each case on its merits."

Parenthetically, where city planners are employed in British ministries they are considered technicians, capable of contributing useful advice on specialized aspects of issues, but not of being entrusted with the power to make decisions.

[22] Chester Barnard, *Organization and Management* (Cambridge: Harvard University Press, 1948), Chap. 4.

[23] It should be clear that when I speak of "planning" in this chapter, I mean the work of determining overall policy guidelines for public activity, and means of implementing them. No single individual or agency makes such determinations alone in an American community. The recommendations of some, however, are bound to carry more weight than those of others. The crucial questions at issue here are (1) whether the views of planning agencies

any one of a number of city officials may qualify better than the planning director to serve as the wise chief advisor of politicians on broad policy issues. The Minneapolis and St. Paul city councils consistently acted on this belief. To the extent that they desired coordination of public works, they normally relied on their city engineers to achieve it. When the Minneapolis City Council decided in 1953 to separate capital budgeting from ordinary budgeting, it set up a committee composed of politicians and civic leaders. The committee was given a small staff headed by a former city councilman. Planners were shut out of the capital budgeting process entirely. When the St. Paul City Council decided that it needed a special advisor on the interstate freeway program, it appointed City Engineer George Shepard, who had been about to retire. When Minneapolis City Engineer Hugo Erickson left the city government for private employ in the late 1950's, his successor proved inadequate (in the City Council's view) for the unofficial task of city public works coordinator. Within a year, the Council lured Erickson back into government, giving him the title of Development Coordinator. Minneapolis planners believed that they should have been given the job, but they could offer no strong arguments to support their view that Erickson was less able to take the overview than they. The politician most responsible for bringing Erickson back told me that the planners thought too abstractly and with insufficient regard to cost, whereas Erickson, though less articulate, understood the infinite, inexpressible complexity of governmental choice. In fairness to the planners, it should be added that Erickson had made his entire career in Minneapolis, looking to the City Council for his raises, perquisites, and promotions. He had risen primarily because of his technical competence, to be sure, but also because the councilmen felt confident that he would not embarrass them politically and that his overriding loyalty was to themselves. Planning Director Irvin, needless to say, could not claim similar qualifications. (Irvin's tactical dilemmas are discussed further in Chapter VII.)

A third defense that planners frequently make of their aspira-

on controversial policy issues should normally be granted presumptive validity in the absence of strong evidence discrediting them; and (2) whether the training and career patterns of professional city planners equip them well for planning at the higher levels.

tion to be more than "mere" specialists is that governmental efficiency is served by having one agency keep track of everything that every city agency does, calling attention to conflicts and to means of coordinating effort for the benefit of all. The distinction between coordination and planning, however, is of practical importance only so long as planners have no power. Without power, they can as coordinators simply try to persuade groups of specialists that their respective interests will be served by improved coordination. As soon as planners begin to impose solutions or advise politicians to impose them, however, they have entered the substantive planning field. That is, they have set their perception of the public interest on substantive matters against those of the specialists who have rejected their advice. Similarly, when planners request authority to prepare a city's capital budget, they cannot justify the request on grounds of "simple efficiency," which would have to be established by the criteria of all the specialists' own goals. They must assert, at least implicitly, that they have some means of choosing among the values entrusted to each operating agency. In other words, they must claim to have goals. And the coordination of action in pursuit of substantive goals, is, if it is anything, substantive planning.

One might say that the planner needs coordinative power only because some specialists stupidly or obstinately refuse to cooperate with others in the interests of "simple efficiency," even though no significant values are threatened. The answer is that no one can determine that this is the case in any particular controversy without examining it in detail. Philip Selznick has illustrated this point clearly in his analysis of the history of the Communist party.[24] The party refused to cooperate with other leftist parties in the decade before the Popular Front, despite the obvious threat of fascism. Yet this period of isolation, Selznick contends, made the party a much more valuable tool to its masters during and after the Popular Front period. During the isolation period, the "character" of the party developed and became incorruptible. This extreme example illustrates a simple point: that cooperation and isolation in themselves have important effects on organizations. If an agency head claims that a measure advanced in the name of efficiency actually threatens important values—and any agency

[24] *The Organizational Weapon* (Glencoe: The Free Press, 1960).

head who refuses the advice of the planning director will say this —no outsider can refute him until he examines the bases of his arguments in detail. If we assume that most agency heads are men of good conscience, we can likewise assume that they will have some reasons that seem genuinely sufficient to them, and that they will seem so as well to at least some reasonable outsiders. In the end, no act of coordination is without its effect on other values than efficiency.

Some planners reading this chapter will no doubt judge that the issues raised in it are "ivory tower stuff," and in the immediate sense perhaps they are—though to me they appeared quite close to the surface in the Twin Cities. The purpose of this chapter, however, has been to challenge the planning profession to reinforce its most fundamental arsenal. In the long run, I suspect, general planning and evaluation will have little effect on American cities unless their goal premises can be established in sufficiently compelling fashion (both politically and intellectually) to make politicians take notice. I shall try to begin the task of reconstruction in the chapters which follow.

VI

The Means of Planning: Reason and Influence in the Public Service

Introduction

Once goals are known, means need only be conducive to their achievement: i.e., rational. I asked in the previous chapter whether the ideal of comprehensiveness was realizable, or even useful as a guide, in the determination of planning goals. I shall ask similar questions in this chapter about the ideal of rationality in the implementation of planning goals. When a planner speaks of implementing goals rationally, he implies that it is possible to demonstrate logically or experimentally the relationship between the proposed means and the ends they are intended to further. Surely such demonstrations are often possible, for practical if not philosophic purposes. The question at issue in this chapter is whether such demonstrations are often possible in general planning contexts.

Let us begin by noting one crucial point about rationality as defined above, namely that demonstrations of the efficacy of means are possible only to the extent that goals are operational. I have already used the word "operational," but a more precise definition than that advanced earlier [1] is required for the discussion which follows: If means of measuring changes in a variable or progress toward a goal are available, we may call that variable or goal op-

[1] See p. 307, above.

erational. The concept is an ideal type. A perfectly operational
goal would be one susceptible of perfect and complete measurement, expressible so that one might say: "We have achieved 31
per cent *of* our goal this year," or "We have covered 31 per cent of
the distance *toward* our goal this year."

Unfortunately, few but the most specialized of social goals approach the ideal of perfect operationalism. Progress toward some,
of course, can be measured in rather sophisticated fashion. The
market analysis of downtown Minneapolis measured business activity (a variable) by levels of sales of goods and services, by numbers of employees and their salaries, by new investment, and so on.
Although none of these scales alone measured overall economic
activity, by using them and many others the analysts hoped to
piece together a composite picture of current activity. At future
points in time, each scale (indicator) might be read again, and the
amount of change that had taken place on it recorded. The idea of
defining economic growth (the goal for downtown) without reference to the available measures of it would have seemed strange to
most people. Therefore, I have called this goal operational.

In view of the relativity of operationalism, students of administration have long had to recognize that value judgments are unavoidably made at all levels and in all branches of bureaucratic
hierarchies. It remains true, nonetheless, that appointed officials in
democratic systems of government have no theoretical justification
for exercising their will in the choice of ultimate criteria for
evaluating their actions Consequently, the political importance of
their being able to make reasoned cases in support of their decisions and recommendations is very great. The remainder of this
chapter will be taken up with an effort to distinguish three kinds
of reasoned cases that public planners may choose to make, and the
situations that provide appropriate settings for each.

The Ideal of Technical Rationality

If an official wishes to persuade his superiors and political critics
that his decisions on a wide range of subjects should be considered
authoritative, his most obvious strategy is to maintain that they
are technical—to maintain, that is, that public policy has been declared in highly operational fashion and that he speaks as an expert interpreter of it. One who qualifies in the purest sense as an

expert—defined here as one who is technically rational—can be judged only according to his competence (assuming that he is honest), not at all according to his personality or character. Give any number of pure experts the same operational objective, and they should come out with sets of specific recommendations that differ insignificantly if at all.

Politicians cannot evaluate every argument presented by any administrative official. They must therefore assess the competence of men and professions, and not, in most instances, arguments. The ideal of expertness serves them as a means of control. The other side of the coin is that it serves the experts as a means of securing freedom from lay criticism. The professional whose claims to expertness are generally accepted rules supreme within his sphere. Moreover, depending on the importance of that sphere and the difficulty of his skill, he is likely to acquire enhanced prestige, self-esteem, and earning power. In real life, of course, no profession quite reaches the goal of pure expertness. Consequently, every professional exercises some judgment. Experienced politicians realize this. When they deem the proportion of judgment in a decision to be a significant determinant of it, they begin to evaluate the man making it. The character of the evaluation is likely to depend on the type of judgment the professional is deemed to exercise. If it does not significantly involve values—that is, if it is essentially technical even though not routinized—the evaluator may simply extend his inquiries into the standing of the official in his own profession. If the judgment is of a broader nature, the evaluator is likely to ask himself whether the official is a wise man.

There are few men in any community whose wisdom is acknowledged by everyone in the community. This is particularly true in a society whose fundamental ideology is as egalitarian as our own. Some men in our society do acquire reputations for being able to make "good" decisions on complex value-impregnated issues, but few of them are civil servants. Most are people who hold or have held positions of great authority—e.g., of corporate and political leadership at the highest levels. American ideology stresses that achievement is by merit, and thus men who achieve great authority are typically believed (at least by those who view them from a distance) to have deserved it. Their salaries, titles, perquisites, and styles of life all keep them socially distant from ordinary men, and reinforce the popular belief.[2] Even those who observe from close by are generally too unclear about what they consider the substance of wisdom and too busy attending to their own affairs to evaluate the decisions of others carefully. They are likely to infer wisdom from little more tangible than impressiveness of bearing, "soundness" of general social and political opinions, acceptance in the right circles, and demonstrated capacity to sense in advance what the direct political consequences of decisions will be. Only those with time, firm philosophic standards, and great confidence in their own judgments are likely to apply less conventional criteria. There are not likely to be many such, nor are they likely to be successful politicians in a democratic polity which lacks a tradition of deference. In consequence, there are not very many members of any public service profession who can wield substantial influence by virtue of their reputations in political quarters for wisdom. The most reliable approach to winning prestige and influence for any entire profession is bound to be by cultivating a reputation for expertness.

How is it possible to establish the sort of rigor in decision-making that I have defined as technical expertness? The only way, it would seem, is to narrow one's criterion of rationality (i.e., one's goal) until the number of variables affecting its achievement is reduced to one or a very few, and they are susceptible of precise measurement. The rigor achieved by the highway engineers may be taken as illustrative. They felt confident that, given a specified amount of money to spend in a given area, they could show expertly—that is, with only a few marginal, and not terribly significant, choices open to dispute—how it should be spent. Up to a certain point, they were even likely to contend that they could recommend highway expenditure itself on an expert basis, by demonstrating that prudent spending would on balance save money. Their methods of forecasting the consequences of choosing particular alternatives were highly impressive indeed. They were able to predict with a high degree of precision the number of vehicles per hour that each portion of any given highway would be able to carry, the number that would actually use it at given future points in time, and the number that would use it if different

[2] See Robert Presthus, *The Organizational Society* (Knopf, 1962), pp. 31-33, 150-155.

locations or designs were chosen. The assertion that they could expertly select "best" highway location and design proposals, however, rested ultimately on a goal assumption: namely, that the exclusive purpose of legislation authorizing highway expenditures was to obtain, for the money appropriated, the maximum amount of "traffic service."

The engineers defined traffic service in terms of vehicle miles traveled on given highways or highway segments in given units of time. The performance of any segment of any highway with regard to this measure was expressible at close, regular intervals along a single continuum from zero to infinity. To the extent that their forecasting methods were reliable, the engineers were able to say precisely how much money would be required to raise the rating of any particular highway by any particular amount on the scale of traffic service. By correlating this information with traffic demand forecasts, they could state the marginal traffic service benefit that it would be possible to achieve with their last available dollar of appropriations—given, of course, the possibilities which had been conceived and considered. Subsequently, their priorities were clear.

The key obstacles to highway engineering rationality, then, were inaccuracies in forecasting. Because the highway engineering profession had defined its interests narrowly, it had been able to focus its research efforts with great intensity on a relatively few prediction problems. This focus had also permitted securing continuous and unambiguous support from pressure groups with an intense interest in highway matters. These groups had been able to obtain large amounts of governmental support for highway engineering research.[3] The result had been truly astonishing progress over the past several decades in the development of highway-related forecasting methods.

Traffic service, needless to say, was a variable. In practical affairs, however, men easily slide into treating familiar variables as ultimate values. The reasons for this psychological shorthand are not difficult to perceive.

Both values and variables are qualities or aspects of things rather than concrete objects. Both are defined by men. The im-

[3] See Alan Altshuler, "The Politics of Urban Mass Transportation," mimeo (November 1963), pp. 2–5.

portant analytical differences between them are two. Values in principle are of ethical significance; variables are not. Variables in principle are measurable; values are not. That is, although men can rank alternatives with regard to a value, they cannot express the implicit measuring process by which they do so. Consequently, observers are forced to treat values not as qualities of objects but as projections of the minds of human subjects. And operational goals are necessarily stated in terms of variables.

The expert's job, strictly speaking, is to measure the effects of action possibilities on variables. His technical conclusions can do no more than provide the factual basis for nontechnical judgments of the significance of alternatives for values. The variables of which operational objectives are composed are related to values, however, and when consensus is sought they often provide the clearest indicators of the values themselves. Moreover, virtually all men feel a need to consider their work valuable, and every particular set of experts has a narrow range of variables with which it is most familiar. It is likely, therefore, to impart exaggerated value significance to these variables, and in some cases to ignore effects on all others entirely.

The profession which consolidates all the measures of its success into one immeasurably enhances its claim to be called expert within its sphere. As the number of measures increases, conversely, the chances decrease at an almost geometric rate that any concrete alternative will show up best on each.[4] All comparisons of alternatives must be based (if not explicitly, then implicitly) on estimates of costs and benefits. If an evaluator can express total relevant cost and total relevant benefit each as a number on a single scale—which is to say, with reference to a single variable—he can express each whole alternative as a cost-benefit ratio and thus rank any number of alternatives "expertly." Unless he can rank alternatives expertly, he is forced to bring intuition into play. The greater the proportion of intuition in a choice, the less possible it

[4] The number of possible conflicts, assuming each measure to be of an independent variable, may be expressed: $x(1/2x-1/2)$, where x equals the number of measures. Given two measures, one conflict is possible; four measures, six conflicts; twenty measures, 190 conflicts; one hundred measures, 4,950 conflicts. Chester Barnard performed similar calculations in *The Functions of the Executive* (Harvard, 1938), Chap. 8, to show the number of possible relationships between members of an organization.

is for the decision-maker to allay all suspicion that his personal preference ruled.

Most politicians are cautious men who make no more decisions than they have to, and who try to make these appear beyond the realm of reasonable controversy. They tend to have a high regard for expertness as a mechanism of consensus: that is, as one which minimizes the number of seriously controversial decisions which politicians have to make. Their favorite programs are likely to be those which are popular in general and uncontroversial in detail. The interstate freeway program may be taken as illustrative. It will displace a million people from their homes before it is completed, but most of those who protest will be persuaded without much trouble that their fate was decreed in the fairest manner possible: by impersonal computers rather than by arbitrary officials.[5]

Even politicians who revel in controversy may support the administrative pursuit of expertness, believing that public agencies should work with the clearest possible premises so as not to confuse lay evaluators of their work about their biases. In this view, the clearer the responsibilities of each specialist, the simpler it is likely to be for politicians to comprehend the values at stake in conflicts between specialists. And more and more, it is conflicts between specialists that give politicians their opportunities to make decisions. The other side of the coin, though, is that in areas of policy where experts do not come into conflict, or where they can resolve their conflicts without resort to political arbitration, decisions are likely to be made on the basis of extremely narrow criteria.

Recognizing the potential dysfunctions of overspecialization, many professions strive conscientiously (though with varying degrees of energy) to resist its lures. They typically contend that they cannot define their central value concerns so as closely to fit the measures they have available, or that they should not try. Psychologists and educators, for instance, note that while they can define intelligence as what they measure on I.Q. tests, they can never be sure that they have measured all that the word "intelli-

---

[5] It may be noted that the engineers' task of persuasion will be facilitated by the unsophisticated nature of most protestants, because of the engineers' conscious search for low-cost rights-of-way.

gence" means to nonspecialists. The same is true even of "educational achievement," and consequently there will always be some people who deny that a proper goal for education is to raise students' scores on tests, even the best that can be devised. As Edward Banfield has asserted, there are bound to be many purposes for which intuitive measurement of the relevant variables (e.g., executive potential) is "better" than judgment based on available objective tests.[6]

Many people would argue as well that vehicle miles do not provide an adequate measure of traffic service. Highway engineers themselves recognize this implicitly when they present data to show that the highways which are most efficient in terms of traffic service (freeways) are in addition the safest of all roads, the easiest on vehicles, the most comfortable for drivers, and so on. They generally act, however, as if these variables never competed for tax dollars. Perhaps the ways in which they do are insignificant. So long as no one argues otherwise, and so long as most people are willing to agree that traffic service is a proper operational objective, highway engineers can convince people that they are very pure experts.

By contrast, city planners have rarely been able to tailor their operational goals to fit their objective measures. Very likely they will never be able to do so on a regular basis without betraying the spirit from which their profession, in the minds of most people, draws its *raison d'être*. The city planning movement arose because of a recognition that the purposeful actions of individuals often produced by-products that harmed the public's interests. Planners, therefore, owe their very professional existence to the problem of by-product control; they cannot argue that the problem is insignificant as they pursue expertness.

Nonetheless, the rewards of expertness in our society are such that many city planners cannot help being attracted by them. Unfortunately, the answer of goal-specialization is hard for them to maintain when they bother to analyze its premises. Consider the most likely planner subject-matter specialty: analysis of the impact of land uses on one another.[7] Suppose that planners tried to use

[6] Edward Banfield, "The Training of the Executive," *Public Policy*, X, 29–32, 42.

[7] I have found it essential in the pages which follow to distinguish two continua of specialization, one having to do with goals and the other with

the knowledge gained in land-use studies to set an operational goal for land-use regulation. What values might they seek to maximize? Traditionally they have resisted goal-specialization and have contended in legal controversies that the courts should consider any public welfare objective a proper basis for land-use regulation. The courts in recent years have finally come to accept this view, at least insofar as the federal constitution is concerned.[8] Planners might now, of course, reverse direction and define the objective of land-use regulation with a high degree of specificity: say, as the maintenance and improvement of property values. They could no doubt within a short while develop claims to expertness as evaluators of proposals rivaling those of highway engineers. They would no longer be generalists in their value orientation, however, and most planners would consider this a step backward for their profession. It seems reasonable, however, to expect that unless professions with relatively broad value orientations can develop persuasive theories to explain the conceptions of rationality which guide them, discipline them, and provide criteria for evaluating their work, they will increasingly be tempted by the political incentive systems in which they operate to pursue the ideal of technical rationality. There is substantial evidence that the narrowing of goals in pursuit of objective measures of success is a phenomenon of virtually all modern professions, but it probably affects those commonly engaged in public controversies most severely. It is extremely difficult to contend publicly with experts who display complex and supposedly conclusive technical justifications of their recommendations when one's own weapons are merely intuitive judgments of the public interest.

It is not impossible, however. Let us turn now to a brief consideration of two conceptions of rationality which goal-generalist pro-

---

subject matter. Maintenance of the distinction throughout is somewhat awkward, but I believe it contributes substantially in the present context to clarity of thought.

[8] The only remaining limitations appear to be that regulation must be "reasonably related" to stated public welfare objectives and must not (in the absence of fair compensation) preclude the use of property for all purposes to which it is reasonably adapted. See *Berman v. Parker*, 348 U.S. 26 (1954); *Vernon Park Realty, Inc. v. City of Mount Vernon*, 307 N.Y. 493 (1954); and *Opinion of the Justices to the Senate*, 333 Mass. 773 (1955). These cases are excerpted in Charles Haar, *Land Use Planning* (Little, Brown and Company, 1959), pp. 175–178, 308–311, 441–445.

fessions might develop to justify resistance to the temptations of technical rationality.

The Ideal of General Evaluative Rationality

The first of these conceptions may be termed that of general evaluative rationality: the capacity to evaluate means in the absence of clear and unambiguous knowledge of ends. This is the problem whose difficulty most clearly distinguishes judicial and administrative decision making at the higher levels from that at lower levels. Judges have faced it most squarely, and commonly emphasize the collective rationality that can come out of incremental growth in the law. American regulatory agencies have typically adopted a judicial approach to their work on similar grounds.[9] Whether or not the incremental approach to change is adopted, however, the problem of changing for the better rather than the worse remains. Its institutional resolution is essentially a matter of establishing qualifications for decision makers.

Ideal qualifications for those who claim rationality in making evaluations under conditions of extreme goal uncertainty are, in their general form, rather obvious. They should be men of the highest integrity. They should be capable of assessing evidence and reasoning clearly. But most of all, they should possess a capacity to sense how the community will react to particular choices, both of values and of risks. Men who possess such qualities are generally considered "wise," not "expert." They may not be wise by the standards of moral philosophy (that is, their judgments may not really be good); but they are conventionally wise—which is to say that they know how to persuade the members of their community that their judgments are good. All societies recognize a need for their kind of "rationality." Unfortunately, as we have noted, conventional judgments of wisdom tend to be based on highly crude indicators (see above, pages 335, 336). Civil servants rarely show up impressively on these indicators. It is thus extremely difficult for them to establish their claims as "rational" evaluators of proposed means unless they can explain the nature of their competence in some highly plausible way.

[9] For a general discussion of the advantages of incremental decision-making, see Charles E. Lindblom, "The Science of 'Muddling Through,'" *Public Administration Review,* XIX, 79–88.

It is obviously impossible to specify technical qualifications for the *most* general evaluators—that is, for those who recognize no limitations on either their goal or subject matter concerns. Agencies charged with general evaluative responsibilities are unlikely to have commensurate political standing unless they are headed by men of great independent eminence, whatever their prior career patterns. This is true most clearly of general planning and budgeting agencies. Herman Somers focused brilliantly on this point in his well-known discussion of Jimmy Byrnes' performance at the Office of War Mobilization, the closest thing to a civilian general staff this nation has ever had.[10] Roosevelt considered Byrnes the perfect man to direct OWM, it will be remembered, essentially because of the virtually unlimited confidence Congress had in him personally. Byrnes recognized the limited nature of the commitment to planning and coordination which Congress had made in creating OWM, and therefore acted in judicial fashion, dealing with only the most important disputes thrust up from below, employing only a few assistants, and making all decisions personally. The heads which OWM had to knock together were invariably among the most persuasive and prestigious in Washington, and Byrnes believed that the agency would quickly lose the superprestige which it required to be effective if it made too many decisions, or if its decisions could not clearly be attributed to himself.

There is a place for specialized as well as comprehensive wisdom, however, and here the goal-generalist professions have their chance. We expect judges to be lawyers as well as men of wisdom. At a level where tradition provides less firm support for a clear role conception, we may return to our example of city planning. Let us suppose that planners spent all their time thinking about the effects of land uses on one another. After awhile, they might claim that their immersion in this subject matter specialty had given them a greater ability to perceive and predict such impacts than most people, and a greater familiarity with the thought of local citizens on what constituted legitimate reason for regulating a man's use of his fixed property. Very few administrative specialists, they might note, have objectives so clearly operational as those of highway engineers. There is no simple or single measure of a

[10] *Presidential Agency* (Harvard, 1950), esp. Chap. 2.

good school, park, or library system. There can be no single measure of a good policy for regulation of land use. At the same time, it
would be *irrational* to forego disciplined analysis of the value
consequences of alternative policies affecting land use.

Objections to this form of specialization may be made from
opposite directions. On the one hand, those oriented toward simple technical rationality will point out that specialists in thought
about land use would not have clear value premises, and thus all
their recommendations (even on seemingly technical questions)
would be potentially controversial. This has to be admitted, and it
clarifies the need for agencies claiming to practice such a specialty
to be headed by men whom the leaders of their respective communities recognize as possessing some personal wisdom as well as professional competence.[11] On the other hand, in the planning
profession at least, those oriented toward the comprehensive tradition will object to any conception of planners as specialists, except
perhaps as specialists in urban life. They will note that a specialist
role conception would require planners to neglect important
problems of urban development outside their specialty. Nor
would it begin to solve the difficulty that planners have in evaluating the work of others, except in terms of land-use relationships.
The assertion that planners should specialize leads logically to the
argument that every city should have a complete set of subject
matter staff agencies, one for every defined "subject" deemed
significant. No one of these agencies could claim a comprehensive
perspective. Politicians would still need pure generalist advisers to
sort out the myriad of points of view, and to formulate them in
terms which would permit the political process to make choices
among them. The validity of this argument too must be admitted,
but we have suggested that overall evaluation is not work for a
profession; it is work for wise men.

---

[11] City planning agencies particularly appear to have suffered frequently
from having directors twenty-five and thirty years younger than other department heads. In addition, local politicians are likely to lack confidence in the
judgments of planning directors on local matters because they tend to be so
new to their areas when appointed. Most department heads in any city have
made their entire careers in it, but the planning director quite commonly has
moved from one city to another every few years during his career.

The Ideal of General Inventive Rationality

The second conception of rationality that goal-generalist professions might develop may be termed that of general inventive rationality: the capacity to widen the range of options open to a political system by redefining problems and by conceiving new means of solving them. The central presupposition of a theory built on this conception would be the simple idea that no serious theory of social rationality in the current era can ignore the problem of conceiving means to evaluate.[12] Not all governments have reason to support basic research, but all have the applied problem of conceiving alternatives. Professions which are oriented toward subject matter specialties without clear goal specialties are necessarily handicapped in expertly evaluating means. They are at no disadvantage, however, in the activity of conceiving interesting means to evaluate. In some circumstances they may be at a positive advantage. The stronger one's commitment to a particular perspective on community problems, the less likely is he to search for, perceive, or absorb evidence pointing to the inadequacy of that perspective. Narrow concerns may be essential to technical innovators in specialized fields, but they are bound to hinder innovation in the realm of general orienting ideas.

This theme is of immediate relevance to the city planning profession. The typical planning agency has the option to choose a broad subject matter as well as goal orientation. If it exercises this option, it should have the potential to define its community's problems freshly and to roam freely in search of alternative approaches to their solution. The best definitions of serious new community problems are seldom likely to coincide with the jurisdictional boundaries of existing operating agencies. A planning director cannot avoid narrowing the concerns and capacities of his staff in particular time periods, of course; but he can avoid doing so carelessly or prematurely. He must decide what mixture of specialists to employ, how to exercise his inescapable influence on their patterns of interaction, and on which problems to focus their central concerns at any time. He can make these decisions in the context of a general planning strategy analysis, however, and he

12 For an extended discussion of this theme, see James G. March and Herbert A. Simon, *Organizations* (Wiley, 1958), pp. 173–199.

can encourage his staff to conceive its basic mission as that of introducing important new ideas into the political system.

Those who produced the *Central Minneapolis Plan* may be
cited as illustrative of planners pursuing the innovative ideal.
They worked on the assumption that their most unique and
salable skill was inventiveness. Businessmen wanted the economic
function of downtown preserved, and the basic strategy of the
Planning Commission was to help them preserve it. The businessmen, however, had no precise proposals to offer; they expected the
planners to conceive a program of action. This was far from easy,
and it might have been beyond the planners' capacities if other
downtown plans had not been produced in great numbers during
the previous decade.

Rodney Engelen, who wrote the plan, believed that formalism
could be his downfall. If he wrote as though the operational goal
were the only element of concern, someone would surely call attention to outrageous side-effects that sprang from this distorted
view. So he tried to put himself in the place of his critics. He
sought means that promised economic returns, but he evaluated
each possibility on the basis of any arguments that struck him as
important. Realizing that he could not foresee all objections, and
that one possible objection might be lack of consultation, he asked
interest group representatives to comment on his ideas before he
incorporated them into his general proposal. He asked not only
whether they objected, but whether they could imagine why *anyone* might object.

In the end, he developed a certain immunity to neat theories
and made the recommendations that intuitively seemed most
defensible to him. He made little effort to draw up formal balance
sheets of pros and cons, but he did point out the noneconomic
arguments for and against each proposal that he thought people
might find significant. In several instances, he suggested particular
methods before asking greater commitment from the persons concerned. Instead of emphasizing statements of abstract goals, he
discussed ways in which public action might influence private
spending and investment decisions. He did not try to set precise
"standards" for other officials, as the St. Paul planners had done in
their *Land Use Plan*. Instead, he explained the ways in which
their work might affect achievement of the downtown operational
goal. In sum, he made no claim to have reduced ends by the appli-

cation of formal procedures, but he linked every recommendation to the plan's operational goal by a chain of reasoning—something the St. Paul land-use planners had not done. This line of reasoning was quite accessible to educated laymen, even though the size of the *Central Minneapolis Plan* seemed sure to deter all but a few specialized opinion leaders from grappling with it in its full complexity.

Engelen recognized that he had made innumerable choices based on his intuition about the preferences of his fellow citizens, and that he had probably failed to foresee some important consequences, including popular reactions, that would flow from execution of the *Plan*. On the other hand, he thought that the need for some public decisions with regard to downtown was obvious, and, this being conceded, that the value of having someone with the daring to conceive and publicize novel recommendations could not be overestimated. He felt confident that he had used his intelligence as well as he knew how, without stultifying his search by the premature acceptance of formal rules. Moreover, he believed that he had trod gingerly, deciding only issues on which local citizens could agree—if they gave the time and study that he had— almost unanimously. He doubted, he said, that he was qualified to plan the resolution of value conflicts within the social system.[13]

[13] Parenthetically, Minneapolis Planning Director Irvin and St. Paul Planning Director Wieland both told me that "reform" should not be the business of city planning. This view is widely accepted in the profession. The late Henry S. Churchill stated the case for it with characteristic vigor: "I do not think," he wrote, "that the task of the planner is to accomplish social or economic reform; that way dogmatism lies, and authoritarianism of whatever complexion, right, left, or religious." ("Planning in a Free Society," *American Institute of Planners Journal*, XX, No. 4 [Fall 1954], 189–191. The quotation is at p. 189.)
In addition, of course, it tends to limit the sources of conflict between planners and articulate interests in their communities. To cite an extreme example of this motive consciously at work: Catherine Bauer Wurster has reported that city planning agencies throughout the country eagerly agreed to let other administrative units be authorized to implement Title I of the 1949 Housing Act because they wanted to avoid involvement in housing controversies ("Redevelopment: A Misfit in the Fifties," *The Future of Cities and Urban Redevelopment*, Coleman Woodbury, ed. [Chicago: University of Chicago Press, 1953], pp. 7–25).
That many planners feel uncomfortable in this ethical position seems clear. Henry Churchill in the very article cited above deplored the widespread and

The value choices he had made in selecting means could have been made as well, he thought, by any citizen whose own mental processes rather well typified the Minneapolis average, and who intuitively understood the degrees of consensus that existed on the issues of concern to planners.

The previous three paragraphs suggest implicitly that the senior planner focusing on innovation will continue to perform a largely evaluative role within the planning staff itself. This is most particularly true of the planning director himself. His central preoccupations are bound to be: (1) which bright ideas of subordinates to approve for development into full-fledged proposals, and (2) which proposals to press assiduously on civic and political leaders. It is in his dealings with the latter that *he* will be able to play an innovative role.

The director focusing on innovation is bound to face several major political handicaps. Like any goal-generalist evaluator, he will rarely be able to base his ultimate defense of any proposal on reasoning as tight as one would expect from an engineer defending recommendations within his specialty. His efforts at persuasiveness will be further hampered, moreover, by his obligation regularly to throw out provocative (and thus potentially controversial) ideas and his need to resist routinization of his concerns (and thus his patterns of argument). By the time consensus envelops any idea, he will no longer have any reason to be interested in it. At best, nonetheless, his reasoning may be akin to that of a judge who in a difficult case makes his central decision intuitively, after examining the available evidence, but who then writes his defense of that decision for all the world to see. The defense is society's safeguard against the uninformed and careless use of intuition.

The proposals flowing from this approach to the planning role are bound to be controversial in many instances and virtually im-

---

continued use of zoning to maintain economic segregation: "I believe planners should do all they can to combat these trends as un-American and un democratic." Most of the planners interviewed for this study who ranked below the director's level refused to accept the argument that reform was outside their professional sphere. One suspects that the argument that it is finds ready acceptance only among planners (academics, with their commitment to dispassion, excluded) who at some time or other have had to worry about the political problems of maintaining an agency.

possible in most for politicians to evaluate quickly. The promise of such planning can only be that it may help to keep curiosity and open-mindedness alive throughout the government and that it may produce a flow of valuable new ideas, of which every government has a chronic shortage. The fact that few individual planners can be expected to originate fundamentally new ideas should not affect this picture. The important thing in each jurisdiction will be the systematic search for ideas already in the public domain but likely to be ignored by existing operating agencies. Competence for the invention-oriented planning practitioner will consist largely of a taste for reading and conversing widely (though with discipline), and a capacity to show imagination in applying the ideas he finds to the setting of his own jurisdiction. The plain fact is that, except within certain narrow specialties, no one else seems to do this in most American state and local governments. Outside the sphere of military and foreign policy, it is probably not done nearly adequately in the federal government, either.

Likely Political Reactions

Both of these alternatives to the ideal of technical rationality are bound to appear threatening to some. To the extent that administrators serve many values, the task of understanding the motives behind their particular recommendations is rendered more difficult. On the other hand, it is far more likely to be undertaken vigorously, because politicians frequently let themselves become mesmerized by the techniques (not to mention the stable if narrow political constituencies) of administrators who serve few values. This is not surprising. The progress of knowledge has made for ever greater specialization; it has led to the ever higher valuation of scientific as opposed to philosophic or commonsensical knowledge; and it has rendered ever more obvious in any event the technical ignorance of would-be general theorists and coordinators.[14] The ideals of "pragmatism" in thought and pluralism in politics are well suited to an age of specialization, and similarly encourage politicians to forego hard thought about the overall

[14] For a systematic exposition of the view that generalists are under severe pressure because of their technical ignorance even in organizations with monocratic rather than democratic formal authority structures, see Victor A. Thompson, *Modern Organization* (Knopf, 1961).

consequences of the aggregate of their decisions. In the absence of immediate crises, it seems sufficient to think about the direct and obvious consequences of specific decisions, treating all as though they were unrelated. This is easiest not only intellectually, but also politically. If pressure groups perceive only their most obvious conflicts of interest, why should politicians stir up hornets' nests by calling other conflicts to their attention? The same considerations are likely to lead politicians to cheer all technical innovations uncritically while ignoring or disparaging ferment in the quarters where general ideas about government, society, and the criteria of utility are pondered.

It is possible to contend that these factors combined have produced an American civilization in which remarkable technical dynamism contrasts starkly with philosophic sterility and political drift. Many political scientists, on the other hand, argue with sophistication that the blindspots of our political system have been fundamental contributors to our social and political peace and ultimately to the viability of our democracy. In the vast middle, those who believe that the balance between pluralism and central direction-giving in our society requires moderate shifting, those who believe that pluralism itself needs to be carefully cultivated if it is not to decline, and those who believe that domestic tranquility and democracy are compatible with a political system organized to think seriously about the adequacy of current institutions, policies, and priorities have a powerful case to make. They need not expect its validity to appear self-evident to American opinion leaders, however. Faith in the "invisible hand" of uncultivated pluralism, and distrust of all goal-generalist planning and evaluation, are bound to die hard in a society traditionally afraid of power and currently devoted passionately to specialization.

A sensible view, however, would appear to be that the potential threat to pluralism and democratic control of goal-generalist evaluation and innovative thinking is not that the planners may be sly, stupid, or unwise, but that the laymen responsible for public decisions may accept their proposals uncritically. This seems a remote danger indeed in the American context. In any event, clarification of the nature of general planning claims would seem to be, in the long run, the best safeguard against it. Clarification would also appear likely to benefit the goal-generalist professions by inducing them to abandon their ambivalent aspirations for "expert" status in favor of the search for provocative and wise ideas.

We might conclude on this note, but I think two other points deserve to be noted.

The first is that the goal-generalist evaluative and inventive roles may be difficult to combine in a single person or even agency. (It is true, as noted previously, that the director of an invention-oriented agency does essentially evaluative work, but his public role is that of advocate of new ideas.) The goal-generalist evaluator makes a claim to rationality which, though it may be limited to a specific area of policy, is essentially a claim to wisdom. He is likely to be taken most seriously, at least in the American political climate, if he cultivates a judicial manner and temperament, and if he presents the image of a skeptic rather than an innovator. The ideal posture for such an official is one of essential, though open-minded, conservatism. Vigorous occupants of the inventive role, on the other hand, would seem almost certain to acquire reputations for being intellectually eager to question accepted doctrines, politically eager to challenge conventional ideas of the possible, and administratively eager to disregard jurisdictional boundaries. These activities are bound to cause a great many people to question the basic soundness of judgment of those performing them. It is probably too much to hope for more than that the critics will concede the value of the inventive function and the need to maintain a few official gadflies. They are most likely to do so, one would hypothesize, where organizational structure aids them by separating the evaluative and inventive roles and claims to value.

This suggests the second point referred to above, namely that professionals who adopt the general inventive role need great patience and a capacity to be satisfied with indirect rather than direct influence on events. It is probably difficult to instill these characteristics in practitioners. C. David Loeks recalled that during his first few years in St. Paul, when he thought he was laying the groundwork for "real" planning by doing simple factual surveys, recommending solutions to specific narrow problems, and establishing friendly relationships, the whole city seemed receptive. When he began to talk about producing plans, however, resistance immediately became apparent. By 1959, when I came on the scene, St. Paul planning was in full stride but few planners believed any longer that they could win approval for proposals that interfered significantly with market forces, or that were likely to cost the city large sums of money. More than half the city's planning personnel were actively seeking other jobs. Even those who were not reported that they had been unprepared emotionally and intellectually on leaving school to meet serious resistance to their plans. Most said they now often wished that they could afford to leave their frustrating profession.

Loeks himself said that he had achieved a measure of contentment by emphasizing the educative role of planning. He claimed to see his whole profession as an articulator of long-ignored problems, rather than of precise solutions. He judged that the primary object of planning should be to educate people to expect their governments to deal with more problems, by more refined means. In this view, it hardly mattered that specific plans were ignored. Periodically, when crises struck, clusters of planning ideas would reach fruition, even if not in the forms anticipated. Planners had to keep on producing new analyses and plans, had to keep the educative process in operation, and had to be ready when the crises came. Loeks pointed out that although particular plans rarely appeared to have much effect on development, many planning ideas about the proper functions of government had become accepted, even if often in distorted fashion, during recent decades. In addition, many planning design principles had been adopted by private developers, even where not compelled by public authorities. Loeks was perfectly aware that no one could determine whether planning ideas as actually and selectively applied had benefited humanity, or whether practicing city planners had contributed much to the acceptance of the ideas. Similar uncertainties plagued all professions, however, and the alternative to accepting them was the most fruitless kind of dissatisfaction.

Most of the planners interviewed, on the other hand, were not satisfied to think of themselves as educators. They wanted to see their plans adopted in roughly the forms they presented them; and they wanted to see the work done before their thrill of creation (or they themselves) died. Rodney Engelen commented that he could bear to think of plan implementation requiring many decades if only he did not have to see, while he waited, things done that guaranteed his plans could never be accomplished. As it was, he saw his city developing and redeveloping in ways of which he disapproved, while his major proposals, which had already been tailored to interest group rather than purely professional specifications, appeared likely to become obsolete before they received serious consideration. He saw little reason to have faith in his ultimate contribution to civic betterment. He had not entered planning to be an educator, but rather to be a planner, a coordinator of human actions. He thought that virtually all recruits to the profession were motivated similarly. He felt certain that good professional planners could devise proposals that would benefit any city. Yet politicians seemed willing to implement only a very few of them, and then only after delaying, diluting, and distorting them to the point where they failed to serve any broad planning objectives. He toyed with the idea that tax-exempt foundations, free from direct democratic control, might take over many of the functions of government concerned with long-range needs. The unreality of his fancy suggested the unreality of his original (and probably typical) aspiration. It also suggested the difficulty of maintaining morale in a profession devoted to political innovation.

To explore the reasons why these experienced planners had come to conceive their potential contribution so modestly, let us turn to an examination of the political setting in which they worked.

VII

Political Restraints
and Strategies

Introduction

Restraints make strategies necessary. And in large part it is by
evaluating the success of strategies that observers try to discover
the importance of particular restraints. In this chapter, I shall deal
primarily with external (political) restraints on planners' actions.
But external restraints can never be separated entirely from internal (or ethical) restraints if we want to explain why certain strategies are chosen rather than others which appear equally plausible.

The thesis of this chapter is that the city planner, like almost
everyone in American politics, controls so little of his environment that unquestioning acceptance of its main features is a
condition of his own success.[1] I shall argue that American city
planners have in recent years escaped charges—such as those
leveled at advocates of national planning—that they are "socialist"
and "dictatorial" *because* they have so well adapted themselves to
the political systems in which they work.

Nor has this come about without awareness on their part.
Robert Walker, in a book known to all planners, recommended
this course to the planning profession two decades ago.[2] He
asserted that planning agencies could never be successful unless

[1] The word "success" is here employed to denote: (1) direct influence on
policy decisions and (2) the prestige that follows from recognition by others
of that influence.

[2] *The Planning Function in Urban Government*, 1st ed. (Chicago: University of Chicago Press, 1941), pp. 366–367.

they cultivated harmonious personal relations with local politicians and operating agency personnel. He expressed this conclusion even more strongly a decade later (1950) in his second edition of the same work. He now advised that planning agencies could not survive if they tried to advocate their own policies or to recruit support for them publicly. The planner's alternatives, he said, were: (1) to flail away ineffectually in the public forum, (2) to deal with issues of slight importance (e.g., zoning to protect property values, or designing individual public works), or (3) to serve as the *confidential* adviser of incumbent officials. Walker found that most planning agencies had lapsed into the second alternative. He personally believed that only by adopting the third could planners make a significant contribution to urban life.

Planning cannot be considered "one among equal public services," Walker continued; its function requires it to be all-inclusive. Planning officials should have direct access to the chief executive, so as to help him formulate the comprehensive policies of his administration. In order best to carry out this task, the planning agency should eschew independent action, since other officials will not be likely to listen sympathetically to the advice of planners who publicly criticize or otherwise embarrass them. The authors of a more recent article have carried Walker's approach one step further, contending that if a city planner believes that "he is being deliberately by-passed, or if he strongly disagrees with managerial policies [of the chief executive], it is his duty to tender his resignation if the differences cannot be resolved." [3]

Walker's work, along with all the literature of recent years showing that politics and administration are inseparable, has no doubt helped to convince city planners that they are ethically justified in playing the political game. Such was not always the case. Walker himself found, and the matter is not open to serious dispute, that a distrust of politics characterized the whole early planning movement.[4] Most early planners seem to have had little doubt that they could judge the public interest, and to have sus-

[3] Peter H. Nash and James F. Shurtleff, "Planning as a Staff Function in Urban Management," *American Institute of Planners Journal*, XX, No. 3 (Summer 1954), 136–147. The quotation is at p. 139.

[4] *Op. cit.*, pp. 143–145. See also T. J. Kent, *The Urban General Plan* (San Francisco: Chandler Publishing Co., 1964), pp. 53–59.

pected politicians who opposed them of having nefarious, or at least ignoble, motives. Today's city planners are less confident of their own infallibility and more respectful of the value of the political process. Moreover, they believe that they cannot be judged as planners without an assessment of their actual influence on community decisions.

The modern planner, therefore, when he reaches positions in which he bears responsibility for formulating the political strategy of his agency, must decide his general approach to the problems posed by politics. With so many values to be concerned about, the planner has a great deal of freedom in choosing his battlegrounds. The avowed specialist has much less discretion. He can fight hard for his program, or present its case phlegmatically. He may, of course, become involved in disputes as to how his program should be carried out. But at least one can predict the kinds of programs with which specialist officials will concern themselves. School officials, park officials, sanitary engineers, and so on, when they choose to fight, engage in characteristic kinds of battles the country over. On the face of things, planners may legitimately fight for any values in the urban environment that they consider worthy of protection. In practice, planners do exercise this discretion to some extent, but they do not exercise it anew on every issue. For the most part, each finds that he must decide his general posture with relation to the political process, and stick with his decision. The bureaucrat who chooses to act as a confidential adviser to government officials cannot change his character at will to fight publicly for independent policies. He may do so occasionally, but only at the risk of jeopardizing his chosen primary role. I shall argue that the "Walker" approach is very likely conducive, as he claims, to the survival and growing respectability of planning in the American political environment, but that it encourages planners to eschew all but the most noncontroversial values and the most predictable effects of actions.

The planner who stirs controversy risks failure, perhaps not only in the particular battle he has chosen to fight but also in budget and program battles for years to come. As a result, when the idea takes hold that a principal component of "good" planning is political success, the temptation is great to choose "easy" political paths. Generalists, because they have so many opportunities for battle from which to choose, are perhaps more easily tempted than specialists, who know at least the most important values they are hired to defend, and can develop clear rationales for defending them.

Implications of "Consensus" Planning

Several implications of the tendency to equate successful planning with good planning may be noted. On the one hand, it reduces the plausibility of arguments that planning threatens established values or the democratic process itself. If this planning does threaten established values, it must do so by means so inadvertent or obscure in intent that intelligent observers cannot foresee the effect at the time the plan is proposed. This very fact, however, undermines the planner's claim to have a comprehensive, or rational, approach. If he must confine himself to the areas of consensus, he can never propose plans that give all values, controversial or not, their proper due. This argument, it should be noted, has nothing to do with the argument advanced earlier that planners cannot discover the overall goals of society. What we are saying here is that even the degree of comprehensiveness that the political city planner can achieve must be distorted in practice by his need to avoid controversial values.[5]

The consequences of the planner's avoidance of controversy are not all unfortunate. His tendency to search for projects on which consensus can be achieved may serve, if he is successful, to focus public attention on areas of consensus rather than conflict. If the planner cannot solve society's disruptive conflicts, perhaps he can reduce their importance by diverting attention from them. Edward Banfield argues in *Political Influence* [6] that ritualistic, platitudinous public discussion of issues that actually turn on potentially disruptive considerations (e.g., racial conflict) may serve a similar purpose. The diversion of attention from threatening conflict can be dysfunctional if it serves to intensify the eventual disruption; but the possibility frequently exists that disruption can be avoided entirely, and the problem will work itself out as well as it might in any event, if public expression of the conflicting interests can be avoided. No one can say in advance for every issue whether

[5] See page 196, above, for an ethical justification of this avoidance.
[6] New York: The Free Press of Glencoe, 1961.

public discussion should be encouraged or avoided. Here is another problem that wise men must deal with anew in every case.

If the planner can truly conceive projects whose foreseeable consequences are favorable by everyone's criteria, then presumably his projects may reasonably be judged to be of net benefit to the community. In this case, though the planner may not be solving the community's most important problems, he may make a definite contribution to its well-being. The possibility always exists, in addition, that the accomplishment of planner objectives will give such satisfaction to community members that other sources of dissatisfaction will seem less important to them. For example, if planners can attract enough investment to maintain full employment in a city, those liberated from the threat of unemployment may worry less about their noneconomic grievances. On the other hand, of course, with their economic worries gone, they may have more time to think about other problems. Planners cannot foresee these long-range effects of change on the human mind any more than politicians. In fact, politicians may plausibly claim to know the minds of their constituents better than planners do. Probably because such effects are so difficult to predict, they are never discussed by planners defending their proposals.

Consequently, the charge may be made that planners who serve the unrelated narrow goals on which consensus exists do not necessarily serve the public interest. By this view, communities are not necessarily logical; any community's consensus on specific points may be inconsistent and self-defeating. The only way to assure that it is not is to relate the community's immediate objectives on which consensus exists to its most profound desires. Planners may achieve political success without taking this latter step. Thus, they cannot prove their wisdom merely by pointing to their political successes. This may be true even though, as I argued in Chapter VI, society for its part can expect no safeguards against unwise recommendations from planners except those of the political decision-making process.

Conditions of Politically Effective Consensus

Beyond a certain point, it becomes fruitless to talk about consensus in the abstract. We must turn to talk of politically effective consensus. In Chapter V, I briefly discussed the veto-group character of American domestic politics, and the unwillingness of politicians to choose in the absence of firm consensus. There I defined consensus as the absence of articulate opposition, not as the presence of unanimous support. If we can achieve some understanding of the conditions under which such opposition to proposals is likely to be absent, we may refine our perception of which values city planners most typically serve, and our understanding of why they serve them.

Marver Bernstein argues that veto-group politics forces proponents of positive governmental action to argue in terms calculated to appease all potentially hostile groups.[7] He bases his generalization on his own study of the histories of the independent regulatory commissions. He finds that every group of reformers that has persuaded Congress to establish a regulatory commission has been forced to prune its goals drastically during its campaign. Each has had to overcome the typical arguments against positive government that characterize our society. The members of each have been called socialists, impractical dreamers, proponents of "big government," and so on. Each has eventually made clear that its reform was intended merely to reestablish free competition. Each commission, once formed, has adopted a judicial procedure and focused on obtaining fairness between the contending parties in cases brought before it, rather than pressing home a conception of society's interest. Each has done so in large part out of recognition that the courts, Congress, and articulate public opinion all favor the protection of individual rights, while harboring at the same time deep suspicions of positive action in the name of that elusive abstraction, the public interest.

Planners cannot adopt a purely judicial procedure because their role, in the eyes of most people, is to propose new policies. Yet many planners in the past have abjured this role to seek a judicial one. Robert Walker found in his 1937–1938 tour of thirty-seven American cities (including the largest ones) that most planning staffs confined their work to zoning administration.[8] Since World

[7] *Regulating Business by Independent Commission* (Princeton: Princeton University Press, 1955).

[8] *Op. cit.*, p. 330.

War II, however, positive planning in the urban sphere has become respectable. The bogey of socialism is almost never raised in responsible circles. Conservative Republicans in the Twin Cities, men who became extremely upset at the thought of federal planning, said without qualm that "we can use some planning here." We must ask what insights into the nature of politically effective consensus have permitted planners to win this respectability.

The most serious barrier to planning success has been, of course, that discussed by Bernstein: the fear of governmental power that pervades American society. Some planners have contended with this fear as New Dealers did several decades back: they have argued that by accepting the modest exercise of public power to save urban investments today, the private sector will retain more power relative to the public sector in the long run than it can by any other means. They constantly reiterate that they can accomplish very little except by providing profitable opportunities for free enterprise. The prudent investor, they say, avoids uncertainty. He prefers not to invest in any section or neighborhood unless he feels that its future is secure. The prime task of planning, it follows, is to assure investors of a public resolve to maintain the quality of given areas and to help investors improve them. They emphasize that all investment occurs in a legal framework and is affected by it. Their proposed ordinances (seldom spoken of as regulations) are designed to make investment less risky. The prospect, they say, is that unless something is done to this end, central cities in large metropolitan areas will be lost as fields for private investment. Yet the cities ultimately are indispensable; as this is realized, government will—unless today's modest plans are accepted—have to take an ever bigger role in reclaiming them.

The power aspect of this analysis is seldom expressed so baldly, because one of the folkways of American politics (referred to explicitly by some of the planners interviewed) is to avoid the mention of power. The proponent of public action who mentions power comes under suspicion by virtue of this alone. Nevertheless, most planners understand very well that they must not ask for significant increases in public power. They know, similarly, that they incur great risks whenever they propose public ownership of a new facility. The word subsidy is even more dangerous, and some planners in the Twin Cities who believed subsidization of public transit to be inevitable dared not say so except in strictest confidence.

On the other hand, there is today widespread acceptance—despite frequent protests from the individuals compelled to sell—of the use of public power to assemble and clear land for private developers. When such a project is finished, the government owns no more than it did before. Surprisingly, the public loss on such transactions is almost never referred to as a subsidy. Planners can generally forestall discussion of the loss by showing that increased tax revenues from the land involved will make up the loss within a few years. Similarly, zoning is justified by its promise to make the environment of private investment decisions more secure. Planners emphasize that subdivision regulation is aimed not at responsible developers but at the outrageous abuses of "hit-and-run" developers who have no interest in the long-term maintenance of property values. Building codes are necessary to assure that a few property owners do not start chains of deterioration that would eventually blight whole neighborhoods. The St. Paul land-use plan urged city officials to make sure that any new private commercial development was based on adequate market analyses; the idea was to save investors from their own mistakes. Those who wrote the *Central Minneapolis Plan* stressed that business needs were satisfied downtown as nowhere else.

Obstacles to "Controversial" Planning

Beyond planning to strengthen the free enterprise system, of course, there are a number of services that Americans traditionally recognize to be within the proper sphere of government. Planners do not risk being charged with socialistic or dictatorial tendencies when they propose alterations in street patterns, purchases of parkland, construction of sewer facilities, and the like. Clear threats to public safety and health are likewise recognized as proper public concerns. But when planners propose novel or expensive projects that cannot be justified by their benefits to property owners, they run afoul of several powerful social mechanisms. Among these are: (1) the necessity of gaining support from politicians who avoid controversy and cooperation from officials in the operating departments who are jealous of their powers; (2) the legal and financial restraints upon the city government, which operate to prevent even some activities in which politicians and agency heads are willing to engage; and (3) the lack of executive authority within the planning agency itself.

First let us consider the tendency among politicians to shy from controversial issues. Incumbent officeholders in the Twin Cities seldom encountered defeat at the polls unless they became identified with unpopular issues. In the absence of party machines or even party labels (both cities used the nonpartisan ballot), they found no asset comparable to a familiar name. They were loathe to risk their natural advantage in a competition based on name familiarity by engaging in controversy. Most were willing, of course, to champion causes certain to increase their popularity; when confronted with new issues, however, they were plagued by uncertainty as to which side, if either, would prove more popular. They inclined to doubt that any novel or expensive proposal could possibly win the support of everyone. They operated frankly on the theory that the gratitude of voters was short-lived, while voter resentment was undying. Given the choice between making one enemy and losing the opportunity to make five friends, almost all (we may infer from their practice) preferred the latter.[9]

[9] Harold Kind, secretary to Minneapolis Mayor P. Kenneth Peterson, explained the Mayor's overall strategy to me in the summer of 1959. The following paraphrase of his account appeared originally in my monograph, *A Report on Politics in Minneapolis* (Cambridge: Joint Center for Urban Studies of Harvard University and the Massachusetts Institute of Technology, 1959).

"Peterson does not actively sponsor anything. He waits for private groups to agree on a project. If he likes it, he endorses it. Since he has no formal power with which to pressure the Council himself, he feels that the private groups must take the responsibility for getting their plan accepted.

"He never attempts to coerce aldermen. Instead, he calls them into his office to reason with them. The Mayor *could* call a press conference, but he has not done so in his two years in office. To do so, he feels, would antagonize people and so actually decrease his influence.

"The Mayor has let citizens' groups use the facilities of his office to work out solutions to certain pressing and highly controversial problems. Such solutions are often then seized upon by him and by the Council and adopted without amendment.

"If the Mayor does not fight his opponents in the Council, neither does he help his friends there. He remains aloof from aldermanic campaigns. It is

These politicians knew that many kinds of characteristic opposition are slow to form, but vehement once formed. Many groups, they realized, neglect to stir until after irreversible steps have been taken. Small property owners in Minneapolis' Lower Loop Redevelopment Area, for instance, confidently assured newspaper reporters until the final months before their buildings came down that the project would never get under way. The politicians knew, finally, that they could not possibly foresee all the kinds of opposition that might arise to haunt them. In this situation, it was most profitable to talk about honest, efficient, economical government, to make sure that one's ward got its share of expenditures for routine public services, and to attend a great many social functions. If the voters occasionally elected a couple of councilmen or a mayor who had grander ideas, they could seldom carry many colleagues with them. Things had been different at various times in the recent past, with the Minneapolis Central Labor Union and the St. Paul Trades and Labor Assembly enforcing a modicum of discipline on matters of importance to them. Both had defined their interests conservatively and narrowly, however. Neither, parenthetically, had shown any interest in planning. Nevertheless, in the city election of 1957 the charge of bossism had cost labor its dominant position in Minneapolis politics. St. Paul's labor leaders took this to suggest that their continued electoral dominance depended on their extracting virtually no price, except on matters of the city's relations with its own unionized employees, from officials elected with the aid of labor endorsement. Despite their caution, labor's endorsed candidates met their worst defeat since before the Depression in the city election of 1960.

The uncertainty as to public reactions that confronted Twin

---

more democratic to let the voter decide on each office, he feels, without being beguiled by candidates who are merely trying to help each other.

"The Mayor will neither argue about an issue nor publicly commit himself. If an alderman inquires publicly about his stand on a particular bill, he is noncommittal. 'We would say it is unfortunate that Alderman so-and-so has chosen to make this suggestion to the newspapers first. Nevertheless, it may be useful. We will conside it.'

"Peterson, nevertheless, has been more active than his predecessor in testifying before legislative committees and in addressing the Hennepin County delegation to the legislature. He lobbies, however, only when the major groups in the city and in the Council are united."

Cities politicians was due in large part to the truncated nature of each city's interest group structure. Where there are representatives of interest groups, they serve to inform politicians of probable reactions to proposals. Few but professional representatives can perform this function well. The professional can spend a large part of his time talking with public officials and with other representatives of interest groups. He learns the devious byways of government. He acquires sophistication in sifting from the proposals pending at any time those that are likely to affect his organization. It is he who, in the first instance, expresses its concern.

The job of maintaining an organization is, of course, an absorbing task in itself. Certain organizations that exert political influence have nonpolitical reasons as the primary justifications of their existence. If they have paid employees, they can quite easily assign one or more to spend time on civic affairs. Business organizations and labor unions fit in this category. It is more difficult, however, to keep up an organization the primary purpose of which is political. A great deal of energy and money is needed to maintain the self-consciousness of members, convince them that their common interests warrant paying dues, inform them of accomplishments, and employ professional representatives. When the number of an organization's potential members is great, a small proportion of them may be able to support the organization at little cost to each individual. When the local level of government is compared with the national, it is obvious that unless the proportion of potential members who support each potential organization is far greater, the number of organizations is likely to be far smaller. Since many interest groups at the federal level operate out of individual lawyers' offices, it may be stated that the minimum cost of supporting an organization is not much less at the local level. Perhaps one might generalize that, other things being equal, government becomes easier to understand as the jurisdiction becomes smaller, but probably there will be fewer interests that have representatives who *do* understand. In Minneapolis and St. Paul, only a few interests consistently kept a professional eye on more than one or two aspects of local government. These were business, "taxpayer," real estate, labor, and "good government" organizations.

The "good government" and labor organizations tended not to become active in controversies about planning proposals. The former had memberships so diverse in political opinion that they tried to avoid taking stands on controversial issues. Like local politicians and newspapers, they inclined to campaign for honest, efficient, economical government. They frequently clashed with politicians about who best understood the requirements of efficient government, but almost never did they commit themselves as organizations on matters of substantive policy. (They might, of course, encourage their members to think about controversial problems as individuals. The Leagues of Women Voters, for example, regularly sponsored debates and round table discussions.) The labor unions knew that most proposals *initiated* by them were sure to be vetoed by the other organized groups. They worried, moreover, about incurring the charge of bossism. Therefore, they tended to narrow their area of concern to such bread-and-butter issues as the wages of unionized public employees and hiring policies on public projects. For the rest, labor in each city was politically inactive except at election times. Minneapolis planners claimed that they knew of no labor representatives with whom they could consult on a continuing basis during the preparation of the *Central Minneapolis Plan.*

Labor leaders, moreover, seldom vetoed proposals for public action. Their initial bias was favorable, especially toward proposals that promised to create employment. Business, taxpayer, and real estate groups, on the other hand, posed strong potential veto threats to any proposal. All three tended to emphasize the tax rate in their thinking; the business and real estate groups inclined to oppose regulatory proposals as well. Their inclination, however, was seldom doctrinaire, though it often sounded as if it were. If they could be convinced that projects were designed to benefit business, or to save taxpayers money in that not-too-long run, they were likely to give their support.

The element of temperament also had its place, of course. Minneapolis businessmen, for instance, seemed more willing to hear out planning proposals then their St. Paul counterparts; the latter tended to suspect that planners were always trying to "put something over" on them. The hostile reaction of downtown businessmen to the St. Paul Central Business District Study, described in Chapter II, may be viewed as a manifestation of this tendency. Also, members of the St. Paul Housing and Redevelopment Authority staff had incurred the displeasure of many businessmen by continuing to produce reports asserting the need for public housing. Some businessmen hardly distinguished between the Housing Authority and the Planning Bureau.

In general, the interest group structure of Minneapolis was far more fully developed than that of St. Paul. One reason may have been that Minneapolis was larger. More important, probably, was that the St. Paul business community had lived for thirty years with a labor-dominated city government. Some observers claimed that it had become a reflex for St. Paul businesses to content themselves with exercising a veto over all proposals for public spending and regulation. Since St. Paul government could hardly do less than it was doing, and since it was not likely to be allowed to do more, public interest in the government had withered. Only in the most recent four or five years had the attitude of business apparently begun slowly to change; the results were still impossible to assess.[10]

Had Twin Cities planners wished to battle the interests of business and taxpayer groups, they would have had to marshal overwhelming support from other elements of the community. Their chances of success would have been minimal. The newspapers would not have been likely to help. Even with their help, the interest of a broad public would have been extremely difficult to create and sustain. The dangers of trying would have been enormous. Any agency that ventured on such a course would almost surely have found its budget and staff cut drastically within a short while. Politicians had enough pressures on them, they felt, without having civil servants go out to recruit more.

Twin Cities politicians, however, seemed no more doctrinaire then businessmen. They could be generous in their forgiveness of administrators whose political efforts turned into political benefits for them as politicians. Some at least recognized that if they

[10] For the background of the assertions in the last four paragraphs, see *A Report on Politics in Minneapolis* and *A Report on Politics in St. Paul* (Cambridge: Joint Center for Urban Studies of Harvard University and Massachusetts Institute of Technology, 1959). I can assert the accuracy of this picture only through September 1960, when I left the Twin Cities.

wanted to shy away from controversial matters, they did well to permit their administrators to seek support for new proposals independently. The administrator who exercised this option had to be prepared, needless to say, to run his risks independently, too. Projects like the redevelopment of the Lower Loop provided campaign arguments for incumbent politicians when they became generally recognized as community assets. The action of Minneapolis city planners in working with businessmen to win support for the *Central Minneapolis Plan* was, seen in this light, within the rules of the game. The planners had a fighting chance (no more!) to reverse the City Council's annoyance at their boldness and actually to gain in stature with it if the friendly attitude of business toward the plan persisted and spread throughout the community. Had they chosen to recruit support for public housing proposals instead, their chances would have been slim indeed.

The planners were restrained further by their perception of the manifest advantages to be gained by acquiring popularity within the city administration. Most administrative officials within each of the Twin Cities had their recognized places in the governmental structure, and their established proportions of the city budget. They were *the* recognized experts within their spheres. No one tried to reduce their share of the budget, and they reciprocated by neglecting to press their own ambitions with much vigor. Most city agencies were headed by veterans of the local civil service, an institution not geared to encourage mavericks. The few positions, such as planning director, which were regularly filled from outside the system were recognized as sources of potential disruption.

The veteran agency-heads all had established relationships of trust with the members of the City Council. The councilmen appreciated the willingness of the civil servants to avoid embarrassing them. In quite a few cases, councilmen and agency heads were close personal friends. They sympathized with each other's problems, and respected each other's working solutions to them as "the best possible." They reinforced each other's views about those who would upset the framework in which they had such secure places.

Most agency heads, of course, had some relations with interest groups. They were governed in these dealings, however, by implicit rules of the game that were no less binding for being unwritten. The rules appeared to be designed for the benefit of City Hall professionals—politicians and administrators both. Their primary functions were to keep down the level of interest group activity— which is to say, demands on government—and to deter maverick administrators from starting jurisdictional battles. The rules, nonetheless, were sufficiently defensible in terms of democratic ideology so that no one could appeal from their effect with assurance of public sympathy. Some of the most important rules, as both satisfied and disgruntled administrators defined them for me, were: An agency may consult with interested groups, but not take the initiative in forming them. It may inform leaders of interest groups of significant developments, but not try to persuade them to arouse their members; it may tell representatives of interest groups in a factual way that a proposal cannot succeed without their support, but it cannot urge them explicitly, let alone put pressure upon them, to give that support. Controversies within City Hall should be kept from the newspapers. Even if the outlines of a dispute become publicly known, no party to it should carry his case to the newspapers; at the same time, no one should use the opposite technique of attracting newspaper interest to an issue by acting conspicuously secretive. The administrator's object, though it may require different tactics in different situations, should be to keep himself unobtrusive. Quite obviously, the boundaries of toleration were not precise, and it was easy for those who were not veterans to cross them inadvertently. Those who administered established programs had the least difficulty. Planners administered nothing, however, and were expected to offer new proposals regularly. They could not avoid running serious risks if they proposed projects likely to stir pressure group and newspaper interest. Their uncertainty as to which of their actions would antagonize the City Hall professionals was in itself an important restraint.

The elective City Hall professionals acted on the assumption that power had to be exercised occasionally if it was to continue to influence action. They willingly paid the price of public criticism for periodic demonstrations of their ability to punish mavericks. The alternative was to run the risk that the mavericks in time would get them into worse trouble, with their constituents if not necessarily with the newspapers. The Minneapolis planning budget, for instance, was cut back in 1960 after five years of rapid rise. The planners believed that they had been disciplined, in part for engaging in a jurisdictional dispute with the city engineer over who should do major streets planning, and in part for neglecting informal City Hall relationships in favor of cultivation of outside groups and the local press. Similarly, the City Hall professionals engaged during 1960 in a battle with the newspaper and good government groups over a proposed charter revision intended to give Minneapolis a "strong mayor" type of government. An engineer in the city's employ was found to have been circulating one of the voter petitions needed to force the referendum. The engineer had not violated any laws or directives, but the City Council canceled an appropriation for him to attend a professional convention. The newspaper editorialized against the Council's action but to no immediate effect. After the newspaper lost interest, and the Council felt its point had been made, it actually permitted the engineer to go to his convention. The latter action was taken so quietly that the newspaper did not even carry news of it. The Council wanted to make clear, apparently, that punishment and advancement within City Hall depended on its favor alone.

Most city officials looked with disfavor on planners' assertions that their view was comprehensive. The heads of other agencies generally said without hesitation that they had no quarrel with planners so long as the planners did not try to tell them how to run their own departments. To planners, this qualifier seemed extremely serious. The Minneapolis planners felt, for example, that they could not possibly develop a downtown plan without considering the handling of traffic. In the end, their most significant proposals had to do with traffic control, much to the annoyance of the city engineer. He took the position that street planning was none of their business. Similarly, the city engineer of St. Paul told me that while he had no objection to letting city planners comment on his proposals for public works, he had no intention of working with them in the conception stage of project planning. He tried to consider the impact of his projects on land use, he said, but he could not share his office's responsibility for proposing public works with anyone.

In both Minneapolis and St. Paul, several operating departments had willingly let the planning agencies make facility location studies for them. They were short of staff for this kind of work, and had no fear that by letting out this work to planners they might imperil their own status. Officials of each reacted with disfavor, however, to the suggestion that planners be given the authority to approve or disapprove their locational decisions.[11] They argued that decisions about the relationships of land uses to each other were no more important than decisions about the quality of each public service. In practical terms, they recognized that their own prestige would suffer if another group of public officials were admitted to have a more comprehensive, or better, view of the public interest than they.

A second mechanism (see above, page 361) restraining planners was the usual requirement that they work within the existing limits of local government powers. These limits were severe. Both Minneapolis and St. Paul had to get along, for example, within spending limits prescribed by their city charters; the charters could be amended only by referendum or vote of the state legislature. As a general rule, the legislature refused to amend any city's charter unless that city's own legislative delegation made the request. With no party machines to discipline them, Twin Cities legislators had no reason to take responsibility for tax increases, and usually preferred to force a referendum. The voters of both cities were so suspicious of charter amendments to raise taxes that they invariably voted "no" if any articulate opposition emerged during the campaign. The more novel and controversial the purpose for which the increase was intended, of course, the less likely was the campaign to be quiet. In the quarter century ending in 1960, the Minneapolis electorate voted on seven proposed tax increases. It approved one, a one-mill Library Board increase in 1942. The St. Paul electorate during the same period rejected ten proposed increases while accepting four.[12]

The cities were also short of nonfinancial power. Most observers

[11] Minneapolis planners did have the power under a 1959 charter amendment to disapprove decisions on the location of schools, subject to overriding by a two-thirds majority of the elective school board.

[12] St. Paul voters had, it should be noted, permitted indebtedness to reach its charter limitation of 10 per cent of full and true valuation. Minneapolis voters did not have to approve bond issues, but the City Council had gradually reduced the city's debt to 3.8 per cent of full and true valuation. The valuations of the two cities appeared to be based on comparable standards.

believed that the same generalization could be made about referenda to increase the scope of city powers as could be made about those on tax increases: namely, that no amendment would pass if any substantial interest group opposed it. Planners found it almost impossible to conceive of large projects that did not run afoul of at least a few provisions of the city charter. During the Central Minneapolis planning process, for example, it was uncertain whether the city possessed power to operate parking facilities. A more urgent situation developed at a late stage in the Lower Loop Redevelopment Project. The city suddenly became aware that there were more than sixty liquor stores in the Redevelopment Area. The total number of liquor licenses had been limited for many years; licenses had been bought and sold for substantial sums; and many of the current licensees claimed that the licenses represented a major part of their capital. City leaders judged that they would make many enemies, and violate common decency, unless they permitted the licensees to relocate. Since 1887, however, the area within which licenses could be issued had been limited, first by state law and later by city charter provision, to a small portion of the city, which most civic leaders now considered supersaturated. The obvious solution was to extend the limits. This approach was finally adopted, but it involved a long and bitter referendum campaign. Good government groups and clergymen supported the proposal, and only a few fundamentalist religious groups opposed it in organized fashion. Nevertheless, the proposal garnered just 3 per cent more than the 55 per cent needed to pass. Because neighborhood opposition showed itself so strongly in the vote tally, the Council, despite its now undoubted power to relocate the licenses, neglected in all but a few cases to do so.

Our list of restraints on city planners cannot omit mention of the fact that every unpopular city action could be challenged in the courts. American courts customarily interpret provisions of a city charter with the utmost severity, on the theory that state legislatures can rectify overstrict interpretations of their intent. In consequence, city officials characteristically tend to be more concerned with the legality of proposals than with their wisdom. The most influential member of the Minneapolis City Council devoted much of a long interview with me to explaining that he would not even peruse the *Central Minneapolis Plan* until the city planners could assure him that all of its recommendations were legal under the existing charter. Planning staff members, on the other hand, protested that although they had tried to remain within the charter, they could hardly write comprehensive plans if in every case they took the narrowest (i.e., safest) view of charter language. They also felt that they could not plan if they had to develop advisory opinions on every potential point of legal controversy.

C. David Loeks recalled that as a young planner he was subjected to courtroom cross-examination by St. Paul's leading trial lawyer, whose clients were challenging an amendment to the zoning ordinance. Loeks had recommended and the City Council had passed the amendment. Even though the decision had been made by elected officials, the city now had to prove in court that it had not acted arbitrarily. Loeks enjoyed telling of how he bested the lawyer, but few planners would incur such an experience deliberately. Similarly, it will be remembered that those who wrote the St. Paul land-use plan explained that they had to use procedures described in reputable publications so that they could demonstrate in court that they had not been arbitrary. This seems to explain in part why they devoted so much effort to fact-gathering and tried to convey the impression that their recommendations flowed necessarily from the application of right principles to the measurable facts. It is extremely difficult to use intuition and still prove in court that one has not been arbitrary. If city officials must be prepared to prove in every case that they acted as technicians, and if it is impossible to make comprehensive planning decisions technically, it is hardly surprising if planners avoid controversy.

Even when the planners win in court, of course, they frequently lose frustrating years to the judicial process. The momentum was eliminated from St. Paul's urban renewal program, for instance, when a group of downtown businessmen halted work for two years with an unsuccessful legal suit. Though the Housing and Redevelopment Authority won the case, it was subjected to a good deal of criticism for having accomplished so little during the years of defending itself in court. Marver Bernstein has made the further point that the movement of political battles to court tends to transfer the focus of attention from social issues to technical findings of fact and law.[13] These bore the general public. Yet the agency which cares to do battle with well-financed interests can do so successfully only by arousing the general public to express its support. It is difficult for those supporters whose interest is sustained only by public spirit to remain attentive during years of legal wrangling. The few individuals and groups who have economic interests at stake are likely to have the field to themselves before the court tests are over.

The final mechanism restraining the planners was their own lack of executive authority. Neither city planning commission could put any recommendations into effect on its own authority. It had to persuade outsiders who did have operating responsibility that *they* should incur the risks of acting on its advice. Had planners had authority to execute their plans unless others objected, they might have won some battles by default. It takes more effort to oppose a proposal than merely to neglect to act upon it. Similarly, had it been assumed—as in planned economies—that the government had to approve *some* plan each year, the planners might again have been more bold. As it was, the likelihood that no action would be taken deterred planners from risking the alienation of any potential supporter.

Politicians saw positive benefits in keeping alive the likelihood of inaction. They understood their operating agencies better than they understood planners. The typical operating agency had a known point of view and a known constituency. Because city planners claimed to champion a wide variety of values, politicians tended to feel that they did well to move slowly and suspiciously in their efforts to discover what values dominated any particular plan. The operating departments seemed to accept the view that only politicians could take the overall view in balancing departmental claims. The city planners often seemed to believe that they had a more disinterested, comprehensive perspective than the politicians. Politicians dealt with this threat of competition by defining the planners' specialties as narrowly as possible. Again and again I was told that planners were specialists in the maintenance of property values by land-use regulation and/or that they were specialists in civic design. By keeping from them the authority to do anything without the explicit approval and active

[13] *Op. cit.,* Chap. 3.

cooperation of others, politicians assured that city planners could not step beyond the boundaries of their specialties without being exposed. The politicians of most cities make in effect a similar point when they withhold from planners the authority to prepare the city's capital improvements program.

Parenthetically, the planning commissions themselves were generally potential rather than active forces restraining the planning staffs. The commission members appeared to have become imbued with planning viewpoints. This is not to say that their support always went much further than that of other restraining groups, but only that it rarely fell short of theirs. Twin Cities planners noted that while most commissioners wished to avoid controversy themselves, they were generally willing to permit the planning staffs to run risks. The planners believed that most commissioners preferred not to antagonize potential customers of their businesses or potential members of their organizations.[14] The members, such as clergymen, who in relative terms were most free and most inclined to favor controversial objectives, generally had the least political influence and the least interest in booster activity to promote plans. The corollary was that the more influential the members of a planning commission, the less "educable" they were likely to be. For example, when the Downtown Council of Minneapolis, the leading organization of the city's businessmen, became interested in city planning, its leaders did set about inducing men of some stature in the business community to serve on the commission. Such men would carry weight when they chose to support planning proposals. This was due, however, at least in part, to *their* constituents' belief that (1) they had a knack of foreseeing objections to proposals, and (2) they shared the essential values of other downtown businessmen. Nonetheless, Planning Director Irvin—a far from timid planner—persuaded his weighty commission to adopt the practice of letting him circulate "tentative" plans without commission approval or disapproval.

Planning Strategies

Given the nature of these restraints, what planning strategies were possible? We shall forego any effort to categorize all the

---

[14] Robert Walker, *op. cit.*, made a similar observation. He seemed to feel that it removed the last argument in favor of retaining the commissions. For my view of this issue, see below, pp. 384–391.

logically possible strategies, and concentrate on some that were tried in the Twin Cities.

Men develop strategies in order to chart paths of least resistance toward their objectives. When an agency has either ill-defined objectives or the option of choosing among alternative objectives, the temptation may be great to choose objectives according to the ease with which strategies for their accomplishment may be devised. Every administrator, obviously, has some choice. Even if he has no freedom in choosing his organization's substantive objectives, he must decide how vigorously to try to achieve each one. His decisions will depend not solely on his expectations of their immediate success, or on his love of battle, but also on his estimate of the effect each strategy will have on the general image he wants his agency to project. Herbert Wieland, for example, believed that planning ideas would gain greater acceptance in the long run if planners acted as team players within City Hall. Others argued that unless the planning department stirred up some excitement occasionally, no one would pay any attention to it, and its own more dynamic staff members would seek other jobs.

The boldest strategy observed in the Twin Cities was that followed by Lawrence Irvin in Minneapolis. Irvin decided that he could not accomplish anything unless he took the risk of upsetting a few members of the City Hall "team." He was not satisfied to comment privately on the proposals of others or to teach city officials about planning principles. He wanted to propose concrete courses of action. He hoped to work with every relevant agency in City Hall, but he refused to be put off by their indifference. When forced to choose between battle and surrender, we have seen that he challenged even the city engineer to a public argument over whether the city had an adequate street plan.

If Irvin refused to halt before the obstacles in City Hall, however, he took great care to avoid battle with influential private groups. When he arrived in Minneapolis in 1958, downtown businessmen were already organized to support planning. Irvin thought of himself as having responsibilities to a much larger public, but he saw nothing wrong with focusing his attention on proposals that simultaneously advanced the public interest and that of his well-organized constituency. The latter greeted his first effort, the *Central Minneapolis Plan*, with apparent enthusiasm, and were well enough organized to ensure its success if they wanted to. He in turn made clear that he wanted to work with the businessmen in revising it. Whether this general harmony could be transferred to proposals for specific actions remained to be seen.

The other side of the picture was that the Minneapolis planning staff had made many enemies within City Hall. Its 1960 budget request was cut almost in half, and below the 1959 appropriation. My interviews revealed strong hostility toward the planning staff among city councilmen and certain agency heads. With the intensive phase of downtown planning over, Irvin's next problem was to win public support for other planning activities. He turned his staff to neighborhood planning, the objective of which seemed primarily to be the conservation of property values. He hoped that neighborhood associations of property owners would in future years provide reliable support for the Planning Department. If he proved correct, the politicians were likely to come around to support planning themselves, in their own self-interest.

A second overall strategy was to neglect the development of broad plans in favor of doing odd tasks that no one else had the time or ability to do, but that everyone agreed should be done. C. David Loeks did a great deal of this during his first years as St. Paul Planning Director. He did site studies for most of the city's operating agencies, and whenever the City Council received a complaint about some problem, they referred it to Loeks for study. Most of Loeks' reports in response to these queries represented several man-weeks of work. Some of the most important were on downtown parking facilities (no recommendations), junk and dismantling yards, billboard control, the feasibility of creating a one-way street system in downtown St. Paul, and recommended priorities for the use of a $38 million bond issue passed in 1953. The last two were more ambitious pieces of work than the others, but still were not part of any general planning analysis. Nevertheless, Loeks must come next after Irvin in this hierarchy of boldness, because he did risk antagonizing fellow officials in a number of instances. His study of billboards, for example, showed that the city architect, despite his clear legal authority to control their spread, had neglected to do so. His demonstration that a one-way street pattern was possible in downtown St. Paul flatly contradicted a series of statements that the then city engineer had made over several decades. Loeks did not try to arouse the Council to refer things to him, nor did he inaugurate dealings with the public, but he did speak frankly when the Council asked his opinion.

Another possibility was to concentrate on factual analyses. Most Americans have faith that fact-gathering is useful. Many types of research are of particular use to businessmen and operating agencies. The newspapers give prominent play to background analyses prepared by city planners, and few people seem inclined to ask persistently what the payoff is supposed to be. On the positive side, everyone who has frequent dealings with the city government finds it convenient to know that one set of officials can locate any fact about the city that anyone has ever collected. An agency with too small a staff for elaborate data collection can publish data compiled by others. The St. Paul planning staff under Loeks did almost no original research, and never had more than two trained planners free from zoning and administrative chores; but in the final two and one-half years of Loeks' tenure it published seven handsome reports. Two were presentations of census data (one on population, one on housing); two explained and "sold" programs of other agencies (urban renewal and freeways); and three proposed procedural, as opposed to substantive, policies ("Selecting Urban Renewal Projects," 1955; "Proposed Planning Districts," 1957; and "Potential Renewal Areas," 1957).

Loeks continued this record of remarkable productivity during and after 1958 as head of the Twin Cities Metropolitan Planning Commission staff (see below). His successor in St. Paul continued to emphasize research, but did not put out so many reports. Wieland believed in thoroughness; when his staff did produce a report, it was as a book compared to Loeks' pamphlets. Loeks in turn believed that the additional detail which took so long to compile and analyze usually contributed little except to deter readers.

Those who publish facts must publish at least a few conclusions, but the conclusions may be of several kinds. Planners may content themselves with stating that problems exist. They may state piously that the facts demonstrate the need for more planning. Or they may go on to propose specific courses of action.

Even those who conclude merely that problems exist can, surprisingly enough, find themselves in trouble unless the balance of their thinking is strongly optimistic. The report on the St. Paul central business district, for example, showed that a declining trend in downtown business activity seemed still to be very much in progress. Downtown businessmen, the newspaper, and many politicians argued that even if this were so—which they preferred to doubt—there was no need to discourage potential investors by saying so. Reports put out under Loeks' auspices generally anticipated this sort of boomerang by showing that every problem was but the handmaiden of booming progress. This strategy was rather difficult to apply in St. Paul, clearly a stagnant city in economic terms. When Loeks moved to the Twin Cities Metropolitan Planning Commission, however, the strategy was perfectly appropriate. The Metropolitan Planning Commission published its first report in December 1958. By the autumn of 1960, it had put out eleven booklets. Two were annual reports, two were guides for local officials in small municipalities of the metropolitan area, and seven dealt with substantive problems of physical (as opposed to social) adjustment to change. Of the latter, two dealt with water resources, one with population, one with land use, one with the area's economic base, one with transportation, and one with the overall "challenge of metropolitan growth." [15]

[15] Loeks, an enormously intelligent and personable man, was in 1960 by all odds, at thirty-seven, the most successful of Twin Cities planners. He had wide contacts in the academic world as well as in the world of practice. His critics, all of whom were friendly, complained that he did everything except plan. This was not entirely fair, however. In his current position as head of a staff agency with area-wide jurisdiction, he had no clear governmental framework within which to push proposals for action.

By way of postscript, it should be noted that as of early 1965 Loeks' posture appeared from afar to be substantially more bold. Following his leadership, the Metropolitan Planning Commission endorsed twenty-nine specific proposals as the 1965 session of the Minnesota legislature convened. The most controversial of these was to establish a public mass-transit agency with the power to tax, float bonds, exercise eminent domain, acquire land and equipment, and develop a mass-transit system for the metropolitan area. In addition, work was far along on an area-wide thoroughfare plan. The "interim" version of this plan, published in December 1964, was simply a summary of state, county, and municipal highway plans for the area. It indicated that two of the problems to be studied in the future, however, were (1) the proper balance between highways and mass transit for the area, and (2) the possibility of using transportation development to encourage alterations of existing urban growth trends in accord with community desires.

Loeks was also at this point national president of the American Institute of Planners.

The Central Minneapolis studies also exuded optimism. They concluded that downtown Minneapolis was in remarkably fine economic health by comparison with other downtowns. The Minneapolis planners did go on with some courage, however, to pinpoint a few weak spots and to propose specific courses of action for dealing with them. The city's hotels, for example, were evaluated by name and in surprising detail, and a new luxury hotel was proposed. The planners were merely following the lead of the downtown's own consultant, however, who had made the original findings and recommendations.

Much of the St. Paul land-use plan exemplified the strategy of recommending more planning. In the summary version of the plan, which was all that they expected interested laymen to read, the planning staff listed three general recommendations: (1) the planning effort should be accelerated, (2) the data collected for the land-use plan should be kept up to date, and (3) the components of the comprehensive city plan "should be reviewed, studied, modified, adopted officially and amended as necessary each year." The plan as a whole was so abstract, as we have seen, that it attracted no comment whatsoever.

Another strategy was to devote the planning staff's efforts to commenting on the proposals of others. The traditional concentration throughout the country of planning staff time on zoning administration—where the proposals are those of private investors —may be viewed as an example of this tendency. The St. Paul planning staff had one planner assigned full-time to studying street and freeway proposals. The rest of the staff was called upon periodically to study other proposals, as, for example, the location and design of the new Ancker Hospital. This might have been perilous work. It was not, however, in this instance. Planning Director Wieland did not think he should pit his firm recommendations against those of other officials; he felt that his staff should confine itself to suggesting points for others to consider. Even in the Ancker Hospital case, he avoided any public expression of firm opinion on the concrete alternatives until consensus had formed among the public officials involved. Some of his subordinates would have liked to be more bold, and of course Housing Authority planners took a great deal of initiative in this case. They made enemies, however, by so doing.

Wieland believed that his approach was the one most likely to benefit the public interest. As mentioned previously, he reasoned that if he challenged agency heads directly, they would defeat him and thereafter close their minds to his suggestions. His approach, however, had its own pitfalls. Every operating official with whom I spoke in St. Paul agreed readily that planning has "a definite role to play" in urban development. None, however, could give concrete examples other than facility site studies of how planners had contributed to their thought. The situation was similar in Minneapolis. I found no member of either city's planning staff except Wieland who believed that planning values were given much consideration in the thinking of departmental officials. Philip Selznick makes a similar observation in *Leadership in Administration*,[16] noting that military personnel frequently on the one hand accept in principle that they should consider the interdependence of politics and war, but on the other hand try consciously to ignore political criteria in making their decisions. By considering only the factors about which they have expert knowledge, they retain their confidence in their own expertness within a defined sphere and preserve their freedom from detailed lay criticism. Selznick terms this "the retreat to technology," and calls it a persistent feature of all administration (to be contrasted with the more frequently noted phenomenon of "empire-building"). Planners themselves, we have seen, are not immune to the temptation to retreat into technology. Unfortunately for them, the technology into which they retreat is not very highly developed, nor can they agree on its proper objectives.

Some planners believe that no one pays serious attention to them unless they issue calls to action. On the other hand, they also arouse the most opposition when they do so. A planning director can retain his budget level and remain secure in his job without ever proposing specific courses of action. As we have seen, he can do detailed staff work for the operating agencies at their request; he can establish a position as the city's major factual resource; he can issue general plans that include no specific calls to action; he may try to make persuasive points when speaking off the record with other public officials. No matter what he does, however, the planner who seeks political approval finds it difficult to be completely candid. We have already discussed the pressures to think

[16] Evanston: Row, Peterson, and Co., 1957.

optimistically and to ignore controversial problems. Now let us turn to one more restraint on planner frankness.

The planners studied found it dangerous to acknowledge uncertainty. The politicians studied felt that they took risks every time they supported a plan proposal. Not even the best efforts to follow the paths of "virtual unamimity" could eliminate all political uncertainty. The easiest way for the politicians to appease critics was to say that experts had deemed their decisions necessary. It will be remembered that many voters who were personally inconvenienced by the freeway accepted the Highway Department's view that the routes could not be changed. One Minneapolis alderman told this writer that the Department had caused unnecessary trouble just by holding public hearings. "These hearings gave people the idea that the experts might be swayed," he said. "Once that was admitted, everyone was encouraged to organize and express his views. Those who lost after going to all that trouble could not bear to take 'no' for an answer; they continued to believe that they might accomplish something by continuing the fight. They expected their alderman to help them." A planner stated the reverse side of the coin: "The politicians force us to oversell ourselves, and to base our sales pitch on the wrong arguments."

The planners' felt need not to acknowledge uncertainty was no doubt an efficient cause of their search, discussed in Chapter VI, for the trappings of expertness. Such a search was bound in turn to produce a reluctance to grapple with unpredictable considerations. The considerations that were most difficult to predict had, usually, to do with social values and individual attitudes. The planners did, of course, argue that their work would increase the general level of civic satisfaction. Rodney Engelen wrote in the *Central Minneapolis Plan,* for example, that if special pedestrian facilities were developed, "persons in the Central Area will gain a more relaxed attitude which will presumably add to their efficiency and improve their general well-being and attitude toward life. Since there are so many of them, this could have a salutary effect on the whole city!" This, however, was an isolated debater's thrust, not part of a careful analysis. It was, further, typical of the tendency of planners to talk as though a few gardens, open squares, and pedestrian malls could alleviate important urban problems. Similarly, the St. Paul planning staff (under Loeks) found it "good" that the landscaped freeway would replace rows of ugly old houses, but never discussed the social consequences of decreasing the supply of low-income housing, of breaking up neighborhoods, or of increasing Negro ghettoization.

Rather than careful analyses of potential indirect effects of proposals, the planners studied generally produced expressions of faith that the costs of progress were unavoidable, that things would work out for the best if technical standards were met. This faith was most evident among the true technicians; the highway engineers expressed it without embarrassment. The city planners were more self-conscious, but ultimately when challenged they too fell back explicitly on it. I suspect that something like this faith is a prerequisite of success in a veto-group system. Comprehensiveness and decisiveness do not go together. The decisive man is one who, after a limited amount of study, can exclude all the arguments he has not considered from subsequently entering his mind. If he is an intuitive actor, he decides on the basis of his feeling or inclination at this point. If he is an expert, he solves the problem in a formal manner, limiting his systematic search for information to several predetermined variables. He knows, however, especially if he is a planner and has often argued in favor of comprehensiveness, that decision by such gross simplification can only be fortuitously wise.

Yet veto-group politics almost requires that action be defended as "necessary." Unless an action is necessary (or insignificant), someone is almost sure to oppose it. A society whose general bias was against action might let the problem lie, but ours is a society whose nonpolitical inclination is to favor action.[17] And the dy-

---

[17] There is no way to prove the existence of this bias, but many observers through the years have noted it. Winston Churchill, for instance, has written of the American insistence on the Burma campaign during World War II over British objections: "We argued that the enormous expenditure of manpower and material would not be worthwhile. But we never succeeded in deflecting the Americans from their purpose. Their national psychology is such that the bigger the Idea, the more wholeheartedly and obstinately do they throw themselves into making it a success. It is an admirable characteristic, provided the Idea is good" (*The Second World War*, Vol. V: *Closing the Ring* [Boston: Houghton-Mifflin Co., 1951], p. 561).

The American public's enormous interest in business executives and in

namic nature of our time requires that numerous important decisions be made. Perhaps the only ways to make them are (1) to abandon democracy, or at least veto-group democracy, as is done in business and most other private organizations, or (2) to cultivate a bias in favor of measurable facts. So long as balance sheets of measurable facts can be drawn, decisions to act can be rendered highly plausible, even if not absolutely noncontroversial.

Were ours a different society, Loeks might have made a reasoned case to the effect that the freeway was an enormous project to undertake when so little in fact was known about the consequences that might spring from it. Had he argued in this way in St. Paul, he would have been called at best overly cautious, more likely an obstructionist. He would have been asked to match the astounding array of facts and figures offered by the Highway Department; and when he failed, his prestige in the city, and that of his whole profession, would have plummeted.

The building of the freeway was exceptional, of course, in that the government that was making important decisions was not the one paying the bill. Ordinarily, our inclination to action in the public sphere is held in some sort of check by fears of "big government" and, more immediately, unwillingness to pay taxes. Organizations of persons who pay large taxes typically provide the most able pleaders in opposition to any proposal. Even when veto-group politics prevails, there are many proposals that can satisfy or neutralize almost all other self-conscious interests. Most of these meet their Waterloo on the budget battleground. The experienced representatives of budget-watching groups do not, needless to say, rely solely on financial arguments to win their points; they seek out and refine all the arguments that have ever been raised against similar proposals at other times and places. When they are removed from battle, as they were in the freeway case, the chances that someone else will do the job as well (especially if city plan-

---

the strong Presidents of our history (who head every list of the "great" Presidents) may be offered as another indicator of the national inclination to admire decisiveness.

To go one step further, these observations suggest that veto group decision-making, for all that it serves the security needs of most politicians and political administrators, is not a way of conducting affairs which most other Americans admire. The low esteem accorded to politicians in American society might tend to support this view.

ners cannot) are slim. In many other societies, temperamentally inclined to resist change, the mere fact that a proposal was non-routine might make its acceptance highly unlikely by businessmen no less than by public officials. In our society, perhaps the representatives of cost-consciousness have replaced the rationalizers of timidity and fatalism as the professional advocates of opposition.[18]

Is Administrative Reorganization the Answer?

In concluding this chapter on restraints and strategies, let us consider one proposed remedy for planner impotence. The remedy, a familiar one to students of American politics, is administrative reorganization. Its most important advocate has been Robert Walker. In his extremely influential book, *The Planning Function in Urban Government,* cited previously, Walker deplored the prevalent organizational arrangement by which planning agencies are responsible to independent boards or commissions. He found that citizen boards tend to shun controversy, to act as watchdogs in their relations with other public agencies, to be biased toward conservatism, and to be uninformed.[19] They have neither the capacity nor the will to impose "an overall point of view" on the work of government. Planning agencies cannot begin to perform this function, he argued, until their organizational status in city

[18] The advantages of having professional advocates on both sides of an issue have been most forcefully expressed by the legal profession, of course. William Beaney has set forth the argument clearly in his book, *The Right to Counsel in American Courts* (Ann Arbor: University of Michigan Press, 1955). Its reasoning runs as follows: Few laymen can argue on equal terms with professionals in the latters' fields. Lawyers are professionals in the law, and courtroom argument is in terms of the law and "legal facts." The layman's sense of which arguments will most affect the decisions of juries and judges is unrefined. His capacity to do legal research and to prepare legally reasoned briefs is extremely limited. The judge and the jury cannot finally make a wise decision unless the relevant facts are brought out with equal skill and vigor on both sides. The ideal of equality is unattainable, but the right to counsel is an attempt to assure some approximation of it.

Political argument in the modern world requires hardly less specialized competence than legal argument. The effective advocate is likely to be one who understands the labyrinths of government, the methods of large organizations and mass communications, and the ways in which politicians try to estimate the representativeness of those who appear before them.

[19] Pp. 151–158.

government is that of close adviser and assistant to the mayor. They cannot effectively be so attached while remaining subject to a citizen board, because executives give their confidence only to subordinates who have no other masters. "Unless it has such confidence, the planning agency cannot hope to be in a position to guide [the executive's] work; . . . it will be financially starved, and its counsel will go unheeded." [20]

Both the Minneapolis and St. Paul planning staffs were formally subject to the direction of independent commissions. There was no apparent reason, however, to attribute the deficiencies of planning in either city to this administrative arrangement. On the contrary, there were reasons for considering it a source of strength. The two commissions gave their staffs full freedom to work harmoniously with other public officials. Neither city's mayor had the authority, and few incumbents had ever had the desire, to coordinate all governmental activity so that it expressed an overall point of view. In St. Paul, the six city departments were headed by the six members of the City Council. They brooked no interference in their spheres from the mayor. Minneapolis city councilmen did not individually have executive responsibilities, but every city department except the Police Department reported directly to the Council rather than to the mayor. The St. Paul city budget was prepared for submission to the City Council by an elected comptroller rather than by the mayor. The Minneapolis city budget was prepared by an official whose position, though mistitled City Research Engineer, was that of chief of staff to the City Council.

Walker of course disapproved of weak mayor systems, but he did

[20] *Ibid.*, p. 177. Walker made clear that his argument against independence applied to agencies concerned with substantive policy, as opposed to "housekeeping," at all levels of government. Thus, he quoted with approval the contention of the President's Committee on Adminstrative Management that " 'the President must be given direct control over and be charged with immediate responsibility for the great managerial functions of the Government which affect all of the administrative departments . . . These functions are personnel management, fiscal and organizational management, and planning management.' " The President's Committee went on to say that the staff agencies dealing with these three functions from an overall point of view should be located in the Executive Office of the President. (President's Committee on Administrative Management, *Report with Special Studies* [Washington: Government Printing Office, 1937], p. 6. Cited in Walker, *op. cit.,* p. 168.)

not qualify his recommendation to apply only to cities with strong mayors. He emphasized that in every city the mayor "more than any other official has the responsibility for taking the overall view of urban government, for coordinatng its various activities, and for planning an integrated future program. Consequently, the planning agency will be most likely to perform its function satisfactorily if it is made immediately responsible to the executive." [21]

We may question, however, whether Walker's prescription would apply to strong mayor cities any better than to Minneapolis and St. Paul. Edward Banfield's portrayal of the governing processes of Chicago, in *Political Influence,* strikingly resembles my description of the governing processes of the Twin Cities. Chicago's mayor is, in fact if not in form, the "strongest" mayor in America today, yet according to Banfield he rarely acts before consensus forms and he manifests no faith in comprehensive planning. Sayre and Kaufman paint an essentially similar picture of the New York political process and the impotence of planning in it.[22]

Philadelphia, on the other hand, is an example of a strong mayor city whose chief executives, at least in the decade after 1952, forcefully championed planning. David Wallace, former Director of Planning of the Philadelphia Redevelopment Authority, recently tried to set forth the bases of their success, and the prospects for Philadelphia planning in the future.[23] He found that the personalities of the "reform" mayors who held office after 1952 were crucial, along with vigorous citizen support. He doubted that any administrative reorganization could assure continued success;

[21] Walker, *op. cit.,* p. 334.

[22] Wallace Sayre and Herbert Kaufman, *Governing New York City* (New York: Russell Sage Foundation, 1960). See especially pp. 474–476 (on the approach of party leaders), 672–676 (on the approach of mayors to their legislative role), and 372–380 (on the dismal history of the City Planning Commission). Sayre and Kaufman emphasized the inadequacies of mayoral power in New York, but even when they wrote (before the 1961 charter revision) New York was generally considered a strong mayor city. The explanation of this discrepancy is that even "strong" American mayors have extremely limited power and security. See also Norman Krumholz, "The Politics of Urban Renewal in Buffalo," unpublished Master's thesis, Cornell University, June 1965.

[23] "Renaissancemanship," *American Institute of Planners Journal,* XXVI, No. 3 (August 1960), 157–176.

and he thought that the Democratic machine, which polled almost 70 per cent for Kennedy in 1960, was feeling safe enough to forego blue ribbon mayoral candidates in the future. But he did not despair. He believed that the gains of planning after 1952 could be secured by

the continued vigor and influence of Philadelphia's "professional citizens." They now act in the democratic process as an additional set of checks and balances outside government, and against manipulation by politicians. Walter Phillips [prominent civic leader and former member of the Philadelphia City Planning Commission] says: "If the politicians' present reaction is anti-planning and anti-renewal, which I think is the case, it is because the citizen effort has been successful through its prestige and influence . . . making it difficult for politicians to have their own way. This I consider a very happy balance as the politician's way at the municipal level seems usually to be slanted toward segmental approaches and special interests.[24]

This is impressionistic evidence, to be sure, but it suggests that Philadelphia may not be as atypical as some planners are still prone to assume. It should be emphasized, moreover, that Philadelphia has a formally independent planning commission. The "professional citizens" to whom Wallace refers started out initially to achieve *both* planning and political reform. They obtained control of the Planning Commission in 1947, and used it as a springboard from which to popularize their ideas. Five years later they captured the mayoralty, at which time the Planning Commission became for the first time a major force in the city government.

The effects that would have flowed from attaching the Minneapolis and St. Paul planning staffs more closely to their respective mayors may be speculated upon. We have discussed at some length the unwillingness of elected officials in both cities to exercise political leadership. It seems likely that a planning agency thought of as part of the mayoral staff would have been denied the opportunity to propose any controversial ideas publicly. It seems probable that it would have been prohibited from taking any initiative in testing public support for its proposals. When members of a mayor's staff release trial balloons, the mayor is assumed to be responsible. Neither the mayor nor any member of his staff

[24] *Ibid.*, p. 174.

demonstrated initiative on any matter of policy during the year in which this study was conducted.

If an occasional mayor had wanted to champion planning ideas, or even to assume leadership of the whole planning process, he would almost surely have been able to do so. The professional planners would have been delighted to have found a political guide, and the planning commissions would have been extremely unlikely to resist. (Indeed, they rarely resisted the leadership of their planning directors alone.) No recent mayor had indicated that he thought there was anything to stop him, nor was this because none had manifested any interest in planning. The 1959 Minneapolis mayoral campaign had been fought in large part on the "issue" of which candidate favored planning more sincerely. (The discussion was purely in the abstract.) Joseph Dillon, mayor of St. Paul from 1954 to 1960, had on several occasions persuaded the City Council to increase the planning budget above the level recommended by the city comptroller. Neither he nor any other Twin Cities mayor in memory, however, appeared to have suggested even privately that reorganization of the planning function would enhance the influence of planning thought.

One may be forgiven for wondering, moreover, how the typical mayor would use a planning agency that was part of his personal staff. Some might be tempted to use it for purposes far removed from planning, such as the study and political clearance of detailed and mainly routine legislative proposals. A mayor with authority to prepare the city budget might make it his budget staff. Another might want it to help him discharge his supervisory responsibilities. Still another might want it to help him establish a dynamic but inoffensive image. One distrustful of city planners might try to occupy the planning staff with busywork. The possibilities are endless, but the mayor who took time from the immediate problems of running his city and winning re-election to worry seriously about long-range planning would probably be rare indeed.

In any event, the cultivation of support for plans is too long and arduous for most mayors. Their terms of office are very short in the lives of big plans. Most successful plans in American urban history have been championed by one or a few prominent people, willing to devote all their energies to the cause for many years. Some observers, in fact, have seen in this need for continuity of leader-

ship a reason for planners to oppose democracy.[25] I have stated
my reasons for considering city planners not to be any threat to
American democracy, but the need for continuous leadership does
pose them a problem. Even the modest decision to build a new
Ancker Hospital evolved over a decade, and the leadership was
taken by men who had been familiar with Ancker's problems for a
generation. Clearly, the civic leadership of most American cities is
far more stable than the mayoral leadership. The exceptions are,
for the most part, cities governed by bureaucratized political machines, which have seldom been noted for their interest in city
planning.

Walker urged in *The Planning Function* that at the very least
the citizen boards should be advisers to the planning agencies
rather than their supervisors. Most Twin Cities planners and politicians disagreed, contending that the value of a planning board
depended on the stature of its members. Planning board members,
they thought, were the most likely people to recruit interest group
support for planning work. Yet only when the board members
were active leaders of community opinion could they do so effectively, or in any other important way facilitate communication
between the planners and the public. The key question was
whether prominent civic leaders would accept membership on a
purely advisory commission. It seemed doubtful that they would.
It was already difficult to invest them. None of the members of
the St. Paul Planning Board were truly active in their city's leadership. The members of the Minneapolis Planning Commission who
were prominent had joined only in the most recent few years, at
the urging of the Downtown Council. Of these, the most prominent member was retired from business.

There were a great many citizen boards and committees in each
city. All had difficulty attracting men who bore heavy responsibilities in their private work. Most of those who did accept appointments preferred posts in which they could make decisions rather
than simply give advice. They came from organizations in which
decision-makers had higher status than their staff advisers, and
they knew perfectly well that they had more status than local offi-

25 See Chester Barnard, *Organization and Management* (Cambridge: Harvard University Press, 1948), Chap. 7, and F. A. Hayek, *The Road to Serfdom*
(Chicago: University of Chicago Press, 1944), Chaps. 5, 11.

cials. Moreover, they probably found it more interesting and obtained more of a sense of accomplishment from making decisions than from merely offering opinions. Planners noted that even now the commissions tended to achieve moderately high levels of interest only when questions were posed to them for decision.

The fact remained, in any case, that neither Twin City planning staff had within memory been prevented by its commission from making a proposal about which the planning director felt strongly. When the commissioners objected strongly to a proposal after hearing the planners' defense of it, the planners were inclined to take the storm as harbinger of much worse to come if they asked for and received permission to publicize their idea anyway.

Did the commission form tend to restrict planner contacts within City Hall? There was no evidence of it. All of the planners studied were alive to the benefits of maintaining friendly contacts with operating departments. In St. Paul Planning Director Wieland's case, this appeared to be his primary political objective, and he was quite successful at it. Lawrence Irvin in Minneapolis made every effort to work with the city's public agencies, and if he refused to let them delimit his area of concern in what he considered excessively narrow fashion, that was his carefully considered decision. He believed that he could initiate ideas with any hope of success only by basing his support outside City Hall. Would he have been less willing to risk antagonizing the City Hall professionals if he had had no commission to back him up? Probably, yes. If his formal lines of responsibility had been confined to the main governmental structure, his discretion to seek support outside City Hall would have been far more limited than it was. The relevant question is whether it was desirable for the planning director to have such discretion.

My inclination is to answer in the affirmative. The case depends on an assumption about what is easy to accomplish in urban politics, and what is difficult. I have no doubt that any city can find a timid planning director if it wants, one who will be awed by the barrier that veto-group politics poses to the initiation of new ideas. The difficult problem is to give a bold planning director room in which to maneuver, to encourage him to take the risks of initiating. No administrative setup can make the role of the initiator easy; all that can be done is to make the risks more bearable for bold men.[26]

[26] I did not read T. J. Kent's book, *The Urban General Plan,* until after this chapter was in final form. Kent discusses very thoughtfully, and in substantial detail, the problem of where to locate the planning agency (pp. 12–18, 53–59). His own position is that the planning staff should be directly attached to the city council rather than to either the mayor or an independent planning commission. I found so little evidence in the Twin Cities to support Kent's view of city councils, discussed previously (Introduction, n.4), that I have not considered it worthwhile to rewrite the chapter in order to incorporate a detailed consideration of his views. My own tentative judgment is that the city councils of the Twin Cities were more nearly typical than the Berkeley, California, City Council, to which Kent constantly refers and of which he is a member.

VIII

Opportunism *vs.* Professionalism in Planning

Introduction

On the one hand, we have seen, planners believe that they should present crucial alternatives for public choice; on the other, they feel that they court political failure by acknowledging uncertainty. They preach that all problems and solutions are interrelated, and emphasize the virtues of honest comprehensiveness; yet they think that political success is possible only if they think optimistically and ignore areas of intense controversy. Thus, aside from the logical and technical barriers to comprehensiveness, there are serious political barriers, consisting of contradictions between the most persuasive abstract justifications of general planning and perceptions by planners of political reality. There are surely no easy ways to overcome these contradictions. Perhaps the very difficulty of the task discourages planners from addressing themselves to it. Only rarely does one find discussions of it in the planning literature. Practicing planners, if those we have studied are typical, easily suppress their awareness that contradictions exist. They cite the virtues of comprehensiveness and in the same breath boast of their political realism.

Protestations of political realism have become *de rigueur* in the planning profession during the past two decades; but few planners associate their brand of realism with opportunism, the abandonment of principle. The planners whose work we have examined were all men of integrity. Knowing that they had little hope of achieving wealth, fame, or power, they derived most of their satisfaction apparently from a pride in their status as professionals and a faith that their work benefited mankind. This pride and faith no doubt helped sustain their belief that they *deserved* more prestige and influence. When asked how they differed from run-of-the-mill civil servants, they referred unhesitatingly to their professional status. When asked to justify political compromises, they spoke always of their need to protect planning as an activity rather than of their own careers. Yet they recognized that their profession offered few clear directional signals for their integrity. This recognition, coupled with their respect for political success, made it particularly difficult for them to resist the lures of opportunism. It also made them peculiarly sensitive to charges that planning was not a profession.

Is Planning a Profession?

Sensitivity on this subject appears to be endemic among planners, despite the fact that planning has all the outward trappings of a profession. The typical planner has his first degree in architecture, landscape architecture, or engineering, all of which are generally considered professional activities.[1] The study of planning itself is usually confined to graduate school. Planners maintain professional associations and journals. And no one would deny that the planning of cities is a task worthy of professional men. Sophisticated planners, however, believe that professionalism consists of more than this.

John T. Howard, when president of the American Institute of

---

[1] Lucien C. Faust, "An Analysis of Selected Characteristics of the American Institute of Planners" (unpublished Master's thesis, University of North Carolina, 1959), p. 151. Faust received 1,415 replies to his questionnaire. He classified the replies into 87 categories, which I have reduced for purposes of simplicity to nine:

24% architecture	6% economics
20% landscape architecture	5% geography
13% engineering (mainly civil)	5% political science
7% city planning	14% others
7% sociology	

I am indebted to Grace Milgram for calling Faust's thesis to my attention. She notes that Faust did not compare age groups in his sample, and that a good many planners are of the impression that the proportion of nonarchitects in the profession is rising.

Planners several years back, offered four reasons why he considered planning work professional: (1) It is tinged with the public interest; i.e., the community has a stake in the way the job is done, regardless of who pays for it. (2) It is predominantly intellectual, and varied in character. (3) It involves the consistent exercise of discretion and judgment. (4) Its practitioners are expected to submerge their own interest to that of their clients, subject only to the primacy of the public interest.[2]

It is noteworthy that in this list Howard stresses the ethical along with the intellectual element of professionalism. He assumes that the professional is able to judge the public interest in his work independently, and has an inescapable responsibility to do so; he is never justified in delegating this responsibility to those who pay him. Howard says nothing, however, about the ways in which professionals are equipped to exercise this responsibility well. As they stand, his points (1) and (4) could surely apply to the work of all public servants as well as to the work of those who are commonly considered professional men.

The late Henry S. Churchill, another planner of national prominence, has expressed the opinion that planning is not a profession. He argued that the essence of professional work is the making of decisions and the acceptance of personal responsibility for them; so long as planners merely perform staff services for decision-makers, they have no right to call themselves professional. Seward Hiltner, a theology professor with a special interest in the ingredients of professionalism, has supported Churchill's contention that planning is not a profession while disputing his definition of professionalism. Hiltner maintains that few professionals can take responsibility for the execution of their recommendations. The clients of doctors, lawyers, and clergymen all frequently ignore professional advice, or look until they find professional men who tell them what they want to hear. In Hiltner's view, the identifying characteristic of a profession is its possession of criteria for making the decisions for which its practitioners *can* take responsibility. The true professional decides according to basic principles, not rules of thumb. Because his criteria are rooted in a coherent theory, he is able to perceive the inadequacy of his techniques. Be-

[2] "Planning Is a Profession," *American Institute of Planners Journal*, XX, No. 2 (Spring 1954), 58–59.

cause he is rigorous about what he knows, he is able to appreciate what he does not know, and adapt creatively to the unique in situations.

Hiltner contends that planners will have difficulty articulating their basic principles until they can grade fields of knowledge by their relevance to planning work. The grading process cannot begin until the core functions planners wish to serve are defined. He finds, however, that in the history of planning the trend has been in just the wrong direction; the core has become increasingly more vague:

The progress of planning has caused [planners] to draw upon more and more areas of knowledge. At the same time, this expansion has seemed to make the center of the enterprise more amorphous. If a planner, in trying to retain a clear focus at the center, should stand against drawing from the various relevant fields of knowledge, he would be an obscurantist. But if he simply seizes eagerly on everything with any degree of relevance, what is he standing on while looking? [3]

Hiltner's own articulations of "the center of the enterprise" hardly provide clarification. For example, he suggests that planners begin with a recognition that their special competence is in recommending rather than executing, or, alternatively, is in "mobilizing and coordinating the relevant technical means toward a particular functional aim."

A similar criticism and solution are offered by Paul Davidoff and Thomas A. Reiner, who write that:

Contemporary urban planning education has been excessively directed to substantive areas and has failed to focus on any unique skills or responsibilities of the planner. Such planning education has emphasized understanding of subject matter: cities, regions, facilities, housing, land use, zoning, transportation, and others. In fact, the student has had thrust upon him a growing list of courses and is perennially in danger of becoming a Jack of all trades (almost all, but never enough), and a master of none. In a few years on the job he sinks into an uninspired and intellectually blunted administrator-generalist or a public relations semi-expert. Planning education, until now, has paid little or no attention to methods for determining ends and relating ends to means. And while some tools of effectuation are studied, their relation

---

[3] "Planning as a Profession," *American Institute of Planners Journal,* XXIII, No. 4 (Autumn 1957), 162–167. The quotation is at p. 165.

to a planning process is largely neglected . . . Planners frequently assert their status of a profession and so implicitly claim a distinct body of knowledge and procedures. Is this claim premature? [4]

Davidoff and Reiner differ from Hiltner in emphasizing planning skills and methods rather than planning principles and functions. In their article, they say a great deal that is extremely pertinent about the need for a body of procedures designed to enable planners to ascertain and serve their clients' values. They say little, however, about how planners should decide what to recommend when their clients cannot or will not lead. They say nothing about how planners should reconcile the demands of candor, idealism, and intellectual boldness with those of strategy when the two conflict. In fact, they do not suggest that planners need strategies. This is not to criticize Davidoff and Reiner; it is just to note that their approach to professionalism in planning is essentially technical, which is to say that it tends to ignore the role of the planner as an independent political actor. We have no reason to be surprised, therefore, that Davidoff and Reiner preface their "Choice Theory of Planning" by stating that it applies as well to business as to public planning. Politics is not a feature of their model.

The Need for a Normative Theory

Where, then, do we stand? Hiltner's answer seems too vague, Reiner and Davidoff's too apolitical, for either to serve by itself as a workable guide for public planners. But it seems to me that in the way they pose the problem these writers do touch the heart of planner disquiet, and the heart of the doubt by others that planners are worthy of great responsibility. The decisive question is not whether planners have or want power, but whether they are well equipped to advise those who have it. Seen in this light, the planner's search for assurance that he is a professional surely represents more than just a striving for status and prestige. It also represents a deep longing for a body of professional theory to show him his competence, his purpose, and his duty, and to give professional content to his integrity. That he should exhibit this longing is not surprising. His work requires him to make potentially mo-

---

[4] "A Choice Theory of Planning," *American Institute of Planners Journal,* XXVIII, No. 2 (May 1962), 103–115. The quotation is at p. 114.

mentous recommendations. He would be insensitive indeed if he felt no desire to justify them in terms of a compelling theory.

It seems clear to me, as to Hiltner, that the theory must be concerned in the first instance with purpose and function rather than with unique knowledge and procedures. The latter are vital to a profession, but they cannot provide criteria of significance to guide the search for new knowledge and they cannot provide principles of choice.[5] The generally acknowledged professions, moreover, are distinguished more clearly by their purposes than their skills. The skills required to practice most professions change drastically, and many of the skills employed by practitioners at any one time are bound to seem unrelated, except by purpose. The professions which consider their approach scientific make a basic tenet of evaluating techniques, however diverse they appear, by their utility; and utility must be assessed by purpose. Thus, Robert Merton has concluded that "medicine is at heart a polygamist becoming wedded to as many of the sciences as prove their worth," [6] and that "the great tradition in medicine is in large part a tradition of commitment to the search for improved, and therefore changing, ways of coping with the problems of the sick. . . . Frequent ceremonies serve to keep alive a sense of the core values of medicine. . . . This helps perpetuate the long term values of medicine and provides the basis for continuing to put these into practice through newly appropriate means." [7]

It seems clear, further, that the acknowledged professions are, as a group, distinguished not so much by refinement of skills as by the uses to which they are put. The professions differ markedly in sophistication of technique and even in capacity to measure achievement. By both criteria, some professions are inferior to some skill groups not generally considered professional. What the professions do appear to share most fundamentally is that their skills serve purposes which society deems worthy of its most serious and high-minded men. This is a normative judgment, which may

[5] Reiner and Davidoff, it should be noted, make the same point indirectly in their unsparing criticism of those who hope to ascertain planning goals from factual surveys and analyses.

[6] "Some Preliminaries to a Sociology of Medical Education," in Robert K. Merton, George D. Reader, and Patricia L. Kendall, eds., *The Student Physician* (Cambridge: Harvard University Press, 1957), p. 32.

[7] *Ibid.*, pp. 6, 7.

be quite at odds with the occupational choices of many of the same society's most able men. There is a moral and aristocratic quality about the conception, and perhaps a cultural lag as well, emphasizing traditional ideas of worthiness and honor rather than more obvious indicators of success. Traditional British values are reflected, for example, in the *Oxford English Dictionary*'s definition of "profession," which lists the four standard professions as being divinity, law, medicine, and the military, and notes that the professions are "considered to be socially superior" to "mercantile occupations." [8]

Changes in the prestige rankings of professions doubtless follow changes in the rankings of values. It is commonplace to note that the prestige of the clergy declines with the secularization of society. The prestige of the law in America corresponds to the priority of the goal of restraining the state. That of the military rises and falls dramatically with the occurrence and passing of wars.

If a profession requires prestige and public support, the first object of its theory must be to define its purposes and explain why society should deem them valuable enough to occupy some of its most serious men. Such a theory of purpose and function is also, necessarily, a theory of role definition. Its most practical expression, therefore, is a complex of principles of professional conduct to guide the members in playing their roles properly. These principles need not be simple or even wholly consistent, but they must fit into a stable pattern which corresponds to the professional self-image and which, therefore, provides as a whole more meaningful guidance in the resolution of value conflicts than any of its parts— i.e., individual principles—could. In the early phase, indeed, it may be easier to evolve the image in an almost literary way without trying to reduce it to a set of principles of behavior. The balance between principles can never be reduced to precise for-

[8] *The Oxford English Dictionary* (Oxford: Clarendon Press, 1933). The definition of "profession" compares profession to trade (Vol. VIII; the definition of "trade" as including mercantile occupations is in Vol. IX). The most authoritative American dictionary reflects this nation's lack of an aristocratic tradition by omitting, in its definition of "profession," all mention of standard professions and social superiority, in favor of considerations of knowledge, skill, long preparation, and systematically maintained high ethical standards (*Webster's Third New International Dictionary of the English Language Unabridged* [Springfield, Mass.: G. C. Merriam Co., 1961]).

mulae in any event. Merton's discussion of medicine is again suggestive. He writes that

the system of values and norms can be thought of as being patterned. . . . For each norm there tends to be at least one coordinate norm, which is, if not inconsistent with the other, at least sufficiently different as to make it difficult for the student and physician to live up to them both. . . . Indeed, the process of learning to be a physician can be conceived as largely the learning of blending seeming or actual incompatibles into consistent and stable patterns of professional behavior.[9]

Inadequacy of Existing Normative Theory

Now, it must be stated that the planners interviewed for this study did share certain beliefs about the meaning of professional planning conduct. Without exception, they recognized a profound obligation to be true to themselves rather than simply to their immediate superiors. They believed that the phrase "public interest" denoted much more than a useful myth, and that no ethical planner would knowingly subordinate it in his plans to anyone's private interest. But these shared beliefs rested on fundamental ambiguity. The values to which planners should be true, the content of the public interest, and the relationship of public and private interests in a democracy were not clarified by them. Some of the planners interviewed perceived the problems of professional identity presented by this situation, but most seemed able to ignore them. In my opinion they were able to do so for three reasons: first, the general indifference of voters and politicians to city planning provided the planners with a common set of frustrations on which to focus attention; second, so long as plans were not executed, the value conflicts concealed within them could comfortably be ignored; and third, the planners were adept at substituting plausible principles of physical design and fashionable types of project for the absent principles of choice among values.

If the doctrine that ineffective planning cannot be good planning continues to permeate planning thought, it seems likely that the plans produced will become more interesting to politicians and civic leaders, and consequently more likely to be put into

---

[9] *Op. cit.*, p. 72. On pp. 73–75, Merton lists twenty-one values of the medical profession with their often incompatible qualifiers.

effect. This development should make it more and more difficult for planners to avoid the hard questions of their goals and the nature of their competence. At the same time, the doctrine tempts them more and more to assume that, for themselves at least, the expedient and the ethical cannot conflict. As we have noted, they are restrained by their image of themselves as professionals from accepting this assumption explicitly. But there is no evidence that most planners understand the need to disavow it explicitly. Several planners wondered aloud during the course of this study why politicians paid so little attention to them at a time when corporate executives were coming to demand more careful planning of important endeavors. To an outside observer, the reason was clear, and it seemed revealing that it was not obvious to the planners. Corporate planners are not expected to divide their loyalties. They act simply as employees, accepting no moral responsibility for the effects of their recommendations on the social system. They can confine their concern with social effects to the management of public relations. When John Howard wrote of city planning, however (see above, pages 393, 394), he had no doubt about the planner's responsibility to a public beyond his political clientele. Similarly, Talcott Parsons has written that "in the immediately obvious sense the essence of professionalism consists . . . of limitations on the aggressive pursuit of self-interest." [10]

Planning in the service of discrete political clienteles can of course be justified quite plausibly in theory. It is possible to argue that such planning is the only kind which can be effective in the American governmental system, and that concentration on this kind of planning would at least aid government to pursue goals on which there is consensus with greater efficiency than at present. Further, specialized planning of this sort would affect controversial values only haphazardly, much as corporate planning does today. The most serious arguments against comprehensive planning might thus be rendered inoperative without abandoning planning altogether.

We have argued that in effect many city planners are acting in accord with this theory today, though they have not permitted

[10] "The Motivation of Economic Activities," *Essays in Sociological Theory Pure and Applied* (Glencoe: The Free Press, 1949), pp. 200–217. The quotation is at p. 200.

themselves to say so. Why have they not? We have indicated several reasons. For one thing, the theory is based on an assumption that planning cannot alleviate the ills of society, other than simple inefficiency. Planners find it difficult (emotionally perhaps more than intellectually) to accept this. In addition, city planners have traditionally defended planning largely on the ground that specialists tend to ignore the wider ramifications of their work. Planners are naturally unwilling to consider the possibility that the specialist approach may have served society better than their own all along. Finally, there is the fact that most city planners are liberal idealists, who believe in their hearts that government should not leave complex social issues to the whims of laissez-faire. As men of political awareness they may eschew controversy in each plan they bring out; but they are unwilling to raise this dictate of expediency to the status of basic dogma. To do so would involve more than a repudiation of their profession's traditional claims; it would require a rethinking of their entire conception of the proper role of government in a free society.

The Profession as Moral Community

Planners, then, have generally rejected theories implying that they should serve noncontroversial goals exclusively, but they have made little progress in defining their approach to controversy. They have continued to assert at the same time that political give-and-take is a poor path to the public interest and that public planners must act as political strategists. How is realistic planning to be distinguished from simple administrative politics? Howard's distinction was clear: the planner's urge to opportunism is restrained by his professionalism. But if established principles of professionalism are lacking, as I have contended, then each individual planner must determine his own professional ethic. An ethic which each man determines for himself, however, can hardly be called "professional."

The distinguished personal ethic is probably rare indeed. Parsons contends, for example, that although "professional" men generally curb their self-interest to a much greater extent than businessmen, the difference is probably not one

of typical motive at all, but [rather] one of the different situations in which much the same commonly human motives operate. . . .

The essential goals in the two cases would appear to be substantially the same, objective achievement and recognition: the difference lies in the different paths to the similar goals, which are in turn determined by the differences in the respective occupational situations.

Parsons goes on to argue that most men give highest priority to the goal of recognition. When they can achieve it by acting unethically, they will be sorely tempted to do so. Money is one such valuable symbol in our society, and men generally seek it "so long as the risk of loss of occupational status is not too great. . . . 'Commercialism' in medicine and 'dishonest' or 'shady' practices in business have much in common as reactions to these strains." [11]

The implication is that lone individuals find it difficult to stand firm for their principles under pressure, or even to know for which principles they should stand firm. Planners are effectively restrained by professional mores from seeking wealth; whether they are effectively restrained from seeking other symbols of success at the expense of meaningful achievement is another matter.

A professional code, based as it must be on a theory of the profession's essential purposes, can take on a sacred quality. Members of the profession can develop a sense that conformance with the code, even when it seems meaningless in individual cases, is of great significance. The ethic can be dramatized to inspire public confidence in the profession. Consider the medical ethic which tells doctors to devote scarce resources to prolonging the lives of incurably diseased people. On a case by case basis, the ethic seems wasteful, but it dramatizes as perhaps nothing else could the medical profession's unswerving devotion to life. Similarly, the legal ethic, which enjoins lawyers to do the most possible for their clients even though they are guilty, and to accept as clients people against whom popular feeling runs high, subjects individual lawyers to great inconvenience in the service of highly unworthy specimens of humanity. But it probably strengthens confidence among leaders of opinion in the overall justness of the legal system. Many individuals succumb of course despite the existence of codes. There are doctors who are careless with life, and lawyers who betray their clients. In the usual case, however, they conceal their behavior and leave public expression to defenders of the code.

[11] "The Professions and Social Structure," *ibid.,* pp. 185–199. The three quotations are from pp. 187, 195, and again 195.

Representatives of the profession elaborate with great care the theories on which the code rests. Critics outside the profession can discuss the ethic's relationship to the public interest. It is a corporate, explicit, ever-growing thing. On the one hand, it restrains the practitioner and gives focus to his integrity. On the other, it enhances his public standing and may provide the means of liberation from certain restrictions which society applies to ordinary mortals. If the members of the profession think that they require special privileges to carry on their work well, they may cite the ethic as insurance to the public against abuse. The clergyman and lawyer claim the right to preserve confidences at their own discretion; the doctor claims the right to violate central sexual taboos of our society; the generalist planner claims to require unusual freedom (for a public servant) from the definition of his role in the political framework. He wishes to avoid defining too narrowly the values in his protection, and the methods he may legitimately use. He says that his work is too creative to be done according to rules, or in the service of any single pressure group or constituency. Public representatives, however, can hardly be expected to concede this freedom without clearly understanding its potential service to society, and without knowing the principles that will guide planners in the absence of political direction.

One would expect the architects of a professional code for city planners to suggest ways of answering at least such general questions as the following: (1) What are the most important ends for planners to serve? (2) How much and what kinds of information should be required to support a professional recommendation for action? (3) Under what conditions and to what extent should planners dilute the ethic of intellectual honesty to engage in political maneuvers? What sorts of compromise are justifiable? Under what conditions? (4) What characteristics of good planning are so essential that individual planners have no right under any circumstances to compromise them?

As the members of a profession become more tolerant of concessions made in the name of expediency, they have all the more need, if their image is not to become entirely blurred, to define principles whose compromise they will not tolerate. Where these principles conflict with one another, reasoned guides to the exercise of prudence can be developed. It is not impossible for prudential decisions, if they occur within a framework of professional purpose, to reinforce a consistent image. But resistance to the clarification of professional purpose is bound to be great. Though all practitioners may ultimately benefit from a clear and shining professional image, each is tempted to undermine it in his own response to many difficult situations. Over the short term, the advantages of unlimited flexibility are substantial and obvious. Limitations on freedom of action are unpleasant, and are particularly difficult for an occupational group to impose upon itself in the absence of external demand. Only the frustration with which planners view their current lack of influence gives any reason to expect that a call for sacrifice of part of an existing asset in the interest of long-run professional standing may receive attention.

Professional conduct cannot be enforced by sanctions alone. They are too blunt for use except against extreme deviations, and all but these are difficult to define when purpose is obscure. Thus, all mature professions are moral communities, and all truly professional education is in large part moral education, designed to mold the student's habits of mind, even his reflexes, to the moral needs of the corporation he wishes to enter.[12] It is this moral core which deters practitioners from developing strategies before objectives. Its delineation requires that the profession decide what its purposes are and what it is competent to do. This painful process of self-limitation must be guided and justified by the profession's philosophers, who are from another point of view its master strategists. Few practitioners can be philosophers, but all can be expected to live by professional standards.

Planners have long understood the use of physical standards to secure the consistent execution of land-use policy; they have exhibited less interest in the use of ethical standards to secure consistency in the execution of professional policy. Surely most planners are ethical men. They condemn acts, such as bribe-taking, that are immoral by the standards of all public servants. They lack distinctive professional standards and principles, however, by which to deal consistently with the more subtle temptations of public life.

12 Cf. Merton, *op. cit.*, pp. 72, 73. For a strikingly similar discussion of professional military education, see John W. Masland and Laurence I. Radway, *Soldiers and Scholars* (Princeton: Princeton University Press, 1957), pp. 197–205.

Consequently, the integrity of even the most ethical planners tends to have a blurred focus. They can hardly judge themselves except by their ability to present material in handsome format, their knowledge of planning fashions, and their immediate political success.

PART THREE

IX

Alternative Perspectives

Introduction

Planning is, in the final analysis, simply the effort to infuse activity with consistency and conscious purpose. All men and organizations plan in this sense, of course, but some plan more systematically and effectively than others. The most distinguishing feature of the bureaucratization of society in recent generations has perhaps been the extent to which planning at the level of governments and large private organizations has gradually become more and more systematized. The proliferation of specialized research and planning staffs in large bureaucracies of all kinds is symptomatic of this trend.[1] Planning becomes "political" only when the efforts of some men and organizations to plan come into conflict with those of others. Needless to say, the larger the organizational system that one chooses to examine, the more likely is it that the plans of subsystems within it will frequently conflict.

The extent to which this potential is realized, and is perceived as a political "problem," will depend on a variety of factors. The following, which are of general relevance but which have admittedly been selected with American metropolitan problems in mind, are illustrative. If the various subsystem actors take for

---

[1] On the significance of growing specialization, see Victor A. Thompson, *Modern Organization* (New York: Alfred A. Knopf, 1961). On the difficulty of planning for highly complex systems, see Robert A. Dahl and Charles E. Lindblom, *Politics, Economics, and Welfare* (New York: Harper & Brothers, 1953), Chaps. 14, 15. See also James G. March and Herbert A. Simon, *Organizations* (New York: John Wiley and Sons, 1958), Chap. 7.

granted the limitations on their capacities to bring about desired results, they and their "publics" may not expect action to deal with the misfortunes produced by lack of coordination. If they have not set up specialized staff agencies to evaluate the long-range effects of their actions and to scan the environment for alternative courses of action, many of these misfortunes are likely in any event to escape their attention. (Needless to say, moreover, fatalistic actors are less likely to establish such agencies than are those who believe in their capacity to change the world. Even where such agencies exist, it will be likely that most of those who consume their reports, and who therefore best understand the biases and blindspots of the existing system, will be those who are most favored by it.) If the cultures of the various subsystems are highly conducive to mutual identification, a great deal of the conflict that is perceived may be dealt with amicably by bargaining or by reference to common values. When important conflicts cannot be resolved by these means, coordination by a superior power is bound to be considered. The loss of autonomy, influence, and prestige that it entails, however, is likely to make this solution appear worse than the "problem" to many of the subsystem actors —unless the misfortunes produced by lack of coordination are so severe as to leave them little alternative. Even when the latter condition prevails, the perceived need for coordination is bound to be greater in some subject matter areas than in others. Those subsystem actors who fundamentally dislike having to give up any power to higher level authorities are likely to try to satisfy the most powerful demands for increased coordination by confining the bodies set up to impose it to the narrowest possible jurisdictions. If the legal procedures for redistributing functions permit these actors to veto more far-reaching proposals, and if it is unfeasible to alter these procedures, then the views of these actors will prevail. Even where legal vetoes cannot be cast, political requirements of consensus may have the same effect. After a number of crises have been brought on by lack of coordination, of course, the great majority of actors in a governmental system *may* decide to generalize from their experience, to move in the direction of comprehensive planning and coordination, and perhaps even to create new general-purpose governments with wider boundaries than those of any existing governments. If they feel strongly enough, they may disregard normal political requirements of consensus and they may mount sufficient pressure to bring about the alteration of any legal procedures which stand in their way.

Obstacles to Comprehensive Planning in the Twin Cities: An Overview

The theme of this book has been that the political culture of the Twin Cities tended to inhibit the development of conditions in which comprehensive planning, even at the level of the city, could have a great deal of impact. Both Minneapolis and St. Paul were run democratically, by politicians who tended to be perceived by their constituents, and to perceive themselves, as servants rather than leaders. They did not sense any significant demand for comprehensive city planning, nor did they feel any obligation to spur such demand. The pattern of existing city agency jurisdictions and services was relatively well fixed. Only infrequently did interagency conflicts arise that could not be settled by informal negotiation among the affected officials. This was not to say that more systematic coordination from above could not have produced genuine benefits, but only that official and public perception of these potential benefits was either lacking or had not yet resulted in demands for action. Nor did this mean that the voters of the Twin Cities were ecstatic about the quality of the local government that they had; it meant only that they gave no appearance of believing that a change in the direction of comprehensive planning would improve that quality substantially. Moreover, to politicians who obtained reelection with great regularity, it appeared likely that such a change would on balance reduce voter satisfaction as measured in the most meaningful currency they knew— votes. Comprehensive planning would probably invite many jurisdictional controversies where few now existed. It would certainly involve additional articulation of city-wide and long-term values that were hard (once articulated) to brush off, but that had less well-organized constituencies than the more narrow and immediate values with which they might often conflict. It was also bound to involve many unusual proposals the ultimate political effects of which were extremely difficult to foresee. So long as the level of voter dissatisfaction, as measured by votes against incumbents, was low, there seemed little reason to advocate substantial change.

We may reasonably ask whether certain special factors may have made the political payoff of planning appear more questionable in the Twin Cities than elsewhere. Several candidates for designation as such factors, some of which have been dealt with at length in previous chapters, come quickly to mind. First, the political culture was favorable to pluralism and the greatest possible autonomy for private groups. Government tended to be perceived by those who shared this culture more as a provider of special services than as a comprehensive designer of the shape of the future.

Second, both cities gave little power—even by American standards—to their chief executives, and party discipline in their city councils was virtually nonexistent. The consequent fragmentation of power discouraged the pursuit of unconventional objectives. No one official or coherent group of officials could reasonably hope to implement such objectives. Moreover, with no one official clearly in the public eye, and with the possibility of dramatization by striking deeds virtually foreclosed, the task of education to make unconventional objectives politically palatable was likely to appear extremely forbidding to anyone who contemplated it. In any event, these political systems did not offer sufficient power or prestige to encourage many men of great independence or imagination to seek elective positions in them. Those who did hold elective positions in them tended to be preoccupied with immediate problems, particularly those of intense concern to their constituents, and in general to be extremely content with things as they were. Not only did they typically believe that the pursuit of ambitious objectives would be politically dangerous; they were also very disinclined to believe that such objectives could be worth pursuing.[2]

[2] This is not to deny that occasionally men of great vigor occupied elective office in the Twin Cities. When Hubert Humphrey was mayor of Minneapolis (1945–1948), he apparently infused the office with unprecedented authority, although critics claimed that his accomplishments were more apparent than real. His primary methods of leadership were speechmaking and helping to organize and lead citizens' groups. By one count, he made 2,500 speeches during his relatively brief tenure. Under his leadership the city government structure was substantially reorganized, the police department was brought under the direct control of the mayor, the city's gambling houses and brothels were closed down, a Mayor's Council on Human Relations was established, and the first Fair Employment Practices ordinance ever passed by an American city was enacted. During the same period Humphrey led the successful

Third, it may have been that the level of functional coordination within departments, and that of mutual accommodation among departments, had risen quickly enough over the years to keep pace with public demands for coordination. There had been no prolif-

---

battle to oust the extreme left wing from the Minnesota Democratic-Farmer-Labor Party, he was a cofounder on the national scene of the Americans for Democratic Action, he spearheaded the successful battle for a strong civil rights plank at the Democratic National Convention of 1948, and he ran successfully for the U.S. Senate. Humphrey benefited from the capacity of the Minneapolis Central Labor Union (CLU) in this period to enforce discipline in the City Council, but even so his career was entirely unique in Minneapolis history. (The CLU had never been previously, and was never after, a reform-minded organization.)

Mayor Arthur Naftalin (1961–), a former political science professor and an influential figure in the state administration of Governor Orville Freeman (1955–1961), has clearly aspired to match Humphrey's record of accomplishment, but he has apparently failed to mobilize substantial citizen support and his efforts to do so have made him more or less anathema to the City Council. One might also pick out two or three city councilmen of the postwar period who appeared to be of unusual quality, but their tenures tended to be short and their impact minimal.

St. Paul has had one mayor in the postwar period (Edward Delaney, 1948–1952) who appeared to have major substantive policy objectives. Like Humphrey, he benefited while in office from the capacity of organized labor to dominate his City Council when it cared to. For reasons too complicated to go into here, however, Delaney projected the image of an old-style machine politician and he eventually met defeat at the polls. One major reason may well have been that his objectives were mainly of the welfare variety. The middle-class ideals of economy, efficiency, and elimination of sin did not, by contrast, move him visibly. (There was no reason to believe that he tolerated corruption in his administration, however.) Particularly as his public housing program threatened racial integration of all-white neighborhoods, he was a rather easy target for conservative snipers. In the end, because Delaney's mode of operation had been to persuade behind the scenes more than to engage in public debates about principles, his vigor as mayor was quickly forgotten. By the time I came on the scene, few but the closest observers of St. Paul politics seemed to remember that Delaney had battled for anything. The usual explanation for his defeat at the polls was simply: poor public image.

One other recent St. Paul politician, Frank Marzitelli, has also been a man of substantial personal force, but he has concentrated on highly orthodox objectives like road building and port development. Though he is greatly respected by just about everyone who knows St. Paul politics as a man who can "get things done," his impact on the public consciousness and the nature of the political system has been minimal. Marzitelli served on the City Council from

eration of departments as city budgets had grown in recent decades. Within each department sufficient power was concentrated at the top to impose any desired level of coordination. Coordination by mutual accommodation among the departments was facilitated by the fact that nearly all the highest departmental officers had spent decades in their city's service prior to achieving their current positions. Their capacities for "getting along" within it had been subject to careful observation and informal cultivation during these long apprenticeships. It was true that many high officials were appointed on the basis of written technical examinations alone, but even they were normally quite well "socialized." This is not to say that all strong public demands for improved interagency cooperation were met adequately by mutual accommodation, or that bitter interagency conflicts never developed. It is to hypothesize an explanation, however, as to why such failures were sufficiently rare so that (1) the elective politicians could take time to handle them individually, and (2) perception of the desirability of new coordinating agencies was held to a low level.

Similarly, at the metropolitan area level there were mechanisms for functional coordination in areas where it was widely deemed to be desirable. The state highway department effectively determined the structure of the major highways network. Three single-purpose metropolitan authorities had been created in recent years to deal with sanitation, airports, and mosquito control. A number of other services were provided jointly by two or more local governments in the area under a Minnesota law which authorized all local governments to perform jointly any functions which they were authorized to perform individually. The services that had been dealt with to some extent in this way included fire-protection, water supply, and recreation.[3]

1950 through 1957, when he resigned to become Deputy Commissioner of the State Highway Department. More recently he has served as the executive vice-president of St. Paul's Port Authority.

Needless to say, the observations in this footnote are purely impressionistic.

[3] See Clarence C. Ludwig, "Planning for Metropolitan Growth," mimeo, May 1954; and Twin Cities Metropolitan Planning Commission, *The Challenge of Metropolitan Growth* (St. Paul: Twin Cities Metropolitan Planning Commission, December 1958), p. 14.

Evaluative Criteria and Factual Perception

To list the factors discussed in the last few paragraphs is to suggest that no evaluation of Twin Cities planning, *circa* 1960, can be very meaningful unless it refers to a carefully specified measure of accomplishment. Throughout this volume I have consciously used the traditional ideal of comprehensive planning as my benchmark. It has the virtue of clarity, and the public image of the city planning profession has been built substantially upon it. Despite the fact that most academic planners today recognize the impossibility of achieving it, practicing planners in the Twin Cities constantly referred to it in their public statements. This was not because they lacked awareness of trends in academia. It was rather because they judged that academics had failed to provide substitute ideals which could guide practitioners, inspire supporters, or have very much persuasive impact upon skeptics. One of my central theses, of course, has been that the planners' steadfastness in the face of political dangers was very much reduced by their lack of strong conviction about the comprehensive planning ideal. They did need some ideal, however, and they had no other. My primary object has been to describe and analyze particular dangers and strategies, but I have found it impossible to determine which were worth discussing without constant reference to the ideal that the planners were supposedly pursuing. (In practice, of course, I have frequently referred to other objectives which they appeared simultaneously to be pursuing, such as the enhancement of their political acceptability and the implementation of specific projects and design principles which, though unrelated to any comprehensive plans, they considered desirable.)

An ideal is, however, an absolute benchmark. Though it may be useful for some purposes to hold current practice up against it, it is vital before essaying practical evaluations to consider real-life trends and comparisons. This is not the place for a systematic analysis of historic trends and comparisons, but the point that such an analysis would probably conclude with emphasis radically different from that of the present study ought to be kept in mind. Assuming that its concerns were political in the first place, such a study would be likely to focus almost solely on the variable "political effectiveness" rather than on the complex interrelationships among political and planning ideals and practices. Moreover, its estimates of political effectiveness would for most of the situations described be quite crude, depending (1) on the most obvious manifestations of political favor—e.g., budgets and numbers of personnel; (2) on highly general accounts of the ways in which "big" decisions had come to be made; and (3) on the extent to which each city's physical features reflected a single guiding hand or set of design values.

These characteristics of the analysis might not apply to every city and period discussed, but they would seem likely to apply to most —for the following reasons. First, standards of the ends of urban physical development planning and of the techniques which ought to be employed in the planning process have always been in constant flux. Second, only very recently have these standards had a self-conscious "profession" to articulate and cultivate them with some semblance of authoritativeness. And third, detailed critical studies of planning processes in earlier periods and other politico-cultural settings are almost entirely lacking. Consequently, it would probably be foolhardy to venture estimates of even the sizes of gaps between ideals and practices in particular cities and time periods, let alone of their causes. One might try, of course, to evaluate the work of the past and of other contemporary cultures —as manifested in extant city plans or in existing physical cities— by the standard of the modern Western ideal of comprehensiveness, but there would be a strong smell of unreality about such an exercise.[4]

A Hypothetical Panoramic Study

What *might* the findings of a panoramic study be if it *did* focus on the variable "political effectiveness"? Let us speculate, dividing our hypothetical study into four parts, dealing respectively with (1) trends in American city planning, (2) trends in American metropolitan area planning, (3) historical examples of effective planning in Western Europe, and (4) the foundations of planning influence in one contemporary Western European nation.

[4] This is not to say that such a study would lack interest if its central concern were the degree of similarity between specific other cultures and our own. It is only to say that it would require one to impose standards on the material that would be completely alien to most of it.

(1) Trends in American city planning. The first part of our survey would no doubt conclude that the trend in American cities was toward a more influential role for general planning. The manifestations of this trend in Minneapolis and St. Paul have been discussed in previous chapters. For indications of its more general character, three citations from standard texts ought to suffice. First, Charles Adrian has written:

In typical American fashion, land-use decisions were, until recently, made by private businessmen, the realtors, land developers, and bankers in particular. Characteristically, nineteenth-century Americans did not believe that a greater community interest stood above that of the profit motives of these men. . . . Because bankers decide who gets loans and realtors decide, through their realty boards, who is to be allowed to buy where, their decisions determined, within the limits of cultural values, the face of American cities. . . . [They] established a basic policy of urban growth through exodus and conversion, so that home construction took place for the higher-income persons only (except in tenements), others taking the vacated property according to their status positions. It was a game of providing according to ability to pay, with little concern for the decaying ugliness at the center.

But as American cities began to mature, this pattern changed. Persons in the community began to become concerned with the growing blight around them. Property owners began to fear for the income value of the older sections. The retreating upper middle class began to run into rural and fringe-area slums. Attitudes toward the uninhibited activities of private business began to change.[5]

Edward Banfield and James Q. Wilson have recently dated, and tried to account for, the most significant changes as follows:

Until the Second World War the typical large-city planning agency was mainly—and often almost exclusively—occupied with zoning and subdivision regulation. . . .
'The record of the 1930's and 1940's speaks for itself,' T. J. Kent has written . 'Piecemeal plans and detailed zoning ordinances that were unrelated to even the sketchiest framework of a general plan were the familiar products of the time.' In those cities where master plans (so-called) were produced, mayors, councils and operating officials filed them and forgot them. With few exceptions the plans were what

[5] *Governing Urban America,* 2nd ed. (New York: McGraw-Hill Book Co., 1961), pp. 457–458.

Norton E. Long has called them: 'civic New Year's resolutions.' Probably not a single city in the United States was significantly influenced
before the end of the Second World War by a master plan even roughly
resembling the ideal held forth by the planning movement.

After the war, master planning received powerful impetus and support from the federal government. Under the Housing and Redevelopment Act of 1949 the government encouraged the cities to undertake
vast new projects that would require planning, and it agreed to pay
much of the cost of this planning. Housing and redevelopment suddenly became as important as zoning in the budgets of many planning
agencies. . . . By 1961 cities could [also] get federal assistance for
planning (and construction of) airports, sewage systems, highways and
other transportation, recreation and open space facilities, and
hospitals. . . .

This is not to say that planning was forced upon the cities against
their will. After the Second World War the general level of local government spending rose very rapidly, and technical and managerial
personnel of other kinds were added to city governments. The increase
in planning personnel was a part of this general increase. But it was
also true that a city which wanted to share in the federal *largesse*—
and which city did not?—had to be able to show that it had made, or
was in the process of making, a master plan.[6]

T. J. Kent agrees with Banfield and Wilson that World War II
was the great divide. Whereas they believe that the main causes of
the change were federal-aid policies, however, he believes that they
were local conditions and perceptions. It will be noted that in his
catalog of causes, which follows, the federal government is not mentioned at all.

During the first decade following World War II, two realities imposed
themselves. . . . First, as a result of the slow but sure effects of the
municipal reform movement, cities throughout the country established
permanent professional planning staffs and began to give continuous,
thoughtful, top-level attention to the job of understanding and
guiding the physical development of their communities. And second,
at the same time, as a result of the pressing demands created by the
wartime postponement of essential public works, by the tremendous
postwar growth of our cities and metropolitan regions, and by the

[6] *City Politics* (Cambridge: Harvard Univerity Press and the M.I.T. Press,
1963), pp. 187, 190, 192. Their citations are from T. J. Kent, *The Urban
General Plan* (San Francisco: Chandler Publishing Co., 1964), p. 46; and
Norton Long, *The Polity* (Chicago: Rand McNally, 1962), p. 192.

natural urge to do constructive tasks after the years of destruction caused by the war, city governments changed from negative to positive their approach to the job of city planning. . . . The reality of the demand for, and the obvious interrelatedness of, the postwar freeway, urban redevelopment, off-street parking, school, recreation, and metropolitan rapid transit projects, coupled with the need for a complete overhaul of the twenty- to thirty-year-old original zoning plans . . . forced civic leaders in American cities everywhere to change their point of view toward city planning. . . . The years of skeleton staffs, of major concern with the administration of crude, first-stage zoning ordinances, and of illogical and misleading piece-meal plans had passed. The first great period of general-plan work and of thorough testing of the general-plan concept had begun.[7]

The present work has explored limitations on the comprehensiveness and on the political impact of contemporary planning. I certainly do not contest the direction of change, however. For what they are worth, my own estimates of the causes of change are similar to Adrian's in their emphasis on special interests in local politics, and to Banfield's and Wilson's in their emphasis on the role of the federal government. As this volume has made clear, I tend also to be extremely skeptical about the amount of influence that general plans are currently having on the physical development of American cities. All we know for sure is that planning agency budgets and numbers of personnel are up, and that plans are being published. In view of these estimates of my own, I find Kent's rhapsodies about enlightened civic leaders, his implicit disparagement of the role of the federal government, and his faith that general planning *is* having a major impact on urban development, rather unnerving. Other scholars will have to judge whether our differences are traceable to error (on one of our parts) or simply to differences in perspective or in the cities we have examined. These differences notwithstanding, however, this part of our hypothetical panoramic study would conclude with a clear finding of a trend favorable to city planning.

(2) *Trends in American metropolitan area planning.* The second part of our survey would no doubt conclude, first, that the planning function is currently far stronger in large central cities than it is anywhere else on the contemporary American urban

---

[7] T. J. Kent, *op. cit.,* pp. 60–61.

scene and, second, that the apparent direction of movement is toward a more influential role for general metropolitan planning agencies.

The former of these generalizations is hardly controversial. Planning has rarely gathered political strength in America before the onset of serious blight in at least large portions of the jurisdictions concerned. This means that is has only infrequently been able to guide the original development of vacant land; its impact has for the most part been confined to ordering the processes of transition and redevelopment in later periods. On the urban fringes, where the great bulk of new development is taking place, planning controls are even today generally very weak and often virtually nonexistent. Prior to the development and the subsequent maturation of community life in the newly developed areas, there are generally no significant forces with a major stake in restraining developers. Even thereafter, as local governments take shape, each unit is likely to be so anxious to outbid other units for "desirable" kinds of development that it is unwilling to risk antagonizing investors. In any event, each is likely to be too weak to deal effectively with major metropolitan forces,[8] and each is likely to develop a highly articulated consciousness of its own special interests which might be threatened by concessions of power to a metropolitan government.

Metropolitan planning agencies are likely to be perceived as harbingers of metropolitan government. Indeed, to a certain extent they are, since they are bound to articulate and publicize the desirability of metropolitan solutions to many problems. In time, they are likely to acquire at least limited vetoes over some local proposals, even if only by informal means, such as their influence with the federal and state officials responsible for approving public works aid applications. To the extent that they fulfill the former potential, they may strengthen local groups favorable to metropolitan government. To the extent that they fulfill the latter, they

[8] Robert Wood has written as follows: "It may not be too far-fetched—though it is certainly an oversimplification—to think of local governments as players at a roulette wheel, waiting to see what number will come up as a result of decisions beyond their direct control" (*1400 Governments* [Cambridge: Harvard University Press, 1961], p. 62).

will actually *become* metropolitan governments, though very weak ones. Even central city officials tend to fear having metropolitan planning agencies come between them and the higher levels of government on which they count heavily for aid.[9] Suburbanites and their representatives tend to have more specific fears. Residents of wealthy suburbs typically fear being taxed to support services for

[9] This fear has been most clearly expressed to date in their opposition to proposals that local applications for federal aid be routed through metropolitan or state planning agencies. Hearings were held in 1963 on S. 855, a bill providing that, effective July 1, 1965, applications for grants-in-aid under seven major federal programs should be accompanied by comments and recommendations from a metropolitan planning agency. The state or local jurisdiction applying for the grant was to be required only to state that it had taken these comments and recommendations into account in preparing its final version of the application. The only significant opposition to the bill came from the American Municipal Association and the U.S. Conference of Mayors (*Metropolitan Planning,* Hearings before the Subcommittee on Intergovernmental Relations, Committee on Government Operations, U.S. Senate, May 21, 22, and 23, 1963).

Similarly, the U.S. Advisory Commission on Intergovernmental Relations recommended in 1964 that "federal grants-in-aid to local governments for urban development be channeled through the states in cases where a state (a) provides appropriate administrative machinery to carry out relevant responsibilities, and (b) provides significant financial contributions." All three mayors on the Commission vigorously opposed this recommendation. They were joined by the Housing and Home Finance Administrator, who tends to be the primary representative of urban (and particularly big city) interests in the federal government (Advisory Commission on Intergovernmental Relations, *Impact of Federal Urban Development Programs on Local Government Organization and Planning* [Washington: U.S. Government Printing Office, January 1964], pp. 30–31).

Nor is it clear that central city officials can be counted on to support thoroughgoing metropolitan government schemes. Scott Greer has recently reported on metropolitan reform campaigns in three major cities: St. Louis, Cleveland, and Miami. In St. Louis and Cleveland, where metropolitan government was rejected, the central city mayors and bureaucracies had opposed it. In Miami, city officials had been badly frightened by a 1953 referendum in which the voters had come within 800 votes of completely abolishing the city government. They had apparently become convinced as a result of this experience that the alternative to supporting a compromise "federal" scheme was eventual total absorption by the higher level (Dade County) government (*Metropolitics* [New York: John Wiley and Sons, 1963], pp. 39–40).

the central city poor.[10] Property owners in nearly all suburbs fear
being compelled to accept minority group tenants and neighbors.
(The other side of the coin is that minority group leaders are
likely to feel that their influence will be far less in a metropolitan
than in a central city political system.) [11] Suburban officials and
newspaper publishers are likely to doubt their capacity to survive
in a centrally governed metropolitan system; if so, they will be
highly motivated to stimulate their constituents to become aware
of whatever suburban interests might be threatened by metropolitan institutions.[12] When problems become so pressing that

[10] Robert Wood pointed out that the municipalities of Teaneck and
Teterboro in Bergen County, New Jersey, were quite close physically, but that
assessed valuation per school child was $33,000 in the former and $5.5 million
in the latter. (It should be noted that the latter, a haven for industry, had a
school enrollment of only two.) This was an extreme disparity, but Wood
contended that it was indicative of a general pattern that prevailed throughout the New York metropolitan region. The most striking feature of this
pattern was that total wealth (measured by business and residential property
values per capita) tended to decrease as one went from less densely populated
to more densely populated communities. Public service needs appeared to vary
in the opposite direction (*1400 Governments*, pp. 50–57).

Scott Greer found in his study of the 1959 St. Louis referendum on a
metropolitan government plan that fears of higher taxes worked against the
plan in the city as well as the suburbs. The plan was defeated by two to one
in the city and by three to one in the suburban areas. In a sample survey
carried out immediately after the election, the argument against the plan
most frequently cited by both city and suburban residents was that it would
result in higher taxes. The organized opponents who obtained publicity for
this argument, however, were predominantly suburbanites (*Metropolitics*, pp.
74–78, 126).

[11] Greer has reported on the responses of the St. Louis and Cleveland
Negro communities to metropolitan government schemes. Both opposed
vigorously. See *Metropolitics*, pp. 80, 90, 94–95.

[12] Greer writes of the suburban opposition to the St. Louis metropolitan
government plan: "The mayors of small suburban municipalities, their councilmen, and their attorneys constituted the cadres that spoke against the plan
and debated with its protagonists. Municipal employees were panicked at the
notice that they might lose their job security in a new and unknown
government. Small businessmen suspected that, should control of streets and
zoning be ceded to a larger government, their own ability to appeal and
influence decisions would wither away. They sensed the loss of 'community
integrity,' which they defined as an asset to their business district—and
business. . . . The suburban community newspapers . . . had both a vested

metropolitan solutions can no longer be avoided, these groups have a stake in pressing for the narrowest possible solutions. Even though some may resist the temptation, it is likely that enough will not to veto most broadly oriented proposals. Once created, metropolitan agencies with narrow responsibilities and constituencies tend to satisfy some of the demand for metropolitan planning and at the same time to provide institutional nuclei of resistance to more comprehensive schemes which might reduce their autonomy.[13]

For all these reasons and more, although two-thirds of the nation's 212 Standard Metropolitan Statistical Areas (SMSA's) supported some general metropolitan planning activity by 1963, most of that activity was, according to a recent authoritative study, "severely handicapped by small and uncertain budgets, insufficient legal power to permit active participation in development decisions, and lack of clear statutory direction."[14] The authors of the

---

interest in the campaign and an interest in its defeat. . . . Here . . . was a major issue which could be used to integrate the paper with the community, against such easy targets as the wicked city politicians, the dying and bankrupt central city, the multitudinous and dangerous strangers who roamed outside the local bailiwick. Furthermore the community newspapers, insofar as the local shopping district and the committed homeowners of the community were their source of revenue and readership, had nothing to gain with the blurring of municipal boundaries. Quite the contrary. The fiction of community autonomy in the suburbs is a powerful legitimizer of the local community press" (*ibid.*, p. 31; see also pp. 74–75).

[13] According to the U.S. Advisory Commission on Intergovernmental Relations, even the federal government, in the course of seeking to assure professional quality performance of specific functions, has frequently encouraged creation of special purpose metropolitan agencies as the most obvious way of achieving its objective (*Impact of Federal Urban Development Programs on Local Government Organization and Planning*, pp. 24, 25).

Five reasons for the recent increase in the popularity of "special districts' are discussed in Advisory Commission on Intergovernmental Relations, *Governmental Structure, Organization, and Planning in Metropolitan Areas* (Washington: U.S. Government Printing Office, July 1961), pp. 27, 28.

See also Robert Wood, "A Division of Powers in Metropolitan Areas," in Arthur Maass, ed., *Area and Power* (Glencoe: The Free Press, 1959); and John C. Bollens, *Special District Governments in the United States* (Berkeley: University of California Press, 1957).

[14] Joint Center for Urban Studies of the Massachusetts Institute of Technology and Harvard University (Charles M. Haar, Project Director), *The*

study in question found no evidence that metropolitan planning agencies had yet had any significant impact on urban development. They did find, however, that by a variety of expedients the American governmental system had "indeed responded to the most serious challenges of urban growth. . . . As a result, the most pressing needs have been met, and few real crises have been allowed to develop." [15]

Nonetheless, a trend in the direction of a more influential role for general metropolitan planning is discernible. Several reasons for it may be suggested. First, as noted previously, the values of coordination as opposed to those of laissez faire have for many years been in the ascendant in our society. Second, as I have argued in Chapter VII, planners and planning agencies have apparently become increasingly adept at cultivating and working with powerful organized constituencies. Third, and of greatest immediate importance, federal aid programs have expanded rapidly and federal officials have become more and more willing to manipulate the incentives at their command so as to encourage general planning in recent years. Total federal grants-in-aid to state and local governments quadrupled between fiscal years 1954 and 1964 [16]—rising from $2.7 to $10.5 billion. Although it is not known with any certainty what proportion of federal grant aid goes to support activities in urban areas, the chairman of the Senate Subcommittee on Intergovernmental Relations has estimated that the total may have been over five billion dollars in fiscal 1963.[17]

The U.S. Advisory Commission on Intergovernmental Relations has recently identified forty-three separate programs of federal financial aid for urban development, administered by a variety

---

Effectiveness of Metropolitan Planning, committee print, Subcommittee on Intergovernmental Relations, Committee on Government Operations, U.S. Senate, June 30, 1964, p. 2.

[15] *Ibid.,* p. 18.

[16] *The Federal System as Seen by State and Local Officials,* committee print, Subcommittee on Intergovernmental Relations (staff study), Committee on Governmental Operations, U.S. Senate, 1963, p. 85; and Legislative Reference Service of the Library of Congress, Supplement, January 4, 1965, to *Catalog of Federal Aids to State and Local Governments,* committee print, Subcommittee on Intergovernmental Relations, Committee on Government Operations, U.S. Senate, May 17, 1965, p. 53.

[17] Senator Edmund S. Muskie, in *Metropolitan Planning,* p. 2.

of bureaus and divisions in five departments and eight independent agencies. Until very recently, it reports, virtually no attention was paid to coordinating the impacts of these programs. Nonetheless, conflicts between programs were minimized by the large gaps between them (due to their highly specialized objectives) and the tendency on the part of administering agencies to expand away from, rather than toward, each other. In recent years, on the other hand, programs—some of which have had rather general objectives (like urban renewal)—have been proliferating and techniques for analyzing the complex ramifications of specialized programs have been improving rapidly.[18]

Federal officials have frequently been criticized for failing to coordinate their programs with each other and with related local programs. In response, many of them have vigorously supported recent efforts to force public officials in each metropolitan area to create institutions able to speak authoritatively for it as a whole in dealings with federal agencies. Most of the top federal officials are, in any case, professionals committed to regional planning of their own functions and identification of as many side effects as possible. Those around the Housing and Home Finance Administrator have, particularly since 1961, been strongly committed to the ideal of comprehensive planning for each metropolitan area. Speaking the language of hostility to waste, and often (though not always) supported by the large-city mayors who tend to personify urban America in Washington—small-city and suburban officials appearing generally to consider federal activity well beyond their range of influence—they have acquired a good deal of Congressional support.

The most tangible evidence of this support has been the urban planning assistance program originally authorized by Section 701 of the Housing Act of 1954. Cumulative appropriations for this program totaled only $16.4 million through fiscal year 1961, but rose to $72.7 million in the following three years.[19] Sections

[18] See Advisory Committee on Intergovernmental Relations, *Impact of Federal Urban Development Programs*, pp. 2–4, 11–12.

[19] *Independent Offices Appropriations for 1963*, Hearings before a Subcommittee of the Committee on Appropriations, U.S. House of Representatives, 87th Congress, Second Session, Part II, p. 1165; and *Independent Offices Appropriations for 1965*, Hearings before a Subcommittee of the Committee on

701(c) and 701(d) of the act as amended make the establishment of metropolitan and regional planning agencies a major objective of the program, and Section 701(a) declares that "the Administrator shall encourage cooperation in preparing and carrying out plans among all interested municipalities, political subdivisions, public agencies, and other parties in order to achieve coordinated development of entire areas." [20] A 1963 survey revealed that 39 per cent of the total revenue available for metropolitan planning in the nation's SMSA's came from federal grants. Even this figure seriously understated the importance of federal aid in spurring planning for those metropolitan areas that spread beyond the confines of a single county. Under one-third of the metropolitan planning agencies served multi-county constituencies, but on the average they served six and one-half times as many people as the others.[21] These agencies received 60 per cent of their revenues from the federal govement, mostly in Section 701 grants, and another 25 per cent from the states. Those serving more than one million people received 95 per cent of their revenues from federal and state sources. Despite these grants from higher levels of government, the mean expenditure per metropolitan planning agency serving more than one million people was less than one-

Appropriations, U.S. House of Representatives, 88th Congress, Second Session, Part II, p. 498.

[20] Quoted, U.S. Advisory Commission on Intergovernmental Relations, *Impact of Federal Urban Development Programs,* p. 62. Only state, metropolitan, and regional planning agencies can receive grants directly from the federal government under this program. Most grants to state agencies are destined for communities of under 50,000 population. Applications for such grants must include a statement indicating that the community's work program has been reviewed by the metropolitan, regional, or county planning agency (if any) serving its area. The state planning agency is charged with supervising and coordinating the use of planning grants channeled through it. For a brief description of the program, and bibliography concerning it, see *ibid.,* pp. 60–64.

[21] U.S. Housing and Home Finance Agency, *National Survey of Metropolitan Planning,* committee print, Subcommittee on Intergovernmental Relations, Committee on Government Operations, U.S. Senate, December 16, 1963, p. 6. Data were available for 125 of the nation's 126 metropolitan planning agencies. (The 126 agencies covered all or part of 142 of the nation's 212 SMSA's.) The average multi-county agency, of which there were thirty-eight, served 1,880,000 people. The average county or city-county agency—the other two categories—served 287,000 people.

quarter of the mean expenditure per city planning agency serving a comparable constituency.[22] Another indication of the lack of local initiative on behalf of metropolitan planning was the average age of the multi-county agencies: only 5.6 years. Most of them, in other words, had come into being *after* the enactment of Section 701.[23]

The trend in federal policy remains clear, however. The Advisory Commission on Intergovernmental Relations reported in May 1964 that only seven of the forty-three federal programs of financial aid for urban development positively encouraged comprehensive city and/or metropolitan area planning. All of these had been enacted since 1949, however, whereas only half of all the federal aid programs had come into being that recently. Of the four which encouraged metropolitan planning, three had come into being since 1961 and the fourth had had its budget quadrupled in the same period. The most important of all federal development programs, highways, was one of these.[24] Since 1934 highway legislation has provided that one and one-half per cent of highway grants-in-aid might be used for planning and research activities. Legislation enacted in 1961 provided that highway research and planning grants might in future be merged with Section 701 planning assistance grants. It also provided that begin-

[22] *Ibid.*, pp. 8–11. The figures (for 1962) were $260,000 for metropolitan planning agencies serving over one million people and $1,074,000 for city planning agencies in the same category.

[23] *Ibid.*, p. 4. The county and city-county agencies had an average age of 10.6 years. It was probable, however, that many of them had begun simply as county planning agencies, only later, as the term had become fashionable, beginning to think of themselves as "metropolitan" planning agencies. The county agencies, of which there were forty-seven, were apparently so categorized (vis-à-vis city-county agencies) because they still did not cover their central cities.

[24] The highway program is included as a post-1961 program in this listing because the relevant provisions of it having to do with urban planning have been enacted since 1961. The other three programs referred to are the open space, mass transit demonstration grant, and urban planning assistance programs. In the open space program, the federal share of any project's total cost is increased by 10 per cent if the project conforms to an officially adopted areawide open-space program (Advisory Commission on Intergovernmental Relations, *Impact of Federal Urban Development Programs*, pp. 16, 17, 20). The regular mass-transit grant program, adopted by Congress in 1964 after three years as a high priority Administration bill, should certainly now be added to the list.

ning in fiscal 1964 one and one-half per cent of highway aid would
be available *only* for research and planning, and that another 0.5
per cent could also be used for these purposes.[25] The Highway
Act of 1962 provided that, effective July 1, 1965, no highway aid
should be approved for projects in SMSA's unless they had
emerged from comprehensive area-wide transportation planning
processes. The extent to which comprehensive transportation
planning and comprehensive development planning more generally conceived will be merged, and carried on in metropolitan
planning agencies, remains to be seen.[26] One can say with confi-

[25] Several points should be noted:

(1) The 1961 amendment permitting joint administration of Section 701
and highway planning grants was preceded by an interagency agreement of
November 1960 providing for the same thing on an "experimental" basis.
The agreement is reproduced in Advisory Commission on Intergovernmental
Relations, *Governmental Structure, Organization and Planning in Metro-
politan Areas,* pp. 81–83.

(2) Highway research and planning grants go mainly to support highly
technical studies of no particular interest to urban planners. For a list of
the kinds of studies supported, see U.S. Bureau of the Budget, *Urban Research
Under Federal Auspices,* committee print, Subcommittee on Intergovernmental
Relations, Committee on Government Operations, U.S. Senate, April 15,
1964, p. 18.

(3) The study just cited was the first survey ever made of the nature and
extent of federally supported urban research activities. *Ibid.,* p. 5. Similarly,
the first study of the impact of federal development programs on local
government organization, coordination and planning appeared in 1964. That
study was: Advisory Commission on Intergovernmental Relations, *Impact of
Federal Urban Development Programs.* See esp. p. 4.

[26] According to one authoritative analysis of the 1962 Highway Act planning
provision (sec. 9):

"Comprehensive planning for urban development, apart from that done
by transportation planners, is not required. However, the comprehensive
transportation plans required in metropolitan areas must assure that highways
are 'properly coordinated with plans for improvements in other affected forms
of transportation and . . . are formulated with due consideration to their
probable effect on the future development of urban areas.' . . .

"The continuing comprehensive transportation planning process requires
either direct participation or adequate representation of each local 'jurisdiction
having authority and responsibility for actions of regionwide significance.'
The Bureau of Public Roads' regional engineers are authorized to determine
what constitutes adequate representation of local government for each urban
area. This planning process can meet all federal requirements without official
urban development plans necessarily being prepared, adopted or adhered

dence only that federal officials have received a clear mandate to coordinate highway and other forms of transportation planning at the areawide level in each SMSA; and that a similar mandate with respect to all forms of urban development planning may be emerging.[27] At the very least, then, the second part of our study would have to conclude that metropolitan planning processes, whether locally initiated or not, appear likely to have a greater impact on urban development in the foreseeable future than they have had in the past.

Whereas the first two parts of our survey would point to the trends in favor of planning in urban America, the third and fourth parts would point, respectively, to instances in history and in other contemporary political systems in which planning controls have been far more influential than they give any promise of becoming in this country. If well done, these parts would make a serious effort to delineate the most important differences between our own political system and those systems in which planning has flourished and is flourishing. They might also attempt to indicate at least the gross differences between the purposes for which these systems have used planning and the central values of modern American society.

---

to. . . . Clarification of the role of official urban planning agencies in transportation planning might . . . be beneficial." (*Impact of Federal Urban Development Programs*, pp. 106, 107. The first internal quotation is from Section 9 of the Highway Act of 1962. The second is from a U.S. Bureau of Public Roads Instructional memorandum dated September 13, 1963.)

[27] Readers may wish to consider the significance of S. 855 again at this point. See above, footnote 9. The bill received Administration support, and the Democratic members of the subcommittee that conducted the hearings seemed to be favorably inclined. (The only Republican who showed up at any of the sessions was Senator Jack Miller of Iowa. His concern was the highway program. He appeared to believe that the Bureau of Public Roads and the various state highway departments were planning well enough as it was.)

It should be noted that since 1952 Congress has required that all federal agency proposals for construction in the Washington metropolitan region be reviewed on an advisory basis by the National Capital Planning Commission. President Kennedy sent a memorandum to all federal agency heads in November 1962 directing them to coordinate their activities with the aim of implementing the general plan for development of the Washington metropolitan region. *Ibid.*, pp. 37, 38.

(3) Historical examples of effective planning. Perhaps the best example of a sophisticated and widely praised historical survey is Lewis Mumford's *The City in History*.[28] Although it deals almost solely with Western European and American cities, it is especially relevant in the present context because, unlike most other histories of urbanism, it seriously considers social, cultural, and political, as well as aesthetic, technological, and economic, causes and values. As a further bonus, Mumford has no fear of stating which examples of "strong" planning were also, in his opinion, examples of "good" planning. In view of his eminence, we may be justified in treating his views as representative of those of at least a significant portion of the American planning profession. (To be sure, there is no way of knowing just how representative Mumford's views are, but it is certainly difficult to think of anyone whose normative judgments would meet with *more* widespread approval in professional planning circles.) [29] *The City in History* has been criticized for judging all historic cities on the basis of a single set of standards, but it is impossible to evaluate without *some* set of standards, and at least Mumford's are both highly plausible and clear. Judgment is, of course, always a dangerous undertaking for those with scholarly pretensions, but those who—like planners—stand in need of principles to guide action have a special need for scholars with points of view. Despite his penchant for evaluating end results, Mumford does not shirk the difficult tasks of description and causal analysis. Even his critics have generally admitted that the quality of his scholarship is extremely high.[30] Let us

[28] New York: Harcourt, Brace & World, 1961.

[29] Actually, as will be indicated below, Mumford's influence has been greater in the United Kingdom than in this country. Many American planners find Mumford's hostility to big buildings and cities, to the automobile, to urban sprawl, and to most other major features of the contemporary American urban scene both quaint and unhelpful. This is, I believe, less because they are strongly committed to other values than Mumford's than because they are unaccustomed to thinking seriously about the desirability of contemporary realities. They do, of course, sometimes favor moderate reorganization and reform proposals, but usually (unless they are disciples of Mumford) on the sole ground that contemporary consensus values—e.g., that property values should be maintained, that the administration of public services should be "efficient"—are being clearly violated.

[30] The question may still be raised whether a relativistic value orientation would have made *The City in History* more useful. I cannot see that it would

inquire as to what the conclusions of the third part of our hypothetical panoramic study might be by analyzing Mumford's judgments and findings.

It should be noted at the start that Mumford has less taste for
mere unity of design in a city than most students of planning. He
writes in the course of his discussion of medieval cities, for example, that "the bastard aestheticism of a single uniform style, set
within a rigid town plan, arbitrarily freezing the historic process at
a given moment, was left for a later period, which valued uniformity more than universality, and visible power more than the invisible processes of life." [31] Consequently, Mumford would seem to
have less reason than most planning theorists to consider centrali-
zation of political power a prerequisite of effective planning.
Nonetheless, to me the most striking thing about Mumford's analysis is not its hostility to size (which strikes most planners), but its
hostility in practice to cultural and political pluralism. This assertion requires a defense, because in principle Mumford is a
vigorous advocate of variety, as the quotation cited above makes
clear. His particular likes and dislikes, however, somewhat belie
this general advocacy.

Mumford reserves his highest praise for the medieval town. Its
plans, he notes, were "more informal than regular," developing
gradually out of organic community needs rather than *a priori*
principles. "Organic planning," he writes, "does not begin with a
preconceived goal: it moves from need to need, from opportunity
to opportunity, in a series of adaptations that themselves become
increasingly coherent and purposeful. . . . Though the last stage
in such a process is not clearly present at the beginning, as it is in a
more rational, non-historic order, this does not mean that rational
considerations and deliberate forethought have not governed

---

have. On the contrary, it would have made the book far less challenging to
criticize and discuss without, probably, enhancing its descriptive validity.
Moreover, unless it had employed constant criteria of relevance throughout,
even the descriptions would have been extremely difficult to compare with
each other. Yet any criteria chosen and articulated would have had to rest
on value judgments comparable to those made so unashamedly by Mumford.
Mumford's values are, of course, fair game for criticism, but until one of the
critics produces a better "City in History" we must take Mumford's as the
prototype of this genre.

31 *The City in History*, p. 312.

every feature of the plan, or that a deliberately unified and integrated design may not result." [32] Thus, the beauty of the medieval town was the product of a highly sensitive incrementalism,
which in turn was disciplined by an underlying consensus on the
purposes of town life and a deep respect by each craftsman for
what had come before.[33]

Mumford does not explore the relationship between the beauty
of medieval towns and their economic stagnation, low standards of living, and lack of pluralism.[34] He does note, however,
that "never since the great dynasties of Egypt had there been such a
religious unity of purpose," and that the social structure of the
medieval town "remained a hierarchical one." [35] As the finest
example of medieval town planning, he chooses Venice. "No other
city," he writes, "shows in more diagrammatic form the ideal components of the medieval urban structure." He calls it "golden
Venice" and notes its "aesthetic glories." [36] Then, in passing, he
goes on to recall that Venice in the period under consideration was
"ruled by an iron-handed patriarchate, ruthless in its centraliza-
tion of power and responsibility," and that "the political order of
Venice was based on an ultimately demoralizing combination of
violence and secrecy: its rulers used private informers and secret
assassination as a commonplace method of control." [37]

Disclaiming romantic nostalgia, Mumford admits that "the
medieval town was no more the successful fulfillment of Christian
hope that it sometimes seemed to pious advocates in the thirteenth
century than it was the unredeemed compound of ignorance, filth,
brutality, and superstition that it seemed to many post-medieval

---

[32] *Ibid.*, p. 302.   [33] *Ibid.*, pp. 302, 303, 316.

[34] He does emphasize, however, that medieval towns were essentially rural.
Most had populations of under 10,000 in the fifteenth century, and London,
the largest city in Europe, had only 40,000 inhabitants (*ibid.*, pp. 300, 314).
He admits that as medieval towns grew in population toward the end of the
middle ages, open spaces were commonly built over and multistory tenements
were constructed—this despite the lack of any provisions for organized waste
disposal. (Nearby farmers did systematically collect human excrement in
many towns for use as fertilizer, but that was only one form of waste.) (*Ibid.*,
pp. 289, 290, 292.) At this point, even Mumford recoils in horror from the
medieval town (*ibid.*, p. 292).

[35] *Ibid.*, p. 316.   [36] *Ibid.*, p. 321.   [37] *Ibid.*, p. 322–324.

commentators." In defense against the latter evaluation, he argues that "if we dismiss medieval culture as a whole because of the torture chamber and the public burning of heretics and criminals, we should also wipe out all pretensions to civilization in our own period. Has not our enlightened age restored civil and military torture, invented the extermination camp, and incinerated or blasted the inhabitants of whole cities?" [38] Displaying a rather typical vice of panoramic historians, Mumford goes no further in relating the seamy side of medieval town life to its aesthetic glories.

Mumford's next section after that on the medieval town deals with the baroque city of the seventeenth and eighteenth centuries. Mumford is generally hostile to the baroque, because its passion for grandeur and formal order rested on the whims of absolute dictators rather than on the "organic" needs of the communities over which they ruled. He finds some examples of baroque planning attractive, however, as the following passage indicates.

How far this new order could go in a direction quite different from the palatial baroque precedents, Craig's plan for the New Town of Edinburgh in 1767 demonstrates. That order and unity were the result of a *unified* attitude toward life, the *unified* ownership of the land, and the *unified* control of the architect and builder. If the land had been first broken up into individual parcels, sold to competitive private owners, each proud of his own tastes, jealous of his own whims, ferocious in defense of his own ideology, the result would have been the chaos that too often prevailed in the late nineteenth century street, urban or suburban. Here . . . the baroque order was at its best: regimentation with a formal bow and a quiet smile.[39]

Mumford also approves of the best baroque residential squares, which, he writes, "performed a new urban purpose, that of bringing together, in full view of each other, a group of residences occupied by people of the same general calling and position." [40] Here again the key to success was apparently unity of outlook, land ownership, and architectural control. Mumford makes clear, of course, that "such upper class planning had almost nothing to contribute to the order of the rest of the city," and that, unfortu-

---

[38] Both quotations in this paragraph are from *ibid.*, p. 316.
[39] *Ibid.*, p. 398. Italics added.   [40] *Ibid.*, p. 395.

nately, even at its best baroque planning "was meant for the better sort." [41] He does not make clear, however, how serious an indictment he considers this to be.

From the baroque Mumford turns to capitalist cities. It seems not unfair to say that his hostility to capitalism is expressed far more intensely than his hostility to any dictatorship discussed in *The City in History*. Thus, he writes as follows: "In relation to the city, capitalism was from the beginning antihistoric; and as its forces have consolidated over the last four centuries, its destructive dynamism has increased. The human constants had no place in the capitalist scheme: or rather, the only constants it recognized were avarice, cupidity, and pride, the desire for money and power." [42]

There are exceptions in every age, however, and Mumford finds that "there is one city that bears witness to the commercial spirit at its best, before it had completely dissociated itself from the customary controls and the collective commitments of its medieval prototype. That city is Amsterdam . . . , one of the greatest examples of the town planner's art . . . , [and] capitalism's one outstanding urban achievement." Amsterdam, he feels, is "the most important example of a city that effected the transition from protectionism to commercial competition without losing form." [43]

Most of the planners with whom I have discussed this matter agree with Mumford's high esteem for Amsterdam, even if not with his low esteem for nearly all other modern cities. The reasons for the success of planning in Amsterdam are consequently worth considering. Several come quickly to mind. First and foremost, there is the fact that most of Amsterdam lies below sea level, protected by a complex system of dikes, locks, sluices, canals, and pumps. The entire city has had to be constructed on piles driven deep into wet sand. Mumford notes that the task of flood protection, plus the expense and difficulty of foundation work, "from the beginning required cooperative management" and "kept the Dutch cities from spreading at the random will of the property owner." "Under municipal direction," he continues, "the growing city was opened up, section by section, and supplied with collec-

[41] *Ibid.*, p. 399.   [42] *Ibid.*, pp. 413–414.
[43] All three quotations in this paragraph are from *ibid.*, p. 439.

tive services. Within this system of collective action and orderly restraint, the dynamic forces of capitalism operated, almost in spite of themselves, toward a public end." [44] The discipline imposed by geography on Amsterdam was, of course, strikingly similar to that imposed on Venice.

The fact that Amsterdam developed originally as a medieval city was also probably a factor helping to account for the tradition of municipal restraint upon capitalist freedom. It may also have been relevant that Amsterdam was in effect an independent nation until the Napoleonic Wars, and that since 1815 it has been the capital of a nation with a unitary constitution and an extremely acute consciousness of limitations on the national supply of land. (The Netherlands is the most densely populated country in the world, nearly eighteen times as densely populated as the United States.[45]) Despite these factors (which he fails to explore), Mumford admits that Amsterdam's working-class quarters, developed in the capitalist period, had none of the amenities of the rest of the city, and in fact were as bad as anything developed anywhere. He concludes that the benefits of even the best planning in capitalist societies, like the best baroque planning, were confined to those with high incomes.[46] He neglects to consider, however, the sources of the cultural tradition that provided wealthy Dutchmen with good taste. He does account for the public planning tradition —"a happy bequest left over from the old medieval economy" [47]— but he says nothing about the obstacles to introducing such a tradition into a capitalist society which has no medieval history.

Mumford's most important prescription for contemporary planning is essentially the "garden city" or "new town" conception first articulated by Ebenezer Howard. Mumford writes:

Against the purposeless mass congestion of the big metropolis, with its slums, its industrial pollution, and its lengthening journeys to

---

[44] *Ibid.*, p. 440.

[45] According to the Dutch government's 1960 population estimate, population density in that year was 888 per square mile. According to the 1960 U.S. census, American population density in the same year was 50 per square mile (*The World Almanac: 1962* [New York: World Telegram Corporation, 1962], pp. 296, 367).

[46] *Op. cit.*, p. 444.   [47] *Ibid.*, p. 444.

work, Howard opposed a more organic kind of city: a city limited from the beginning in numbers and in density of habitation, limited in area, organized to carry on all the essential functions of an urban community, business, industry, administration, education; equipped too with a sufficient number of public parks and private gardens to guard health and keep the whole environment sweet. To achieve and express this reunion of city and country, Howard surrounded his new city with a permanent agricultural greenbelt, . . . [intended] not merely to keep the rural environment near, but to keep other urban settlements from coalescing with it: not least, it would, like the ancient vertical wall, heighten the sense of internal unity. . . .

He saw that, once it has achieved an optimum size, the need for the individual town is not to increase its own area and population, but to be part of a larger system that has the advantage of large numbers and extensive facilities.[48]

As this is written, late in 1964, the garden city (as opposed to the purely residential suburb) appears to be coming to the United States for the first time. According to a recent article in *The New York Times,* written with the aid of the Housing and Home and Finance Agency staff, "this country is on the verge of a New Town boom. About 20 of these planned communities are in the design or construction stage. They are beginning to add up to a coast-to-coast trend of particular importance at a time when soaring population and the flight from cities have created two of the most serious problems of the century—the urban explosion and the rapid consumption of land. The New Town offers a hopeful solution, because it substitutes planned, orderly expansion for chaotic, uncontrolled sprawl."[49] My impression is that American city planners find this development extremely exciting, even though not all the New Towns will have provisions for employment. What is more striking about the projected American New Towns, however, is that they are all to be private developments. Thus, their developers will not be subject to any political limitations on their aspirations for planning control.

Tight planning control by private developers is, of course, not new even in America. John Delafons reports that the use of pri-

[48] *Ibid.,* pp. 515, 516.
[49] *The New York Times,* February 17, 1964, p. 17. See also "New Urban Plans Stir California," *ibid.,* December 25, 1964, p. 24.

vate restrictive covenants to govern the character of neighbor-hoods dates in America to the 1880's, and that it is an extremely common practice.[50] He finds the classic example of its success in Houston, the largest American city with no public land-use con-trols whatever. Interviewing bankers, real estate men, and city planners in Houston in 1961, he found them agreed "that on the whole the large-scale developer, the builder of higher-income homes, and the better educated home-buyer were all aware of the need to protect their investments, and that private covenants were adequate for the purpose." [51] At the end of a discussion of the extraordinary controls promulgated in authoritarian fashion by Levitt and Sons for each of their Levittowns (which have popu-lations of over 50,000), Delafons concludes that there is no demo-cratic country in the world in which *public* control of the uses of private property could go so far.[52] It is of course true that plan-ning by private developers is only for those who can afford new private housing, but the New Towns contemplated for America appear unlikely to mark any change in this respect. In fact, as some of the projected American New Towns will not even have substantial economic bases, and as none will provide housing for the low income employees of their businesses and industries, it may be that many of them will differ from the existing Levittowns only in aesthetic quality and expense.

A number of other democratic nations, however, particularly Britain, Holland, and the Scandinavian countries, have built New Towns as public ventures since World War II. These are fre-quently cited as indicative of what comprehensive planning can

[50] John Delafons, *Land-Use Controls in the United States* (Cambridge: Joint Center for Urban Studies of the Massachusetts Institute of Technology and Harvard University, 1962), p. 76.

William Ashworth has described the development of the 112 acre Bedford estate in Bloomsbury, London, beginning in 1774, as follows: "Twenty acres were first laid out as gardens for the use of lessees, the intention being that the buildings should be grouped around greens scattered over the whole area. . . . No lessee was allowed to put up any sign or to use a house as a shop or restaurant; the entrances to the estate were closed by gates, and persons with no business in Bloomsbury were not admitted. Thus was the character of the quarter preserved, and all the more easily as only a small portion of leases expired at any one time" (*The Genesis of British Town Planning* [London: Routledge & Kegan Paul, 1954], p. 36).

[51] Delafons, *op. cit.*, p. 81.   [52] *Ibid.*, pp. 76–79.

accomplish when given its head. They are *certainly* symbols of the great influence of planning in some contemporay democratic polities by comparison with the American. Let us speculate in the fourth part about the sources of that influence in one such polity, namely Great Britain.[53]

(4) *Foundations of planning influence in Great Britain.* First, there seems little doubt that the British receptivity to planning, like that of the Dutch, is associated with an acute sense of land shortage. British population density on a national basis is eleven times as great as American population density, and to the extent that cultural lag exists it is the Americans who live psychologically

[53] British planning was selected for consideration not because it is "stronger" or in any way more admirable than Scandinavian or Dutch planning, but rather because I know more about it.

Parenthetically, I have judged that this chapter is not the place for a substantive criticism of the British New Town plans themselves. Perhaps the most balanced assessment by one not himself part of the New Towns movement is still that ventured by Lloyd Rodwin in his book, *The British New Towns Policy* (Cambridge: Harvard University Press, 1956). Rodwin concluded that the conception of the New Towns policy had been bold and imaginative, but that the execution to date had been quite melancholy. He agreed with the many critics who had found most New Town architecture dreary, who had noted the apparent unconcern of the New Town planners for the economics of industrial and commercial location, and who had emphasized the failure of the New Town theorists to deal adequately with the relationships among such variables as the length of journey to work, community size, economic stability, employment mobility, industrial dynamism, the standard of living, and easily accessible urban variety.

Many British planners have been inclined to write off such criticisms on the ground that these mistakes of the pioneers can be corrected in future New Town planning, and that in any event even the first New Towns have provided much better living environments than the cities from which their residents came. Peter Self, for example, noted several years ago that there had been virtually no experience of New Town families returning to London. He admitted, however, that some of the New Towns were one class, working class, communities, and that just about all were very short of social and cultural facilities. (*Cities in Flood,* 2nd ed. [London: Faber and Faber, 1961], pp. 88–91. The chapter in question was originally published in 1957.) (Self, it may be noted, is a political scientist rather than a planner by profession, but in practice he is also a leading figure in British planning. As this is written, he is chairman of the executive committee of the Town and Country Planning Association.) So far as I know, no studies have been done comparing the satisfactions of ordinary suburbanites with those of New Town residents.

in a still less crowded past.[54] Moreover, Great Britain is a food importing country, and one that has come close to being starved out for lack of capacity to feed herself in wartime twice in this century.[55] By contrast, the great American farm problem has consistently been how to control and finance surpluses. Although each year American urban development absorbs perhaps thirty-five times as much land as does the British,[56] the capacity of American farmers to produce surpluses continues to grow. Planners may see land shortages on the distant horizon; laymen appear to find it impossible.

Second, capitalist ideas have never, except perhaps for several decades in the middle of the nineteenth century, triumphed in Britain to the extent that they have in the United States. Capitalism has been opposed in Britain, first by a strong aristocratic tradition of *noblesse oblige* and more recently by a powerful socialist movement. With respect to the first of these checks, it may be noted that land ownership and beautification have long been particular preoccupations of the British ruling classes. There is relatively little sympathy in Britain for those who would despoil the landscape in the name of any "right" to pursue profits. In any event, the British political tradition has—at least by comparison with the American—always stressed "rights" less than responsibilities.[57]

[54] According to the 1961 census, British population density was 559 to the square mile. According to the 1960 census, American population density was 50 to the square mile (*The World Almanac: 1962*, pp. 296, 314).
From 1871 to 1961, British population increased by 92 per cent. From 1870 to 1960, American population increased by 365 per cent.

[55] For a discussion of the impact of these wartime experiences on British planning, see Lewis Keeble, *Town Planning at the Crossroads* (London: Estates Gazette, 1961), pp. 53, 54. More generally, see G. P. Wibberley, *Agriculture and Urban Growth* (London: Michael Joseph, 1959), esp. Chaps. 6, 7.

[56] Delafons, *op. cit.*, p. 5.

[57] The practical impact of this aristocratic heritage has been summed up by Charles Haar as follows:
"One of the important strands in English planning has been the eighteenth-century aristocratic interest in landscape, estate planning, village preservation, and the development of city squares. Often the examples of large-scale private enterprise have been stimulants to the planning movement; thus the few model factory towns of the nineteenth century are to some extent forerunners of the New Towns. Another factor has been the traditional English love for the

Despite the significance of this aristocratic heritage, the impact of socialism on recent planning developments can hardly be over-estimated. The New Towns Act of 1946 and the Town and Country Planning Act of 1947, which together form the foundations of postwar British planning, were the work of a government most of whose energies were directed to nationalizing major industries. The New Towns were to be located and financed by the national government, constructed and managed by instruments (public corporations) of the national government. It is perhaps not sur-prising that, despite nearly universal rhetorical support for the New Town idea, fourteen New Towns were begun during the five years 1946–1951, and only one more during the succeeding decade of Conservative rule.[58] Two of the most important features of the Town and Country Planning Act were its provisions for control

---

countryside and concern with preservation of the beauties of nature; this latter movement has been fostered by many societies and associations which have exerted important political influence on the passage of town and country [planning] legislation. . . .

"The common acceptance by the major political parties in England of the need for central direction of the use of land, and, in general, the apolitical nature of town and country planning is surprising to the American observer. The pre-1947 legislation had been fostered by different governments. The Barlow Commission, which gave such a tremendous impetus to planning, was appointed by Neville Chamberlain, the then Prime Minister. The pledge in Parliament to establish a central planning authority was made by a Con-servative, Lord Reith. The first Minister of Town and Country Planning was a conservative, W. S. Morrison. . . . Considering the scope of the 1947 Act, there was a remarkable degree of agreement in both Houses. Conservative speakers, no less than the Laborite, echoed the fact that it is possible for the great mass of people to have a fair and decent life only by planning of land uses." Charles M. Haar, *Land Planning Law in a Free Society* [Cambridge: Harvard University Press, 1951], pp. 3, 4. On the eighteenth and nineteenth century traditions of town improvement, see Ashworth, *op. cit.*, pp. 33–46. With regard to the aristocratic heritage of emphasizing duties rather than rights, see M. Ostrogorski, *Democracy and the Organization of Political Parties* [New York and London: Macmillan and Co., 1902], Vol. I, pp. 14–23.

[58] As will be noted presently in the text, six more were begun in 1962–1964. For descriptions and assessments of the first eighteen New Towns by two leaders of the New Towns movement, see Frederick J. Osborn and Arnold Whittick, *The New Towns: The Answer to Megalopolis* (London: Leonard Hill, 1963). For a brief rundown of up-to-date statistics on the New Towns, see *Town and Country Planning*, XXXIII, No. 1 (January 1965), 28–29, 36–37.

by a national ministry of the location of all significant new industrial construction and its nationalization of development values in land.

Under the location of industry provision, no application to a local planning authority for permission to construct more than 5,000 square feet of industrial floor space was to be considered unless accompanied by a clearance certificate from the Board of Trade. The primary purpose of this policy was to direct employment to Britain's depressed areas rather than to serve specific town planning objectives—thus, administration by the Board of Trade. Nonetheless, British planners have always considered the distribution of population and employment around the country, and between various sized communities, a central concern of planning. Moreover, since a high priority objective of postwar planning was to stem the flow of population to London and Birmingham—both areas of very low unemployment—the policy was of great immediate interest to them.[59]

Under the land nationalization provision, owners of land were to be compensated once and for all for existing development values.[60] In the future, all increases in the value of any particular piece of land, except those attributable to the actual investments of its owner, were to accrue to the state. The purposes of this

[59] See Haar, *Land Planning Law in a Free Society*, pp. 24-26, and Peter Self, *The Planning of Industrial Location* (London: University of London Press, 1953), esp. Chap. 1. It should be emphasized that the Board of Trade has consistently administered the policy so as to alleviate pockets of unemployment even where this has meant discouraging emigration from obsolete, overcrowded, and blighted areas to much pleasanter communities short distances away. It has also at times discouraged industrial development in New Towns because they happen to be in areas of low unemployment. Consequently, it seems fair to say that coincidences between the location of industry policy and planning policies have been largely fortuitous—this despite their common origin in the Planning Act. In view of the immense political significance of unemployment, and the desire of most communities (however obsolete and uninviting in the eyes of observers) to hold their young people, this is probably not surprising. Nonetheless, at least insofar as it has discouraged immigration to the Birmingham and London regions, the location of industry policy has served British planners.

[60] The "development value" of a piece of land is that part of its "fair market value" attributable to speculation about new uses for which it may be in demand at some future time.

provision were (1) to reduce the cost of future land-use controls so restrictive as to require public purchase under existing law, (2) to eliminate all financial incentives for property owners to oppose even less restrictive controls, and (3) to destroy land speculation. The assumptions behind the provision were (1) that most future development would be public, (2) that therefore most future land sales by private owners would be compulsory, and (3) that consequently price would no longer have any significant function as a mechanism for nudging land toward its most productive uses. When the Conservatives, as part of their policy of encouraging private enterprise, repealed the nationalization of development values in 1954, most British planners were aghast.[61]

When a new Labor Government took office in October 1964, it was committed to a policy of nationalizing all land as it came up for development in the future.[62] It had also promised to enforce

[61] The Conservatives themselves experienced great difficulty in deciding just how far back they wished to turn the clock. The Town and Country Planning Act of 1954 set up a dual land market. Sellers of land to private purchasers were to be permitted to retain whatever price they could get. Those compelled to sell to public agencies, however, were to be paid only on the basis of 1947 use value. The indignation of those forced to sell to public agencies was finally recognized by the Town and Country Planning Act of 1959, which provided that henceforth public agencies should pay full market value for any land they acquired. (See Charles M. Haar, "Planning Law: Public v. Private Interest in the Land," in *Land Use in an Urban Environment* [Liverpool: Liverpool University Press, 1961], pp. 107–108.)

On reading this section, John R. James, Chief Planner of the Ministry of Housing and Local Government, commented that he thought most British planners had come by 1954 to realize that total nationalization was politically and administratively unfeasible. They were "aghast," in his view, only at the blatantly unfair "two price" system and at the totality of the retreat with respect to private land sales. James noted, however, that by 1962, when I conducted my interviews, land prices had risen so steeply that most planners again favored nationalization. This might, he thought, have affected their memories of their 1954 views.

[62] The 1947 scheme had involved nationalization of development values only, with imposition of a 100 per cent tax on future increases. By the spring of 1965 the Government appeared to have abandoned the idea of nationalization. The national budget announced in April 1965 introduced a 30 per cent capital gains tax on sales of all property—including land—held for more than one year. Profits on sales of property held for less than one year were to be taxed as ordinary income. It should be noted that Great Britain had not previously taxed capital gains at all. It was henceforth, according to *The Economist* (April 10, 1965), to tax them at the highest rate in the world.

location of industry controls much more vigorously—i.e., with less sympathy for the pleas of investors—and to vastly increase the magnitude of the subsidies offered to induce industries to locate in the depressed areas. Finally, one of the first acts of the new Government was to impose national restrictions on office development in the Greater London region, extending roughly forty miles in every direction from Charing Cross. Office developments involving more than 2,500 square feet of new floor space were henceforth to require an office development permit from the Board of Trade as well as local planning permission. The Government indicated that the new policy would be applied very restrictively, particularly with respect to London itself.[63]

A third general factor which should be mentioned is the unitary nature of the British constitution. Histories of British land-use planning invariably focus on national rather than local policies, and with good reason.[64] All local authority powers derive from national legislation, and all significant local authority decisions are subject to being overruled by national ministries—the Ministry of Housing and Local Government in the case of planning. When, in 1947, the national government wished to reduce the fragmentation of local planning responsibilities, it reduced at one stroke the number of local authorities empowered to plan from more than 1,400 to 145. More recently, another piece of legislation has brought metropolitan government to the London region. No one even thought of suggesting an area-wide referendum.[65] The major

[63] For a clear statement of the case for office location controls, see *The Paper Metropolis* (London: Town and Country Planning Association, 1962). The fundamental assumption behind industrial and office location controls, of course, is that the best way to influence the distribution of people around a nation is to influence the distribution of employment opportunities.

[64] See William Ashworth, *op. cit.;* Patrick Abercrombie, *Town and Country Planning*, 3rd ed., revised by D. Digby Childs (London: Oxford University Press, 1959); Lewis Keeble, *Planning at the Crossroads*, Chaps. 2–4; M. P. Fogarty, *Town and Country Planning* (London: Hutchinson's University Library, 1948), Chaps. 1–5; and the historical discussions (sprinkled throughout) in Nathaniel Lichfield, *Economics of Planned Development* (London: Estates Gazette, 1956).

[65] Needless to say, however, a Royal Commission first held extensive hearings and deliberated at length; then the Government held lengthy additional hearings; and finally the Government modified the Royal Commission's recommendations in numerous—though fundamentally minor—ways to make them more palatable. (See Royal Commission on Local Government in Greater

objectives of British land-use planning are national, and local development plans are expected to comply with them. In particular, the policies of discouraging population movement from declining areas of the United Kingdom to Southeast England, of encouraging the maintenance of greenbelts around large urban areas, of encouraging compact and orderly rather than chaotic suburban development, and of encouraging employment to follow population to the suburbs, are all primarily national rather than local.[66]

Fourth, it should be noted that in Britain government is an upper- and middle-class, not an all-class, affair; and although the governing classes have internal disagreements about particular questions of policy, their degree of consensus on the components of good communities and good lives is extremely striking by American standards. This consensus is probably nowhere more striking than in the policy area of planning. Controversy within the British planning profession is confined to quite minor issues. Consequently, despite the great influence of planning policy on urban development, planning theory is extremely rudimentary— theoretical elaboration and revision tends to be neglected in the absence of controversy.[67] Nearly all British planning ideas emerge

---

London, *Report* [London: Her Majesty's Stationery Office, Cmnd. 1164, October 1960]; Peter Self, "The Herbert Report and the Values of Local Government," *Political Studies*, X, No. 2 [June 1962], 146–162; The Editors. "The London Government Bill," *The Political Quarterly*, XXXIV, No. 2 [April–June 1963], 115–120; and Frank Smallwood, *Greater London: The Politics of Metropolitan Reform* [New York: The Bobbs-Merrill Co., 1965], esp. pp. 10–33, 309–310.)

[66] At the same time, it should be emphasized that the national government is often criticized for having only very vague and poorly formulated goals, or for being unwilling to resolve conflicts among its many specific goals. Few British planners deny, however, that to be effective planning *needs* national policy guidance.

[67] It has frequently been remarked that British political philosophy as a whole tends to be antiphilosophic in its frequent assumptions that the fundamental truths are commonplace and that they are hardly in need of defense because they are already known to and accepted by all enlightened Englishmen. For a recent example and defense of this antiphilosophic philosophical tradition, see Michael Oakeshott, *Rationalism in Politics* (New York: Basic Books, 1962). For a discussion of the distrust of philosophic speculation on the British Left, see R. H. S. Crossman, "Towards a Philosophy of Socialism," in R. H. S. Crossman, ed., *New Fabian Essays* (London: Turnstile Press, 1952).

from the Town and Country Planning Association, originally founded to advance the garden city ideas of Ebenezer Howard and still very much under their influence. Its chief source of supplementary ideas in recent decades has been Lewis Mumford.[68] Not only do nearly all British planners appear to accept its "line," but it seems fair to say that whatever resistance comes from generalist administrators in the Ministry of Housing and Local Government and from Conservative politicians is based not on any alternative conception of the nature of "good" urban communities but rather on a desire to restrict the role of public power.[69]

A fifth, and very closely related, factor is the great prestige of politicians and high civil servants in Britain. Part and parcel of this prestige is the assumption by nearly all British subjects that discretionary public power will—especially when it is lodged in national ministries—be exercised with scrupulous honesty and concern for the public interest. There is little evidence that this trust is misplaced. Where government is respected and trusted, many policies and practices become feasible that would not otherwise be so. In particular, effective regulation of the uses of privately owned land requires vesting tremendous discretionary authority in public officials. The exercise of this authority in large part determines relative land values within any jurisdiction. Where development

[68] These generalizations are based on interviews conducted in the summer of 1962 and on Donald L. Foley, "Idea and Influence: The Town and Country Planning Association," *Journal of the American Institute of Planners,* XXVIII, No. 1 (February 1962), 10–17. It should be noted, by the way, that the Town and Country Planning Association is not the British town planners' professional association. The Town Planning Institute, however, which is, has historically concerned itself with maintaining and upgrading the technical qualifications of planners. It has left "value" matters to the TCPA.

On reading this section, John R. James commented that, in his view, the TCPA was only the primary "seller" of planning ideas in Great Britain. Their ultimate origins, on the other hand, were quite varied. He also thought that controversy within the British planning profession tended to be more spirited than my account suggested. I suspect that our differences are mainly a function of our perspectives. James is an "insider," naturally impressed with the complexity of his professional world. As an "outsider," and one writing for an American audience, I have had to simplify, and I have kept American comparisons constantly in mind while writing this section.

[69] See Donald L. Foley, "British Town Planning: One Ideology or Three," *British Journal of Sociology,* XI, No. 3 (September 1960), 211–231.

values are privately owned, enormous profits are often available to those who can influence regulatory decisions, and substantial losses are often incurred by those who cannot. Once the suspicion gets around that some land-use control decisions are being made in response to political pressures and/or outright payoffs, the political viability of the control system is bound to become extremely precarious.[70]

In the United States, such suspicion is so endemic that it has become part of our political culture. Consequently, pressures are brought to bear with great intensity, politicians find it difficult to explain resistance to them, and the ideal of platonic governance is generally scoffed at even by academic political scientists.[71] At the same time, in order to offset the assumed corruptibility of each decision-making individual and institution, great efforts are made to express legal regulations as uniformly and precisely as possible, and to provide elaborate appeals mechanisms—first administrative, then judicial—for dissatisfied property owners. These efforts tend to permeate each land-use control system with rigidity and red tape, and at the same time to facilitate strategies of circumvention.

The British planning system, by contrast, emphasizes the need for planners to decide every issue "on its merits" and well insulated from outside influences. Even the process of determining broad planning principles for any jurisdiction is generally well insulated (by American standards) from public participation. Local authority planning committees invariably keep their proceedings secret, and local newspapers show no interest in inspiring or reporting "leaks." The development plans themselves emphasize detail; their supporting explanations tend to be extremely cryptic, leaving outsiders virtually no basis for raising issues general enough to attract much public attention. Citizens dissatisfied

[70] See Delafons, *op. cit.*, pp. 8, 9, 38.

[71] See, for example, Frank Sorauf, "The Public Interest Reconsidered," *Journal of Politics*, XIX, No. 4 (November 1957), 616–639; and Glendon Schubert, "The 'Public Interest' in Administrative Decision-Making," *American Political Science Review*, LI, No. 2 (June 1957), 346–368. For a review of the most recent literature on responsibility and the public interest, see Herbert J. Storing, "The Crucial Link: Public Administration, Responsibility, and the Public Interest," *Public Administration Review*, XXIV, No. 1 (March 1964), 39–46.

with a local development plan at the time of its appearance can testify at the Ministry's inquiry (hearing) on it, but the Ministry's decision processes are even more effectively shrouded in secrecy and insulated from local pressures than those of local authorities.[72] Subsequent denials of permission to develop may be appealed by aggrieved property owners to the Ministry on the ground that national policies have been ignored. Until 1958, local authorities did not have to state the reasons for any denial until the Ministry's inquiry on it took place. Since 1958 they have been required to state their reasons for any denial *which has been appealed* well in advance of the inquiry—the purpose being, of course, to aid the lawyers of appellants in preparing their cases. The Ministry now—also since 1958—explains its decisions in very general terms in letters to the parties concerned. It neither publishes them with any regularity, however, nor admits that even those published have any value as precedents. Officially, it decides each case "on the merits," uninfluenced by precedents.[73] There is no evidence whatever that any significant segment of the British public doubts the efficacy of this system, though Conservatives and Laborites do split on the weight that the system should give to the goal of cultivating private initiative in conceiving and financing development schemes.

Sixth, and finally, the influence of war on British planning must not go unmentioned. One well-known British planner, trying to assess the prewar history of British town planning (dating from the first Town and Country Planning Act, that of 1909), has gone so far as to write:

[72] This is the stage at which red tape frequently creeps in, however. The Ministry regularly takes one to two years, and has taken up to five years, before approving local development plans. Consequently, the plans have often been out of date before acquiring official status. Moreover, because of the complexity of the national review procedure, continuous updating is discouraged. The law requires a review only every five years (dating from the Ministry's approval).

[73] See Lewis Keeble, *Principles and Practice of Town and Country Planning*, 2nd ed. (London: Estates Gazette, 1959), pp. 278–283, 287; and Daniel Mandelker, *Green Belts and Urban Growth* (Madison: University of Wisconsin Press, 1962), p. 20. The first chapter of Mandelker's book, by the way, is the best discussion available of the relationship between law and discretion in British planning.

In retrospect we can see that the years 1909–39 were the formative years: they raised great hopes, but also led to many disappointments. By 1939 it was clear that Town and Country Planning had no very definite results to show.[74]

During the war, however, one of the government's more important ways of building public morale was to promise frequently and poetically that out of the ashes would emerge a beautified, rationalized, and more comfortable Britain.[75] To dramatize the wartime coalition government's commitment, a separate Ministry of Town and Country Planning was created in 1943.[76] The great Abercrombie Plan of London was issued in the same year. Other, only slightly less dramatic, gestures were made and widely publicized throughout the war. There was severe doubt in the planning world that a postwar Conservative Government would actually pay more than rhetorical attention to planning ideals, but as it happened the war's end also produced the first majority Labor Government in British history.

The Labor Government came to power with a landslide majority, an enthusiastic commitment to planning, and a great arsenal of rationing powers left over from the war, including control of all building licenses.[77] With much of the nation, particularly its central city cores, in ruins, and with austerity the overriding theme of national life, the need for continued rationing of investment resources was almost universally accepted. If resources were to be rationed, the case for rationing according to plan was overwhelming, especially to a socialist government. As it was, the Labor Gov-

[74] D. Rigby Childs, "The First Half-Century of British Planning," epilogue to Patrick Abercrombie, *op. cit.* The quotation appears at p. 250.

[75] I am indebted to John Reps for emphasizing the great importance of this point to me.

[76] Most of the national government's responsibilities having to do with local government were transferred to the Ministry (from the Ministry of Health) early in 1951. Simultaneously, the Ministry's name was changed to Local Government and Planning. When the Conservatives took over the government in the autumn of 1951, they wished to emphasize their campaign promises to step up housing construction and to de-emphasize restrictive planning controls. Consequently, they renamed the Ministry that of Housing and Local Government. (See *Report of the Ministry of Housing and Local Government for the period 1950/51 to 1954* [London: Her Majesty's Stationery Office, Cmnd. 9559, August 1955], p. 1.)

[77] See Lloyd Rodwin, *op. cit.,* p. 20.

ernment was not content merely to regulate; it believed that public objectives were likely to be served best by publicly *owned* enterprises. Moreover, one of the most popular national investment priorities was housing, and Labor policy was to conceive housing as a public service rather than as an ordinary economic product. The extent of its commitment in this direction was indicated by the fact that even as late as 1950 and 1951 (taken together) only 13 per cent of all new housing in England and Wales was built under private auspices.[78] The popularity of this policy was such that even the Conservative government after 1951 had to abandon it very gradually. Not until 1958 did private housing construction exceed public.[79] In any event, the point to note is that planning is rather easier in a society where most housing is publicly built and where the principle is established that nearly all construction should be licensed in accordance with national investment priorities than it is in a predominantly private enterprise economy. Where land development values have also been nationalized, as they were in Britain after 1947, the obstacles presented by private enterprise to planning may be all but invisible.

The consensus among British planners has been that the period of the Labor Government (1945–1951) marked the zenith of their influence to date. The Conservative Government that came to power late in 1951 left most of the planning machinery intact, but in terms of substantive policies and priorities it did rather sharply shift direction. It moved resolutely to increase the role of private as opposed to public investment in land-use development, to end

---

[78] *Report of the Ministry of Housing and Local Government . . . 1950/51 to 1954,* p. 127. The percentage is of new permanent dwelling units completed. Nathaniel Lichfield has noted that housing accounted for about one-half of all British construction (by the measure of value) in this period. In 1951, 84.2 per cent of all housing construction was public, and 58.7 per cent of all other construction was also public (Lichfield, *op. cit.,* p. 5).

[79] *Report of the Ministry of Housing and Local Government, 1959* (London: Her Majesty's Stationery Office, Cmnd. 1027, June 1960), p. 180. It may be noted that the Labor Government's policy had been to have 175,000 new dwelling units a year completed in England and Wales The Conservatives promised in the 1951 campaign to raise that figure to 300,000 units a year. They in fact approached their target in 1953 and surpassed it in 1954. This emphasis on stepping up the overall pace of building necessitated a slower transition from public to private building than might otherwise have been possible.

both rationing and the licensing of construction, and (as mentioned previously) to repeal the nationalization of land development values. It retained the location of industry regulative machinery, but most observers agree that it employed it (1) gingerly, and (2) with an eye almost solely to holding down unemployment rates in depressed areas.[80] Moreover, as knowledge accumulated that office construction was a far more important harbinger of central city congestion than industrial construction in the postwar economy, the Conservatives resisted all suggestions that they enact a location of office construction policy. They refused even to deal with one of the monumental loopholes in the 1947 Town and Country Planning Act, the provision that owners of older buildings should automatically be permitted to increase their *cubic* content by 10 per cent on rebuilding. As most older office buildings had very high ceilings, wide corridors, and so on, this provision often permitted increases of up to 40 per cent in floor area on redeveloped sites. Only one New Town was begun by the Conservatives in the first decade of their rule, and their alternative policy of subsidizing expansion of existing small towns

[80] Both changes, if they in fact took place, were only matters of degree, of course. Data on the geographic distribution of industrial development are available, and they strongly support the hypothesis. The Board of Trade's decision processes are completely shrouded in secrecy, however, so it is impossible to separate political from economic factors with assurance in accounting for the trend. A study based on interviews with industrialists might have provided useful evidence, but to my knowledge none was conducted. On the basis of his impressions, though, Peter Self wrote the following in 1956: "From 1948 onwards, the momentum of Government policy slackened. The Board's powers of control were used more sparingly, particularly after the advent of a Conservative Government in 1951. By stages, the threat of compulsion gave way to an almost exclusive reliance upon persuasion until, by mid-1956, the application for an industrial development certificate (IDC) had become, in almost all cases, a mere formality. . . . Inducements to settle in the development areas continued to be offered, but on a somewhat reduced scale" (*Cities in Flood,* pp. 129–130; see also Lewis Keeble, *Principles and Practice,* p. 284).

Parenthetically, it may be noted that from 1949 through 1957 the average unemployment rate in Great Britain was 1.5 per cent. The unemployment rate in the depressed areas (officially known as development areas) was 2.9 per cent. (J. Sykes, "Location of Industry and Population," *Journal of the Town Planning Institute,* XLV, No. 6 [May 1959], 126–130. The reference is to p. 128.)

appeared to be prosecuted half-heartedly in the same period.[81]
The one major planning policy which the Conservatives did pros-
ecute vigorously in the decade after 1951 was that of establishing
and conserving agricultural greenbelts around every significant
urban unit. This policy was, of course, in accord with the aristocratic tradition mentioned previously. Summing up the Conservative approach to planning in this period, most observers agreed
that it was "marking time" or operating the planning machinery
as a "necessary evil." [82] (It should be noted that something of a
change took place in the early 1960's, as concern about British
resistance to modernization became a national "fad." The Government responded with numerous headline-catching initiatives,
some involving both economic and town planning. Among other
things, six additional New Towns were designated in the years
1962–1964. The far bolder intentions announced by the new—at
this writing—Labor Government have been mentioned previously.
If it carries them out, it will be the first British government in
history to show great zeal for town planning in the midst of a long
period of peace and prosperity.)

Concluding Remarks

What has been the point of these speculations on what the conclusions of a panoramic survey might have been? It has been two-
fold: first, to mitigate the rather harsh conclusions of the study
which occupies the main body of this book by clarifying their

[81] The expanded towns program required local authorities wishing to "ex-
port" industry and population to reach agreements with those willing to
"import." The Ministry did not give any lead or exercise any compulsion.
Few agreements of significance were reached. See Lewis Keeble, *Principles
and Practice,* pp. 297–298.

[82] The quotations are from D. Rigby Childs, *op. cit.,* p. 250, and Peter
Self, *Cities in Flood,* p. 166. Most writers agree that the change from the late
1940's to the decade of the 1950's was more than one of party. They contend
that a major shift in national mood was involved as well, and frequently
point to the fact that the Labor Government itself made some moves toward
relaxation of planning controls in 1950 and 1951. See Lewis Keeble, *Town
Planning at the Crossroads,* pp. 45–46. Self argues similarly in *Cities in Flood,*
pp. 166–170. The Conservatives were whipping on and exploiting this shift,
however, whereas apparently the Laborites were trying to keep their concessions minor while riding it out.
On the early postwar mood, see Lloyd Rodwin, *op. cit.,* p. 20.

452 The City Planning Process

relationship to the demanding (though, in my opinion, highly relevant) criteria of "good" planning employed throughout the study; and second, to suggest at least a few of the ways in which differently focused studies of planning by political scientists might have produced fundamentally different conclusions. The section would probably not have been written if a significant number of politically oriented historical and comparative studies of planning had been available. In fact, however, such studies are virtually nonexistent.

Two consequences of this dearth appear to me to be the following. First, American city planners tend to have their horizons limited almost entirely by contemporary American practices and short-term estimates of political feasibility. Second, when they do report historic and contemporary examples of "good" civic design, they tend to neglect analysis of the cultural, political, and economic factors which produced them. Until a serious effort is made to remove these blinders, the imagination of the American planning profession is bound to be severely confined, its perception of political opportunities and obstacles is bound to be quite shallow, and (probably most important) its sense of the difficulty of truly comprehensive evaluation—at the politician's level—is bound to remain rudimentary.

It may plausibly be maintained, of course, that the typical American city planner already has enough difficulty avoiding paralysis of will, that any deeper perception of obstacles or more sophisticated sense of complexity would totally ruin him. This may be true. The traditional task of the scholar, however, has been to remind his readers of the unsavory aspects of this conclusion. Today it is fashionable among "realistic" students of decision making to point out that the only way men can make decisions is to narrow their concerns and perspectives.[83] I cannot help noting

[83] See, for example, James G. March and Herbert A. Simon, *op. cit.*, Chap. 6; and Charles E. Lindblom, "The Science of 'Muddling Through,'" *Public Administration Review*, XIX, No. 1 (Spring 1959), 79–88. March and Simon, whose views are of greater interest here, write as follows:

"From a phenomenological viewpoint we can only speak of rationality relative to a frame of reference; and this frame of reference will be determined by the limitations on the rational man's knowledge. . . . The organizational and social environment in which the decision maker finds himself *determines*

that it is easy to learn this lesson too well, to become smug about one's parochialism. The prospect of lives and cities being planned by multitudes of technicians with a positive distaste for social, political, and historic complexity, moves me to foreboding. The orientation of this volume has been dictated in large part by my belief that at least those who call themselves "comprehensive" planners ought to be broadly learned and thoughtful—even though technically qualified—men. The question is not *whether* decisions must be made on the basis of simplified assumptions about the real world; it is rather *which* complicating factors shall be de-emphasized, *how* significance shall be judged, and *what* the substance of the assumptions shall be.

---

what consequences he will anticipate, what ones he will not; what alternatives he will consider, what ones he will ignore. . . .

"The theory of rational choice put forth here incorporates two fundamental characteristics: (1) Choice is always exercised with respect to a limited, approximate, simplified "model" of the real situation. We call the chooser's model his "definition of the situation." (?) The elements of the definition of the situation . . . are themselves the outcome of psychological and sociological processes" (pp. 138–139; italics added).

Bibliography

The following is simply a list of the works cited in this volume, and is not intended as a general bibliography on urban planning. Those interested in such a bibliography would do well to begin with T. J. Kent, *The Urban General Plan* (San Francisco: Chandler Publishing Co., 1964), pp. 189–210.

Abercrombie, Patrick. *Town and Country Planning.* London: Oxford University Press, 1959.

Abrams, Charles. "The Housing Order and Its Limits." *Commentary,* XXXV, No. 1 (January 1963), 10–14.

Adrian, Charles. *Governing Urban America,* 2nd ed. New York: McGraw-Hill Book Co., 1961.

Altshuler, Alan. "The Politics of Urban Mass Transportation." Revised version of a paper delivered at the 1963 annual meeting of the American Political Science Association. Mimeo. November 1963.

——— *A Report on Politics in Minneapolis.* Cambridge: Joint Center for Urban Studies of the Massachusetts Institute of Technology and Harvard University, 1959.

——— *A Report on Politics in Saint Paul.* Cambridge: Joint Center for Urban Studies of the Massachusetts Institute of Technology and Harvard University, 1959.

American Institute of Planners. *The Role of Metropolitan Planning.* Metropolitan Planning Conference, Findings and Recommendations. Chicago, 1962.

American Public Health Association. *Planning the Neighborhood.* Chicago: Public Administration Service, 1948.

Aschman, Frederick T. *The Function and Organization of City Planning in Minneapolis.* Report to the Minneapolis City Planning Commission. May 1957.

—— and Richard L. Nelson. *Real Estate and City Planning.* Englewood Cliffs: Prentice-Hall, 1957.

Ashworth, William. *The Genesis of British Town Planning.* London: Routledge & Kegan Paul, 1954.

Banfield, Edward C. *Political Influence.* New York: The Free Press of Glencoe, 1961.

——"The Training of the Executive." *Public Policy,* X (1960), 16–43.

—— and James Q. Wilson, *City Politics.* Cambridge: Harvard University Press and the M.I.T. Press, 1963.

Barnard, Chester. *The Functions of the Executive.* Cambridge: Harvard University Press, 1938.

—— *Organization and Management.* Cambridge: Harvard University Press, 1948.

Bartholomew, Harland. *Land Uses in American Cities.* Cambridge: Harvard University Press, 1955.

Barton, George, and Associates. *The Freeways in Minneapolis.* Appraisal prepared for the City Council and the City Planning Commission of Minneapolis. Evanston, 1957.

Barton-Aschman Associates. *Nicollet Avenue Study: Principles and Techniques for Retail Street Improvement.* Report prepared for the Downtown Council of Minneapolis. Evanston, 1960.

Beaney, William. *The Right to Counsel in American Courts.* Ann Arbor: University of Michigan Press, 1955.

Bernstein, Marver. *Regulating Business by Independent Commission.* Princeton: Princeton University Press, 1955.

Blessing, Charles A. "Perception in Planning." *Journal of the American Institute of Planners,* XXVI, No. 1 (February 1960), 2–4.

Bollens, John C. *Special District Governments in the United States.* Berkeley: University of California Press, 1957.

Browning, Clyde. "Recent Studies of Central Business Districts." *Journal of the American Institute of Planners,* XXVII, No. 1 (February, 1961).

Chapin, F. Stuart. *Urban Land Use Planning.* New York: Harper and Bros., 1957.

Chase, Edward T. "Revolution in Hospitals." *Architectural Forum,* CXI, No. 2 (August 1959), 127–129, 178 ff.

Childs, D. Rigby. "The First Half-Century of British Planning," epilogue to Patrick Abercrombie, *Town and Country Planning.* London: Oxford University Press, 1959.

Churchill, Henry S. "Planning in a Free Society." *Journal of the American Institute of Planners,* XX, No. 4 (Fall 1954), 189–191.

Churchill, Winston. *The Hinge of Fate,* Vol. IV of *The Second World War.* Boston: Houghton-Mifflin Co., 1950.

—— *Closing the Ring,* Vol. V of *The Second World War.* Boston: Houghton-Mifflin Co., 1951.

City of Minneapolis Planning Commission. *Central Minneapolis Cordon Count: 1958.* Minneapolis, 1959.

—— *Central Minneapolis Master Station Count.* Minneapolis, 1959.

—— *Comprehensive Planning for the Loring Park Neighborhood.* Minneapolis, 1959.

—— *First Report on the Central Minneapolis Plan.* Minneapolis, 1959.

—— *Goals for Central Minneapolis.* Minneapolis, 1959.

—— *Land and Space Use Survey, Central Commercial Area.* Minneapolis, 1959.

—— *Parking Survey: 1958, Central Commercial Area.* Minneapolis, 1959.

—— *Pedestrian Count: 1958, Central Commercial Area.* Minneapolis, 1959.

City Planning Board of St. Paul. *New Life in St. Paul.* St. Paul, 1956.

—— *The Proposed Freeways for St. Paul.* St. Paul, 1957.

—— *St. Paul's Central Business District.* St. Paul, 1958.

—— *St. Paul's Preliminary Land Use Plan.* St. Paul, 1959.

Crossman, R. H. S. "Towards a Philosophy of Socialism," *New Fabian Essays,* ed. R. H. S. Crossman. London: Turnstile Press, 1952.

Dahl, Robert A., and Charles E. Lindblom. *Politics, Economics, and Welfare.* New York: Harper & Brothers, 1953.

Davidoff, Paul, and Thomas Reiner. "A Choice Theory of Planning." *Journal of the American Institute of Planners,* XXV, No. 3 (August 1959), 133–42.

De Mars, Vernon. "Townscape and the Architect: Some Problems of the Urban Scene," *The Future of Cities and Urban Redevelopment,* ed. Coleman Woodbury. Chicago: University of Chicago Press, 1953.

Delafons, John. *Land-Use Controls in the United States.* Cambridge: Joint Center for Urban Studies of the Massachusetts Institute of Technology and Harvard University, 1962.

Dewey, John. *The Public and Its Problems.* New York: Henry Holt and Co., 1927.

Dunham, Allison. "A Legal and Economic Basis for City Planning." *Columbia Law Review,* LVIII (May 1958), 650–671.

Dyckman, John. *Readings in the Theory of Planning: The State of Planning Theory in America.* (Forthcoming.)

Editors, *The Political Quarterly.* "The London Government Bill." *The Political Quarterly,* XXXIV, No. 2 (April–June 1963), 115–120.

Faust, Lucien C. "An Analysis of Selected Characteristics of the American Institute of Planners." M.A. thesis, University of North Carolina, 1959.

Fogarty, M. P. *Town and Country Planning.* London: Hutchinson's University Library, 1948.

Foley, Donald L. "British Town Planning: One Ideology or Three." *British Journal of Sociology,* XI, No. 3 (September 1960), 211–231.

———— "Idea and Influence: The Town and Country Planning Association." *Journal of the American Institute of Planners,* XXVIII, No. 1 (February 1962), 10–17.

Frank, Charlotte. "Politics in the Nonpartisan City." M.A. thesis, University of Chicago, 1958.

Greer, Scott. *The Emerging City.* New York: The Free Press of Glencoe, 1962.

———— *Metropolitics.* New York: John Wiley and Sons, 1963.

Gruen, Victor. "Save Urbia for the New Urbanites." *Journal of the American Institute of Architects,* February 1960, pp. 35–38.

Haar, Charles M. *Land Planning Law in a Free Society.* Cambridge: Harvard University Press, 1951.

———— *Land-Use Planning: A Casebook on the Use, Misuse, and Reuse of Urban Land.* Boston: Little, Brown and Company, 1959.

———— "The Master Plan: An Inquiry in Dialogue Form." *Journal of the American Institute of Planners,* XXV, No. 3 (August 1959), 133–142.

———— "Planning Law: Public v. Private Interest in the Land," *Land Use in an Urban Environment.* Liverpool: Liverpool University Press, 1961.

Hayek, F. A. *The Road to Serfdom.* Chicago: University of Chicago Press, 1944.

Hiltner, Seward. "Planning as a Profession." *Journal of the American Institute of Planners,* XXIII, No. 4 (Autumn 1957), 162–167.

Hobbs, Edward H. *Behind the President.* Washington, D.C.: Public Affairs Press, 1954.

Holmans, A. E. *United States Fiscal Policy 1945–1959.* London: Oxford University Press, 1961.

Howard, John T. "The Planner in a Democratic Society—A Credo." *Journal of the American Institute of Planners,* XXI, No. 3 (Spring–Summer 1955), 62–65.

———— "Planning Is a Profession." *Journal of the American Institute of Planners,* XX, No. 2 (Spring 1954), 58–59.

Isaacs, Reginald. "Goals for 2012." Minneapolis: University of Minnesota School of Architecture, 1962. This pamphlet was originally delivered as a lecture on April 6, 1962.

Joint Center for Urban Studies of the Massachusetts Institute of Technology and Harvard University (Charles M. Haar, Project Director). *The Effectiveness of Metropolitan Planning.* U.S. Senate, Committee on Government Operations, Subcommittee on Intergovernmental Relations, committee print. June 30, 1964.

Keeble, Lewis. *Principles and Practice of Town and Country Planning.* London: Estates Gazette, 1959.

———— *Town Planning at the Crossroads.* London: Estates Gazette, 1961.

Kent, T. J. *The Urban General Plan.* San Francisco: Chandler Publishing Co., 1964.

Key, V. O., Jr. "The Reconversion Phase of Demobilization." *American Political Science Review,* XXXVIII, No. 6 (December 1944), 1137–1153.

Krumholz, Norman. "The Politics of Urban Renewal in Buffalo." M.A. thesis, Cornell University, 1965.

Legislative Reference Service of the Library of Congress. *Catalog of Federal Aids to State and Local Governments.* U.S. Senate, Committee on Government Operations, Subcommittee on Intergovernmental Relations, committee print. Washington, D.C., April 15, 1964.

———— Supplement, January 4, 1965, to *Catalog of Federal Aids to State and Local Governments,* committee print. Washington, D.C., May 17, 1965.

Lichfield, Nathaniel. *Economics of Planned Development.* London: Estates Gazette, 1956.

Lindblom, Charles E. "The Science of 'Muddling Through.'" *Public Administration Review,* XIX, No. 1 (Spring 1959), 79–88.

Long, Norton. *The Polity.* Chicago: Rand McNally, 1962.

Ludwig, Clarence C. "Planning for Metropolitan Growth." Mimeo. May 1954.

Masland, John W., and Laurence I. Radway. *Soldiers and Scholars.* Princeton: Princeton University Press, 1957.

Merriam, Charles E. *Chicago: A More Intimate View.* Chicago: University of Chicago Press, 1929.

———— "The National Resources Planning Board: A Chapter in American Planning Experience." *American Political Science Review,* XXXVIII (December 1944), 1075–1088.

Merton, Robert K. "Some Preliminaries to a Sociology of Medical Education," *The Student Physician,* eds. Robert K. Merton, George D. Reader, and Patricia L. Kendall. Cambridge: Harvard University Press, 1957.

Meyerson, Martin. "Research and City Planning." *Journal of the American Institute of Planners,* XX, No. 4 (Autumn 1954), 201–205.

Mitchell, Robert B. "The New Frontier in Metropolitan Planning." *Journal of the American Institute of Planners*, XXVII, No. 3 (August 1961), 169–175.

Moynihan, Daniel P. "New Roads and Urban Chaos." *The Reporter*, XXII, No. 8 (April 14, 1960), 13–20.

Mumford, Lewis. *The City in History*. New York: Harcourt, Brace & World, 1961.

Nash, Peter H., and James F. Shurtleff. "Planning as a Staff Function in Urban Management." *Journal of the American Institute of Planners*, XX, No. 3 (Summer 1954), 136–147.

Nelson, Richard L. *The Selection of Retail Locations*. New York: F. W. Dodge Corporation, 1958.

Oakeshott, Michael. *Rationalism in Politics*. New York: Basic Books, 1962.

Osborn, Frederick J., and Arnold Whittick. *The New Towns: The Answer to Megalopolis*. London: Leonard Hill, 1963.

Ostrogorski, M. *Democracy and the Organization of Political Parties*. New York and London: Macmillan and Co., 1902.

Parsons, Talcott. *Essays in Sociological Theory Pure and Applied*. Glencoe: The Free Press, 1949.

Praeger, Polly. "Extinction by Thruway: The Fight to Save a Town." *Harpers*, No. 1303 (December 1958), 61–71.

President's Committee on Administrative Management. *Report With Special Studies*. Washington, D.C.: Government Printing Office, 1937.

Presthus, Robert. *The Organizational Society*. New York: Knopf, 1962.

Problems of Decentralization in Metropolitan Areas. Proceedings of the First Annual University of California Conference on City and Regional Planning, 1953. Berkeley: Department of City and Regional Planning, University of California, 1954.

Real Estate Research Corporation. *Central Area Housing Market Analysis*. Chicago, 1959.

—— *Economic Development Study of Downtown Minneapolis*. Chicago, 1959.

Rodwin, Lloyd. *The British New Towns Policy*. Cambridge: Harvard University Press, 1956.

Royal Commission on Local Government in Greater London. *Report*. London: Her Majesty's Stationery Office, Cmnd. 1164, October 1960.

Sayre, Wallace, and Herbert Kaufman. *Governing New York City*. New York: Russell Sage Foundation, 1960.

Schubert, Glendon. "The 'Public Interest' in Administrative Decision-Making: Theorem, Theosophy, or Theory." *American Political Science Review*, LI, No. 2 (June 1957), 346–368.

Self, Peter. *Cities in Flood*, 2nd ed. London: Faber and Faber, 1961.

——— "The Herbert Report and the Values of Local Government." *Political Studies*, X, No. 2 (June 1962), 146–162.

——— *The Planning of Industrial Location*. London: University of London Press, 1953.

Selznick, Philip. *Leadership in Administration*. Evanston: Row, Peterson, and Co., 1957.

——— *The Organizational Weapon*. Glencoe: The Free Press, 1960.

Simon, Herbert. *Administrative Behavior*, 2nd ed. New York: Macmillan Co., 1957.

——— *Models of Man*. New York: John Wiley and Sons, 1957.

——— "Theories of Decision-Making in Economics and Behavioral Science." *American Economic Review*, LXIX, No. 2 (June 1959), 253–283.

——— and James G. March. *Organizations*. New York: John Wiley and Sons, 1958.

Smallwood, Frank. *Greater London: The Politics of Metropolitan Reform*. Indianapolis: The Bobbs-Merrill Co., 1965.

Somers, Herman. *Presidential Agency*. Cambridge: Harvard University Press, 1950.

Sorauf, Frank. "The Public Interest Reconsidered." *Journal of Politics*, XIX, No. 4 (November 1957), 616–639.

Storing, Herbert. "The Crucial Link: Public Administration, Responsibility, and the Public Interest." *Public Administration Review*, XXIV, No. 1 (March 1964), 39–46.

——— "The Science of Administration: Herbert Simon," *Essays on the Scientific Study of Politics*, ed. Herbert Storing. New York: Holt, Rinehart and Winston, 1962.

Sykes, J. "Location of Industry and Population." *Journal of the Town Planning Institute*, XLV, No. 6 (May 1959), 126–130.

Thompson, Victor A. *Modern Organization*. New York: Knopf, 1961.

Town and Country Planning Association. *The Paper Metropolis*. London: Town and Country Planning Association, 1962.

United Kingdom. *Report of the Ministry of Housing and Local Government, 1959*. London: Her Majesty's Stationery Office, Cmnd. 1027, June 1960.

United Kingdom. *Report of the Ministry of Housing and Local Government for the period 1950/1951 to 1954*. London: Her Majesty's Stationery Office, Cmnd. 9559, August 1955.

U.S. Advisory Commission on Intergovernmental Relations. *Governmental Structure, Organization, and Planning in Metropolitan Areas*. Washington, D.C.: Government Printing Office, July 1961.

——— *Impact of Federal Urban Development Programs on Local*

Government Organization and Planning. Washington, D.C.: Government Printing Office, January 1964.

U.S. Bureau of the Budget. *Urban Research Under Federal Auspices.* U.S. Senate, Committee on Government Operations, Subcommittee on Intergovernmental Relations, committee print. Washington, D.C., April 15, 1964.

U.S. Congress. *Message from the President of the United States Relative to a National Highway Program.* 84th Congress, 1st sess., House Document No. 93. Washington, D.C., 1955.

―――― *The Federal System as Seen by State and Local Officials.* U.S. Senate, Committee on Government Operations, Subcommittee on Intergovernmental Relations, committee print. Washington, D.C., 1963.

―――― *Metropolitan Planning.* U.S. Senate, Hearings before the Subcommittee on Intergovernmental Relations, Committee on Government Operations. Washington, D.C., May 21–23, 1963.

U.S. Housing and Home Finance Agency. *National Survey of Metropolitan Planning.* U.S. Senate, Committee on Government Operations, Subcommittee on Intergovernmental Relations, committee print. Washington, D.C., December 16, 1963.

Walker, Robert. *The Planning Function in Urban Government,* 2nd ed. Chicago: University of Chicago Press, 1950.

Wallace, David. "Renaissancemanship." *Journal of the American Institute of Planners,* XXVI, No. 3 (August 1960), 157–176.

Wibberley, G. P. *Agriculture and Urban Growth.* London: Michael Joseph, 1959.

Wood, Robert. "A Division of Powers in Metropolitan Areas," *Area and Power,* ed. Arthur Maass. Glencoe: The Free Press, 1959.

―――― *1400 Governments.* Cambridge: Harvard University Press, 1961.

Wurster, Catherine Bauer. "Redevelopment: A Misfit in the Fifties," *The Future of Cities and Urban Redevelopment,* ed. Coleman Woodbury. Chicago: University of Chicago Press, 1953.

Index